10

Story and Art by
Rumiko Takahashi

Characters

TAISHO ERA

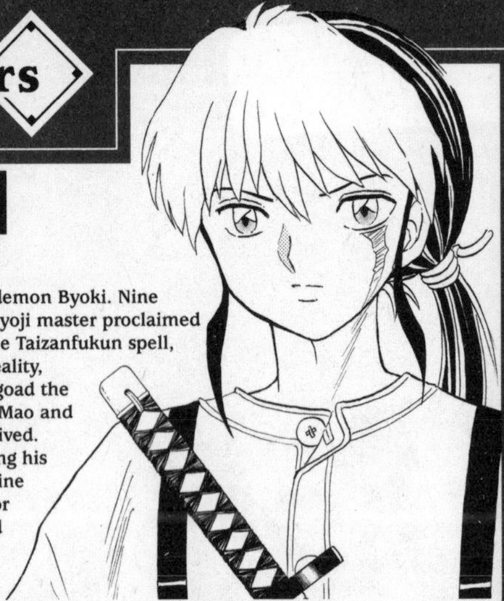

MAO

An exorcist cursed by the cat demon Byoki. Nine hundred years ago, Mao's onmyoji master proclaimed Mao his successor to inherit the Taizanfukun spell, which controls life spans. In reality, the master's intention was to goad the other five trainees into killing Mao and each other until only one survived. Then Mao was accused of killing his master's daughter, Sana. For nine centuries, Mao has searched for Byoki to uncover the truth and purge his curse.

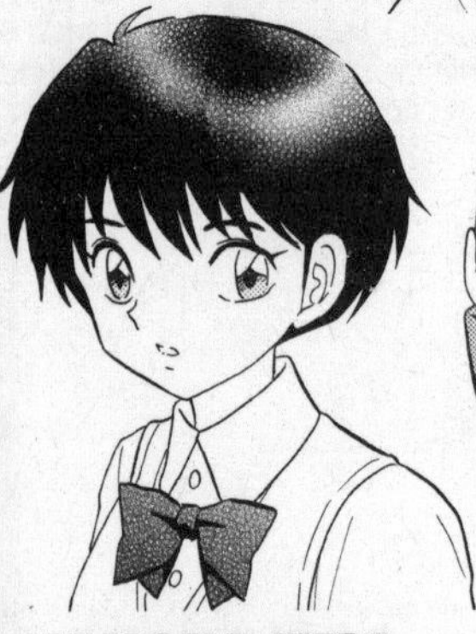

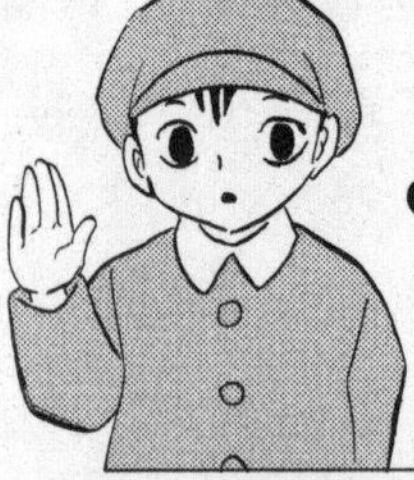

OTOYA

Mao's hardworking shikigami.

NANOKA KIBA

A first-year high school student living in the present day. Like Mao, she was cursed by Byoki, becoming part ayakashi as well as a potential vessel for him to inhabit. Her blood is capable of healing Mao.

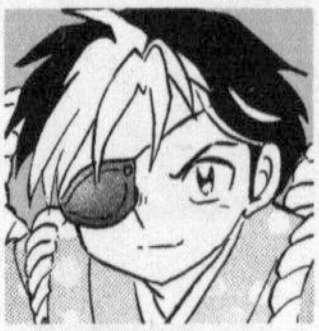

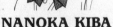

HYAKKA

Mao's senior apprentice. Wields fire spells.

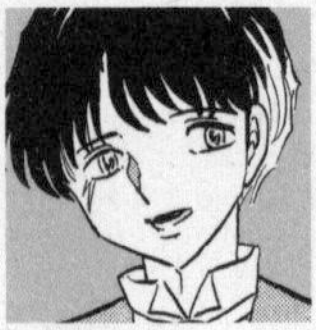

KAMON (KUCHINAWA)

Mao's senior apprentice. Wields tree spells.

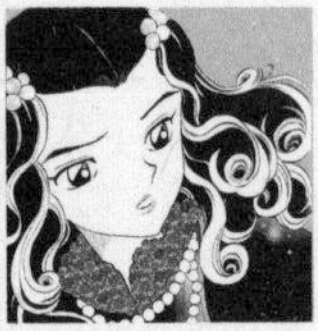

YURAKO

The Goko clan's vessel for curses. She looks exactly like Sana and works for Shiranui.

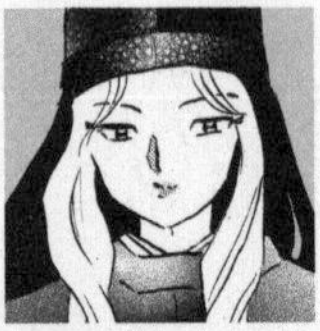

SHIRANUI

Mao's senior apprentice. Wields water spells. Seeks vengeance on Mao.

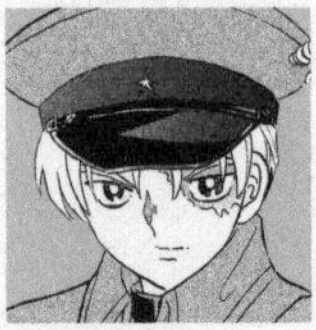

HAKUBI

Mao's senior apprentice. Wields metal spells. Works for Shiranui.

HEIAN PERIOD

HOUSE OF GOKO

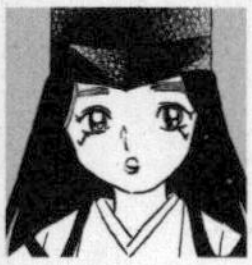

MASAGO
A Goko clan onymoji. The most powerful wielder of water spells.

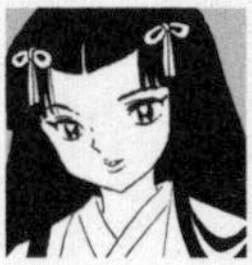

SANA
The master's daughter. Betrothed to Mao by her father. Murdered, possibly by Mao.

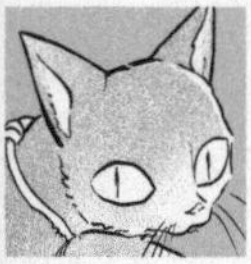

HAIMARU
Sana's beloved cat. Only liked her and Mao.

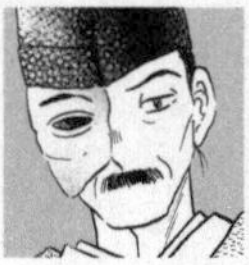

MASTER
The head of the Goko clan and Mao's former master. Wields forbidden spells and attempted to sacrifice Mao for his own ends.

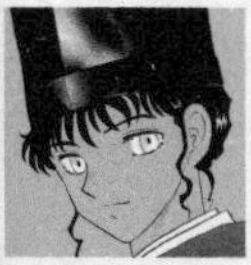

DAIGO
Mao's senior apprentice. He invited Mao to join the Goko clan. An experienced exorcist, he was slain during the battles to become the master's successor.

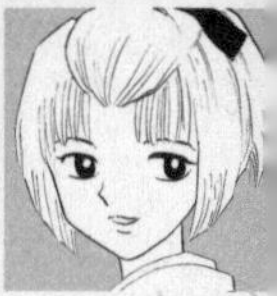

NATSUNO
Mao's senior apprentice. Wielc earth spells.

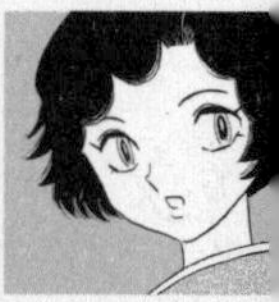

TENKO
Mao's ayakashi informant.

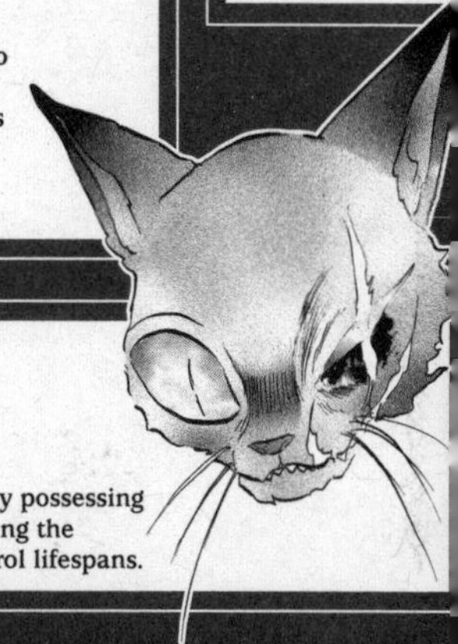

PRESENT DAY

BYOKI

The kodoku cat who cursed Mao and Nanoka. Survives by possessing human bodies. After eating the forbidden scroll containing the Taizanfukun spell, he gained the ability to use it to control lifespans.

Story thus far...

When Nanoka Kiba was seven, she was orphaned in a violent accident. At 15, she is transported to the Taisho era, where she joins forces with exorcist Mao to find Byoki, the cat demon who has cursed them both. Centuries ago, Mao's master pitted Mao's fellow apprentices against him. Now Mao is allied with some of them and battling others to prevent the Goko clan from reascending to power.

Months have passed, and Nanoka is starting high school. Kagari, one of Hakubi's underlings, uses her puppet needle to bring Nanoka to Yurako. There, Nanoka learns the story of Yurako's tragic past...

CONTENTS

Chapter 1:
Kindness

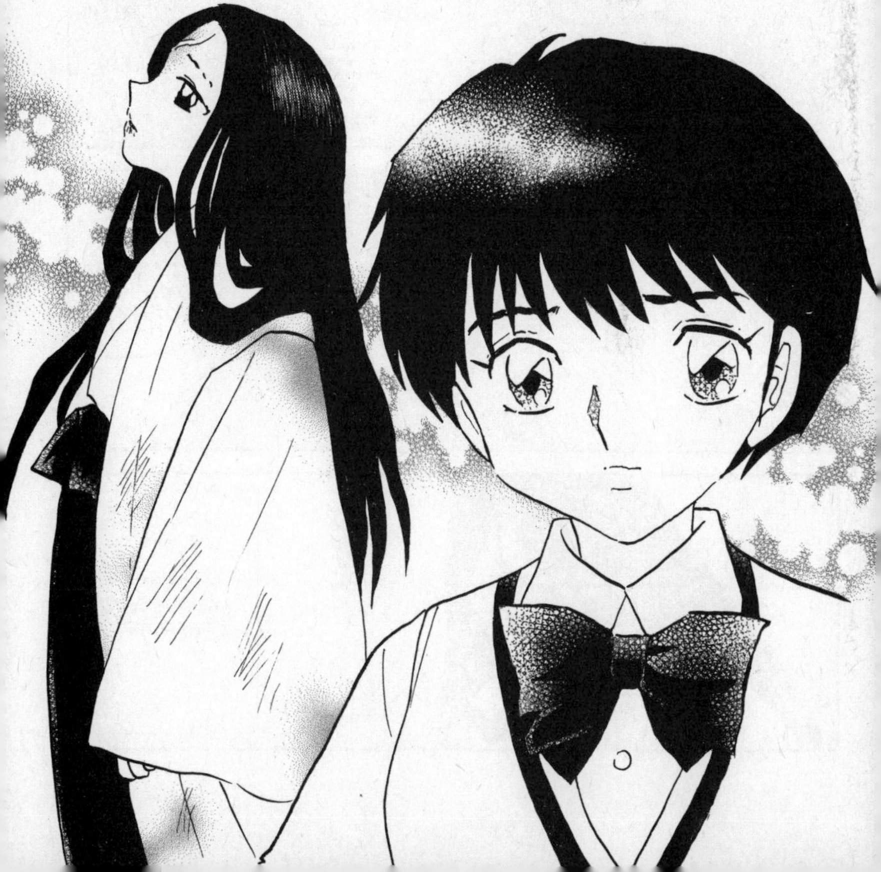

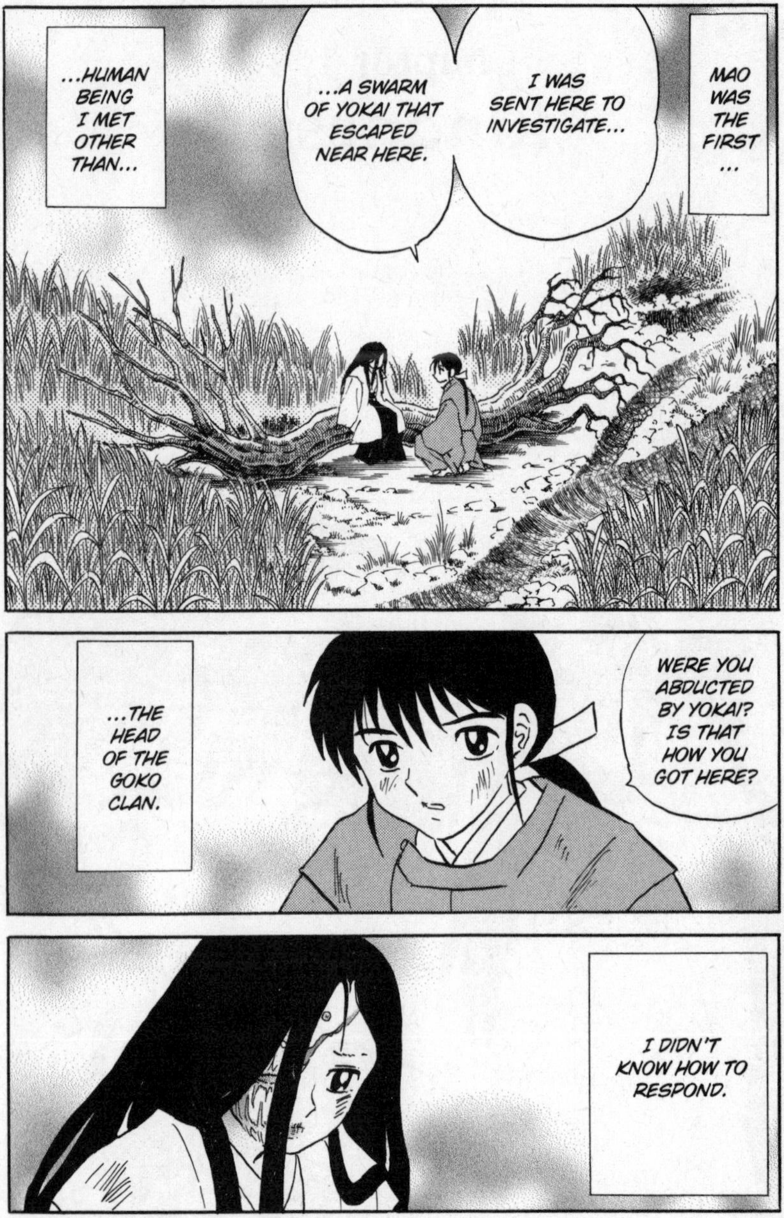
MAO WAS THE FIRST ...
I WAS SENT HERE TO INVESTIGATE...
...A SWARM OF YOKAI THAT ESCAPED NEAR HERE.
...HUMAN BEING I MET OTHER THAN...
WERE YOU ABDUCTED BY YOKAI? IS THAT HOW YOU GOT HERE?
...THE HEAD OF THE GOKO CLAN.
I DIDN'T KNOW HOW TO RESPOND.

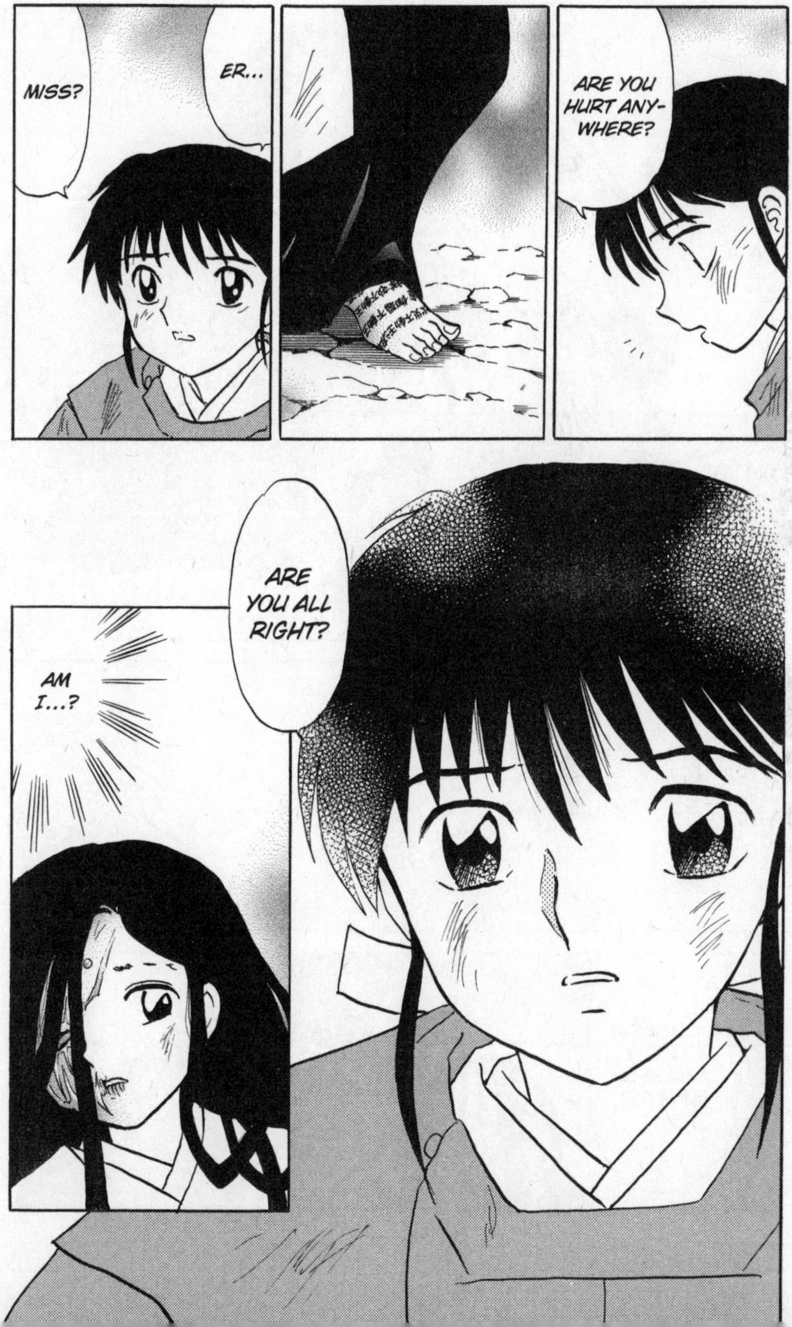
ARE YOU HURT ANYWHERE?
ER...
MISS?
ARE YOU ALL RIGHT?
AM I...?

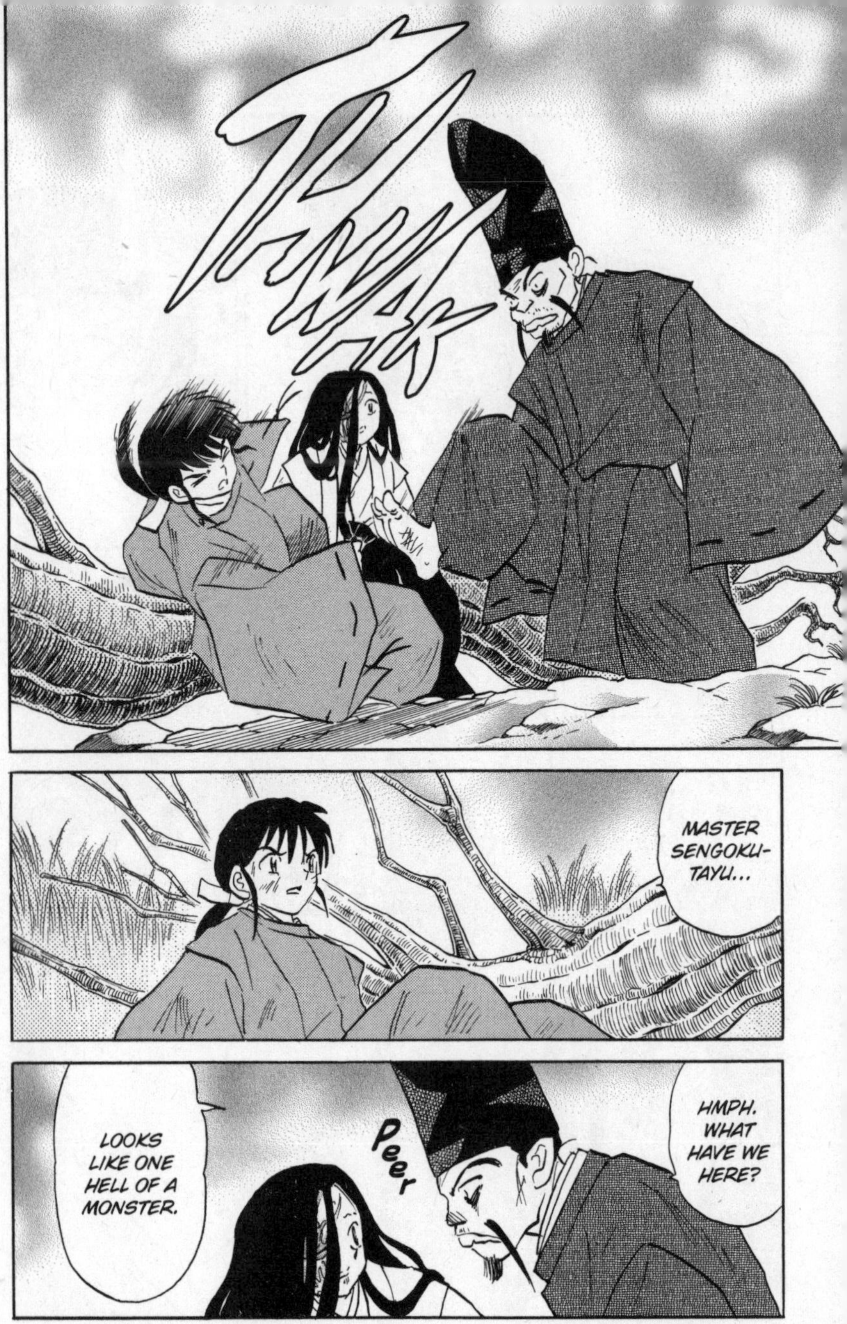
THWAK
MASTER SENGOKU-TAYU...
HMPH. WHAT HAVE WE HERE?
Peer
LOOKS LIKE ONE HELL OF A MONSTER.

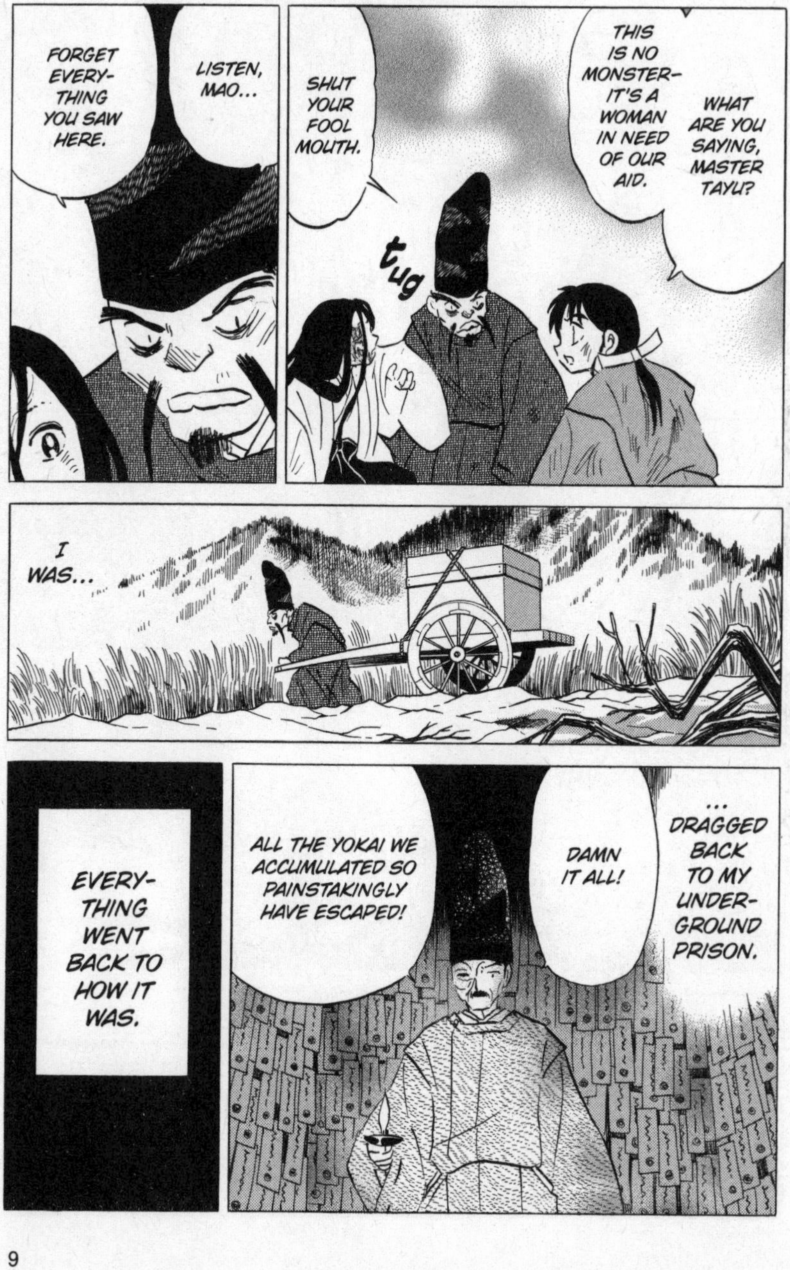
WHAT ARE YOU SAYING, MASTER TAYU?
THIS IS NO MONSTER–IT'S A WOMAN IN NEED OF OUR AID.
SHUT YOUR FOOL MOUTH.
tug
LISTEN, MAO...
FORGET EVERY-THING YOU SAW HERE.
I WAS...
...DRAGGED BACK TO MY UNDER-GROUND PRISON.
DAMN IT ALL!
ALL THE YOKAI WE ACCUMULATED SO PAINSTAKINGLY HAVE ESCAPED!
EVERY-THING WENT BACK TO HOW IT WAS.

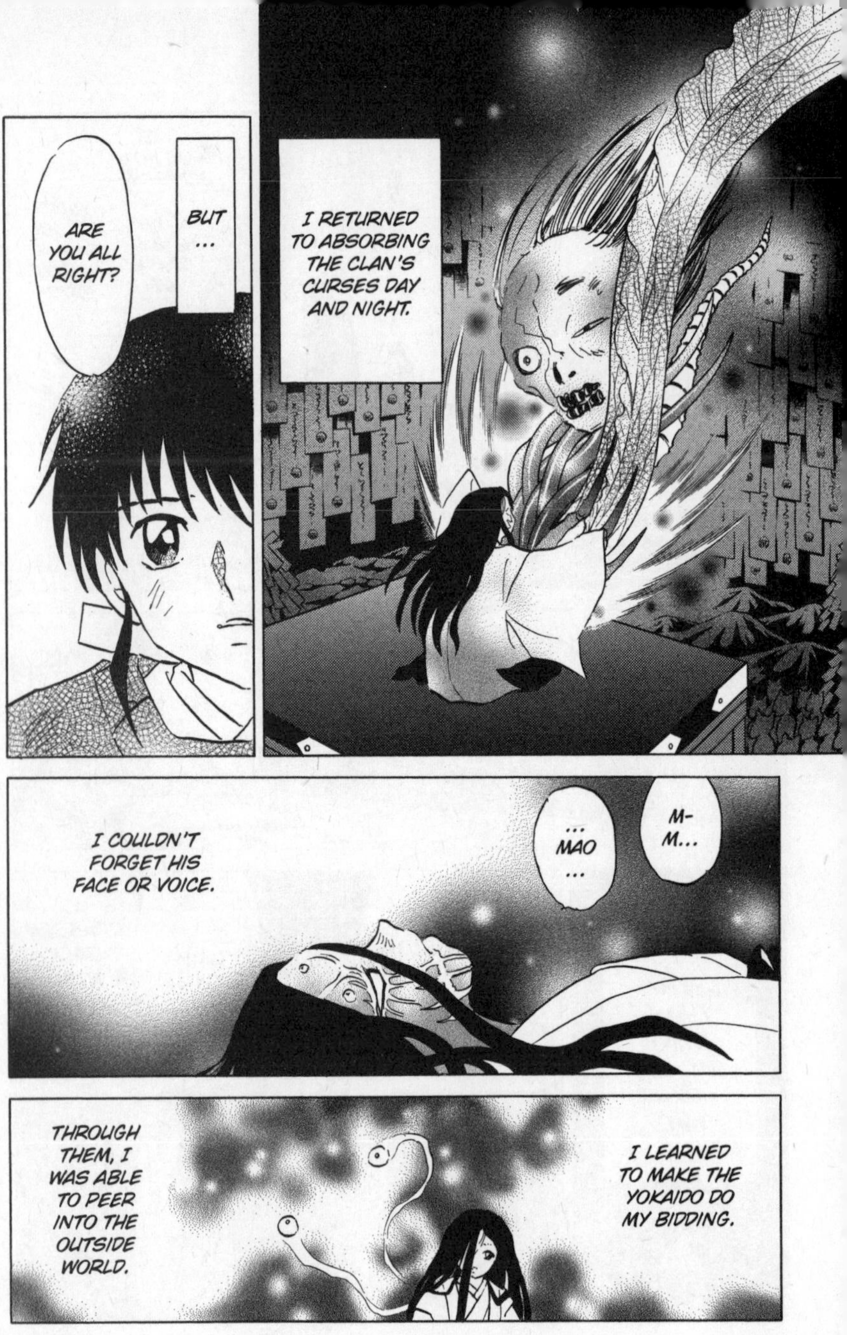
I RETURNED TO ABSORBING THE CLAN'S CURSES DAY AND NIGHT.
BUT ...
ARE YOU ALL RIGHT?
M-M...
... MAO ...
I COULDN'T FORGET HIS FACE OR VOICE.
I LEARNED TO MAKE THE YOKAIDO DO MY BIDDING.
THROUGH THEM, I WAS ABLE TO PEER INTO THE OUTSIDE WORLD.

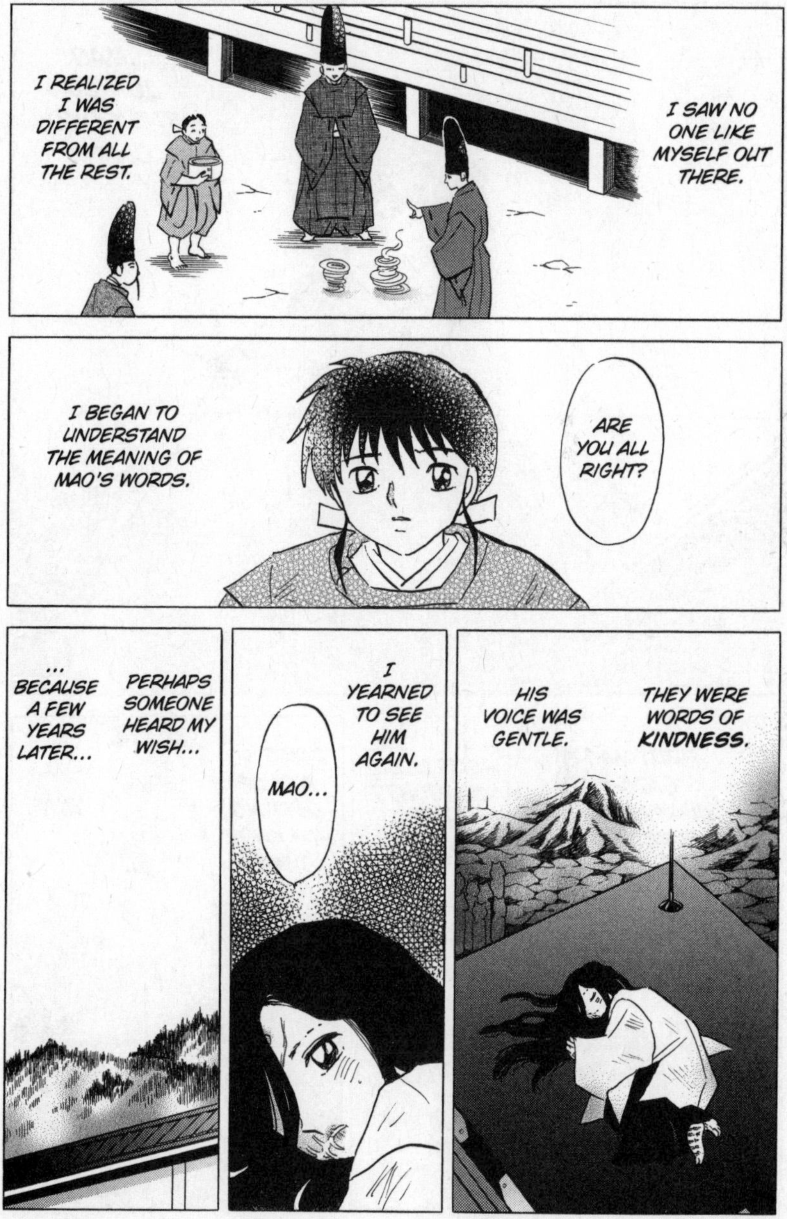
I SAW NO ONE LIKE MYSELF OUT THERE.
I REALIZED I WAS DIFFERENT FROM ALL THE REST.
ARE YOU ALL RIGHT?
I BEGAN TO UNDERSTAND THE MEANING OF MAO'S WORDS.
THEY WERE WORDS OF KINDNESS.
HIS VOICE WAS GENTLE.
I YEARNED TO SEE HIM AGAIN.
MAO...
PERHAPS SOMEONE HEARD MY WISH...
...BECAUSE A FEW YEARS LATER...

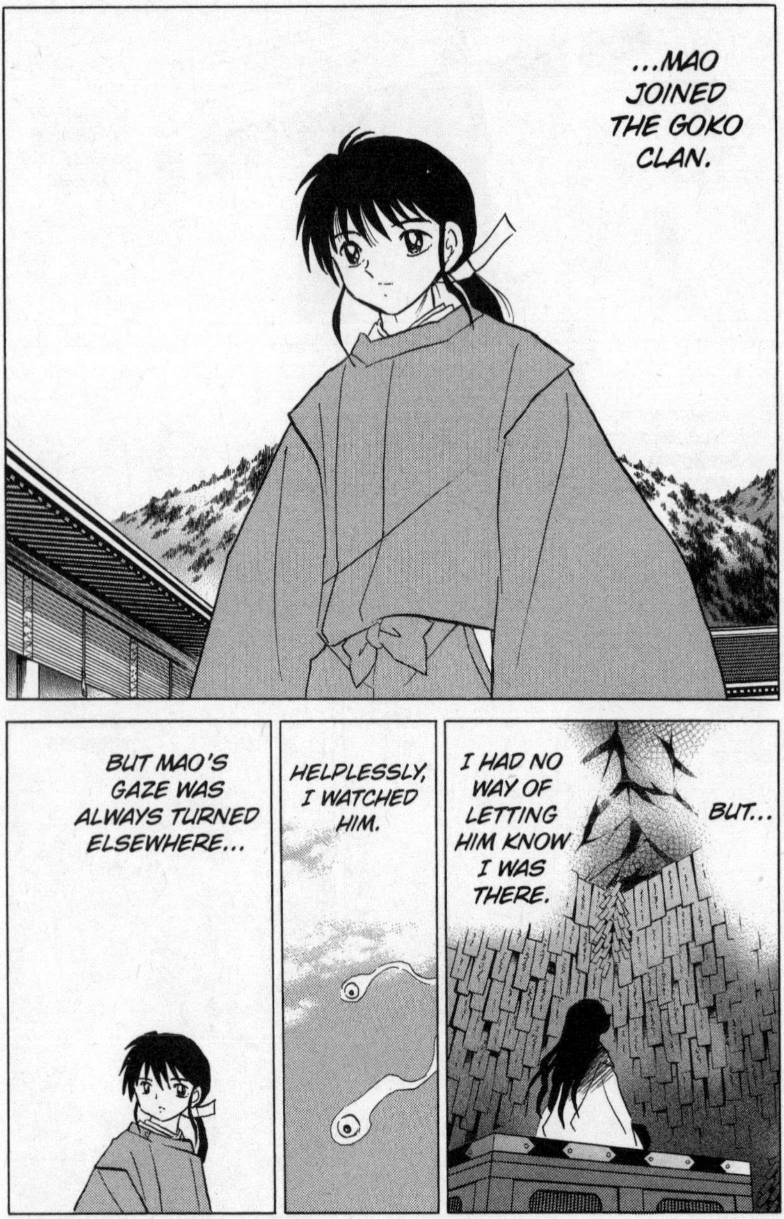
...MAO JOINED THE GOKO CLAN.
BUT...
I HAD NO WAY OF LETTING HIM KNOW I WAS THERE.
HELPLESSLY, I WATCHED HIM.
BUT MAO'S GAZE WAS ALWAYS TURNED ELSEWHERE...

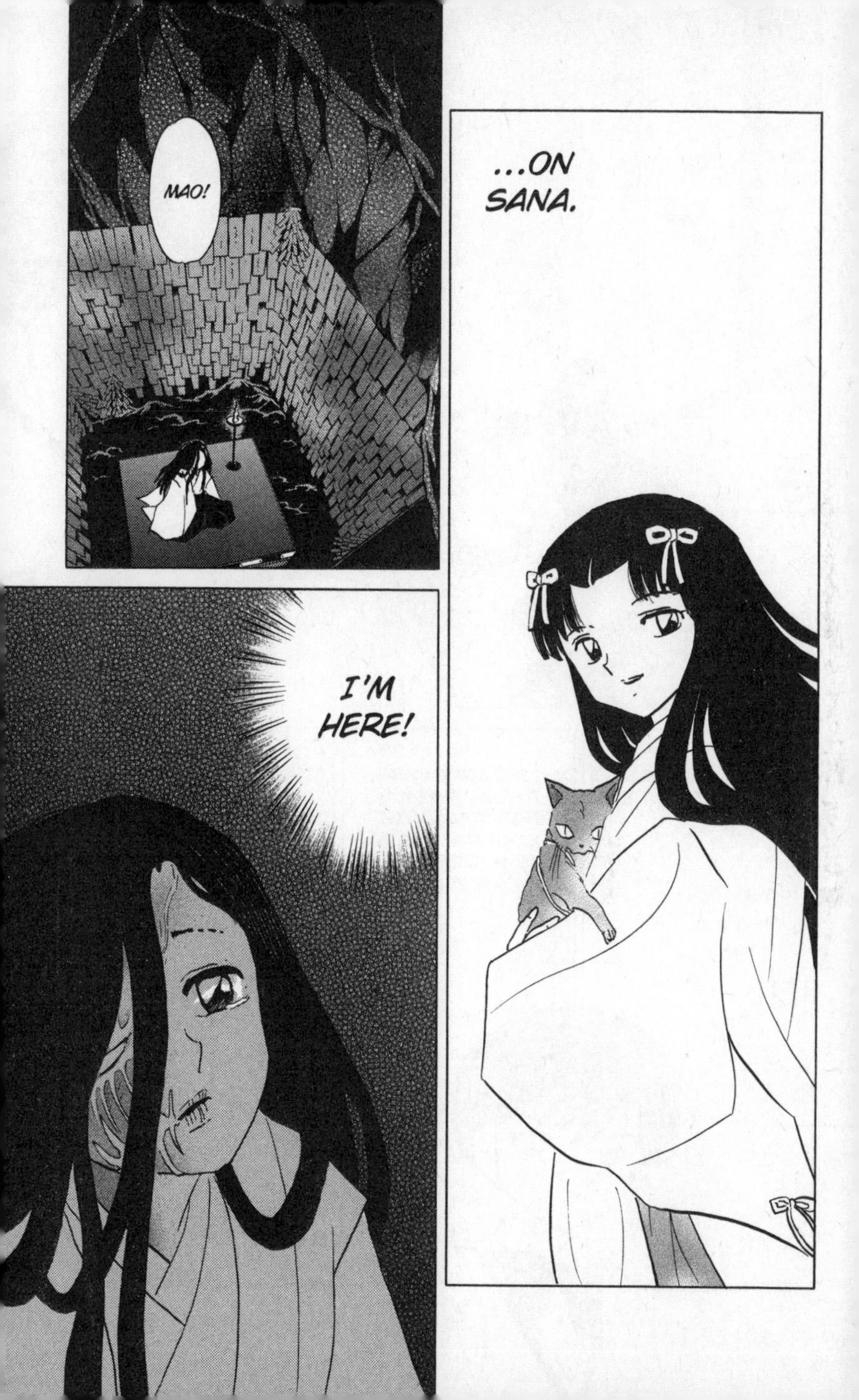
...ON SANA.
MAO!
I'M HERE!

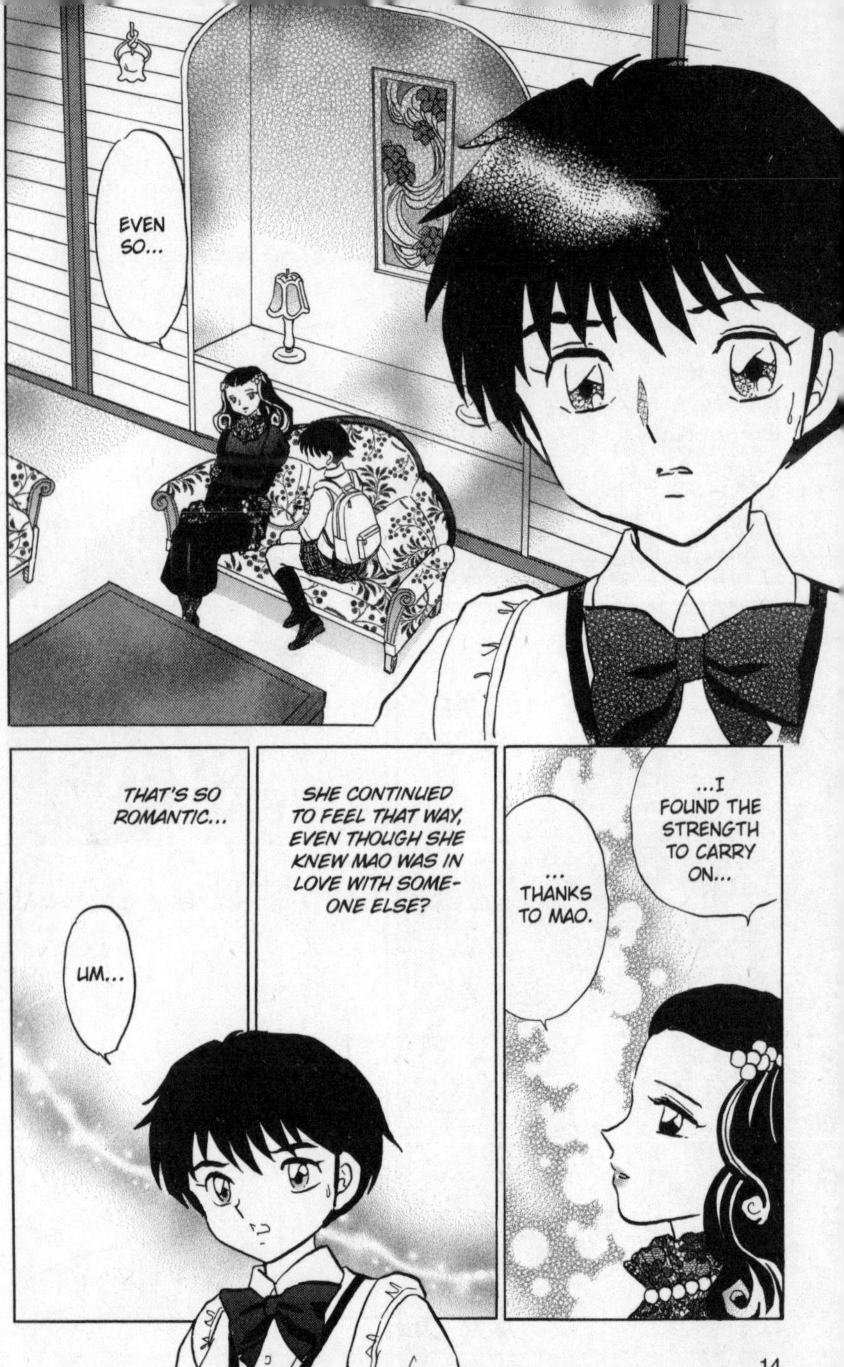
EVEN SO...
...I FOUND THE STRENGTH TO CARRY ON...
...THANKS TO MAO.
SHE CONTINUED TO FEEL THAT WAY, EVEN THOUGH SHE KNEW MAO WAS IN LOVE WITH SOME-ONE ELSE?
THAT'S SO ROMANTIC...
UM...

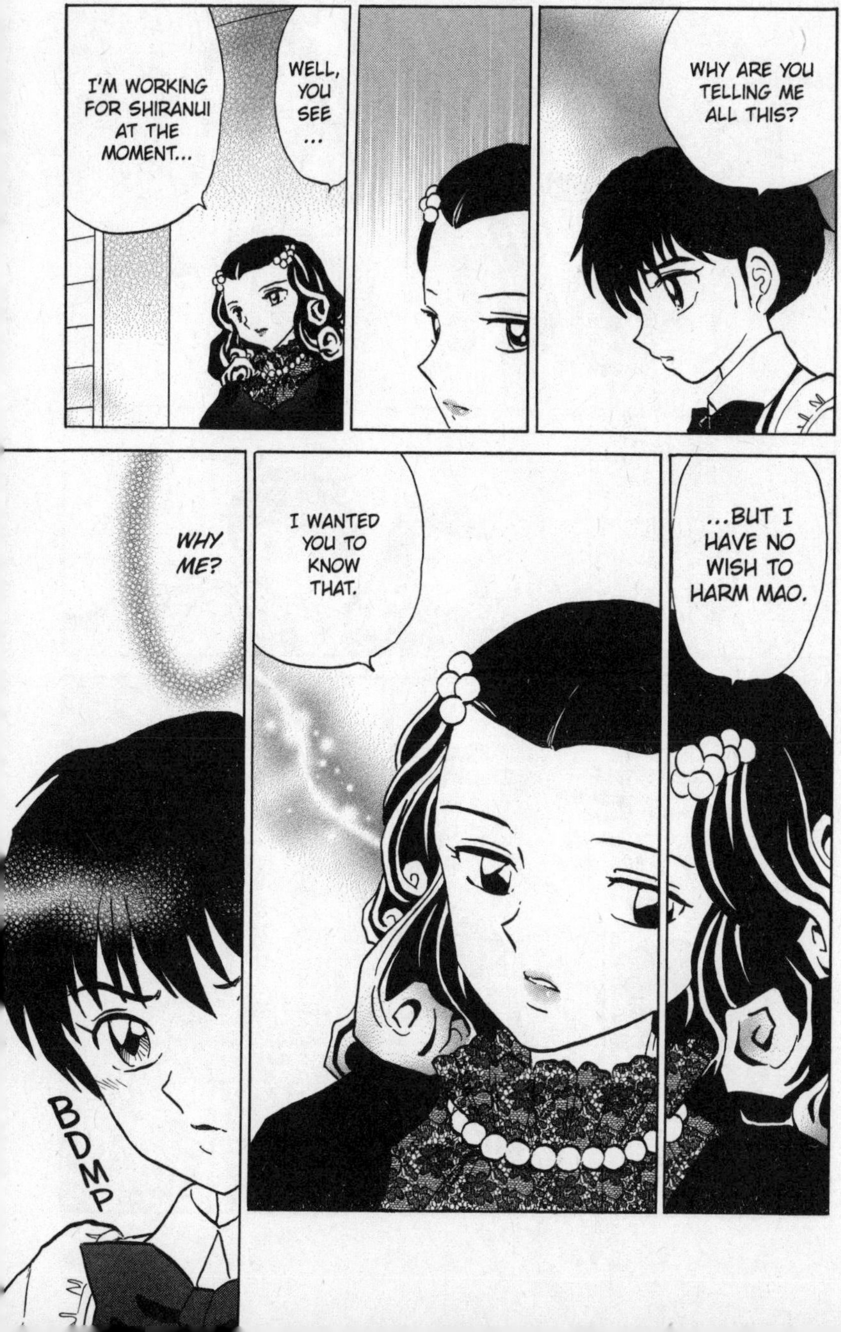
WHY ARE YOU TELLING ME ALL THIS?
WELL, YOU SEE ...
I'M WORKING FOR SHIRANUI AT THE MOMENT...
...BUT I HAVE NO WISH TO HARM MAO.
I WANTED YOU TO KNOW THAT.
WHY ME?
BDMP

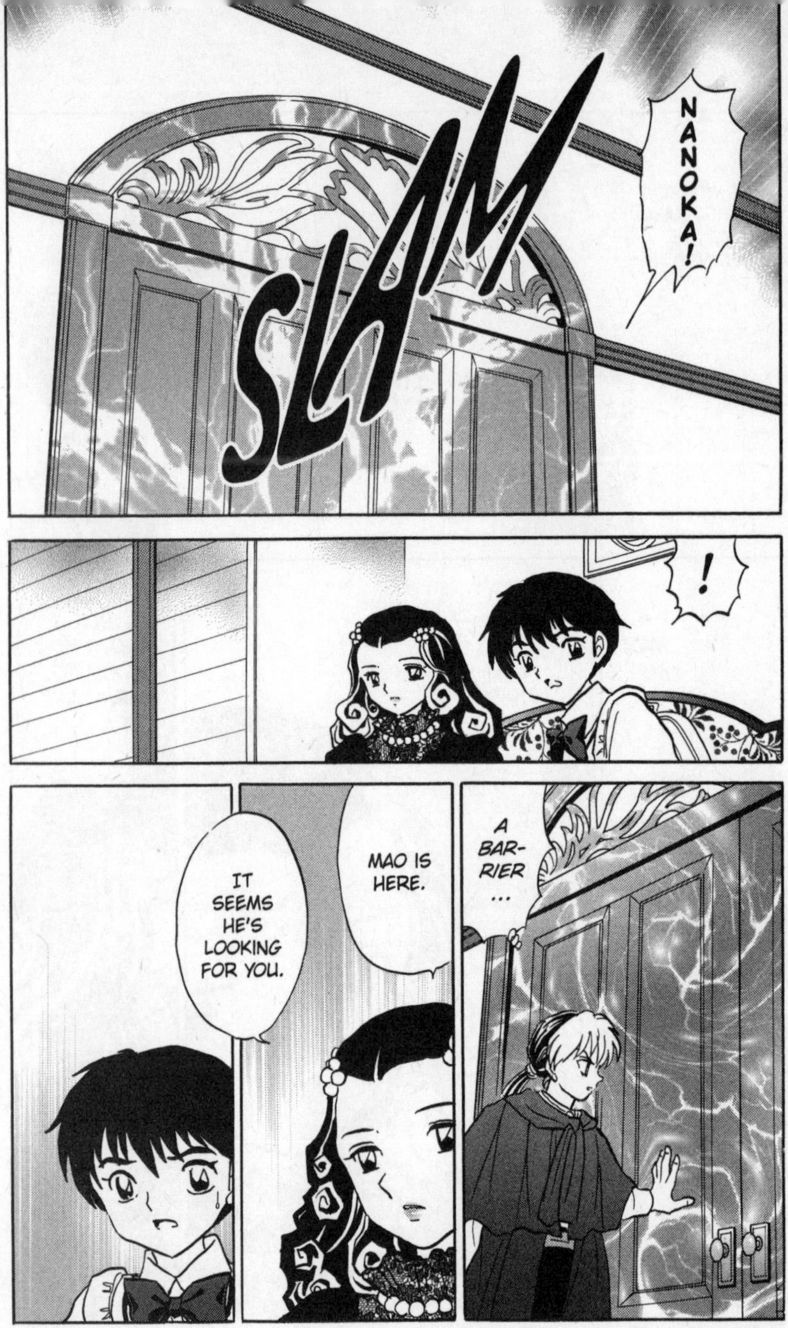
NANOKA!
SLAM
!
A BARRIER ...
MAO IS HERE.
IT SEEMS HE'S LOOKING FOR YOU.

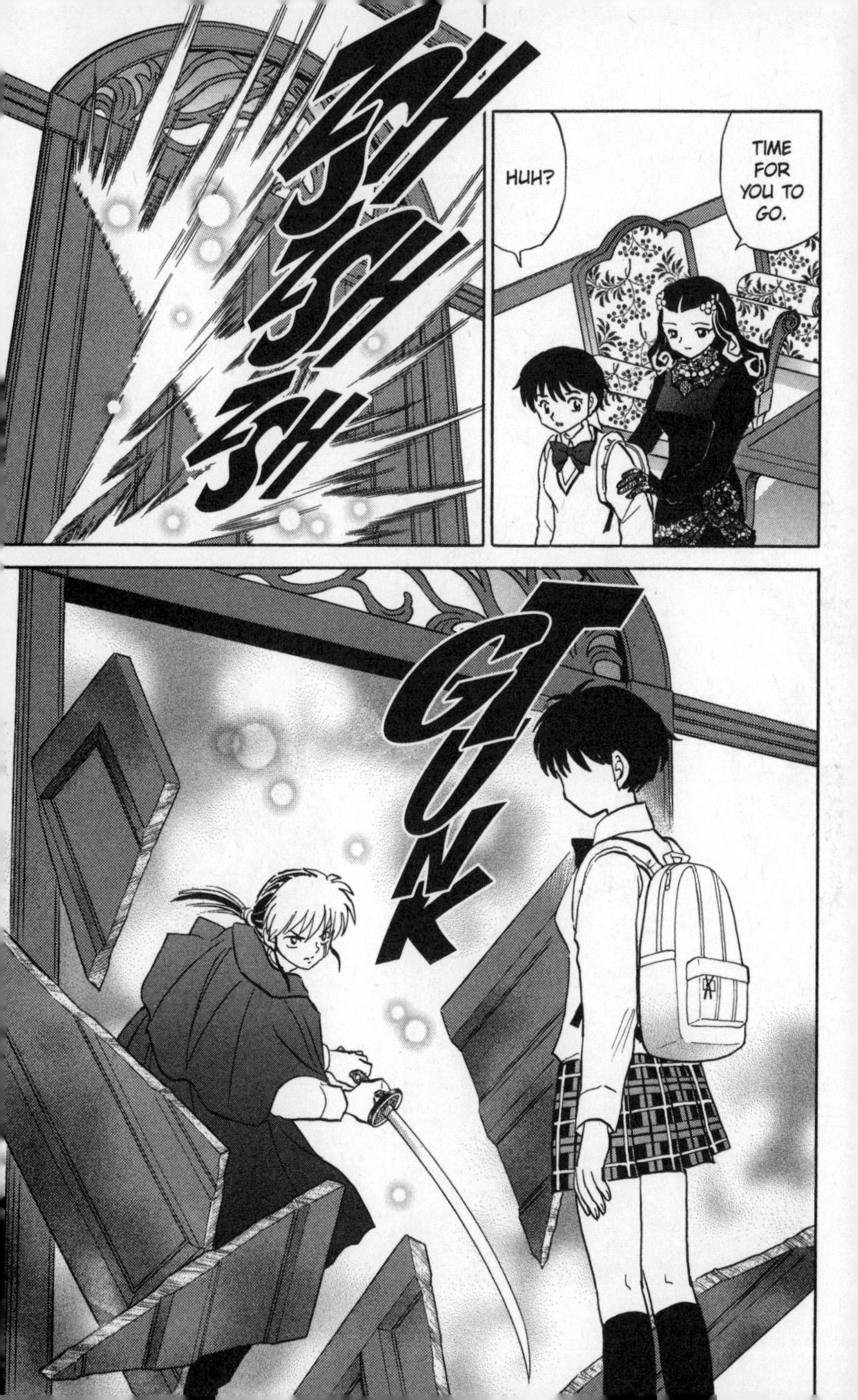
TIME FOR YOU TO GO.
HUH?

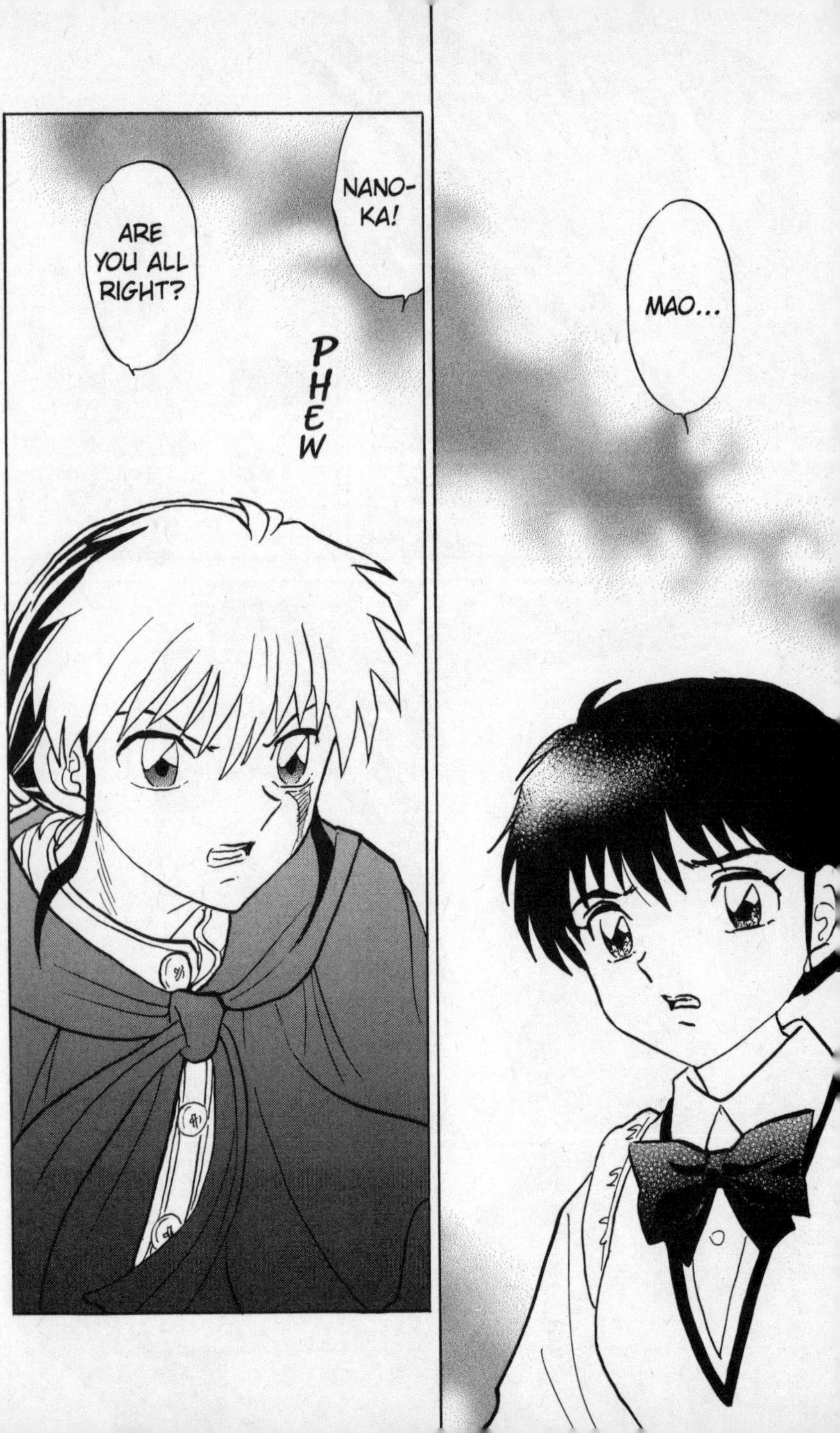
MAO...
NANO-KA!
ARE YOU ALL RIGHT?
PHEW

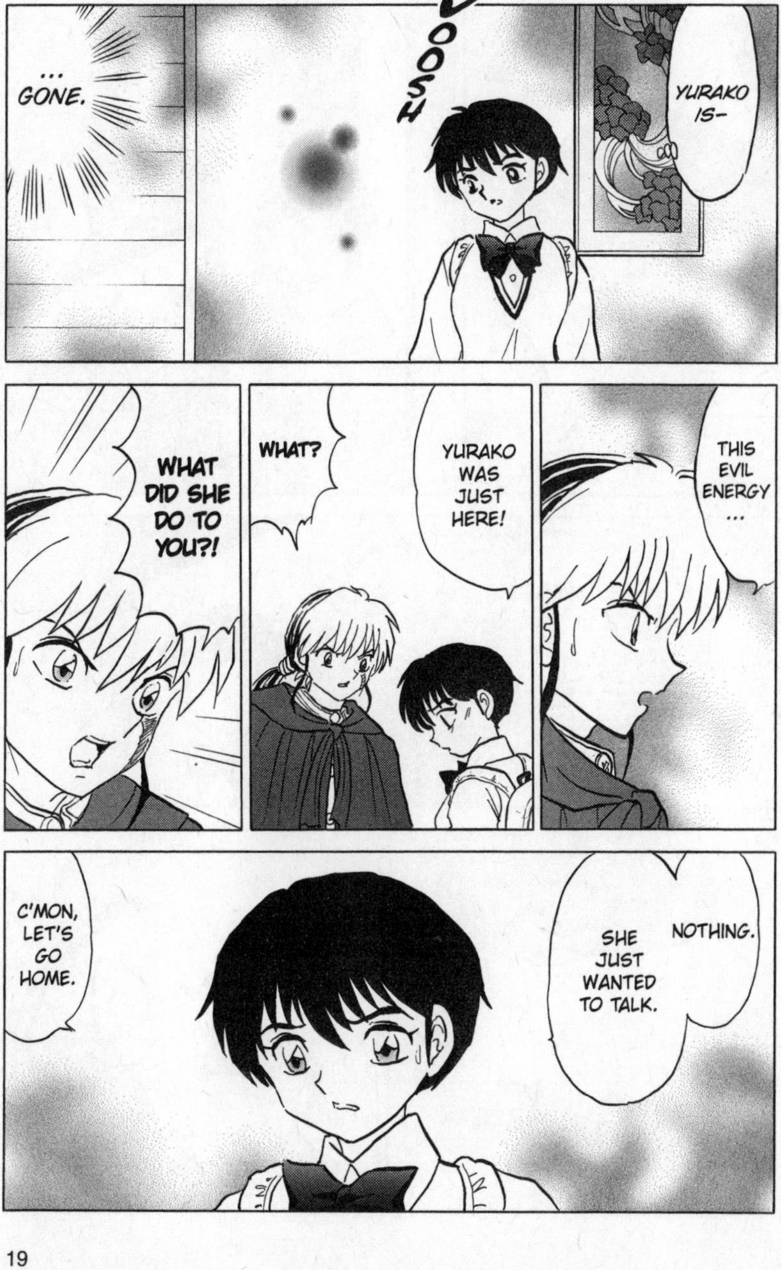
YURAKO IS-
VOOOSH
... GONE.
THIS EVIL ENERGY ...
YURAKO WAS JUST HERE!
WHAT?
WHAT DID SHE DO TO YOU?!
NOTHING.
SHE JUST WANTED TO TALK.
C'MON, LET'S GO HOME.

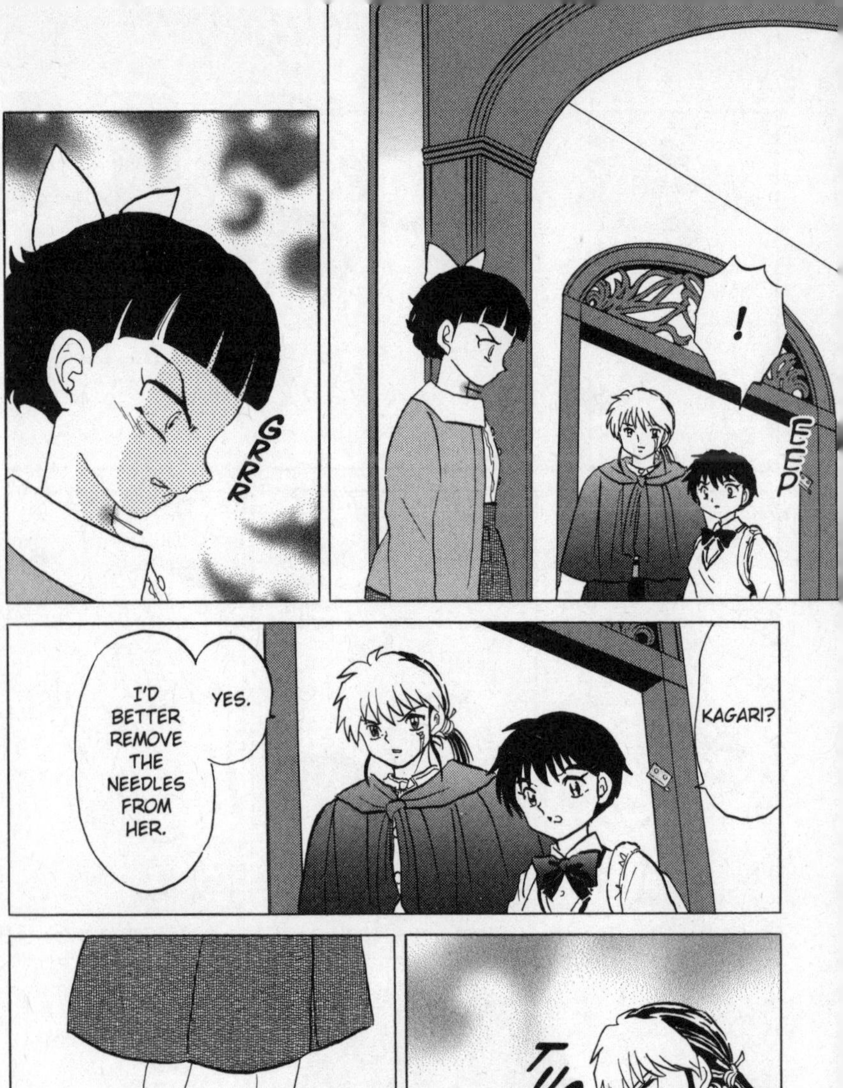
!
EEP
GRRR
KAGARI?
YES.
I'D BETTER REMOVE THE NEEDLES FROM HER.
TUG
TINK TINK
TINK

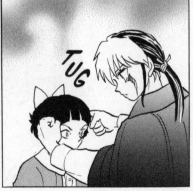

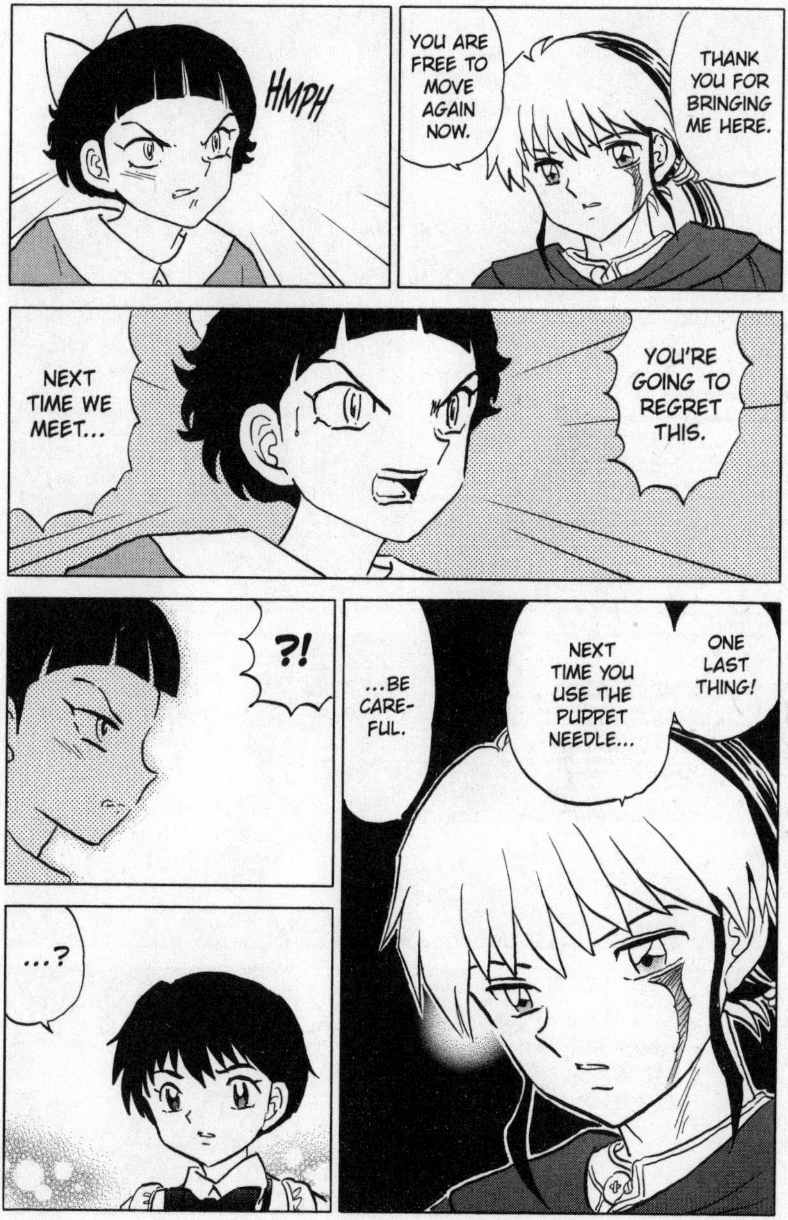
THANK YOU FOR BRINGING ME HERE.
YOU ARE FREE TO MOVE AGAIN NOW.
HMPH
YOU'RE GOING TO REGRET THIS.
NEXT TIME WE MEET...
ONE LAST THING!
NEXT TIME YOU USE THE PUPPET NEEDLE...
...BE CARE-FUL.
?!
...?

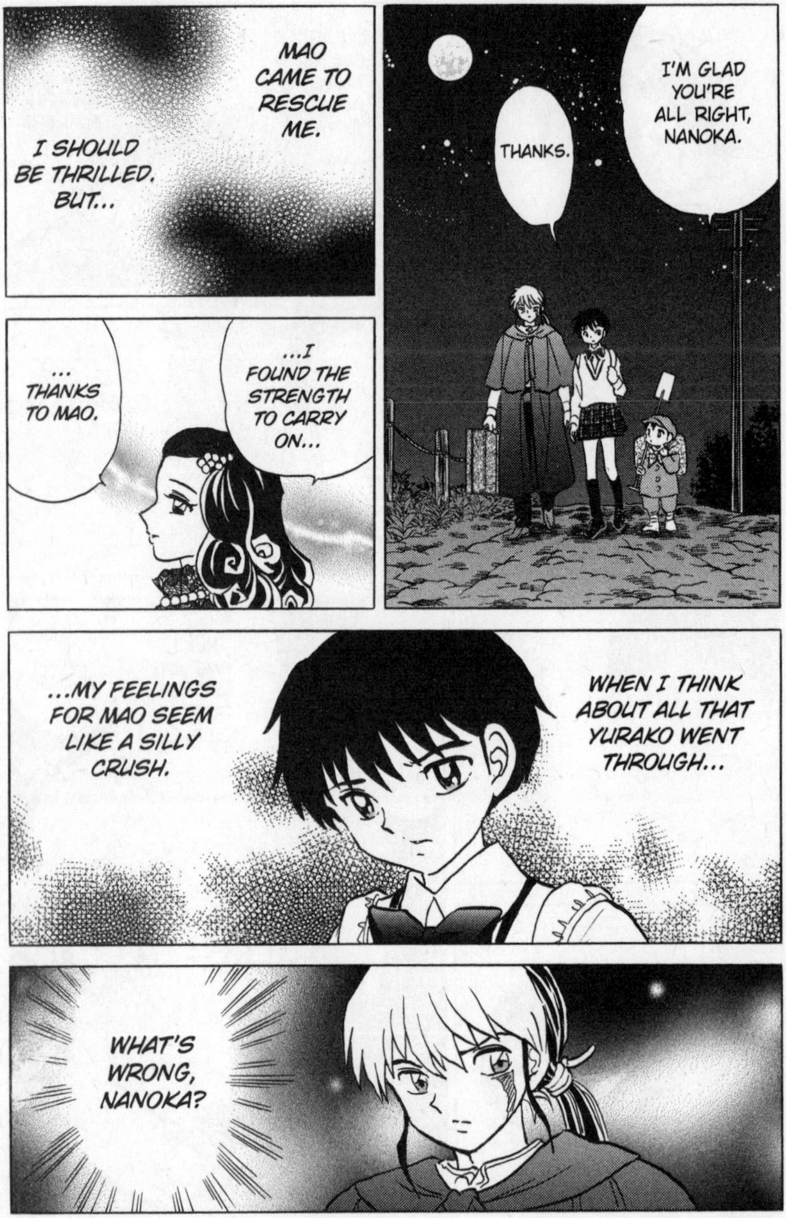
I'M GLAD YOU'RE ALL RIGHT, NANOKA.
THANKS.
MAO CAME TO RESCUE ME.
I SHOULD BE THRILLED. BUT...
...I FOUND THE STRENGTH TO CARRY ON...
... THANKS TO MAO.
WHEN I THINK ABOUT ALL THAT YURAKO WENT THROUGH...
...MY FEELINGS FOR MAO SEEM LIKE A SILLY CRUSH.
WHAT'S WRONG, NANOKA?

Chapter 2:
Words Can Curse

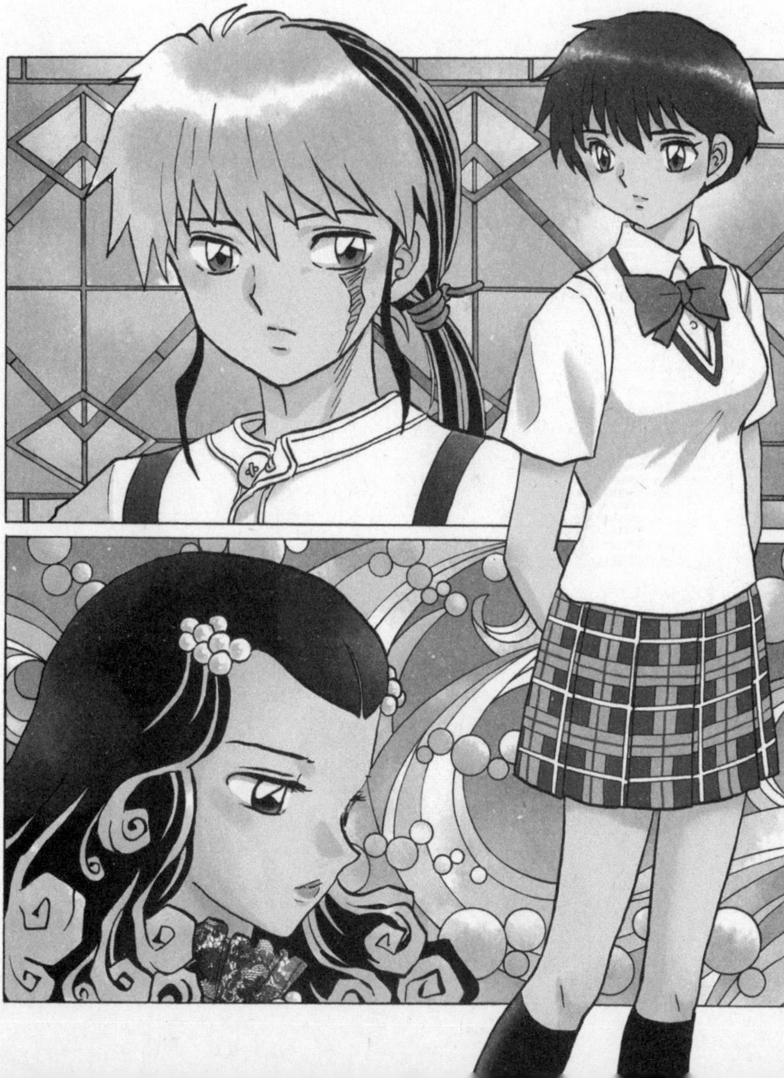

MAO

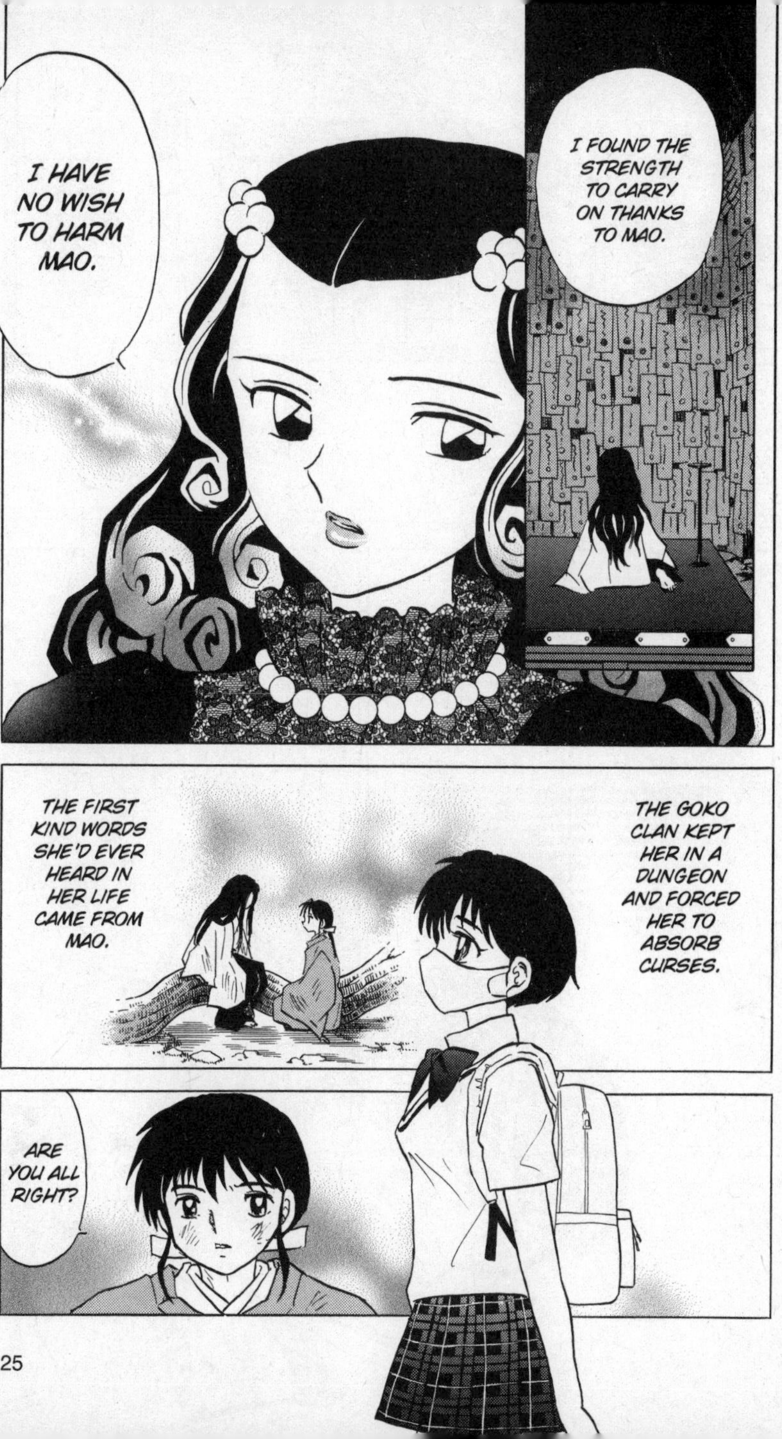
I FOUND THE STRENGTH TO CARRY ON THANKS TO MAO.
I HAVE NO WISH TO HARM MAO.
THE GOKO CLAN KEPT HER IN A DUNGEON AND FORCED HER TO ABSORB CURSES.
THE FIRST KIND WORDS SHE'D EVER HEARD IN HER LIFE CAME FROM MAO.
ARE YOU ALL RIGHT?

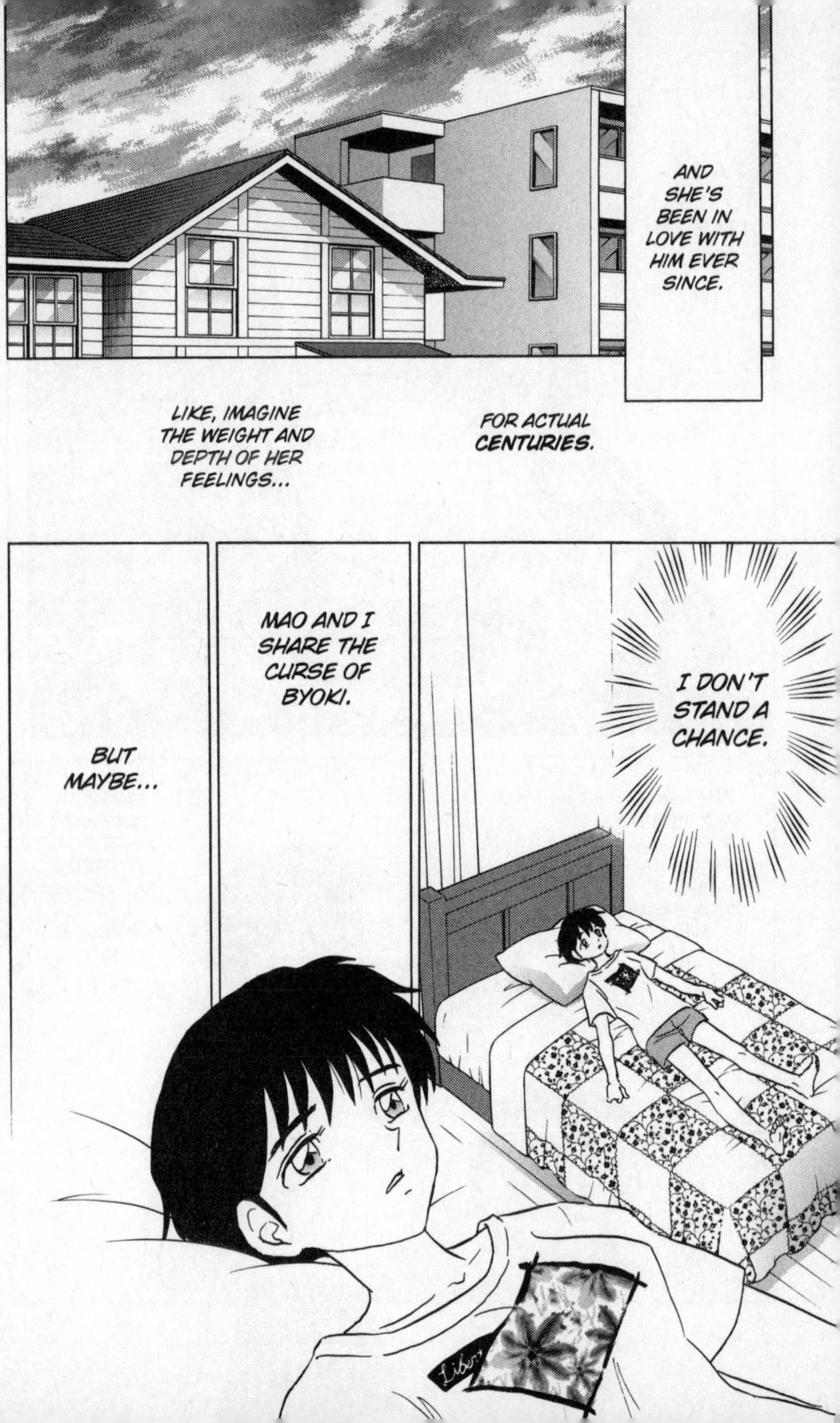
AND SHE'S BEEN IN LOVE WITH HIM EVER SINCE.
FOR ACTUAL CENTURIES.
LIKE, IMAGINE THE WEIGHT AND DEPTH OF HER FEELINGS...
I DON'T STAND A CHANCE.
MAO AND I SHARE THE CURSE OF BYOKI.
BUT MAYBE...

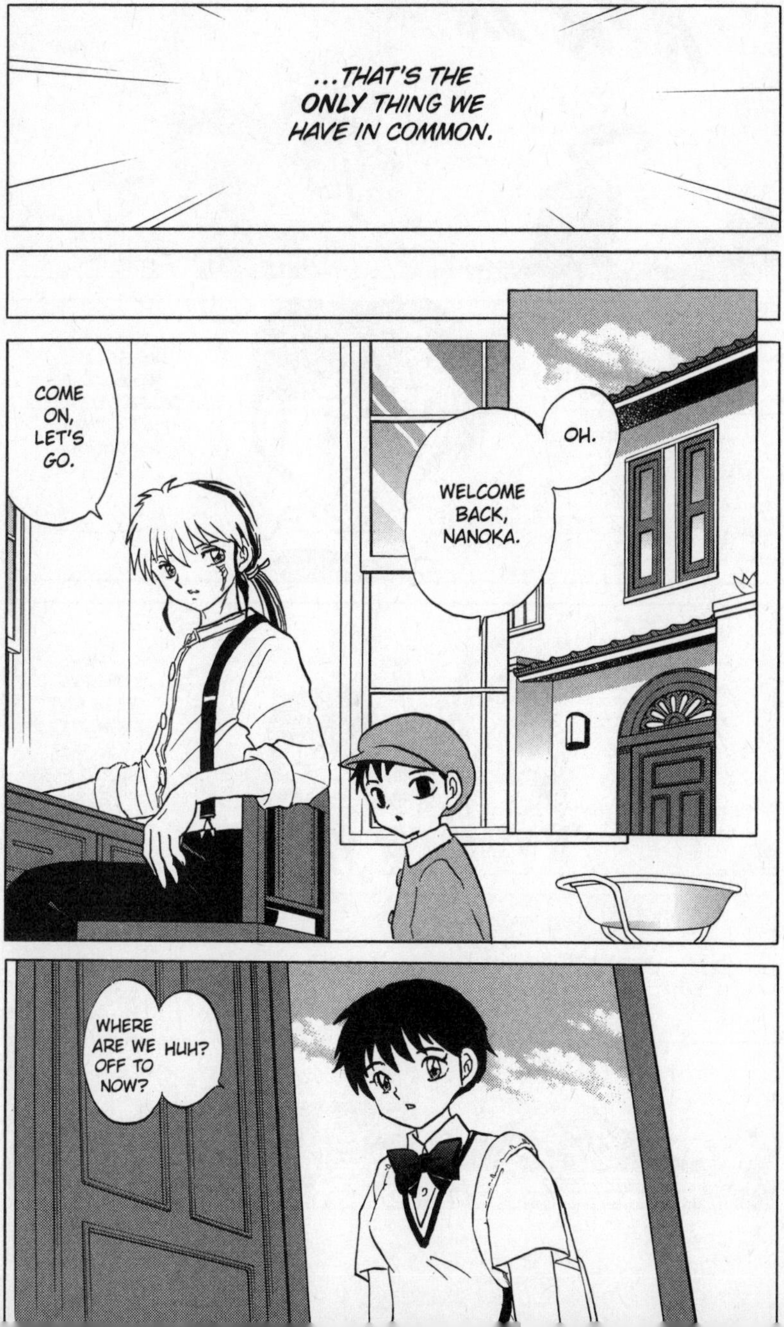
...THAT'S THE ONLY THING WE HAVE IN COMMON.
OH.
WELCOME BACK, NANOKA.
COME ON, LET'S GO.
HUH?
WHERE ARE WE OFF TO NOW?

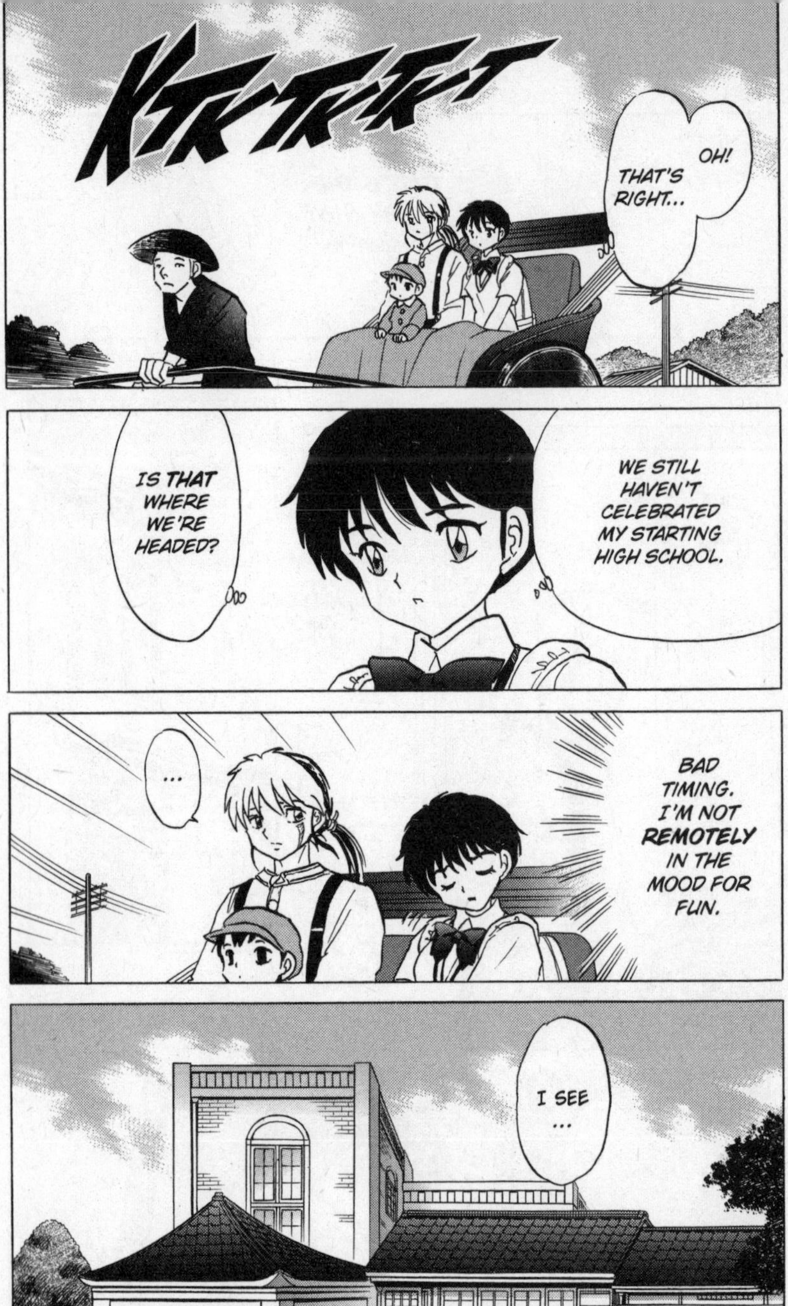
KTR-TR-TR-T
OH! THAT'S RIGHT...
WE STILL HAVEN'T CELEBRATED MY STARTING HIGH SCHOOL.
IS THAT WHERE WE'RE HEADED?
BAD TIMING. I'M NOT REMOTELY IN THE MOOD FOR FUN.
...
I SEE ...

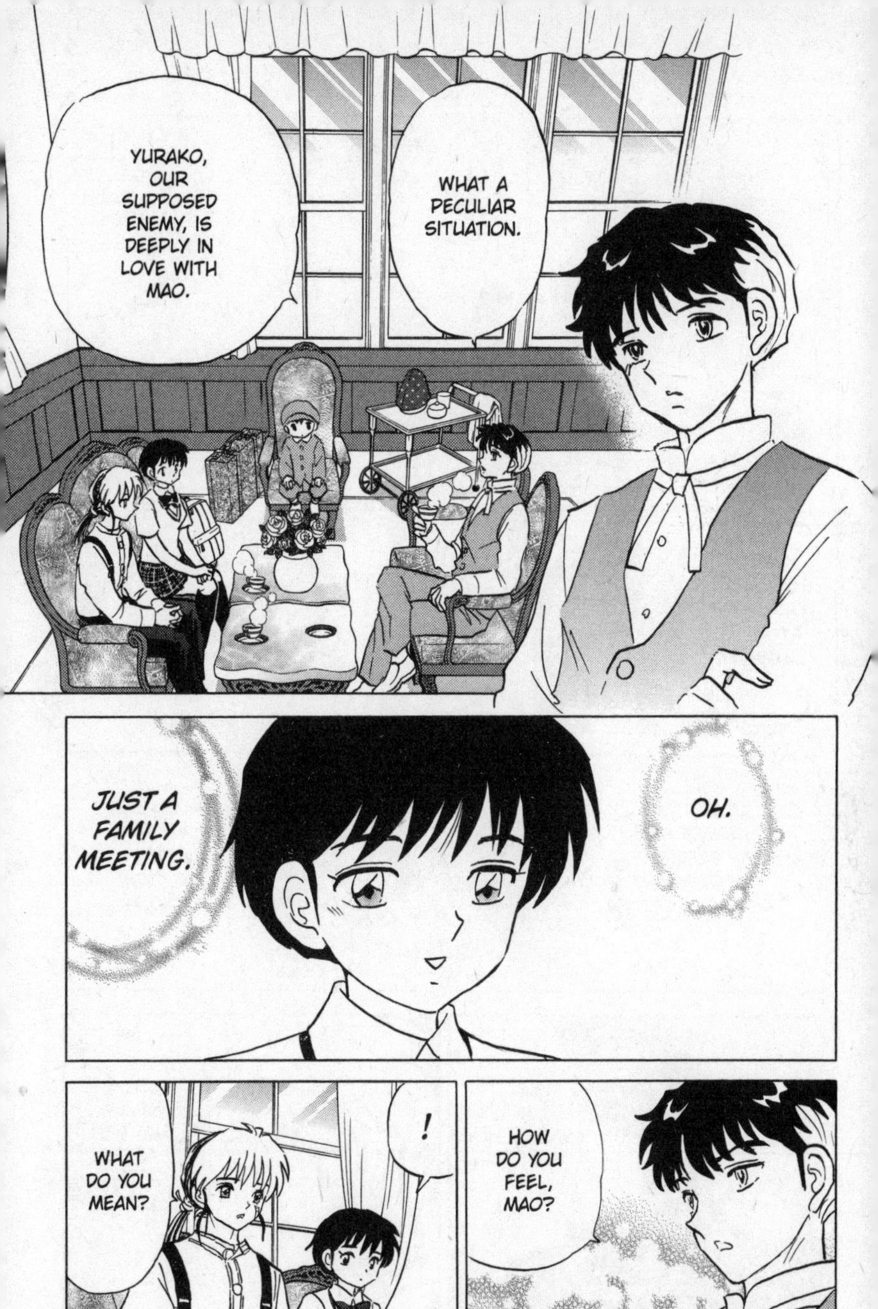
WHAT A PECULIAR SITUATION.
YURAKO, OUR SUPPOSED ENEMY, IS DEEPLY IN LOVE WITH MAO.
OH.
JUST A FAMILY MEETING.
HOW DO YOU FEEL, MAO?
!
WHAT DO YOU MEAN?

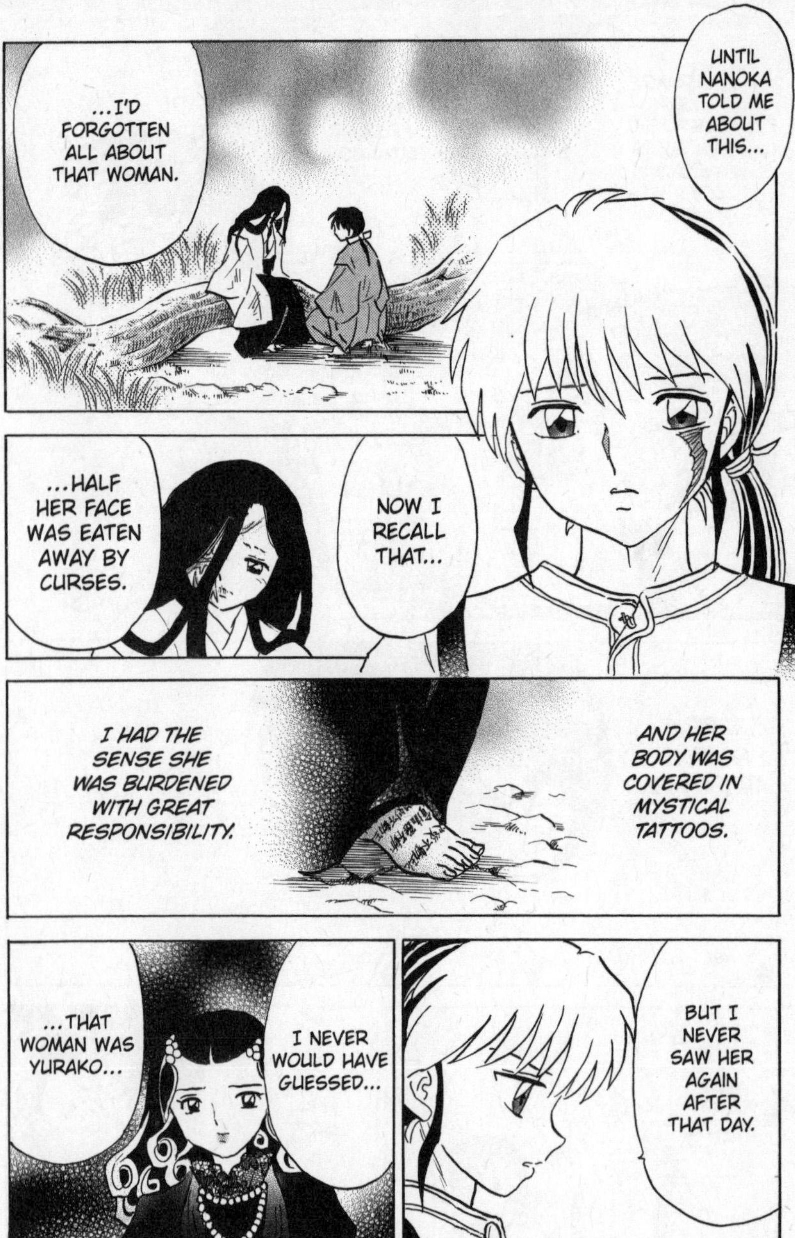
UNTIL NANOKA TOLD ME ABOUT THIS...
...I'D FORGOTTEN ALL ABOUT THAT WOMAN.
NOW I RECALL THAT...
...HALF HER FACE WAS EATEN AWAY BY CURSES.
AND HER BODY WAS COVERED IN MYSTICAL TATTOOS.
I HAD THE SENSE SHE WAS BURDENED WITH GREAT RESPONSIBILITY.
BUT I NEVER SAW HER AGAIN AFTER THAT DAY.
I NEVER WOULD HAVE GUESSED...
...THAT WOMAN WAS YURAKO...

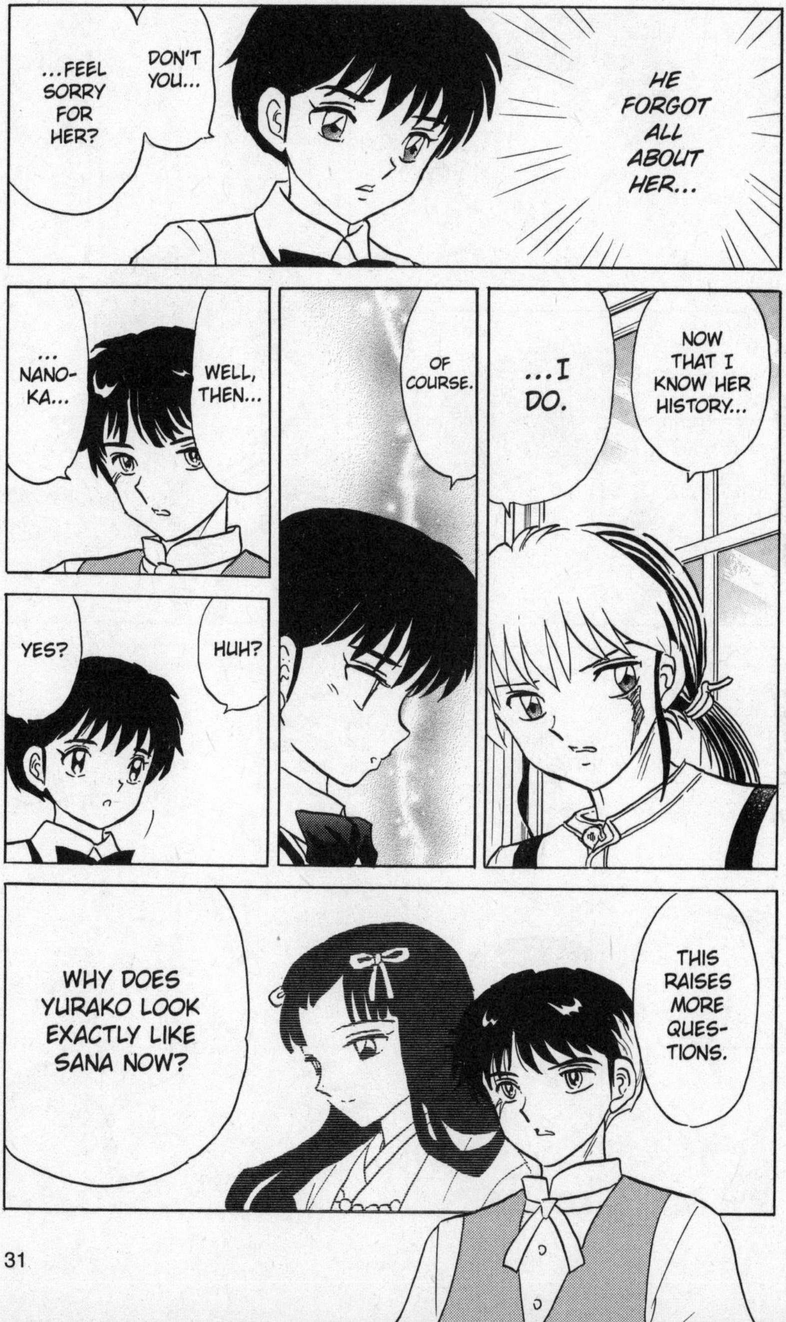
HE FORGOT ALL ABOUT HER...
DON'T YOU...
...FEEL SORRY FOR HER?
NOW THAT I KNOW HER HISTORY...
...I DO.
OF COURSE.
WELL, THEN...
...NANO-KA...
HUH?
YES?
THIS RAISES MORE QUES-TIONS.
WHY DOES YURAKO LOOK EXACTLY LIKE SANA NOW?

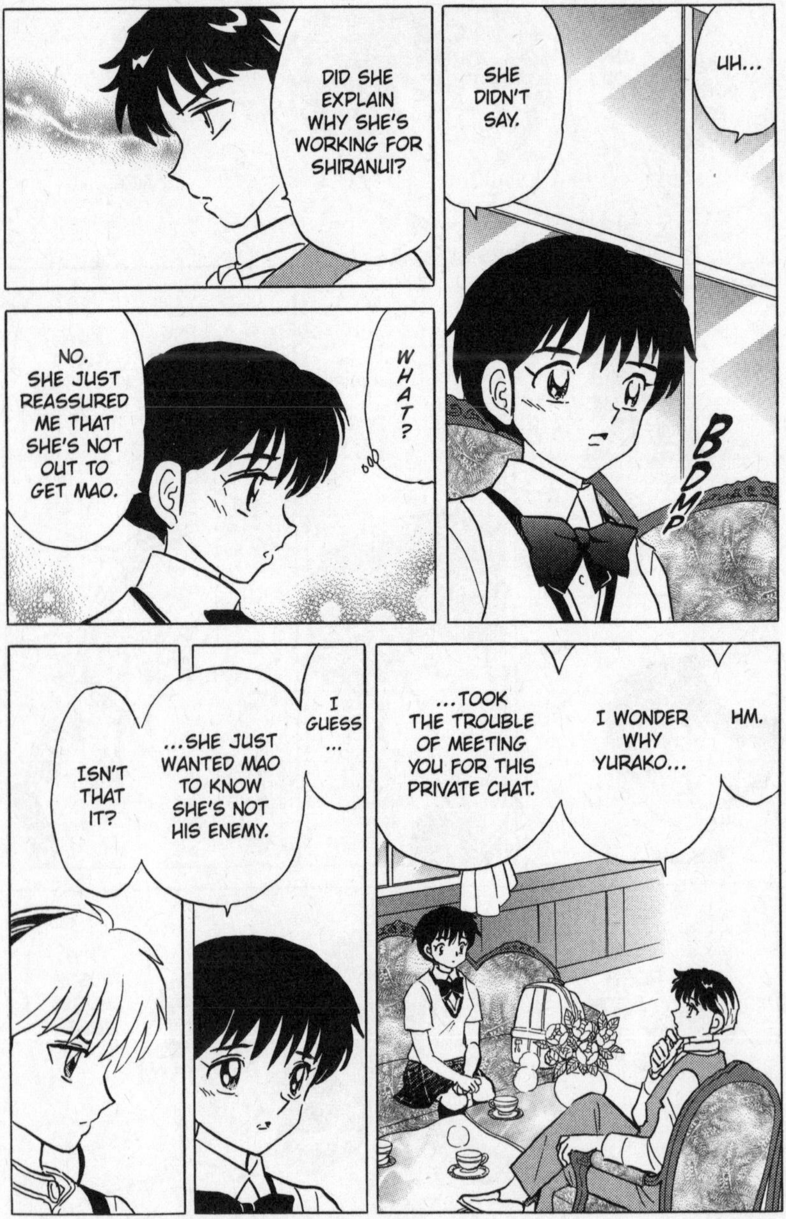
UH...
SHE DIDN'T SAY.
BDOMP
DID SHE EXPLAIN WHY SHE'S WORKING FOR SHIRANUI?
WHAT?
NO. SHE JUST REASSURED ME THAT SHE'S NOT OUT TO GET MAO.
HM.
I WONDER WHY YURAKO...
...TOOK THE TROUBLE OF MEETING YOU FOR THIS PRIVATE CHAT.
I GUESS...
...SHE JUST WANTED MAO TO KNOW SHE'S NOT HIS ENEMY.
ISN'T THAT IT?

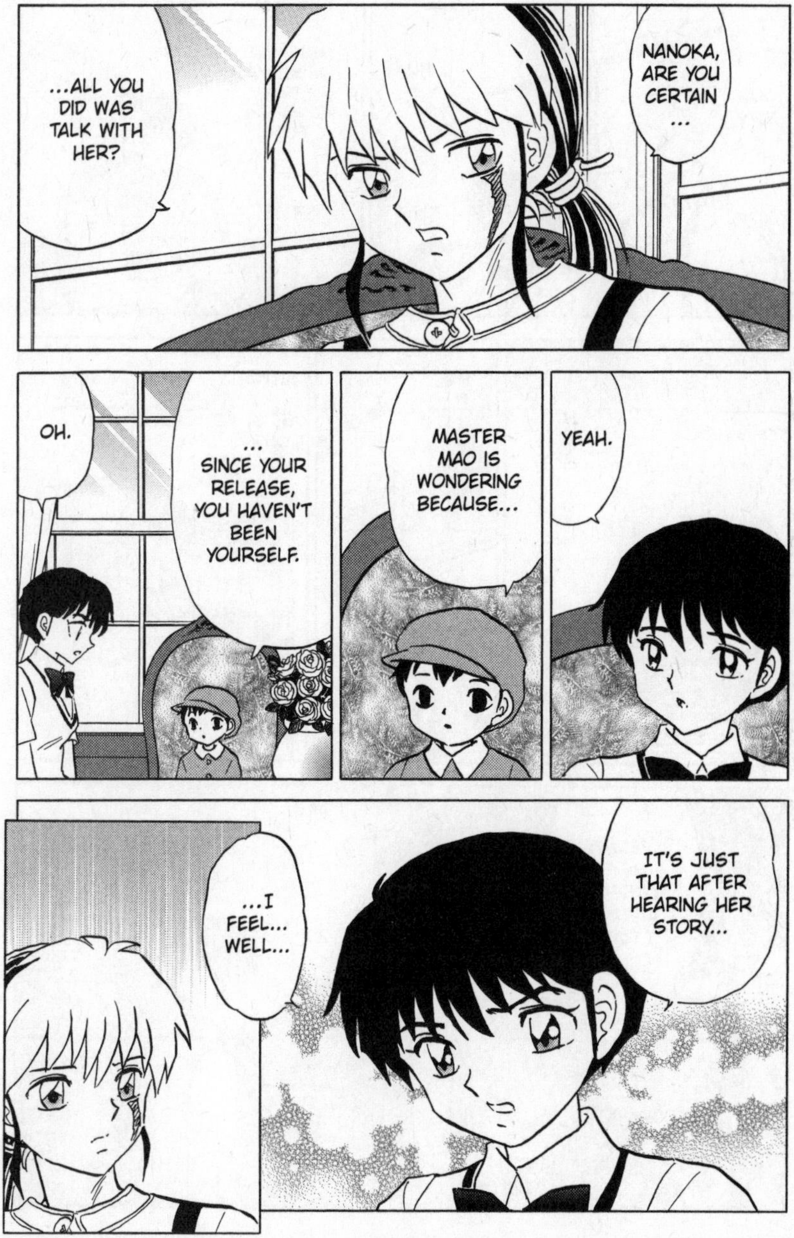
NANOKA, ARE YOU CERTAIN ...
...ALL YOU DID WAS TALK WITH HER?
YEAH.
MASTER MAO IS WONDERING BECAUSE...
... SINCE YOUR RELEASE, YOU HAVEN'T BEEN YOURSELF.
OH.
IT'S JUST THAT AFTER HEARING HER STORY...
...I FEEL... WELL...

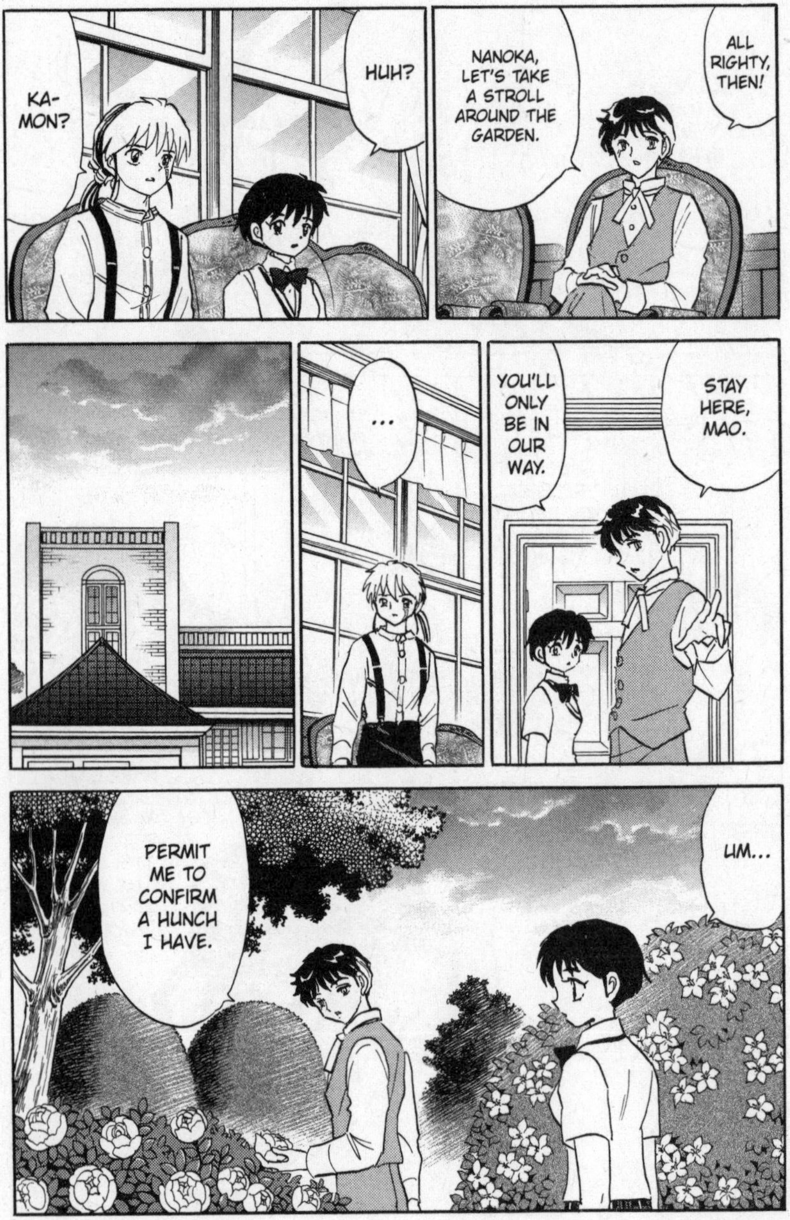
ALL RIGHTY, THEN!
NANOKA, LET'S TAKE A STROLL AROUND THE GARDEN.
HUH?
KA-MON?
STAY HERE, MAO.
YOU'LL ONLY BE IN OUR WAY.
...
UM...
PERMIT ME TO CONFIRM A HUNCH I HAVE.

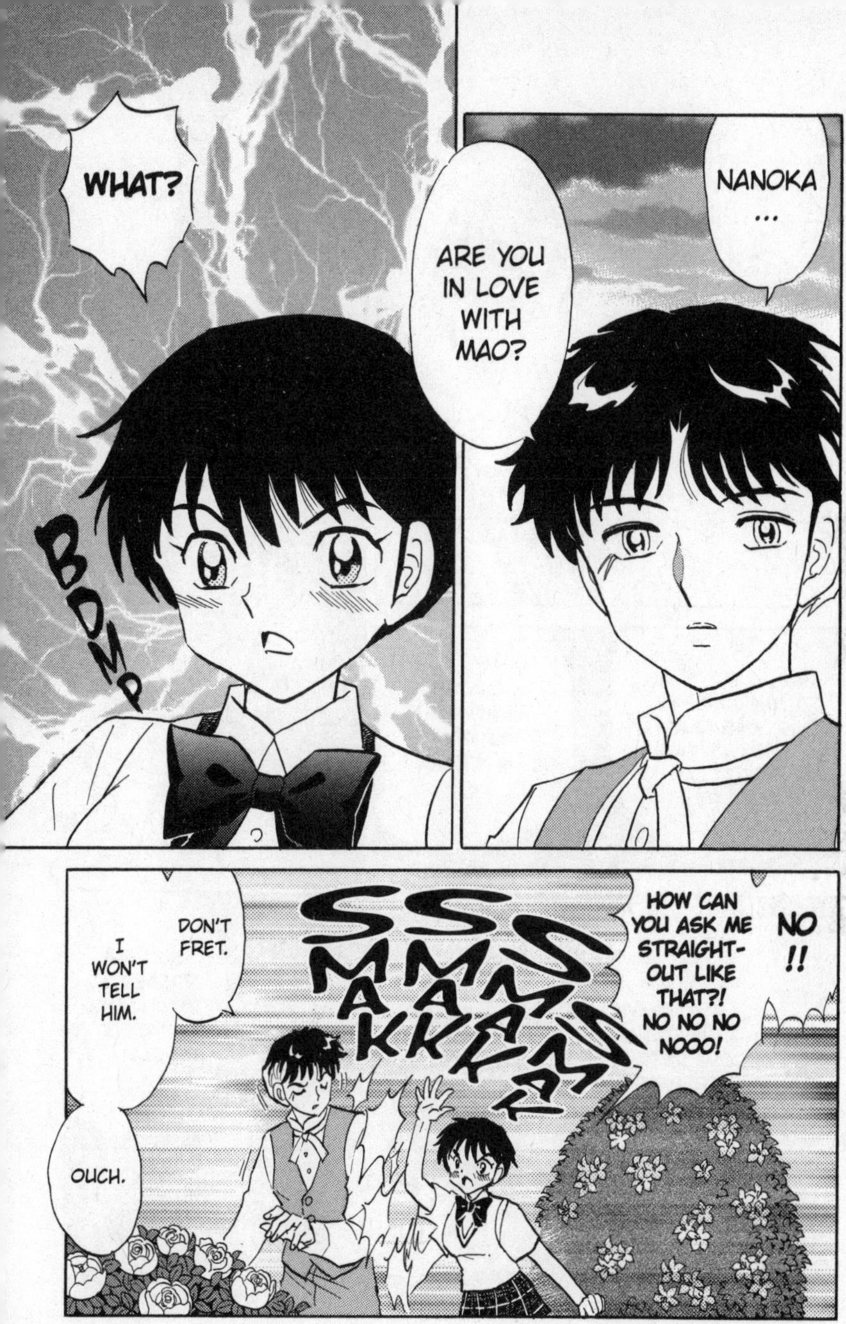
NANOKA ...
ARE YOU IN LOVE WITH MAO?
WHAT?
BDMP
NO !!
HOW CAN YOU ASK ME STRAIGHT-OUT LIKE THAT?! NO NO NO NOOO!
DON'T FRET.
I WON'T TELL HIM.
OUCH.

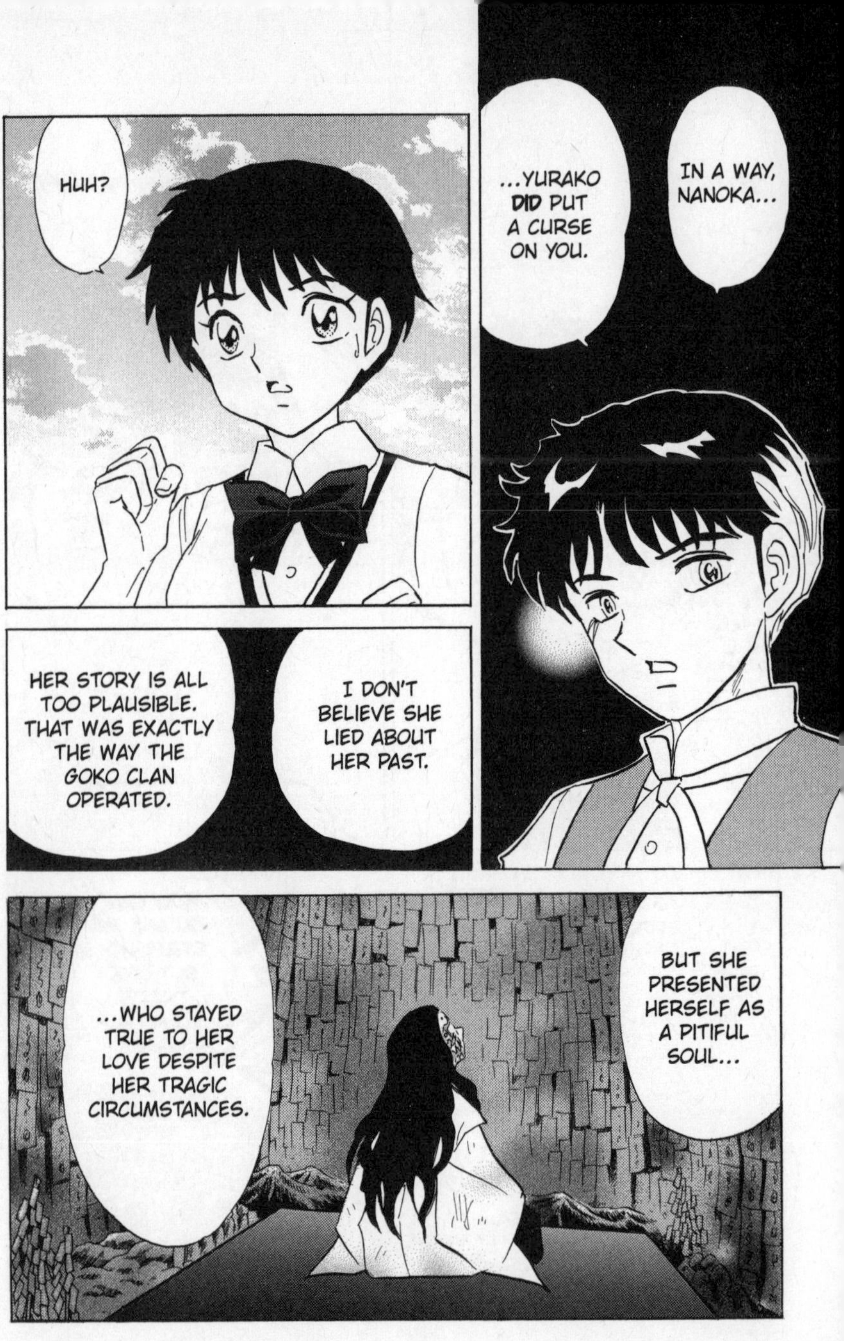
IN A WAY, NANOKA...
...YURAKO **DID** PUT A CURSE ON YOU.
HUH?
I DON'T BELIEVE SHE LIED ABOUT HER PAST.
HER STORY IS ALL TOO PLAUSIBLE. THAT WAS EXACTLY THE WAY THE GOKO CLAN OPERATED.
BUT SHE PRESENTED HERSELF AS A PITIFUL SOUL...
...WHO STAYED TRUE TO HER LOVE DESPITE HER TRAGIC CIRCUMSTANCES.

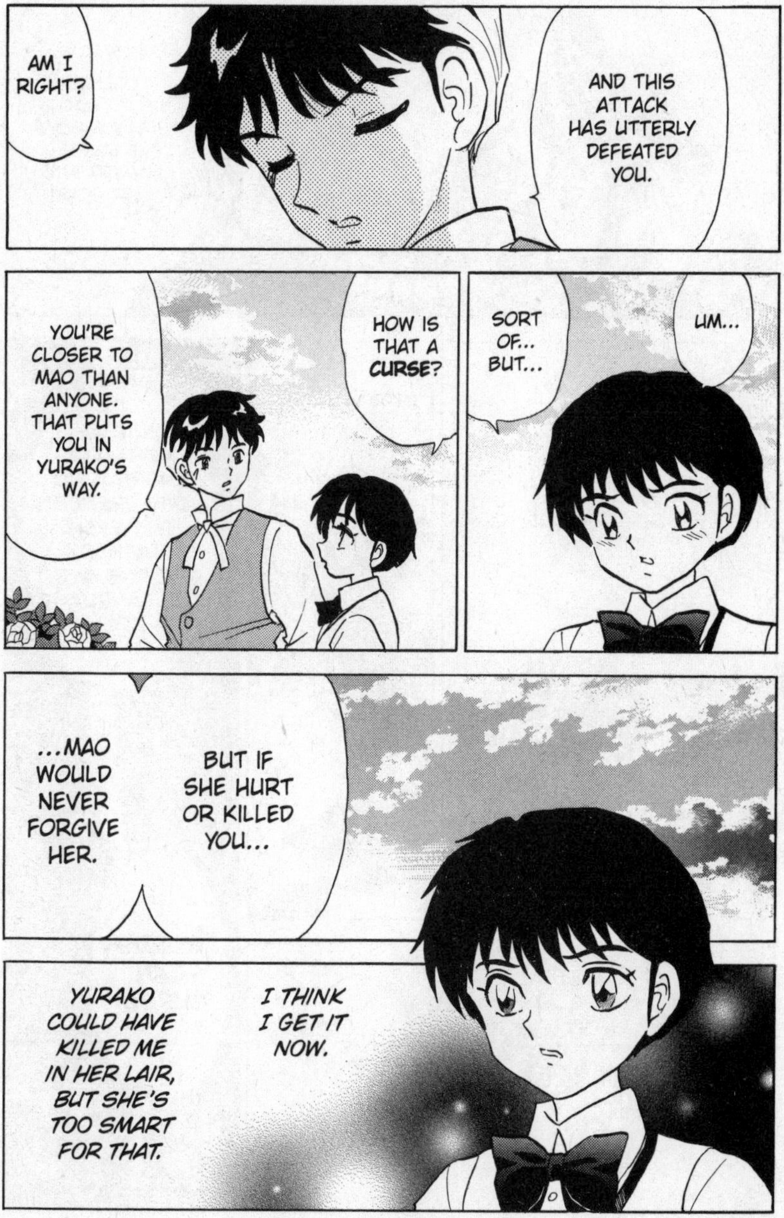
AND THIS ATTACK HAS UTTERLY DEFEATED YOU.
AM I RIGHT?
UM...
SORT OF... BUT...
HOW IS THAT A CURSE?
YOU'RE CLOSER TO MAO THAN ANYONE. THAT PUTS YOU IN YURAKO'S WAY.
BUT IF SHE HURT OR KILLED YOU...
...MAO WOULD NEVER FORGIVE HER.
I THINK I GET IT NOW.
YURAKO COULD HAVE KILLED ME IN HER LAIR, BUT SHE'S TOO SMART FOR THAT.

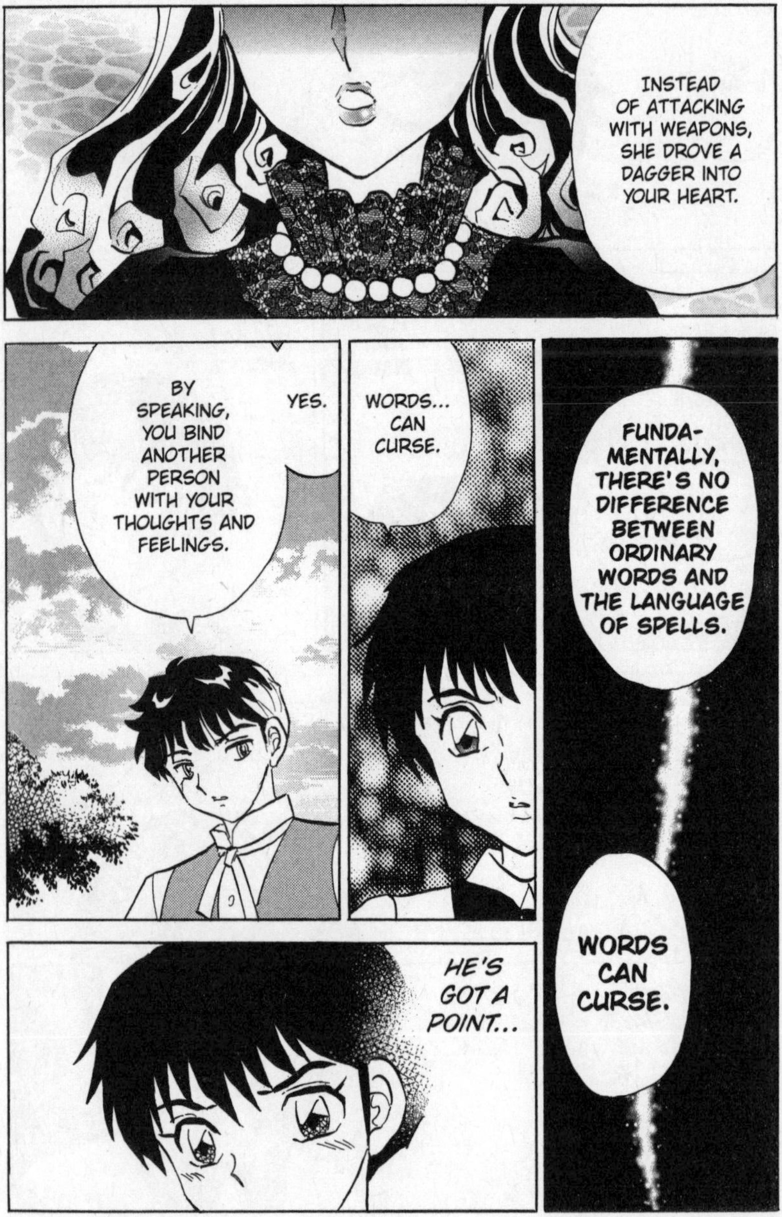
INSTEAD OF ATTACKING WITH WEAPONS, SHE DROVE A DAGGER INTO YOUR HEART.
FUNDA-MENTALLY, THERE'S NO DIFFERENCE BETWEEN ORDINARY WORDS AND THE LANGUAGE OF SPELLS.
WORDS CAN CURSE.
WORDS... CAN CURSE.
YES.
BY SPEAKING, YOU BIND ANOTHER PERSON WITH YOUR THOUGHTS AND FEELINGS.
HE'S GOT A POINT...

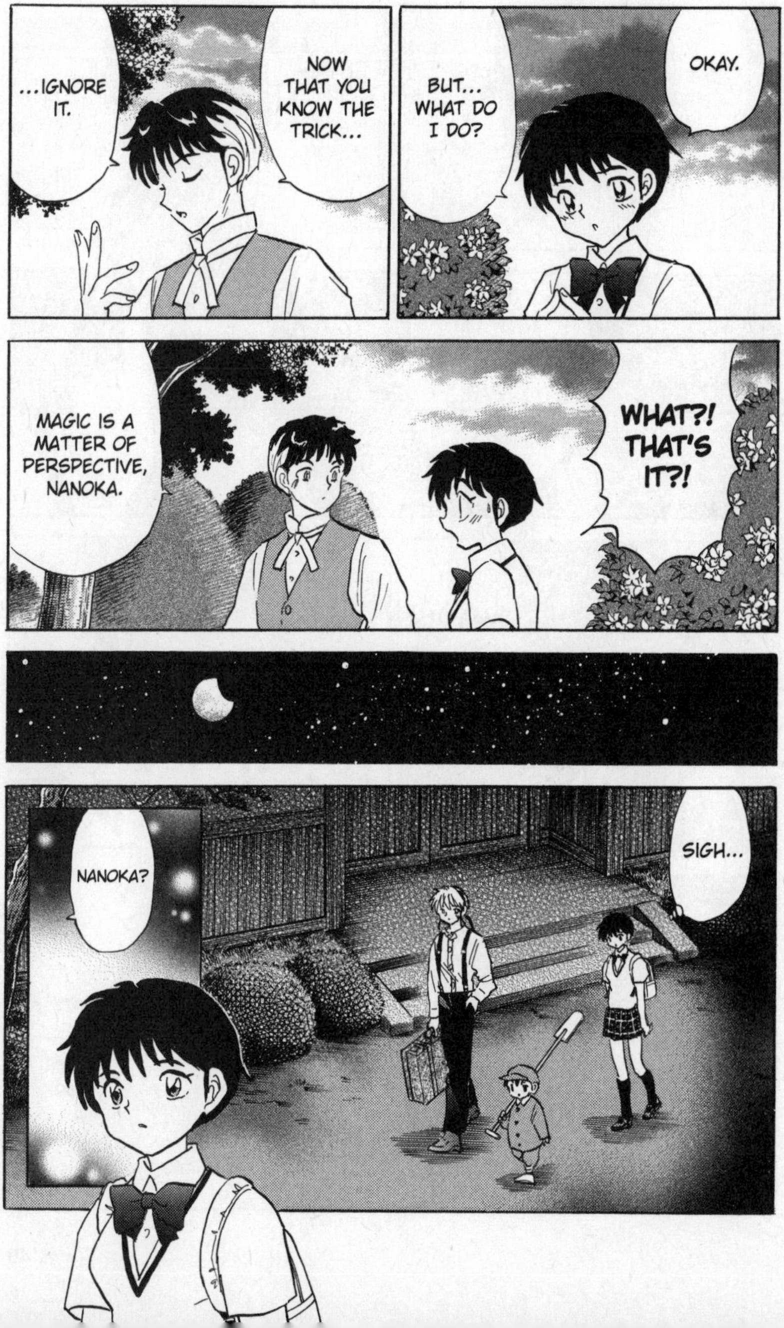
OKAY.
BUT... WHAT DO I DO?
NOW THAT YOU KNOW THE TRICK...
...IGNORE IT.
WHAT?! THAT'S IT?!
MAGIC IS A MATTER OF PERSPECTIVE, NANOKA.
SIGH...
NANOKA?

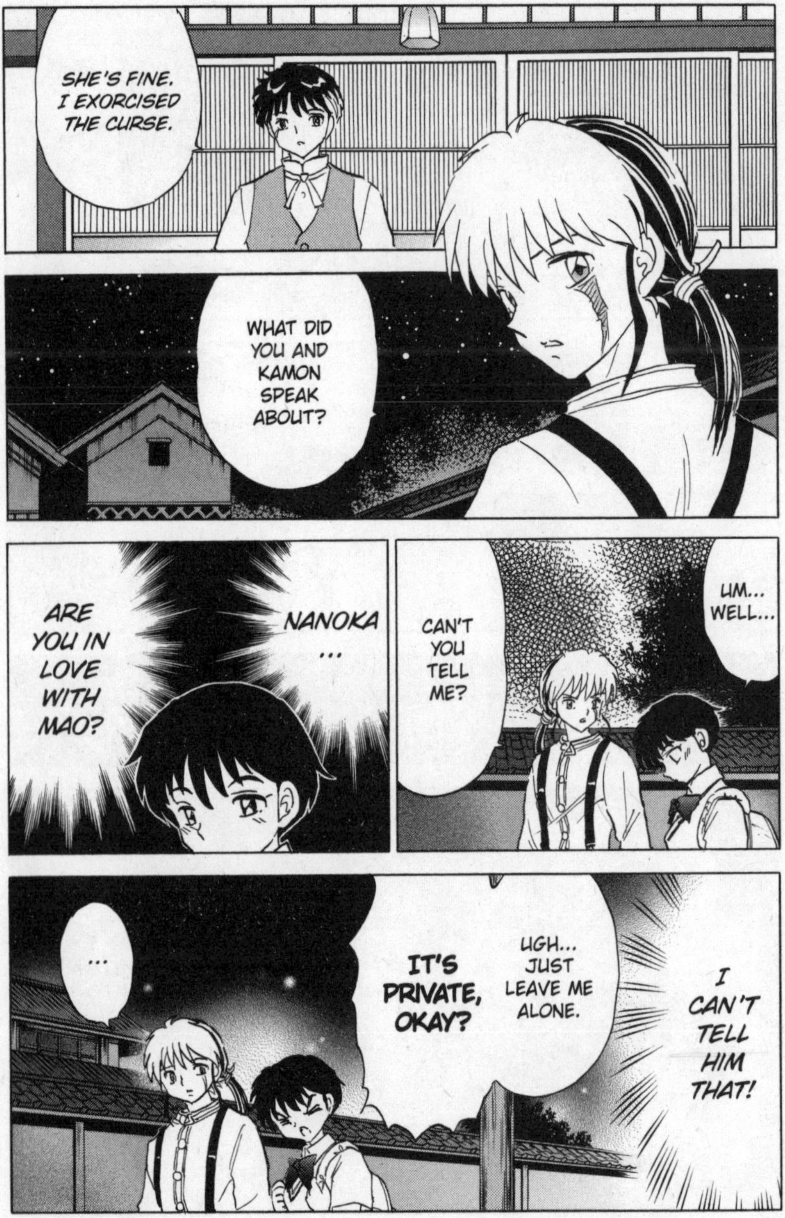
SHE'S FINE. I EXORCISED THE CURSE.
WHAT DID YOU AND KAMON SPEAK ABOUT?
UM... WELL...
CAN'T YOU TELL ME?
NANOKA...
ARE YOU IN LOVE WITH MAO?
I CAN'T TELL HIM THAT!
UGH... JUST LEAVE ME ALONE.
IT'S PRIVATE, OKAY?
...

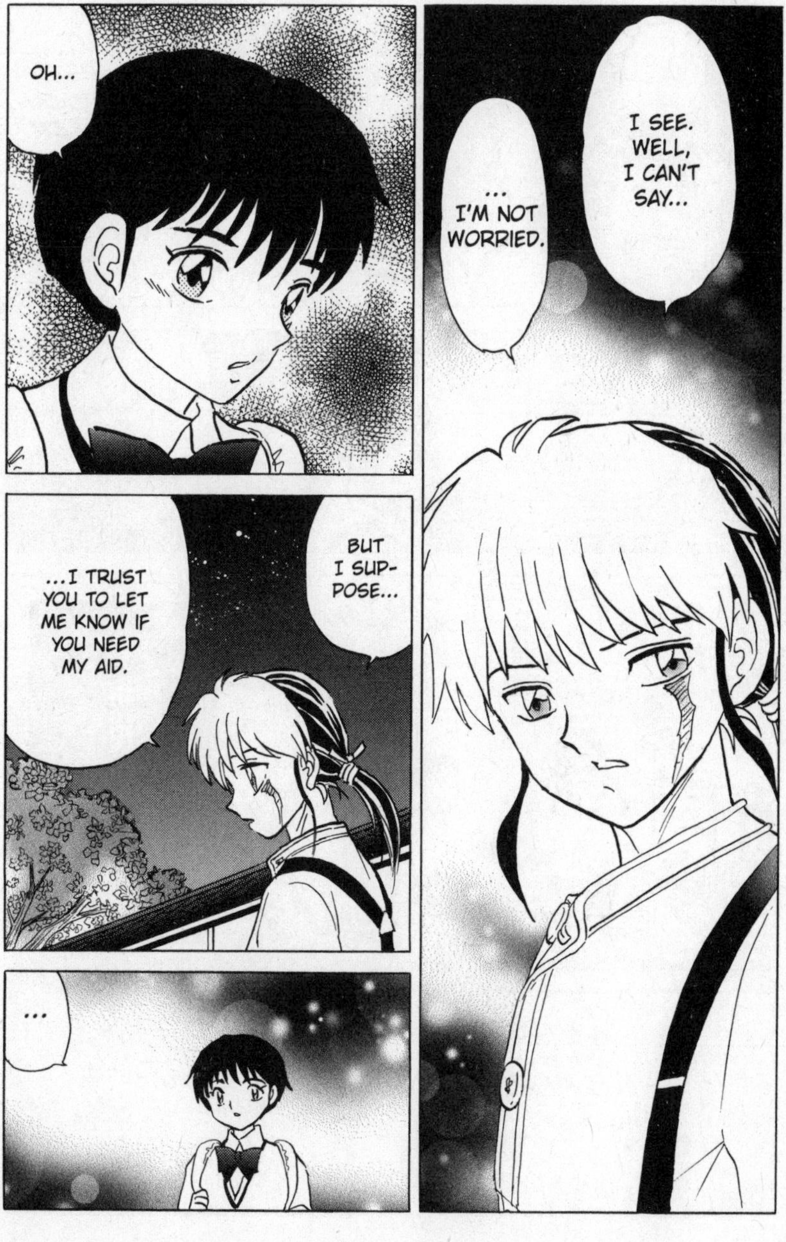
I SEE. WELL, I CAN'T SAY...
... I'M NOT WORRIED.
OH...
BUT I SUPPOSE...
...I TRUST YOU TO LET ME KNOW IF YOU NEED MY AID.
...

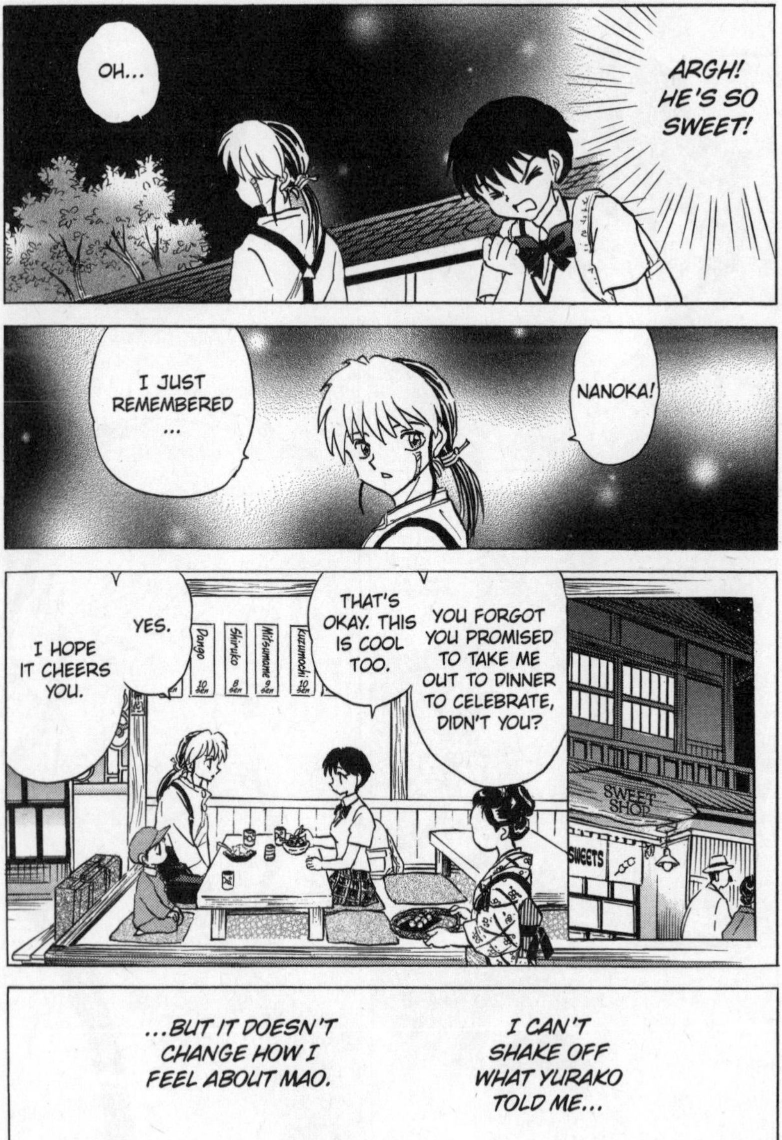
ARGH! HE'S SO SWEET!
OH...
NANOKA!
I JUST REMEMBERED ...
YOU FORGOT YOU PROMISED TO TAKE ME OUT TO DINNER TO CELEBRATE, DIDN'T YOU?
THAT'S OKAY. THIS IS COOL TOO.
YES.
I HOPE IT CHEERS YOU.
Kuzumochi 10 sen
Mitsumame 9 sen
Shiruko 8 sen
Dango 10 sen
SWEET SHOP
SWEETS
I CAN'T SHAKE OFF WHAT YURAKO TOLD ME...
...BUT IT DOESN'T CHANGE HOW I FEEL ABOUT MAO.

Chapter 3:
Kakachu

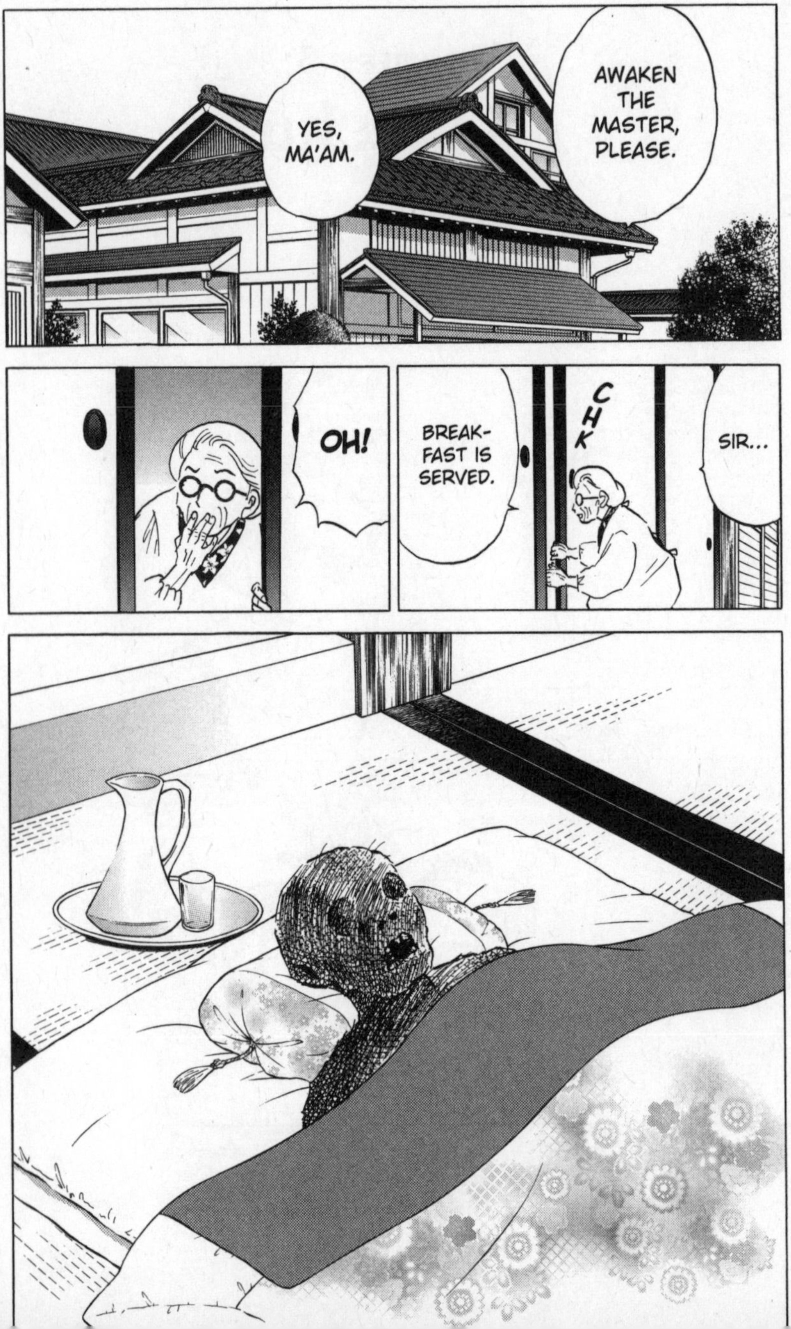
AWAKEN THE MASTER, PLEASE.
YES, MA'AM.
SIR...
CHK
BREAK-FAST IS SERVED.
OH!

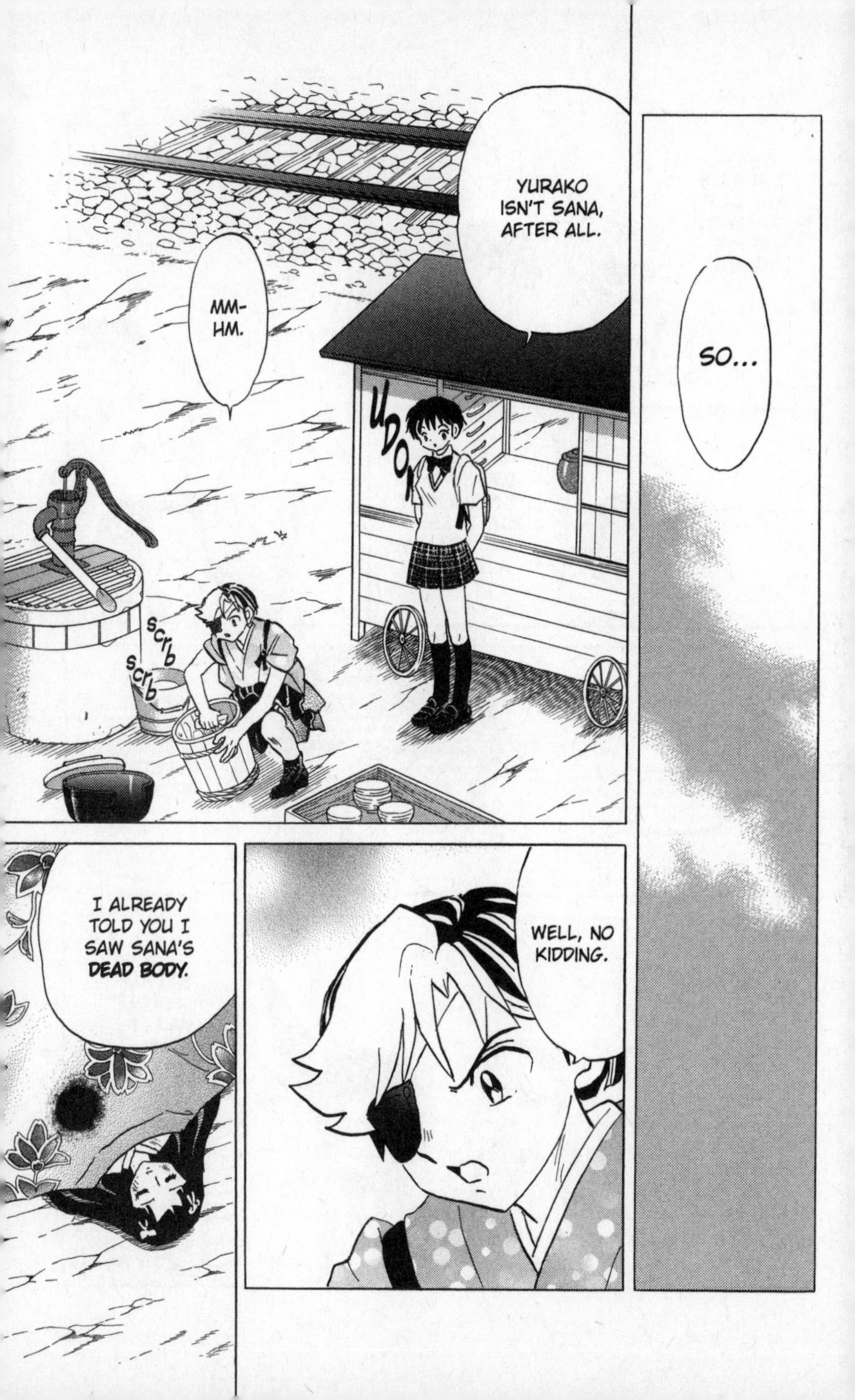
SO...
YURAKO ISN'T SANA, AFTER ALL.
MM-HM.
UDON
scrb scrb
WELL, NO KIDDING.
I ALREADY TOLD YOU I SAW SANA'S **DEAD BODY.**

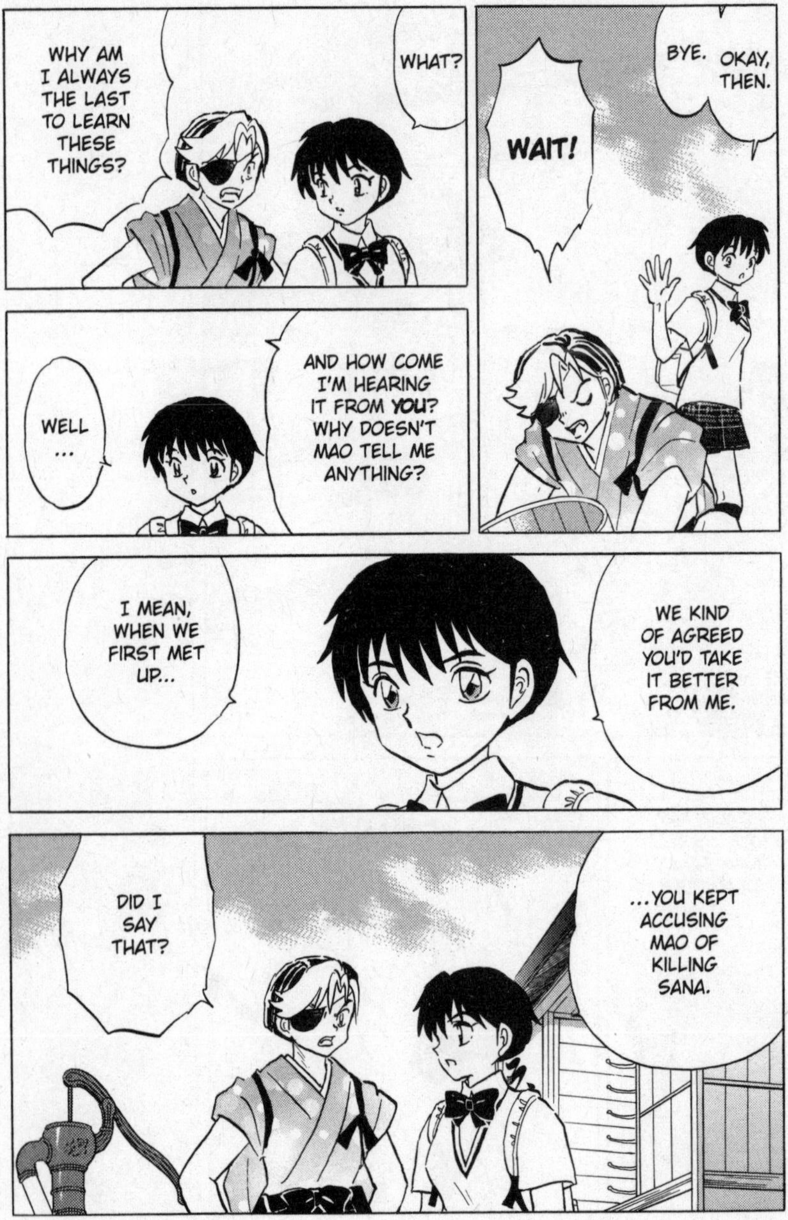
OKAY, THEN.
BYE.
WAIT!
WHAT?
WHY AM I ALWAYS THE LAST TO LEARN THESE THINGS?
AND HOW COME I'M HEARING IT FROM **YOU**? WHY DOESN'T MAO TELL ME ANYTHING?
WELL ...
WE KIND OF AGREED YOU'D TAKE IT BETTER FROM ME.
I MEAN, WHEN WE FIRST MET UP...
...YOU KEPT ACCUSING MAO OF KILLING SANA.
DID I SAY THAT?

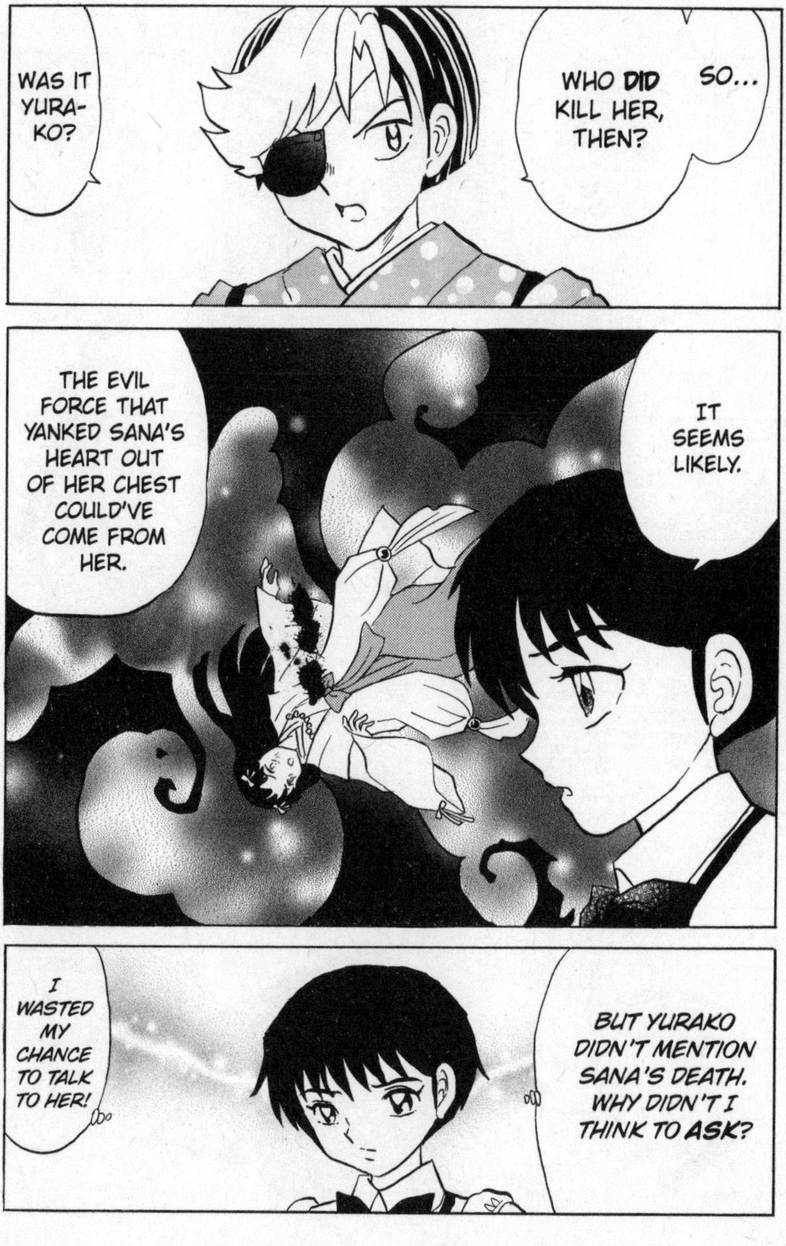
SO...
WHO DID KILL HER, THEN?
WAS IT YURA-KO?
IT SEEMS LIKELY.
THE EVIL FORCE THAT YANKED SANA'S HEART OUT OF HER CHEST COULD'VE COME FROM HER.
BUT YURAKO DIDN'T MENTION SANA'S DEATH. WHY DIDN'T I THINK TO ASK?
I WASTED MY CHANCE TO TALK TO HER!

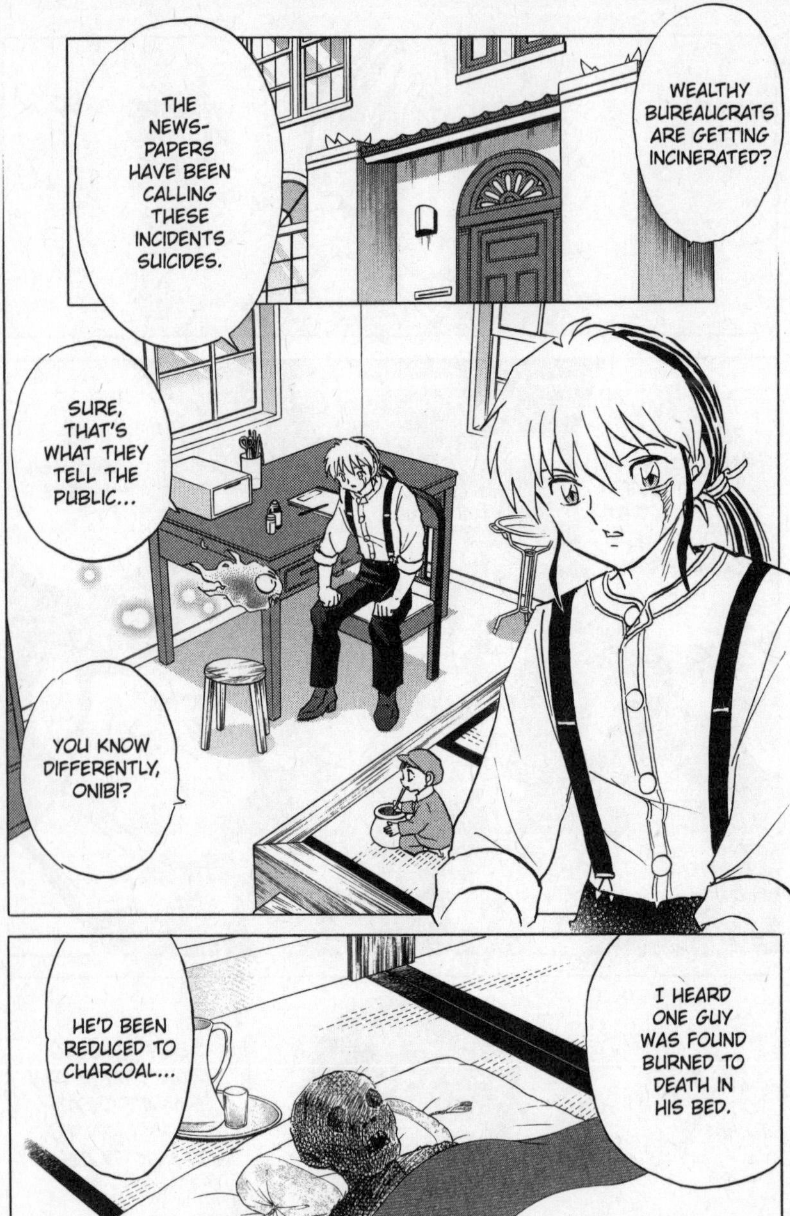

WEALTHY BUREAUCRATS ARE GETTING INCINERATED?
THE NEWS-PAPERS HAVE BEEN CALLING THESE INCIDENTS SUICIDES.
SURE, THAT'S WHAT THEY TELL THE PUBLIC...
YOU KNOW DIFFERENTLY, ONIBI?
I HEARD ONE GUY WAS FOUND BURNED TO DEATH IN HIS BED.
HE'D BEEN REDUCED TO CHARCOAL...

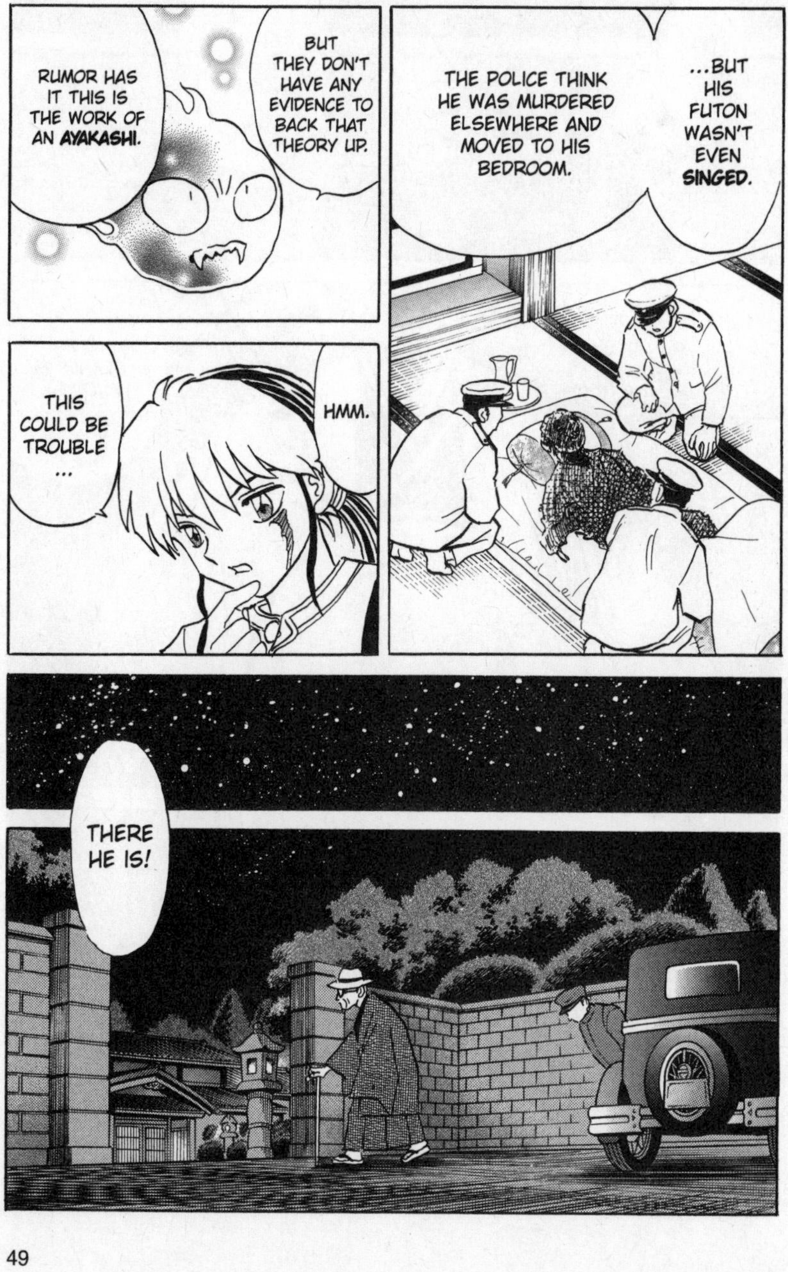
THE POLICE THINK HE WAS MURDERED ELSEWHERE AND MOVED TO HIS BEDROOM.
...BUT HIS FUTON WASN'T EVEN SINGED.
RUMOR HAS IT THIS IS THE WORK OF AN AYAKASHI.
BUT THEY DON'T HAVE ANY EVIDENCE TO BACK THAT THEORY UP.
HMM.
THIS COULD BE TROUBLE ...
THERE HE IS!

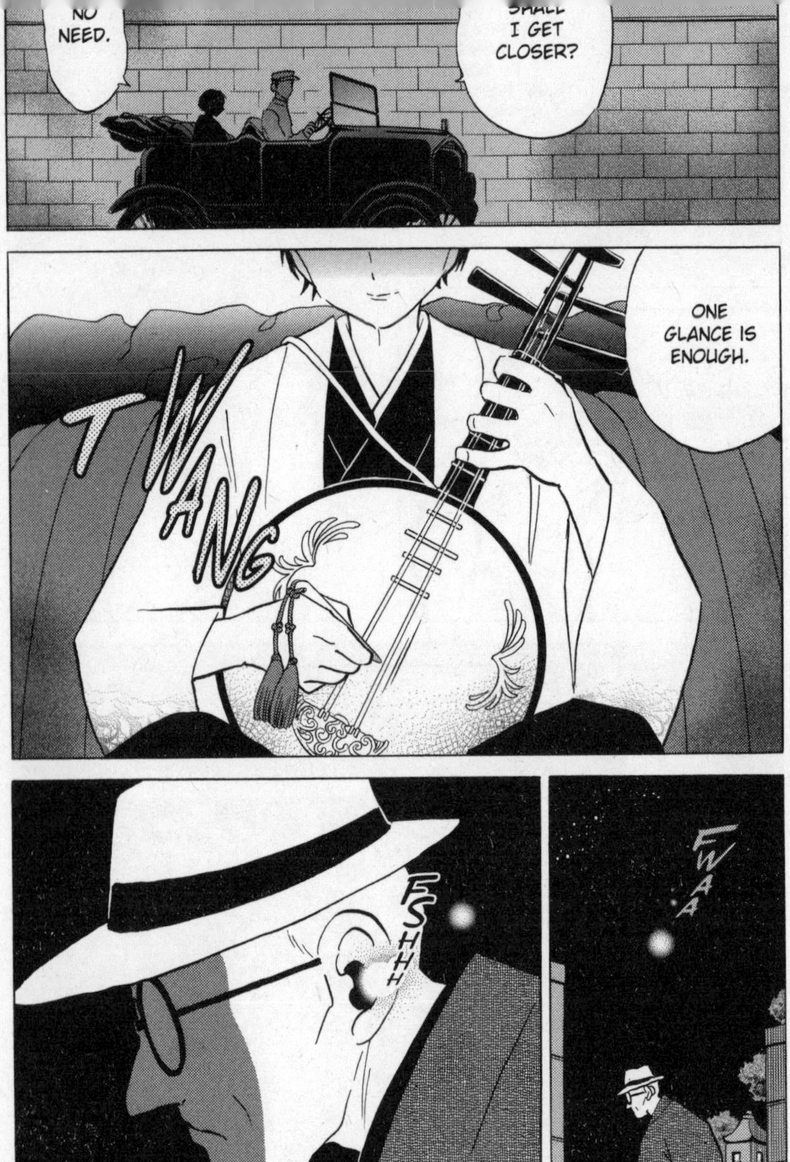
SHALL I GET CLOSER?
NO NEED.
ONE GLANCE IS ENOUGH.
TWANG
FWAA
FSHHH

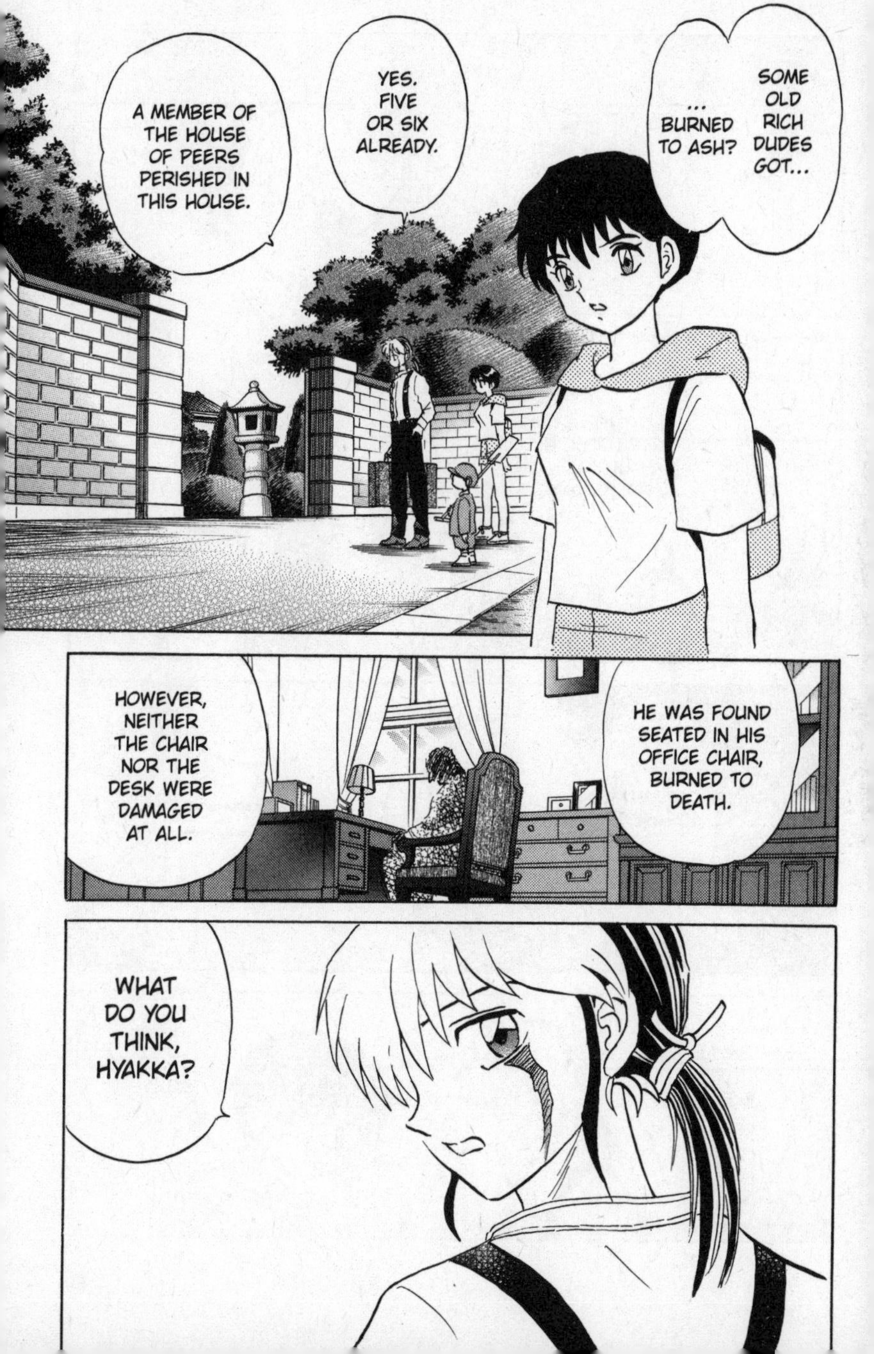
SOME OLD RICH DUDES GOT...
...BURNED TO ASH?
YES. FIVE OR SIX ALREADY.
A MEMBER OF THE HOUSE OF PEERS PERISHED IN THIS HOUSE.
HE WAS FOUND SEATED IN HIS OFFICE CHAIR, BURNED TO DEATH.
HOWEVER, NEITHER THE CHAIR NOR THE DESK WERE DAMAGED AT ALL.
WHAT DO YOU THINK, HYAKKA?

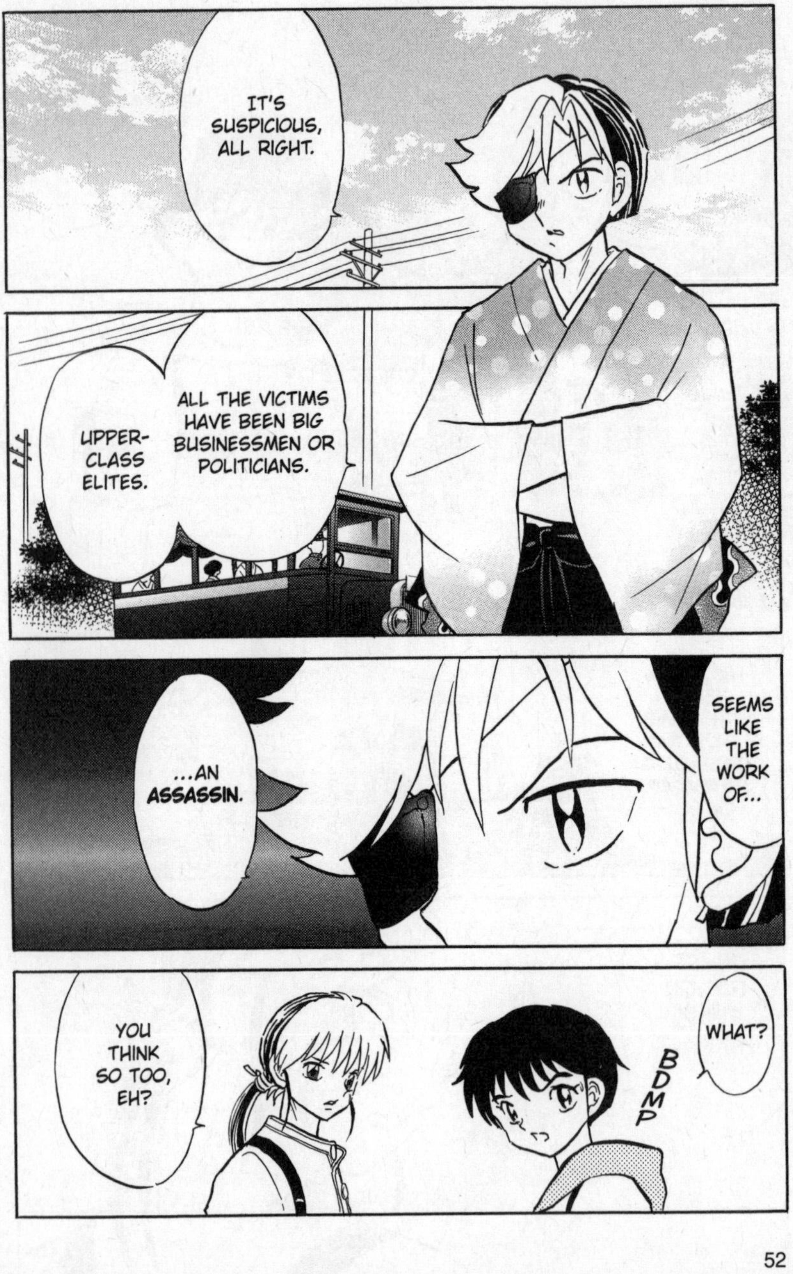
IT'S SUSPICIOUS, ALL RIGHT.
ALL THE VICTIMS HAVE BEEN BIG BUSINESSMEN OR POLITICIANS.
UPPER-CLASS ELITES.
SEEMS LIKE THE WORK OF...
...AN ASSASSIN.
WHAT?
BDMP
YOU THINK SO TOO, EH?

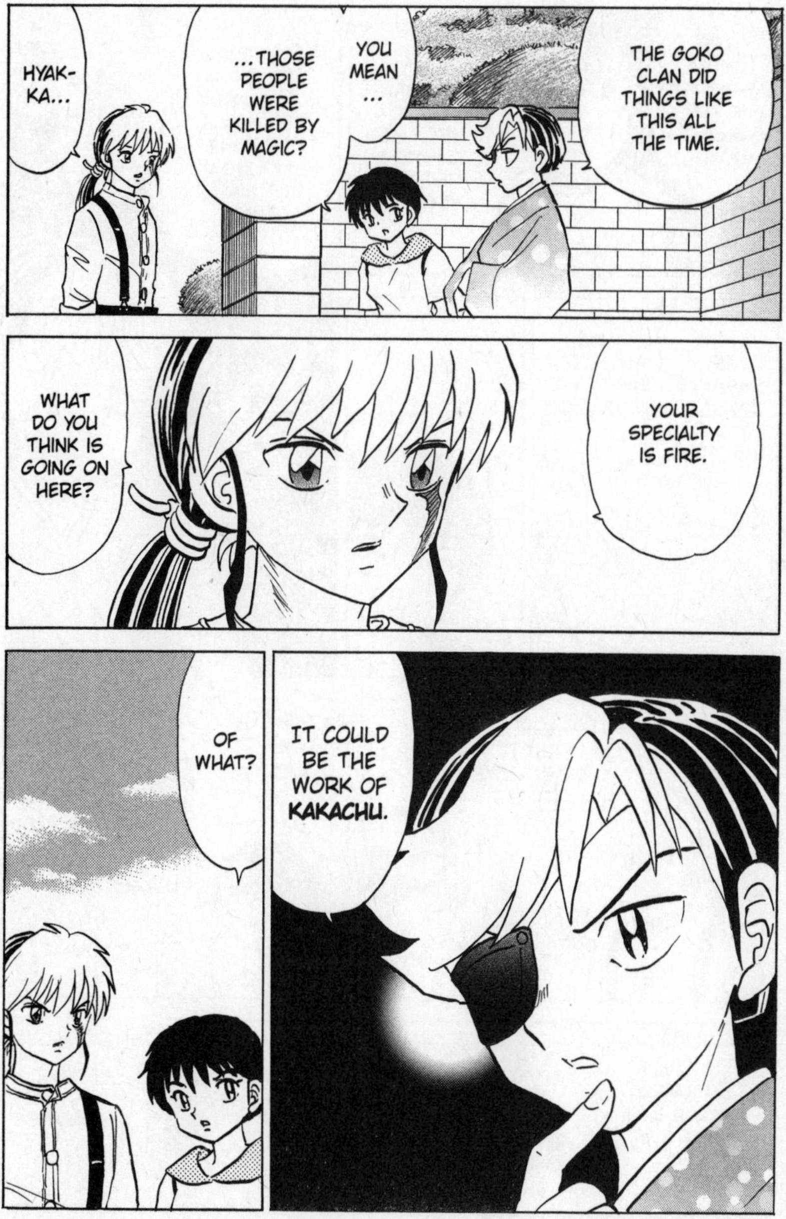
THE GOKO CLAN DID THINGS LIKE THIS ALL THE TIME.
YOU MEAN...
...THOSE PEOPLE WERE KILLED BY MAGIC?
HYAK-KA...
YOUR SPECIALTY IS FIRE.
WHAT DO YOU THINK IS GOING ON HERE?
IT COULD BE THE WORK OF **KAKACHU.**
OF WHAT?

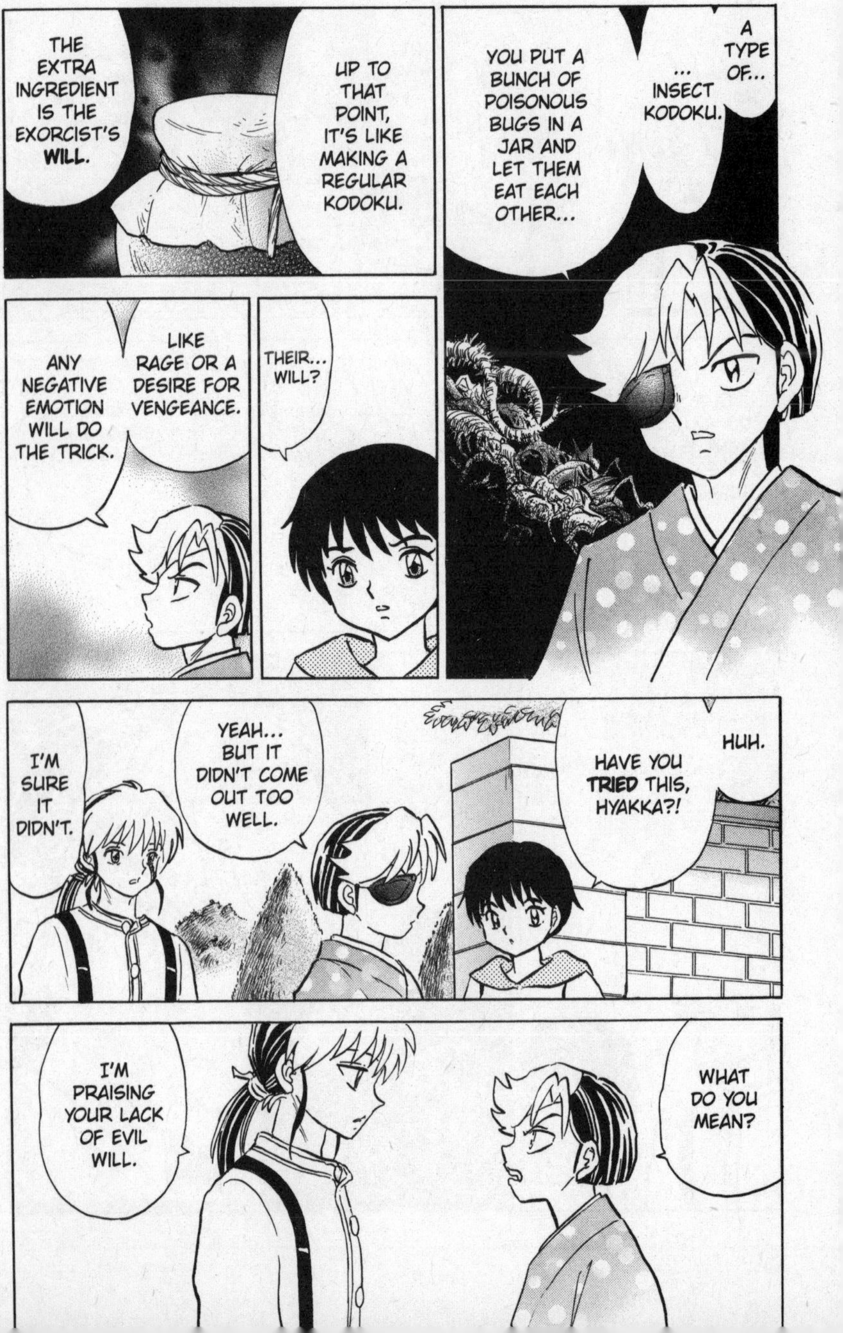
A TYPE OF...
... INSECT KODOKU.
YOU PUT A BUNCH OF POISONOUS BUGS IN A JAR AND LET THEM EAT EACH OTHER...
UP TO THAT POINT, IT'S LIKE MAKING A REGULAR KODOKU.
THE EXTRA INGREDIENT IS THE EXORCIST'S **WILL.**
THEIR... WILL?
LIKE RAGE OR A DESIRE FOR VENGEANCE.
ANY NEGATIVE EMOTION WILL DO THE TRICK.
HUH.
HAVE YOU **TRIED** THIS, HYAKKA?!
YEAH... BUT IT DIDN'T COME OUT TOO WELL.
I'M SURE IT DIDN'T.
WHAT DO YOU MEAN?
I'M PRAISING YOUR LACK OF EVIL WILL.

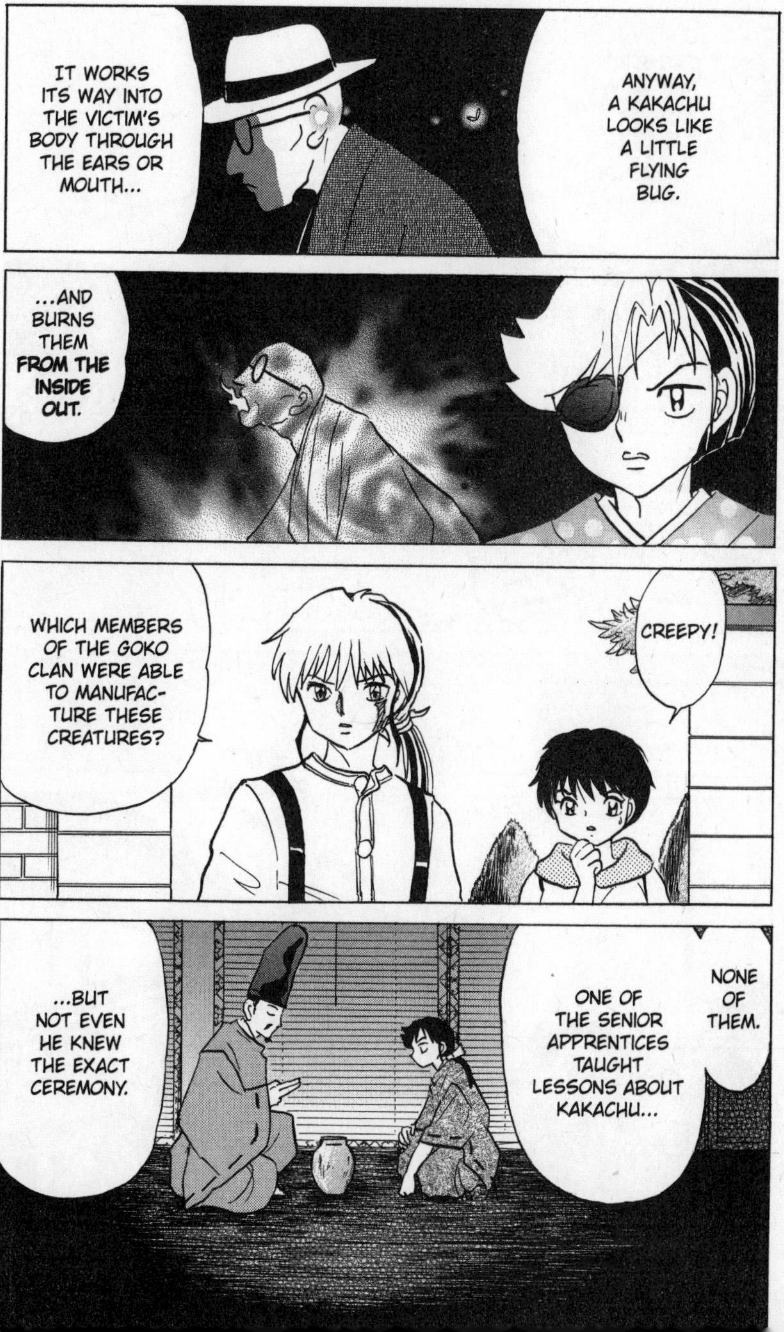
ANYWAY, A KAKACHU LOOKS LIKE A LITTLE FLYING BUG.
IT WORKS ITS WAY INTO THE VICTIM'S BODY THROUGH THE EARS OR MOUTH...
...AND BURNS THEM FROM THE INSIDE OUT.
CREEPY!
WHICH MEMBERS OF THE GOKO CLAN WERE ABLE TO MANUFAC-TURE THESE CREATURES?
NONE OF THEM.
ONE OF THE SENIOR APPRENTICES TAUGHT LESSONS ABOUT KAKACHU...
...BUT NOT EVEN HE KNEW THE EXACT CEREMONY.

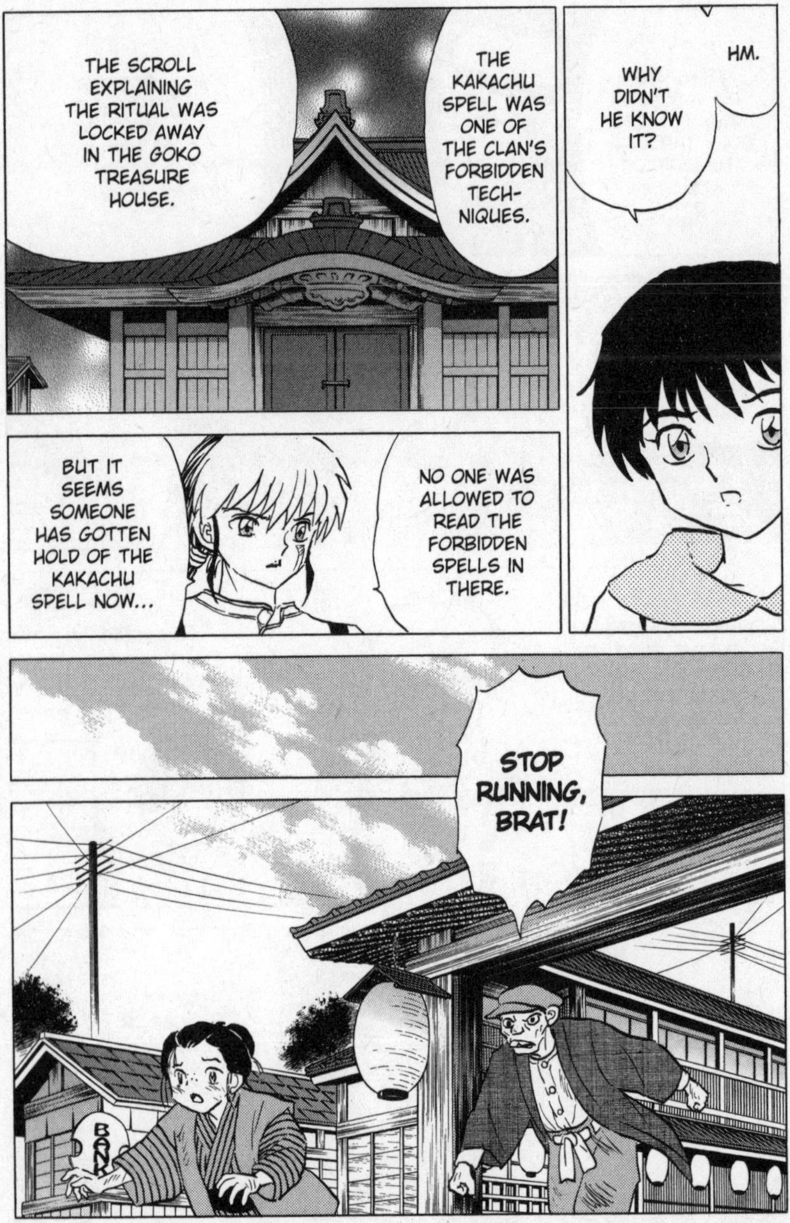
HM.
WHY DIDN'T HE KNOW IT?
THE KAKACHU SPELL WAS ONE OF THE CLAN'S FORBIDDEN TECH-NIQUES.
THE SCROLL EXPLAINING THE RITUAL WAS LOCKED AWAY IN THE GOKO TREASURE HOUSE.
NO ONE WAS ALLOWED TO READ THE FORBIDDEN SPELLS IN THERE.
BUT IT SEEMS SOMEONE HAS GOTTEN HOLD OF THE KAKACHU SPELL NOW...
STOP RUNNING, BRAT!
BANK

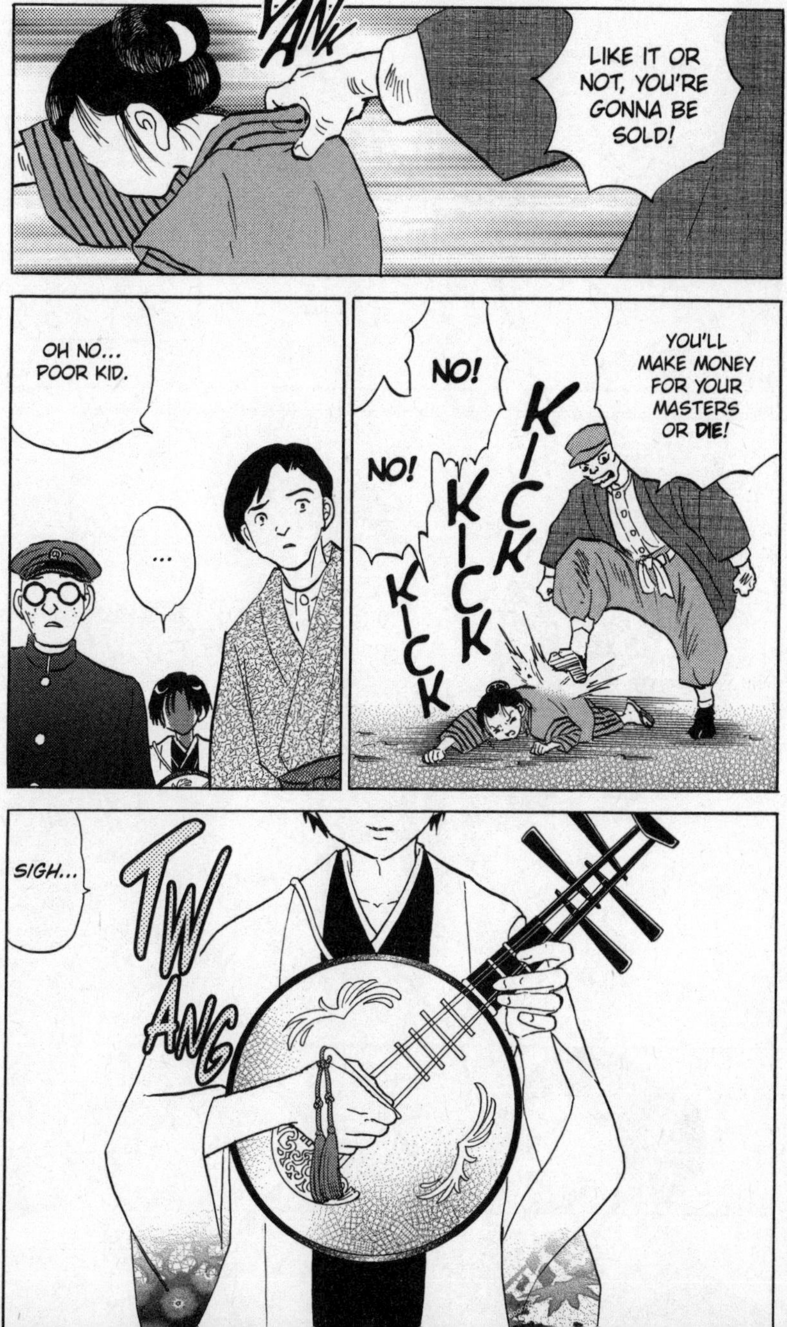
YANK
LIKE IT OR NOT, YOU'RE GONNA BE SOLD!
YOU'LL MAKE MONEY FOR YOUR MASTERS OR DIE!
NO!
NO!
KICK
KICK
KICK
OH NO... POOR KID.
...
SIGH...
TWANG

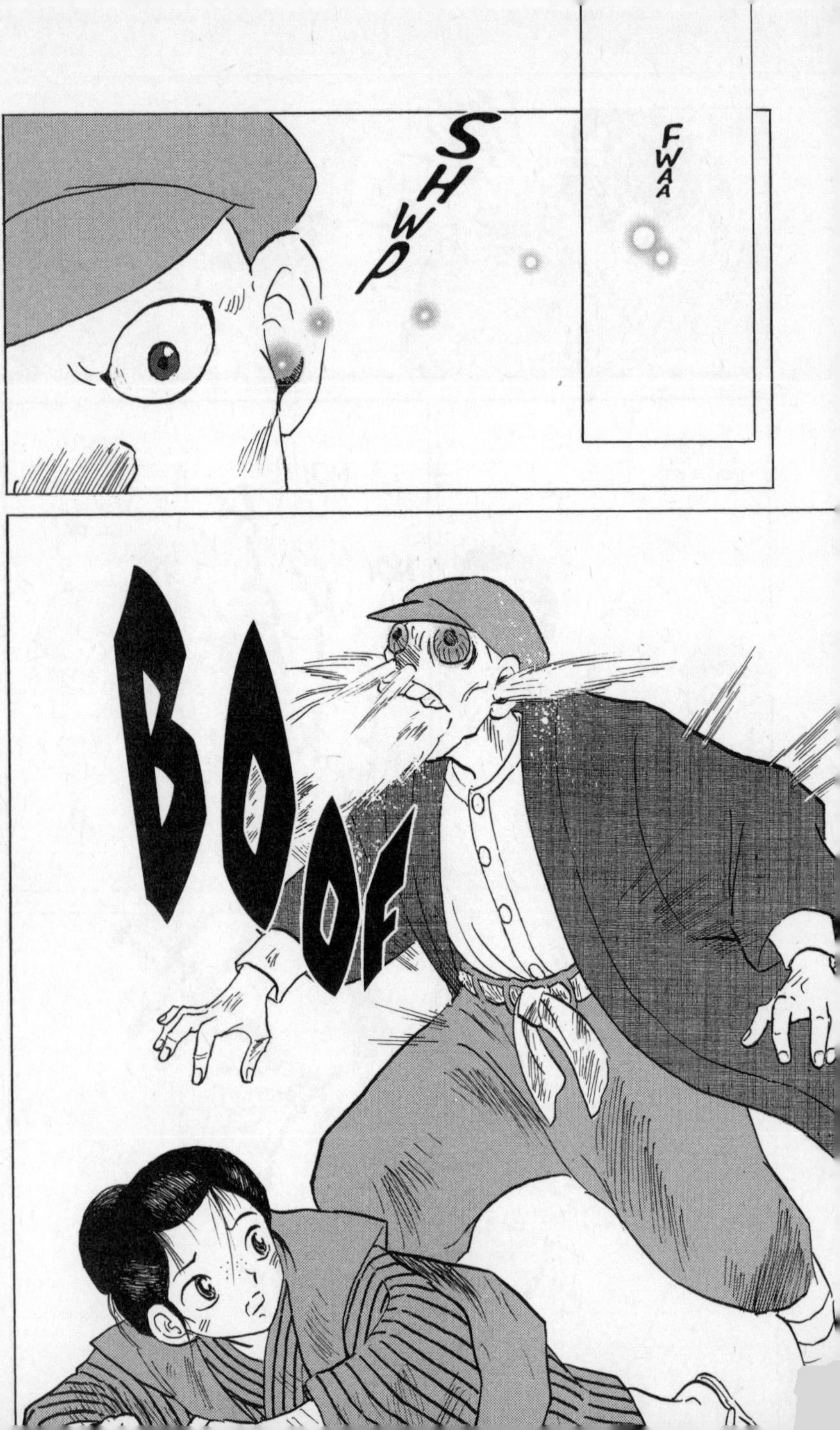
FWAA
SHWP
BOOF

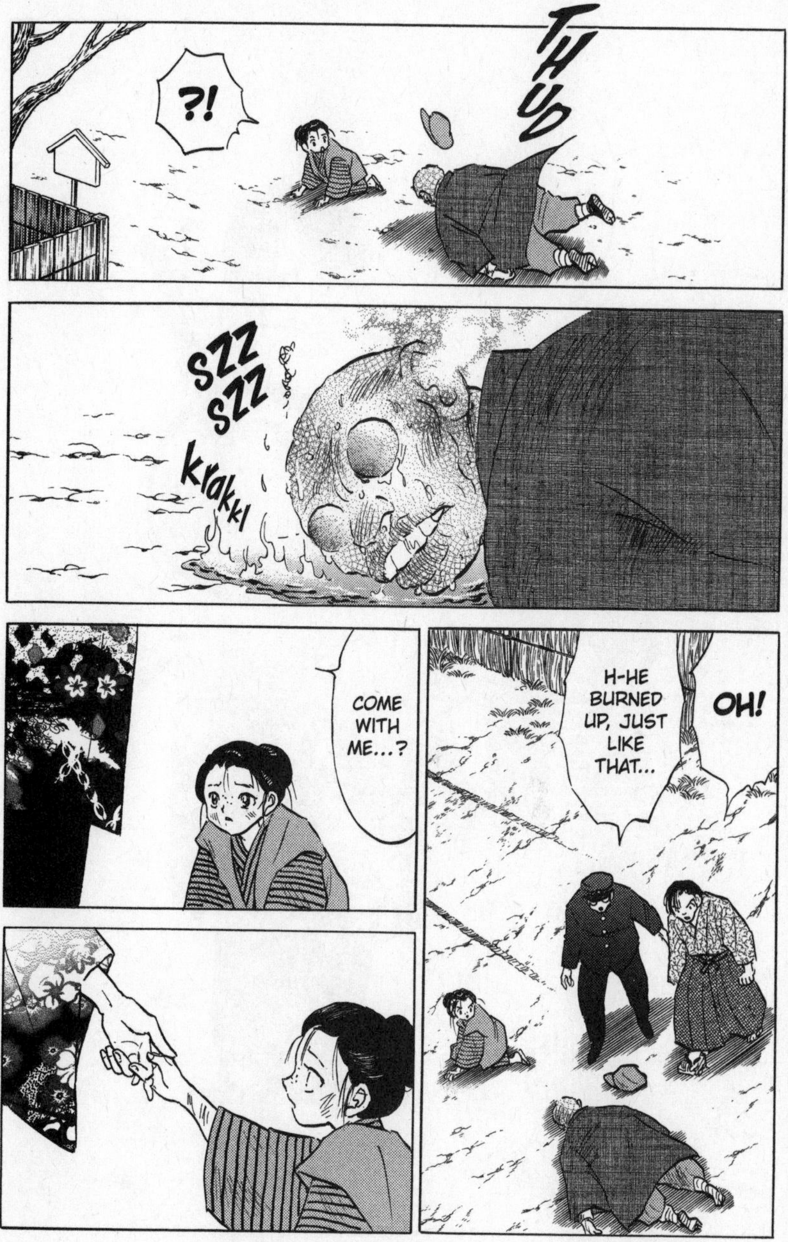
THUD
?!
SZZ SZZ
krakki
OH!
H-HE BURNED UP, JUST LIKE THAT...
COME WITH ME...?

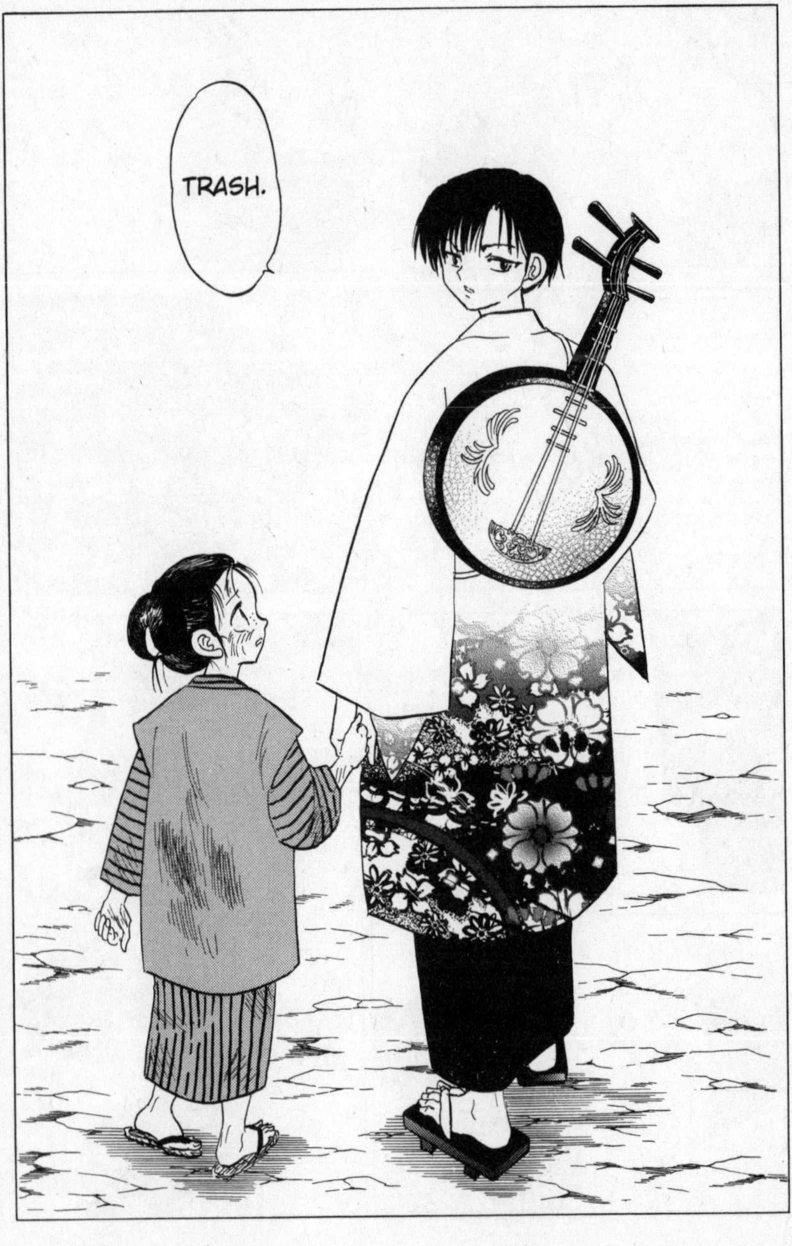
TRASH.

Chapter 4:
Renji

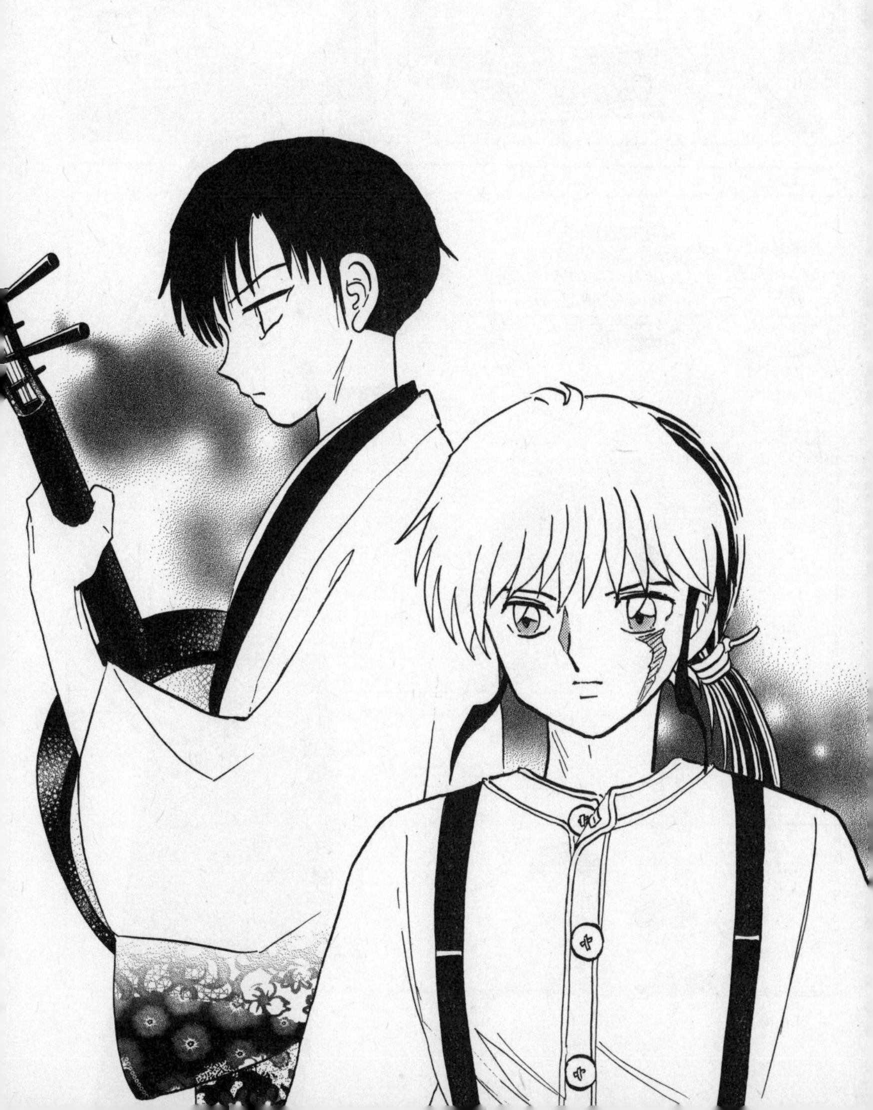

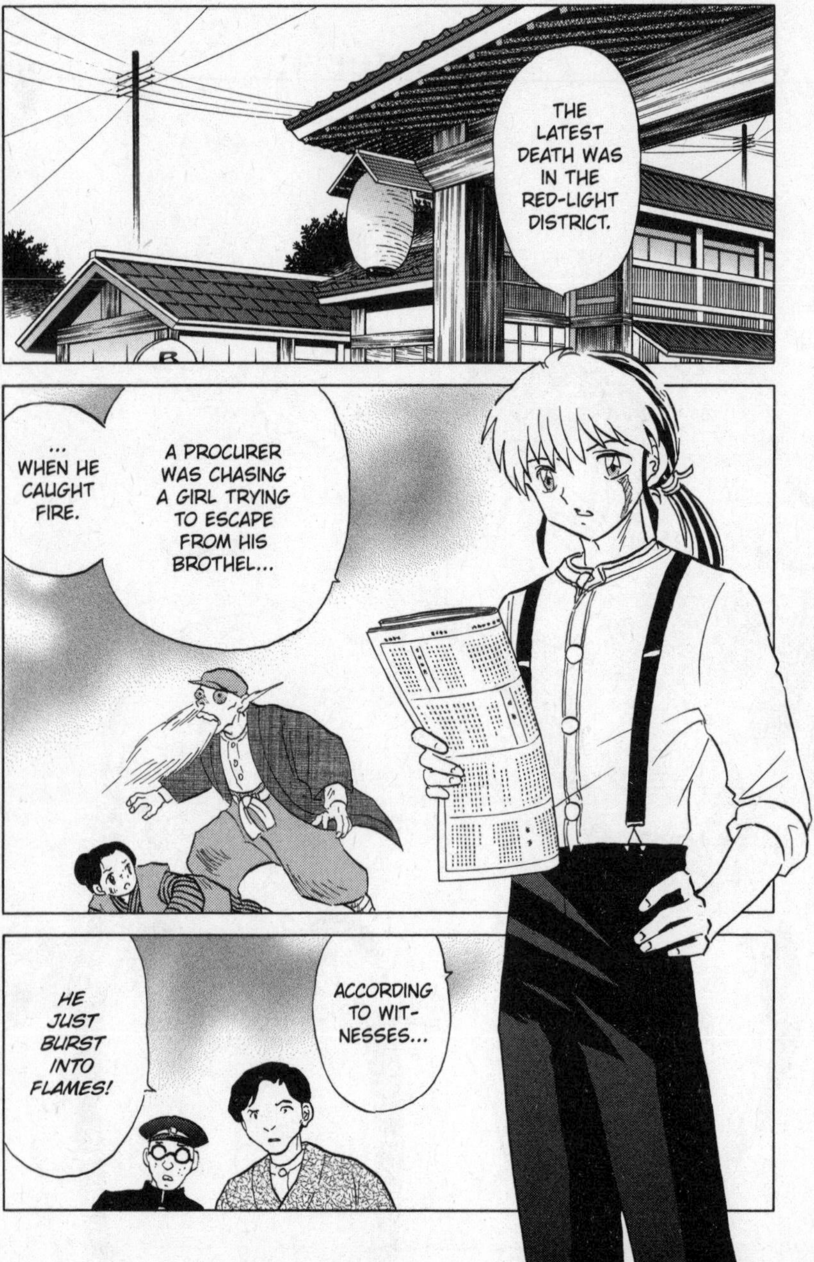
THE LATEST DEATH WAS IN THE RED-LIGHT DISTRICT.
A PROCURER WAS CHASING A GIRL TRYING TO ESCAPE FROM HIS BROTHEL...
... WHEN HE CAUGHT FIRE.
ACCORDING TO WIT-NESSES...
HE JUST BURST INTO FLAMES!

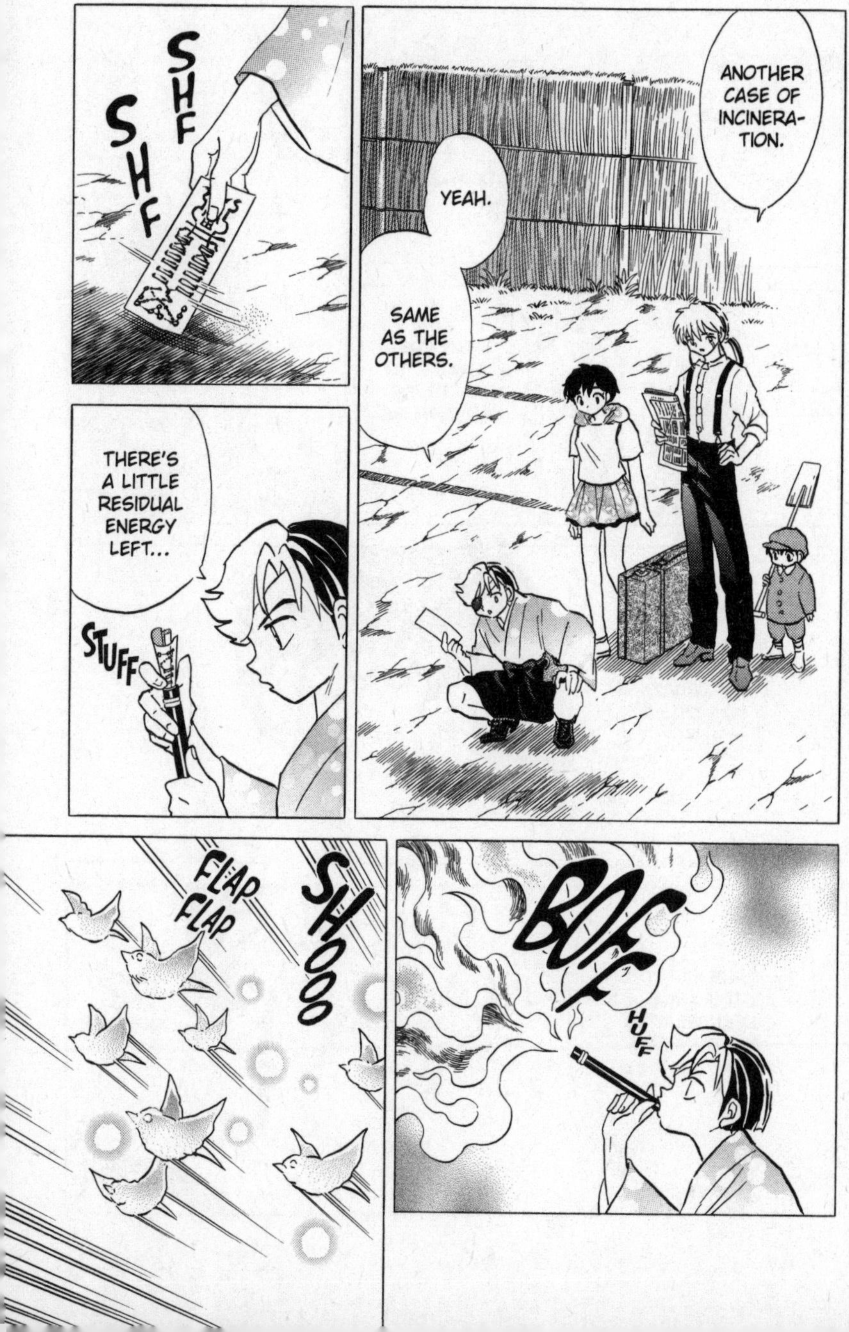
ANOTHER CASE OF INCINERA-TION.
YEAH.
SAME AS THE OTHERS.
SHF SHF
THERE'S A LITTLE RESIDUAL ENERGY LEFT...
STUFF
BOFF
HUFF
SHOOOO
FLAP FLAP

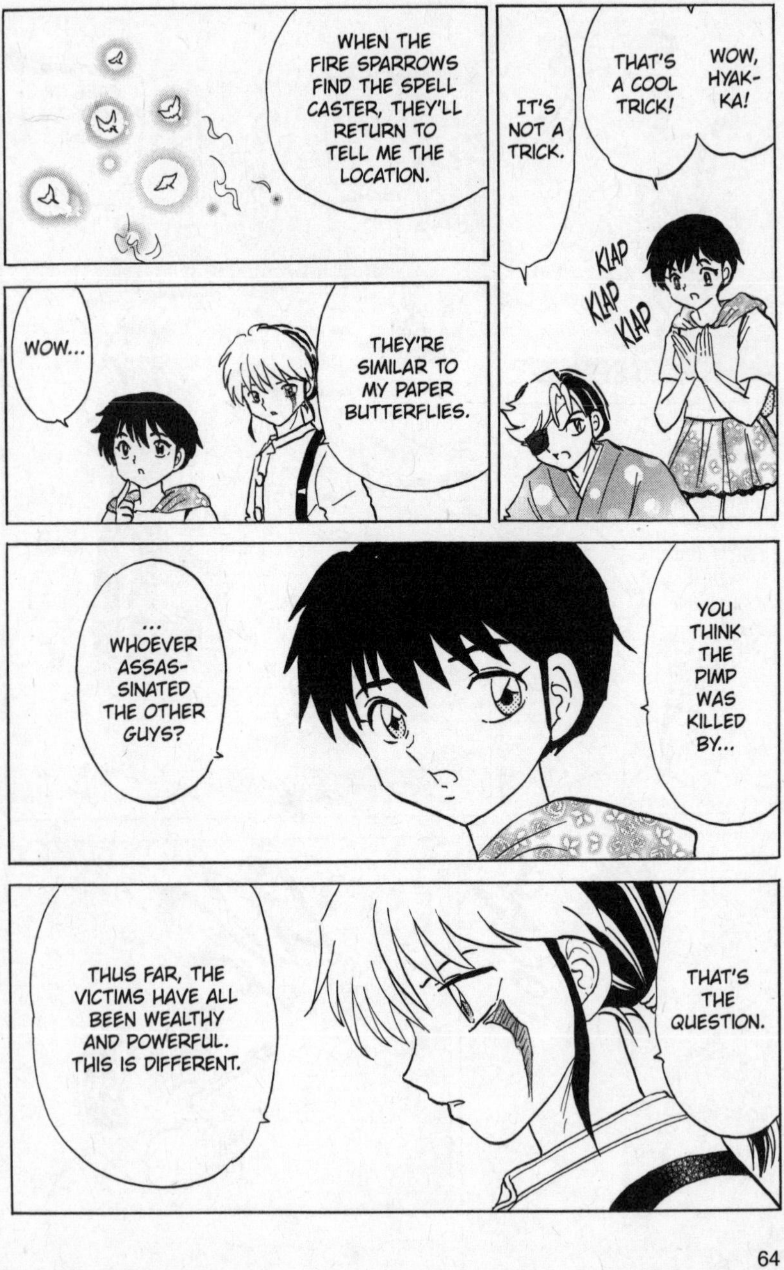
WOW, HYAK-KA!
THAT'S A COOL TRICK!
IT'S NOT A TRICK.
KLAP KLAP KLAP
WHEN THE FIRE SPARROWS FIND THE SPELL CASTER, THEY'LL RETURN TO TELL ME THE LOCATION.
THEY'RE SIMILAR TO MY PAPER BUTTERFLIES.
WOW...
YOU THINK THE PIMP WAS KILLED BY...
...WHOEVER ASSAS-SINATED THE OTHER GUYS?
THAT'S THE QUESTION.
THUS FAR, THE VICTIMS HAVE ALL BEEN WEALTHY AND POWERFUL. THIS IS DIFFERENT.

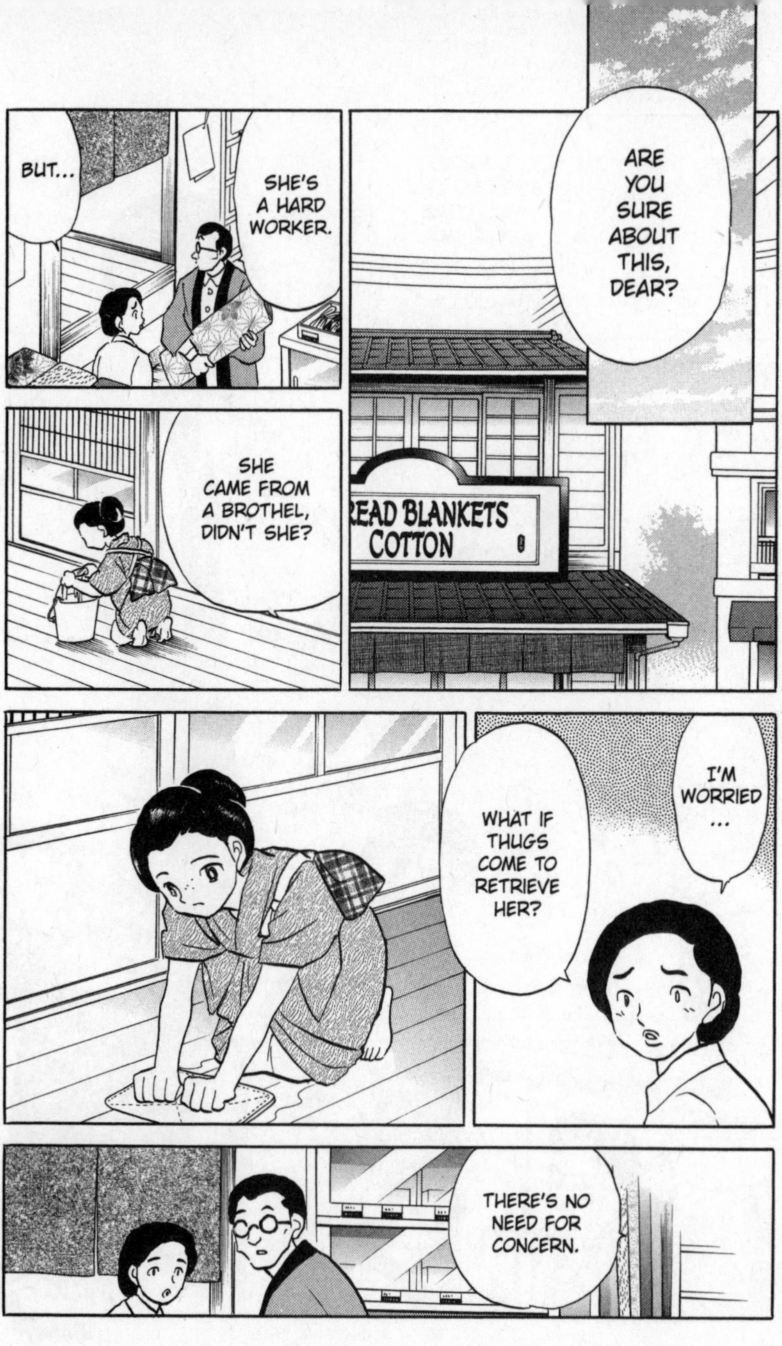
ARE YOU SURE ABOUT THIS, DEAR?
READ BLANKETS COTTON
SHE'S A HARD WORKER.
BUT...
SHE CAME FROM A BROTHEL, DIDN'T SHE?
I'M WORRIED...
WHAT IF THUGS COME TO RETRIEVE HER?
THERE'S NO NEED FOR CONCERN.

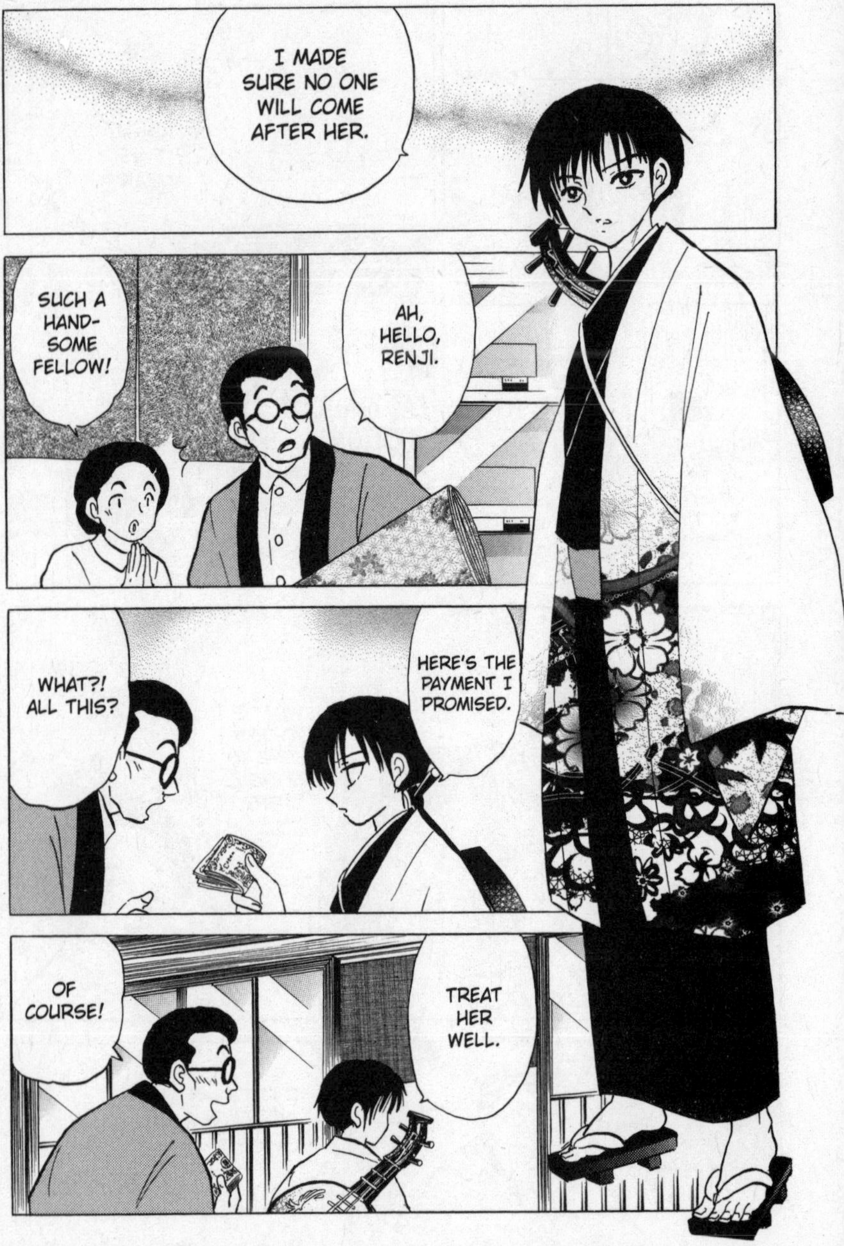

I MADE SURE NO ONE WILL COME AFTER HER.
AH, HELLO, RENJI.
SUCH A HAND-SOME FELLOW!
HERE'S THE PAYMENT I PROMISED.
WHAT?! ALL THIS?
TREAT HER WELL.
OF COURSE!

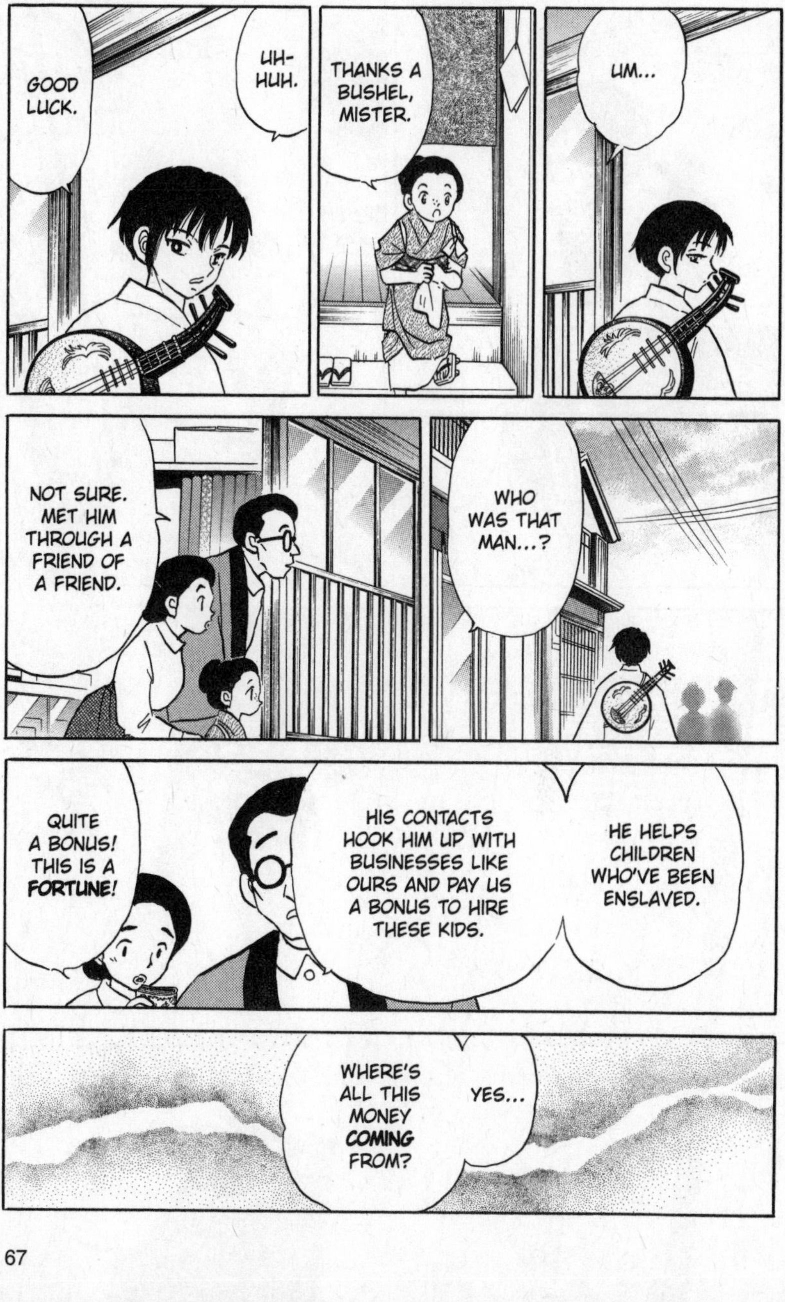
UM...
THANKS A BUSHEL, MISTER.
UH-HUH.
GOOD LUCK.
WHO WAS THAT MAN...?
NOT SURE. MET HIM THROUGH A FRIEND OF A FRIEND.
HE HELPS CHILDREN WHO'VE BEEN ENSLAVED.
HIS CONTACTS HOOK HIM UP WITH BUSINESSES LIKE OURS AND PAY US A BONUS TO HIRE THESE KIDS.
QUITE A BONUS! THIS IS A FORTUNE!
YES...
WHERE'S ALL THIS MONEY COMING FROM?

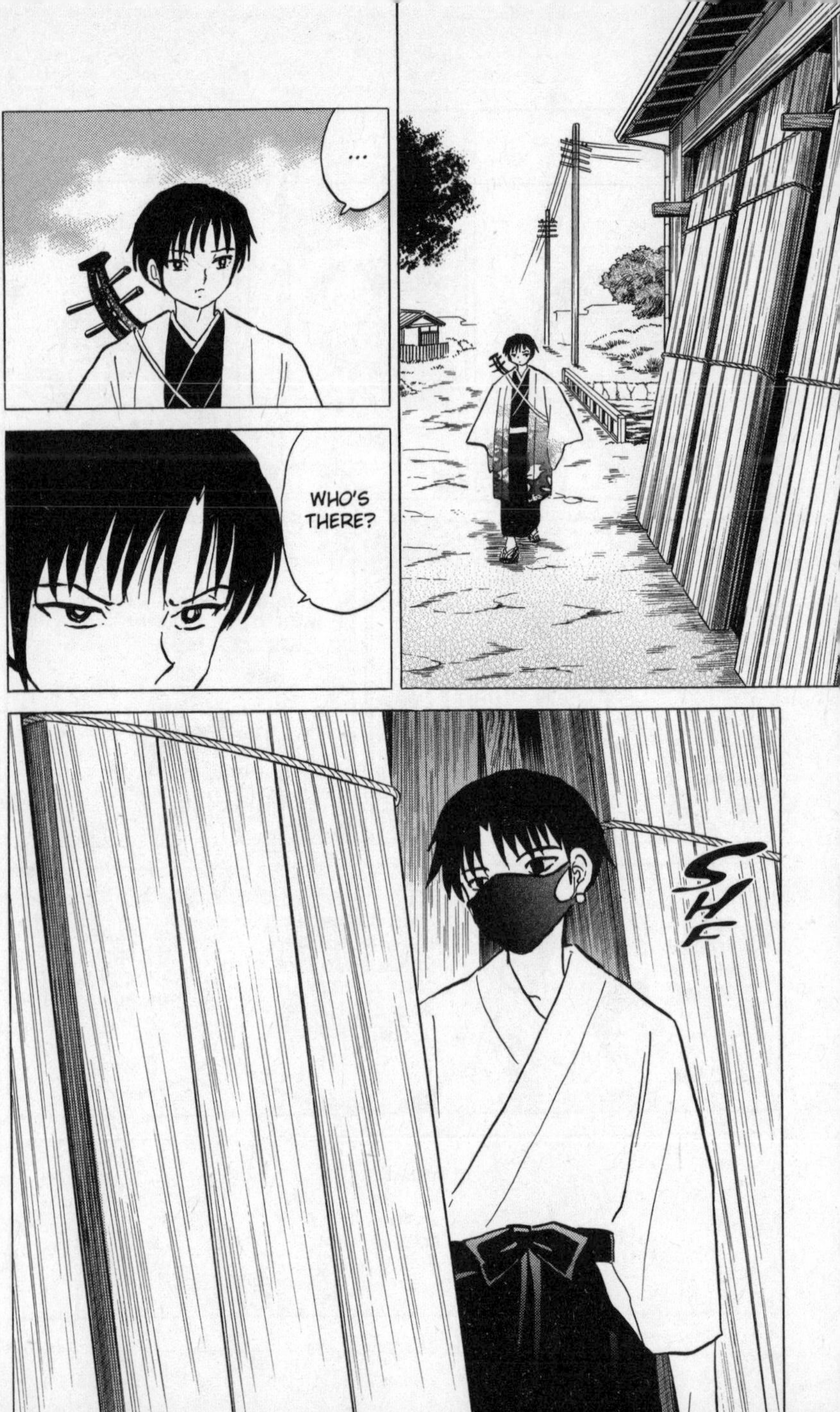
...
WHO'S THERE?
SHF

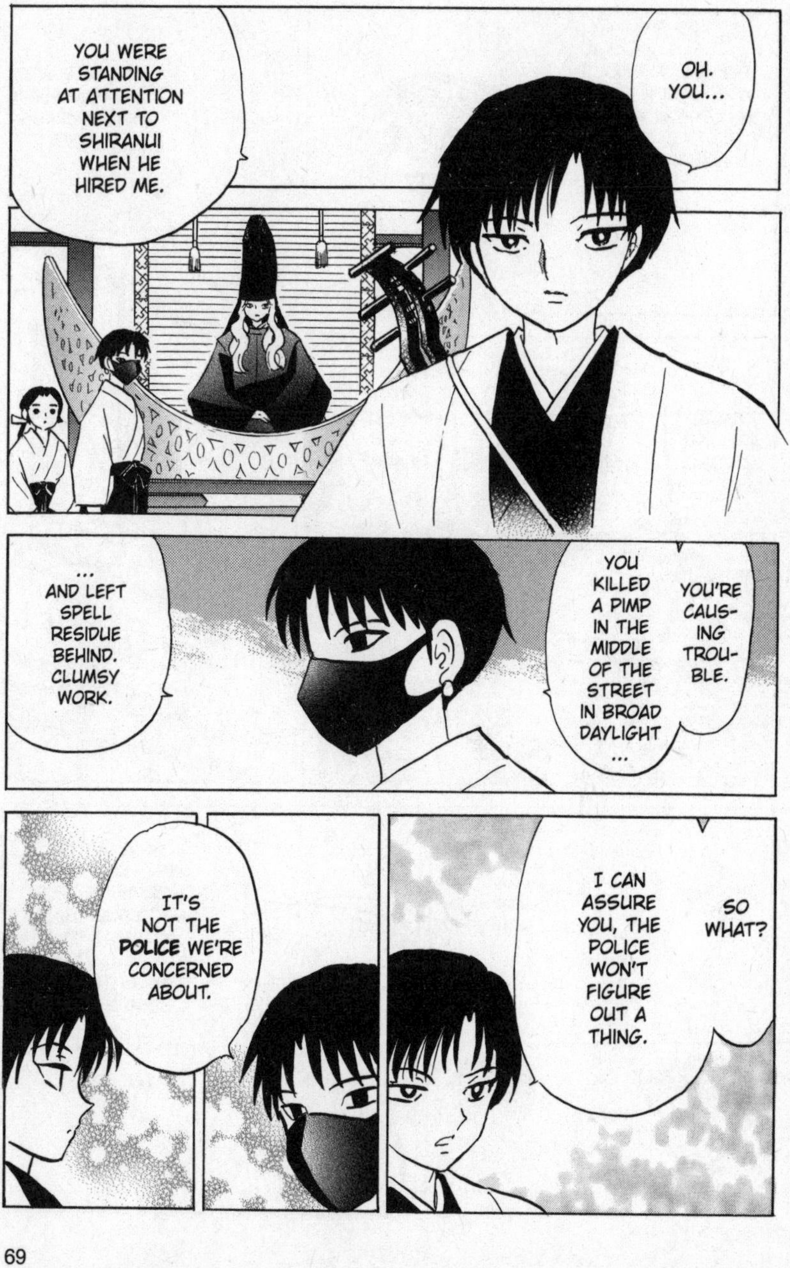
OH. YOU...
YOU WERE STANDING AT ATTENTION NEXT TO SHIRANUI WHEN HE HIRED ME.
YOU'RE CAUS-ING TROU-BLE.
YOU KILLED A PIMP IN THE MIDDLE OF THE STREET IN BROAD DAYLIGHT ...
... AND LEFT SPELL RESIDUE BEHIND. CLUMSY WORK.
SO WHAT?
I CAN ASSURE YOU, THE POLICE WON'T FIGURE OUT A THING.
IT'S NOT THE **POLICE** WE'RE CONCERNED ABOUT.

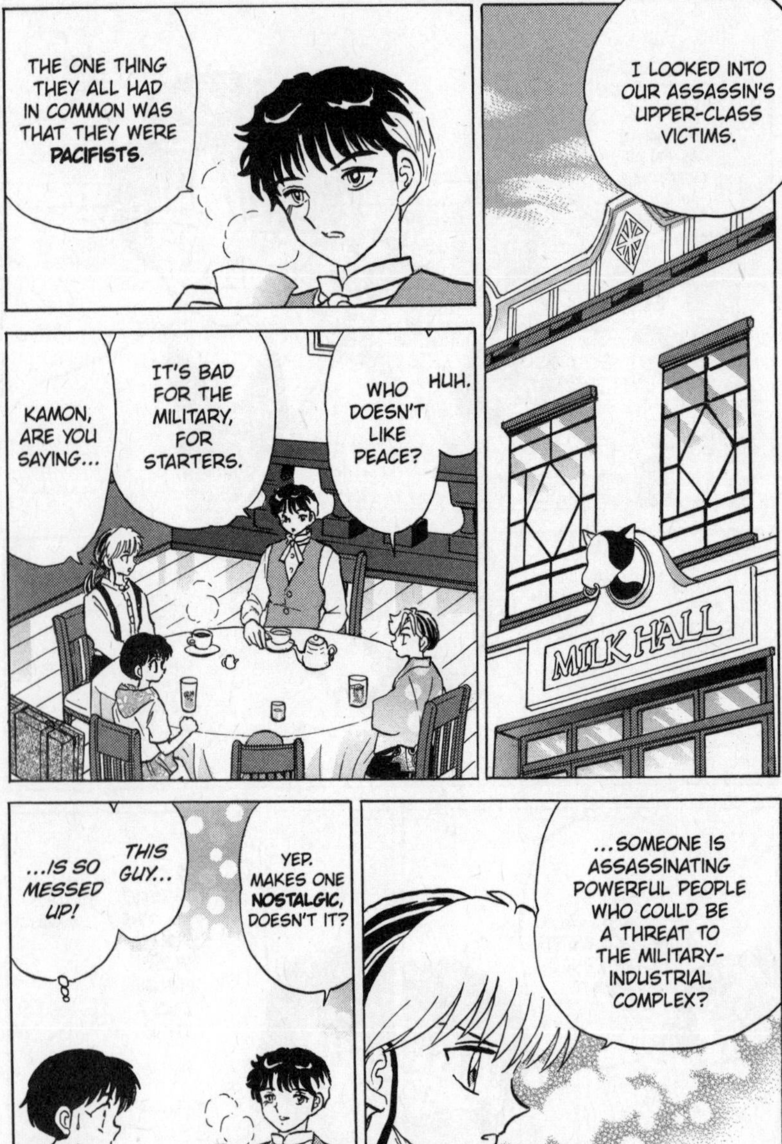

I LOOKED INTO OUR ASSASSIN'S UPPER-CLASS VICTIMS.
THE ONE THING THEY ALL HAD IN COMMON WAS THAT THEY WERE **PACIFISTS.**
HUH.
WHO DOESN'T LIKE PEACE?
IT'S BAD FOR THE MILITARY, FOR STARTERS.
KAMON, ARE YOU SAYING...
MILK HALL
...SOMEONE IS ASSASSINATING POWERFUL PEOPLE WHO COULD BE A THREAT TO THE MILITARY-INDUSTRIAL COMPLEX?
YEP. MAKES ONE **NOSTALGIC,** DOESN'T IT?
THIS GUY...
...IS SO MESSED UP!

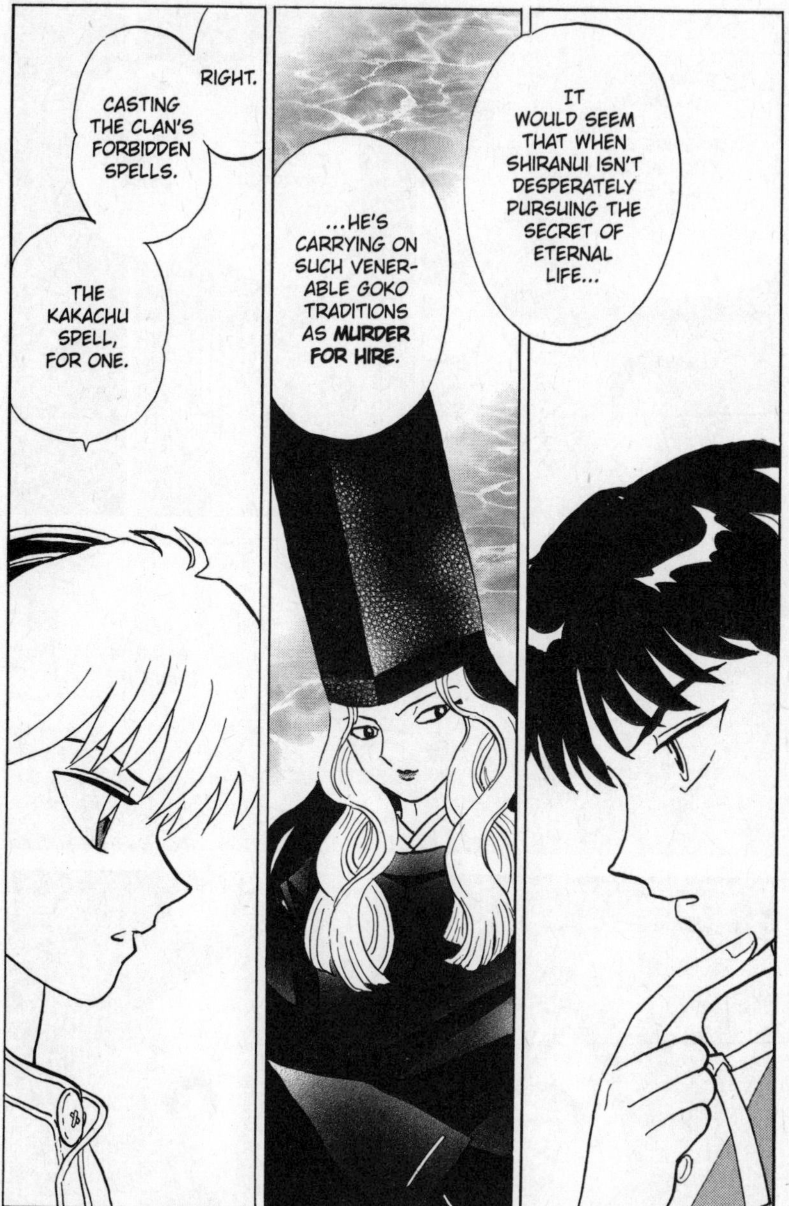
IT WOULD SEEM THAT WHEN SHIRANUI ISN'T DESPERATELY PURSUING THE SECRET OF ETERNAL LIFE...
...HE'S CARRYING ON SUCH VENER-ABLE GOKO TRADITIONS AS **MURDER FOR HIRE.**
RIGHT.
CASTING THE CLAN'S FORBIDDEN SPELLS.
THE KAKACHU SPELL, FOR ONE.

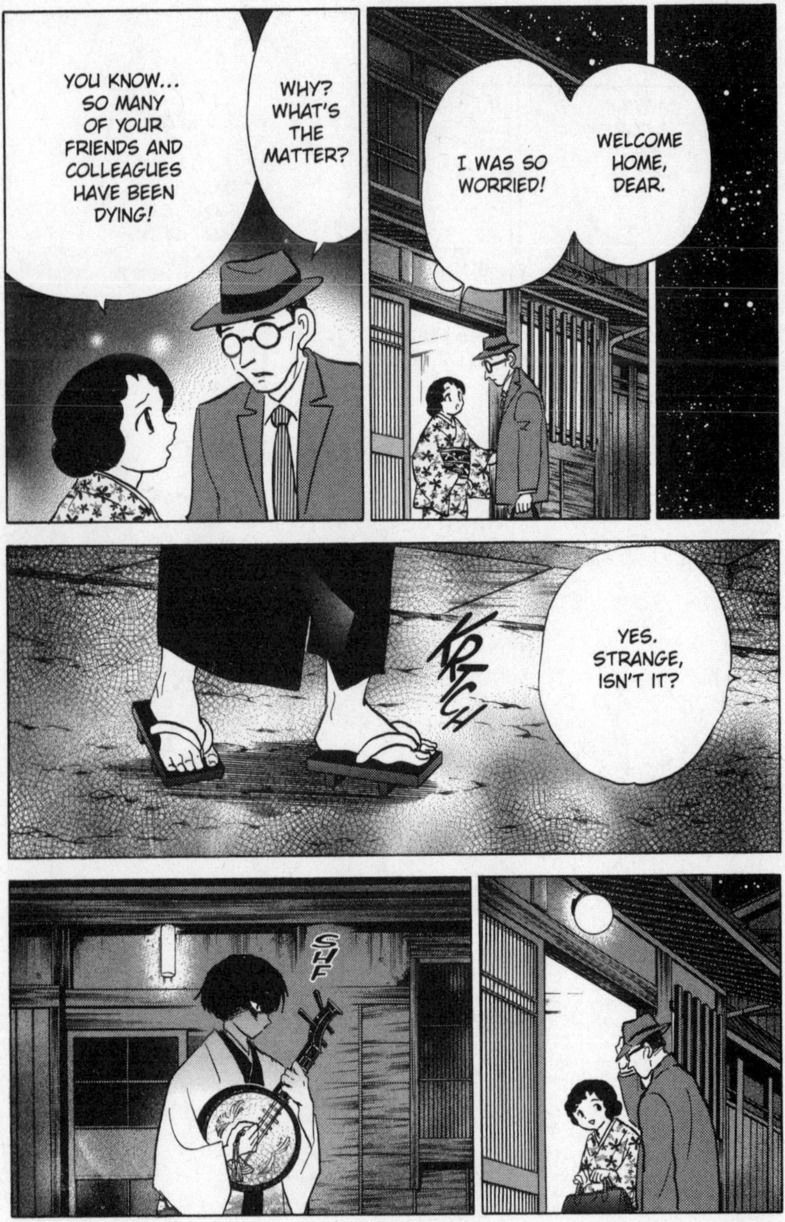
WELCOME HOME, DEAR.
I WAS SO WORRIED!
WHY? WHAT'S THE MATTER?
YOU KNOW... SO MANY OF YOUR FRIENDS AND COLLEAGUES HAVE BEEN DYING!
YES. STRANGE, ISN'T IT?
KRTCH
SHF

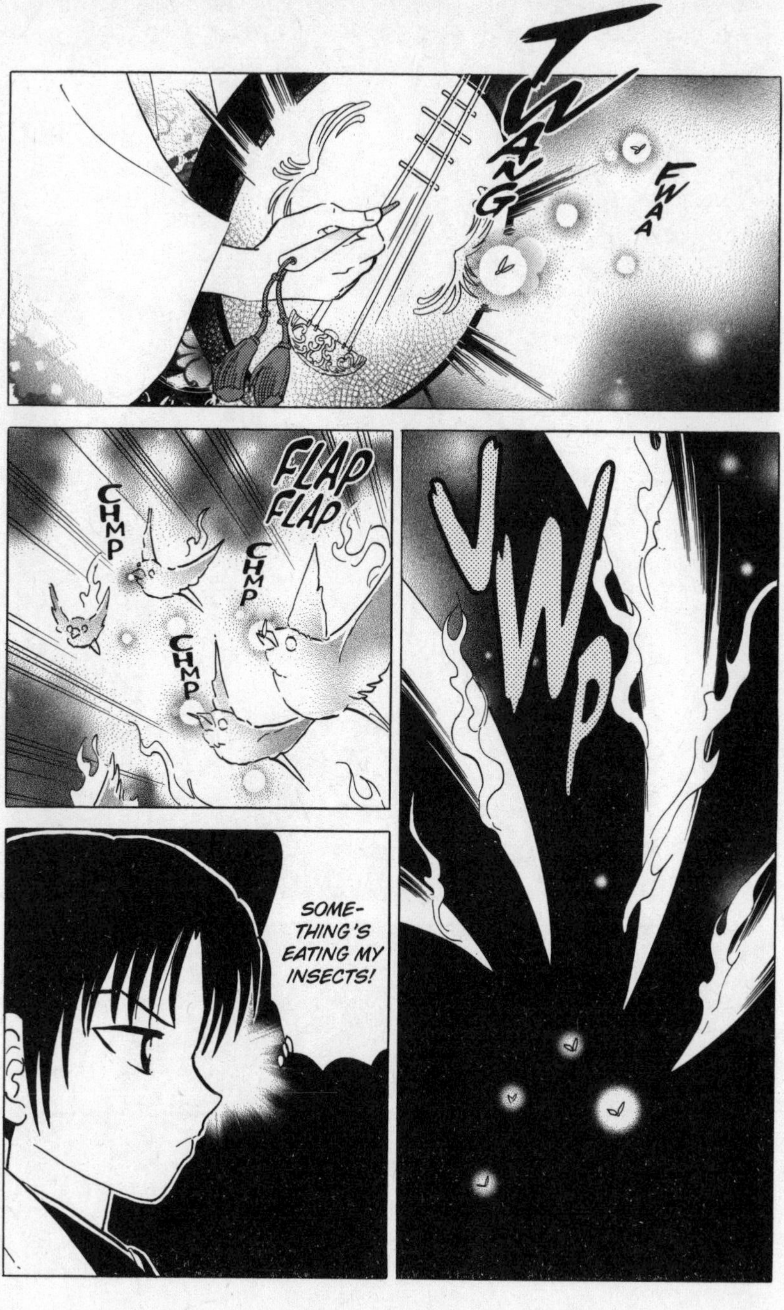
TWANG
FWAA
VWP
FLAP FLAP
CHMP
CHMP
CHMP
SOME-THING'S EATING MY INSECTS!

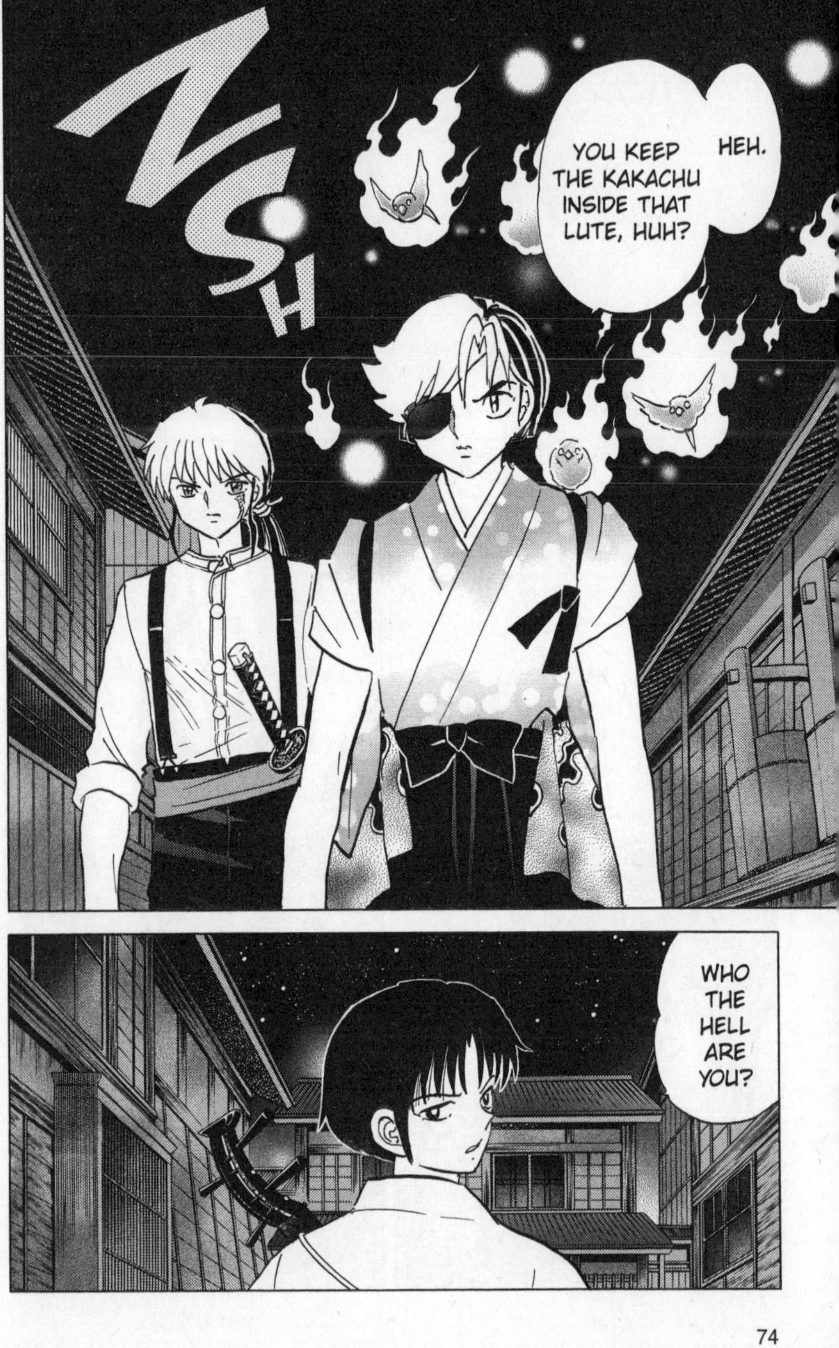
HEH.
YOU KEEP THE KAKACHU INSIDE THAT LUTE, HUH?
NSH
WHO THE HELL ARE YOU?

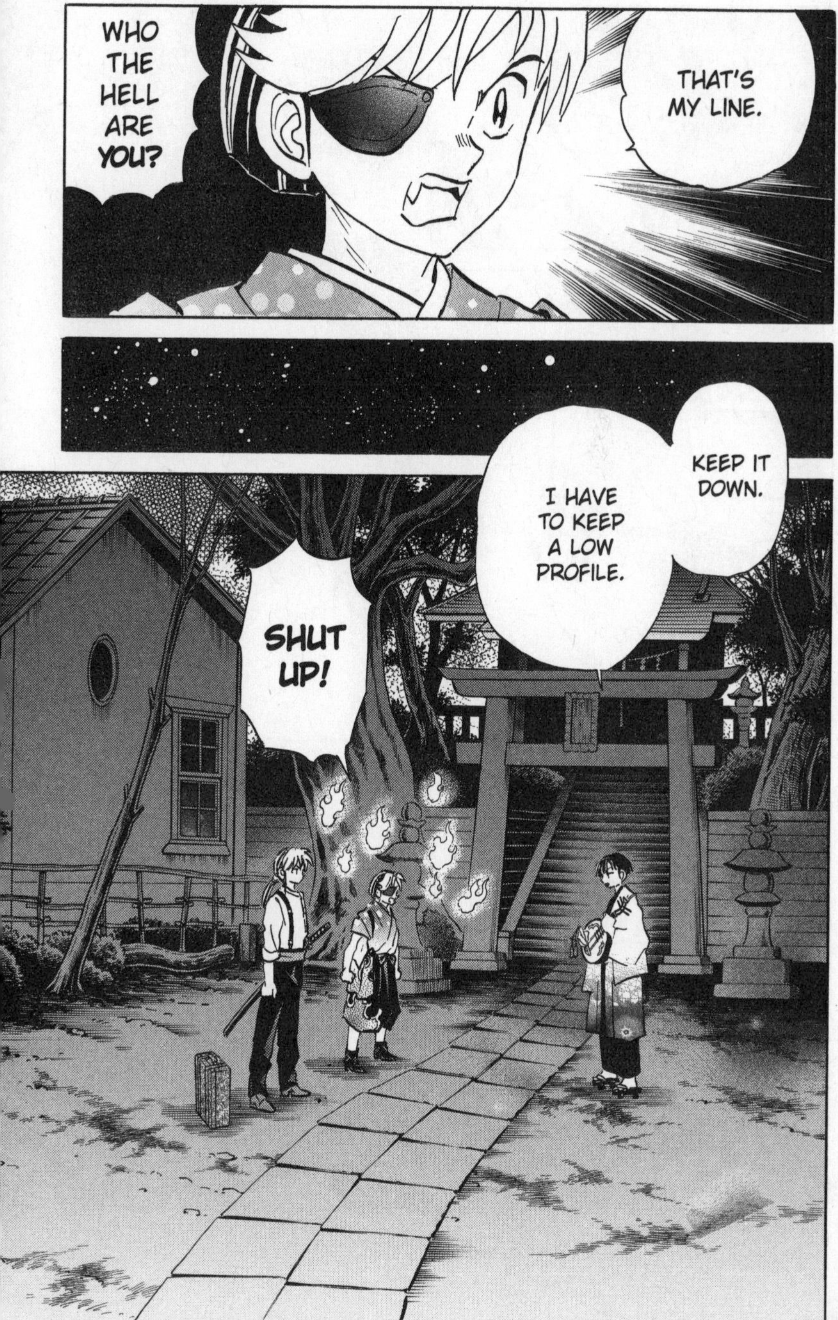
THAT'S MY LINE.
WHO THE HELL ARE YOU?
KEEP IT DOWN.
I HAVE TO KEEP A LOW PROFILE.
SHUT UP!

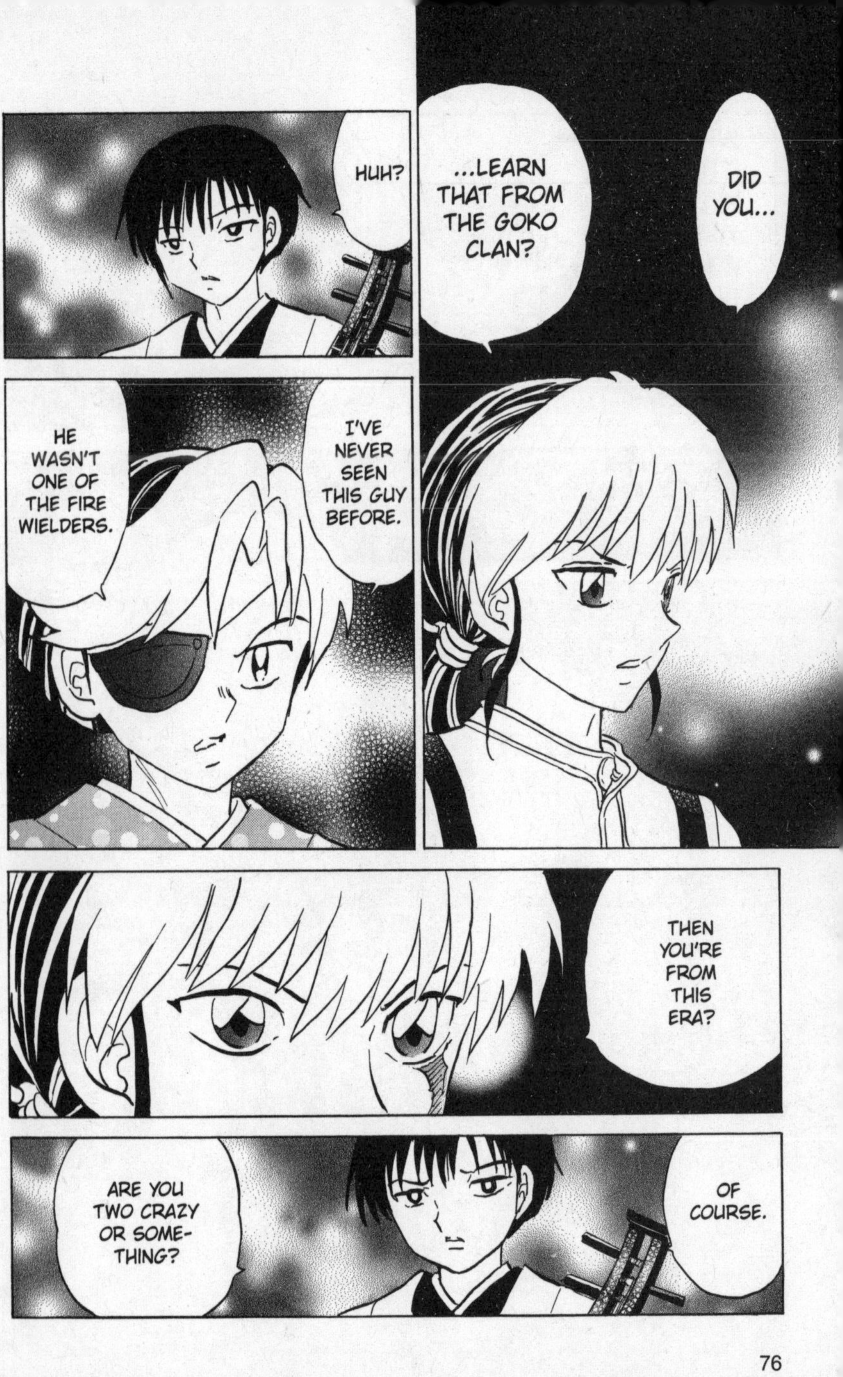
DID YOU...
...LEARN THAT FROM THE GOKO CLAN?
HUH?
I'VE NEVER SEEN THIS GUY BEFORE.
HE WASN'T ONE OF THE FIRE WIELDERS.
THEN YOU'RE FROM THIS ERA?
OF COURSE.
ARE YOU TWO CRAZY OR SOME-THING?

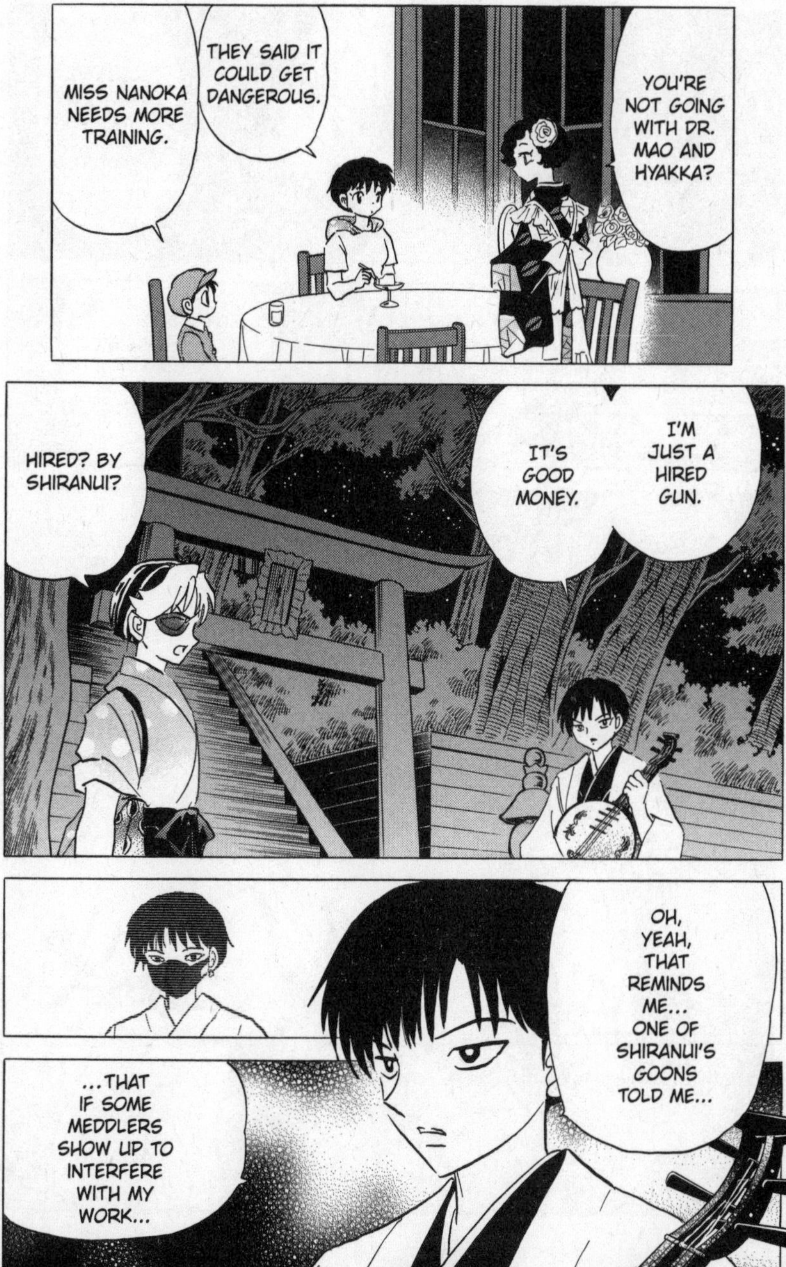
YOU'RE NOT GOING WITH DR. MAO AND HYAKKA?
THEY SAID IT COULD GET DANGEROUS.
MISS NANOKA NEEDS MORE TRAINING.
I'M JUST A HIRED GUN.
IT'S GOOD MONEY.
HIRED? BY SHIRANUI?
OH, YEAH, THAT REMINDS ME... ONE OF SHIRANUI'S GOONS TOLD ME...
...THAT IF SOME MEDDLERS SHOW UP TO INTERFERE WITH MY WORK...

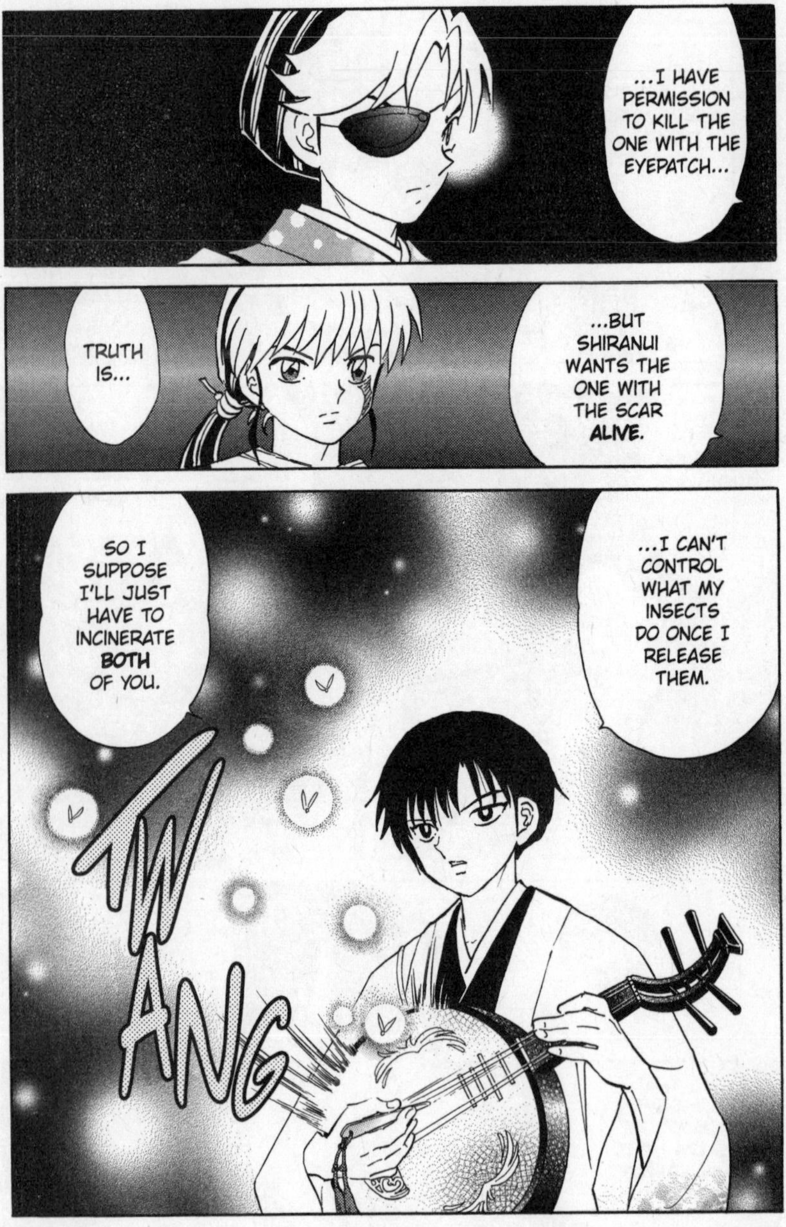
...I HAVE PERMISSION TO KILL THE ONE WITH THE EYEPATCH...
...BUT SHIRANUI WANTS THE ONE WITH THE SCAR **ALIVE.**
TRUTH IS...
...I CAN'T CONTROL WHAT MY INSECTS DO ONCE I RELEASE THEM.
SO I SUPPOSE I'LL JUST HAVE TO INCINERATE **BOTH** OF YOU.
TWANG

Chapter 5:
Life or Death

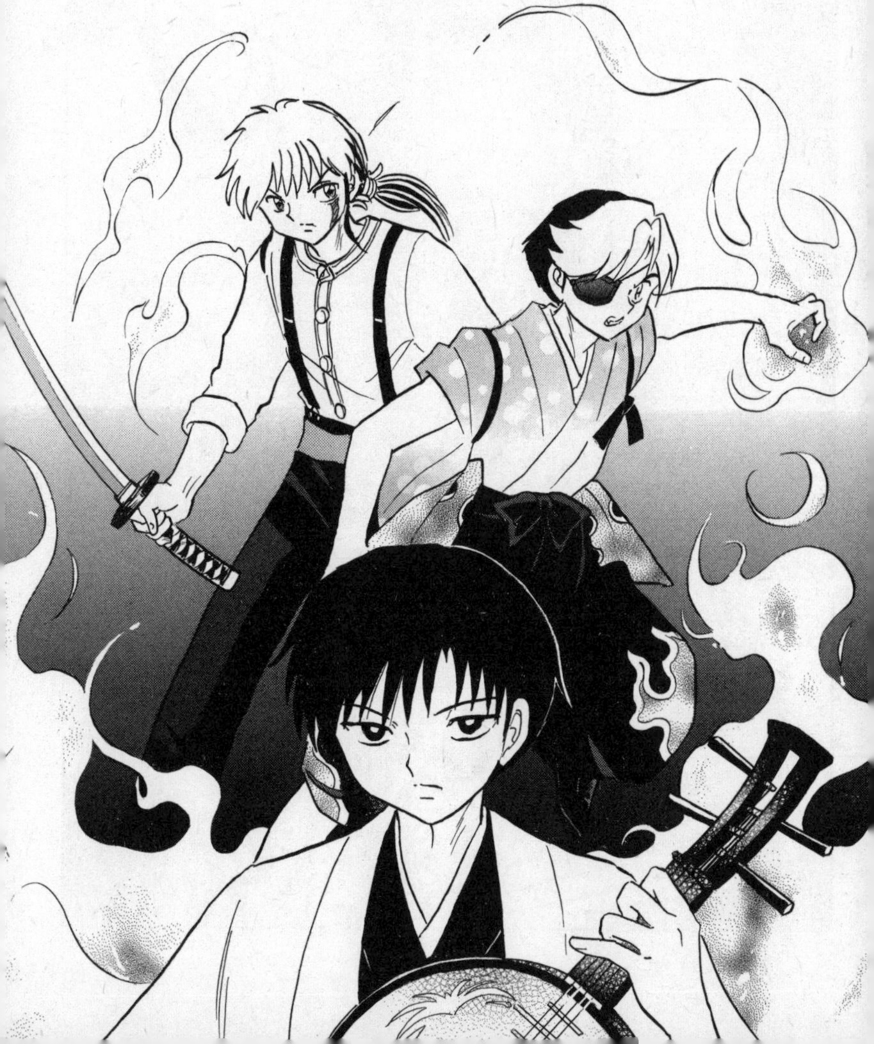

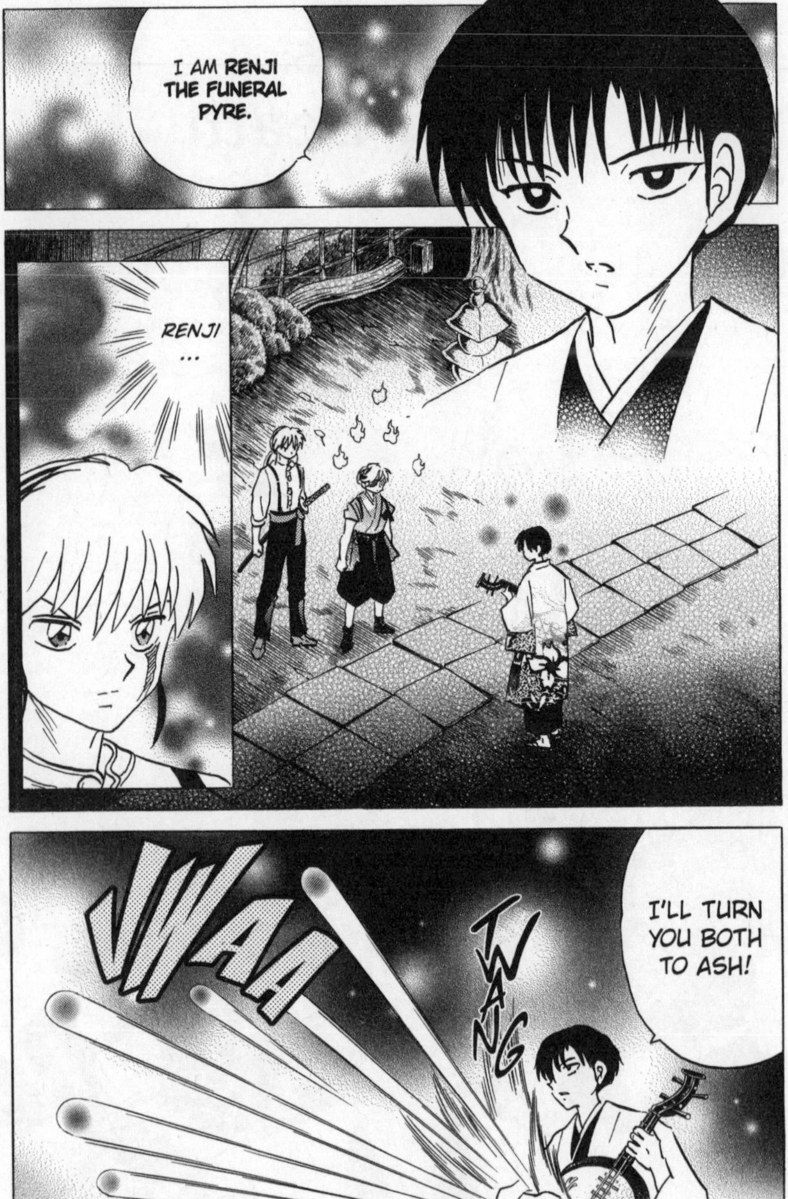
I AM RENJI THE FUNERAL PYRE.
RENJI ...
I'LL TURN YOU BOTH TO ASH!
TWANG
JWAA

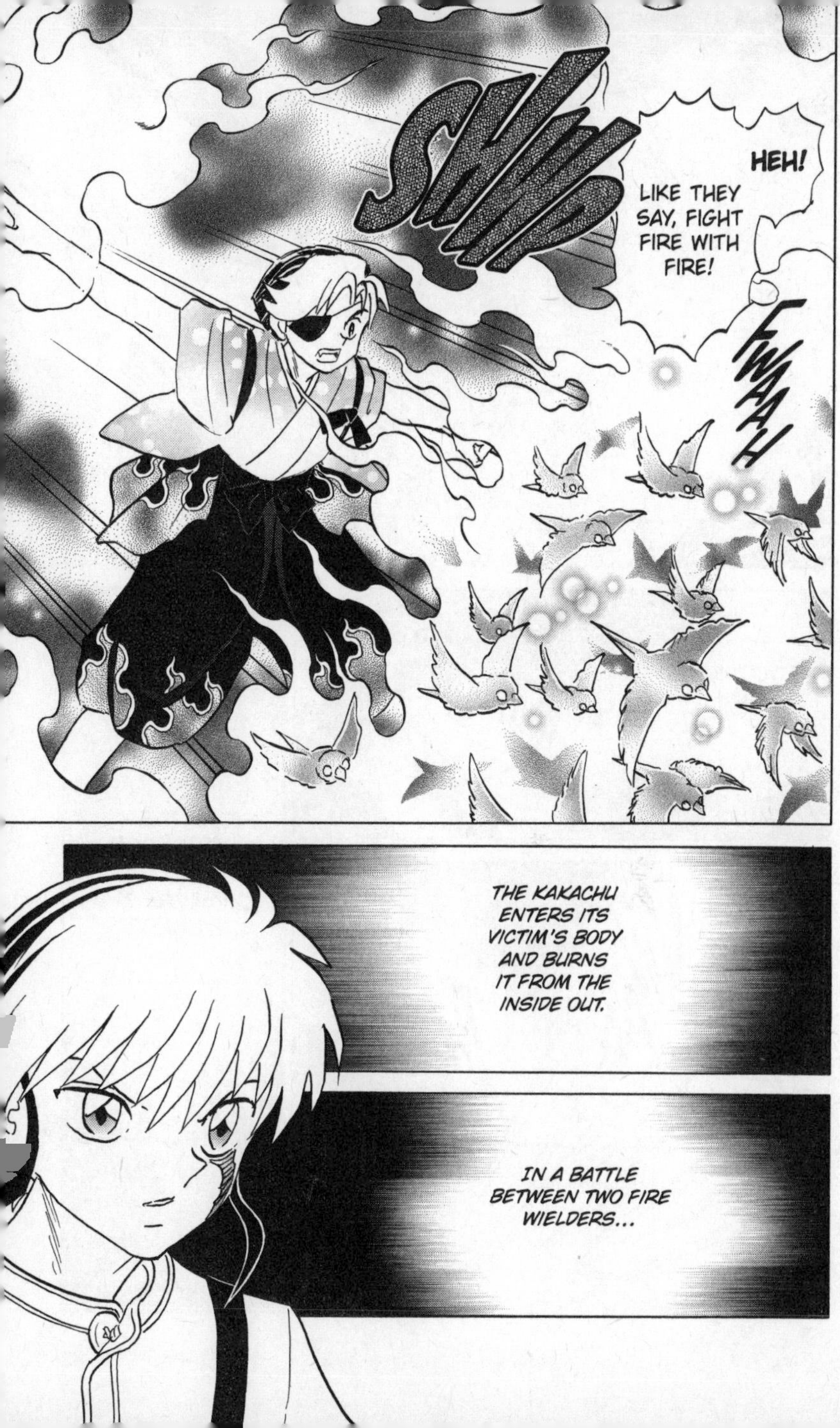
HEH!
LIKE THEY SAY, FIGHT FIRE WITH FIRE!
SHWP
FWAAAH
THE KAKACHU ENTERS ITS VICTIM'S BODY AND BURNS IT FROM THE INSIDE OUT.
IN A BATTLE BETWEEN TWO FIRE WIELDERS...

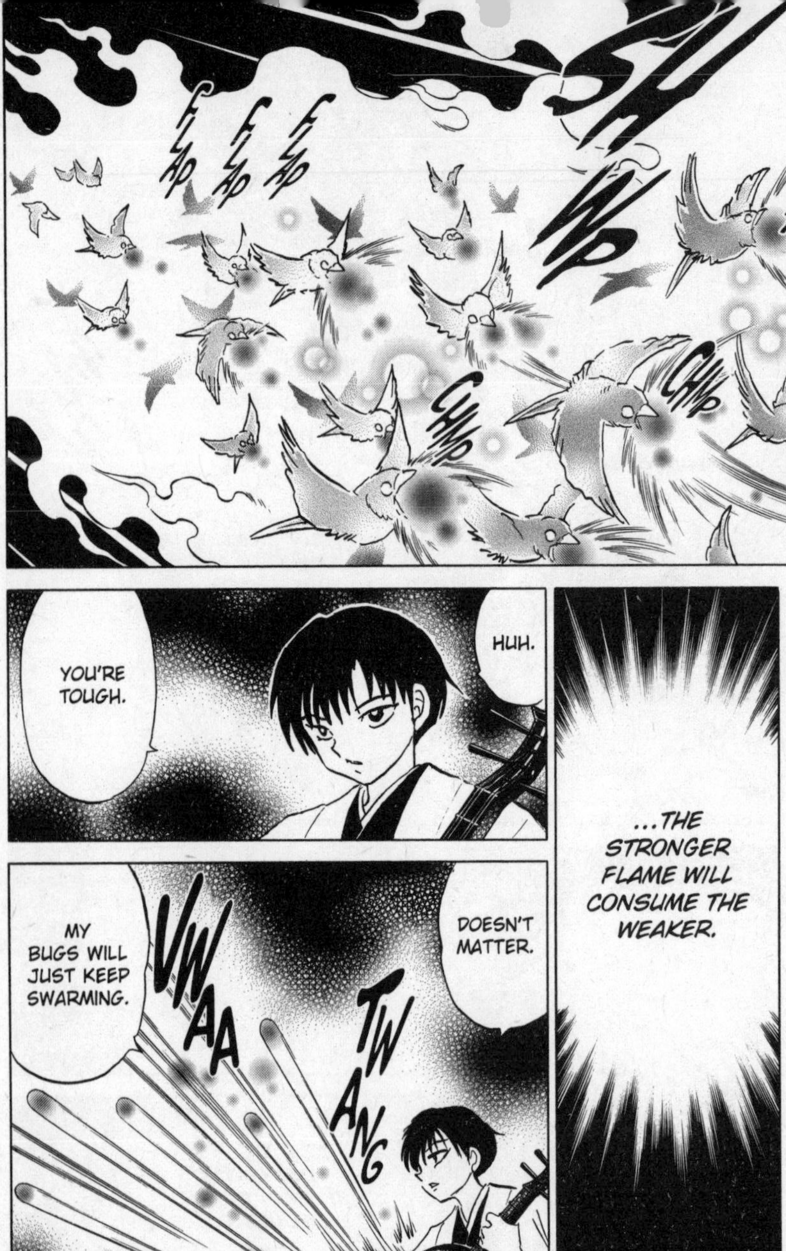
SHWNP
CHMP
FLAP
FLAP
FLAP
CHMP
CHMP
...THE STRONGER FLAME WILL CONSUME THE WEAKER.
HUH.
YOU'RE TOUGH.
DOESN'T MATTER.
TWANG
VWAA
MY BUGS WILL JUST KEEP SWARMING.

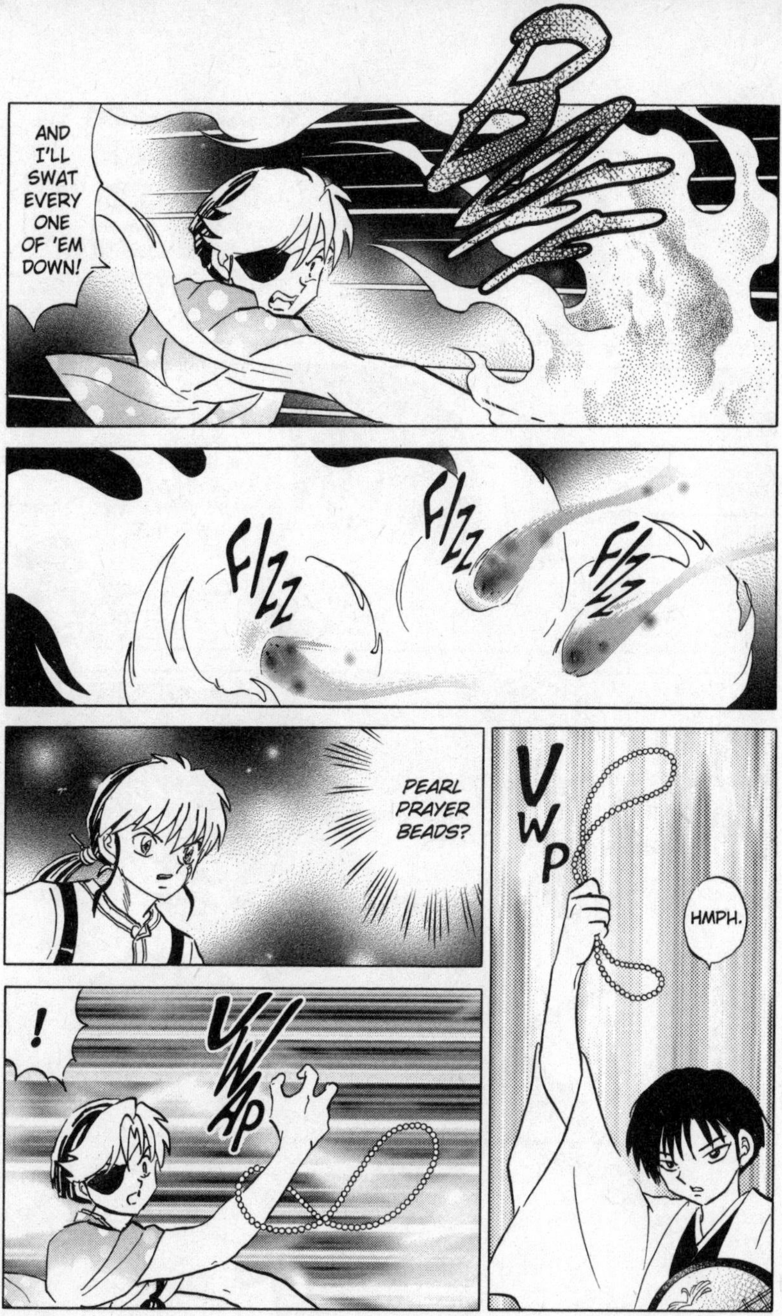
AND I'LL SWAT EVERY ONE OF 'EM DOWN!
FIZZ
FIZZ
FIZZ
VWP
HMPH.
PEARL PRAYER BEADS?
!
VWAP

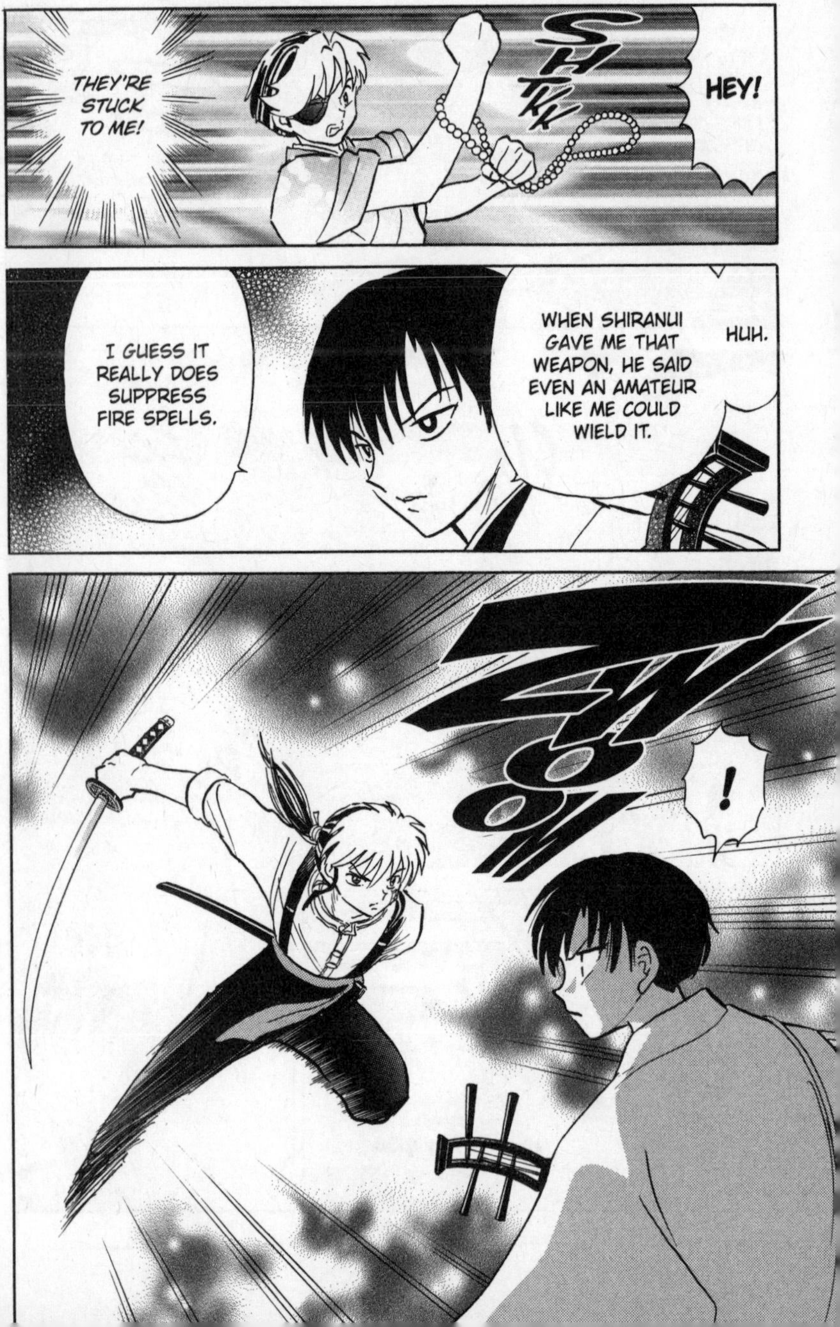
HEY!
SHTKK
THEY'RE STUCK TO ME!
HUH.
WHEN SHIRANUI GAVE ME THAT WEAPON, HE SAID EVEN AN AMATEUR LIKE ME COULD WIELD IT.
I GUESS IT REALLY DOES SUPPRESS FIRE SPELLS.
!

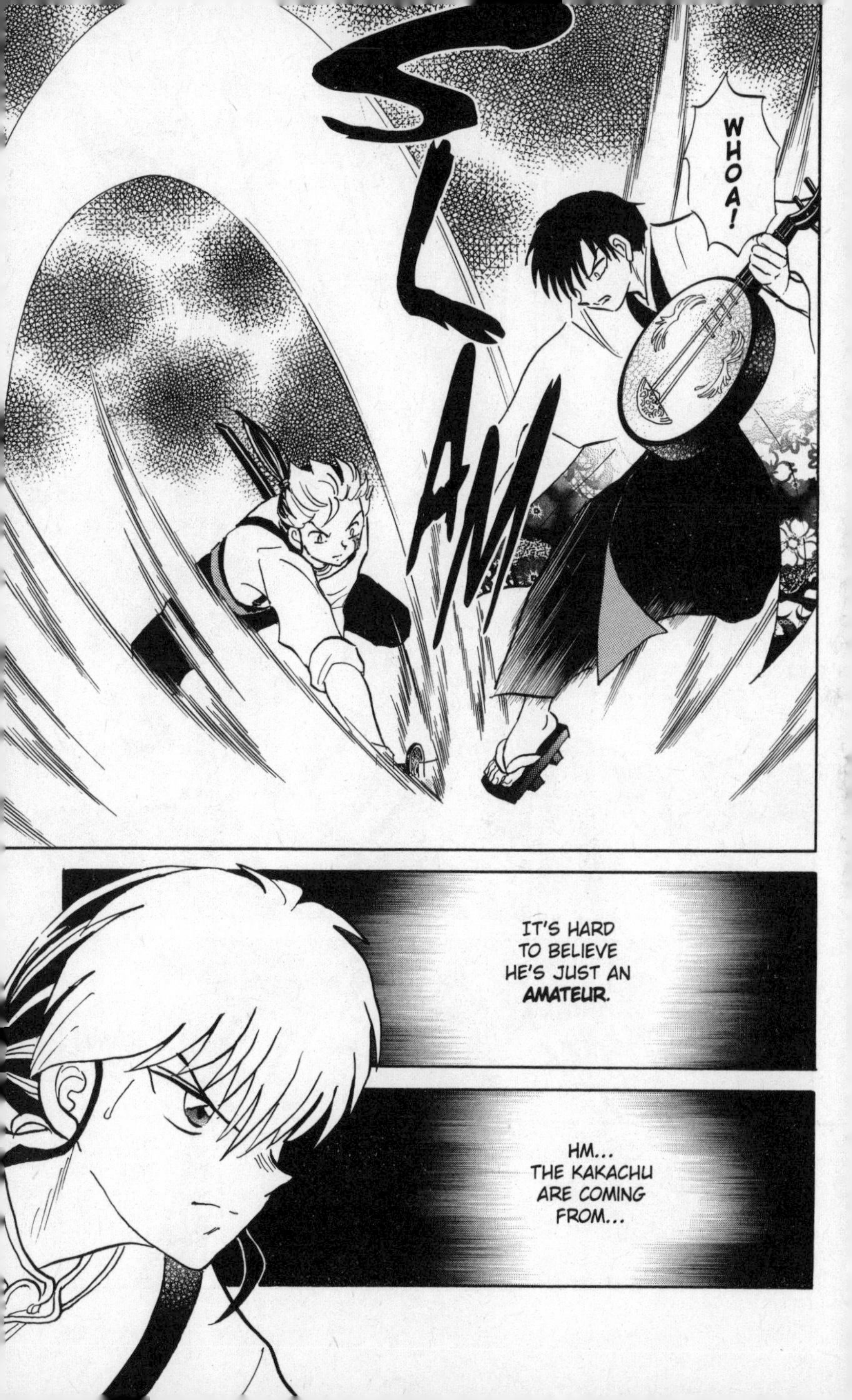
SLAM
WHOA!
IT'S HARD TO BELIEVE HE'S JUST AN AMATEUR.
HM... THE KAKACHU ARE COMING FROM...

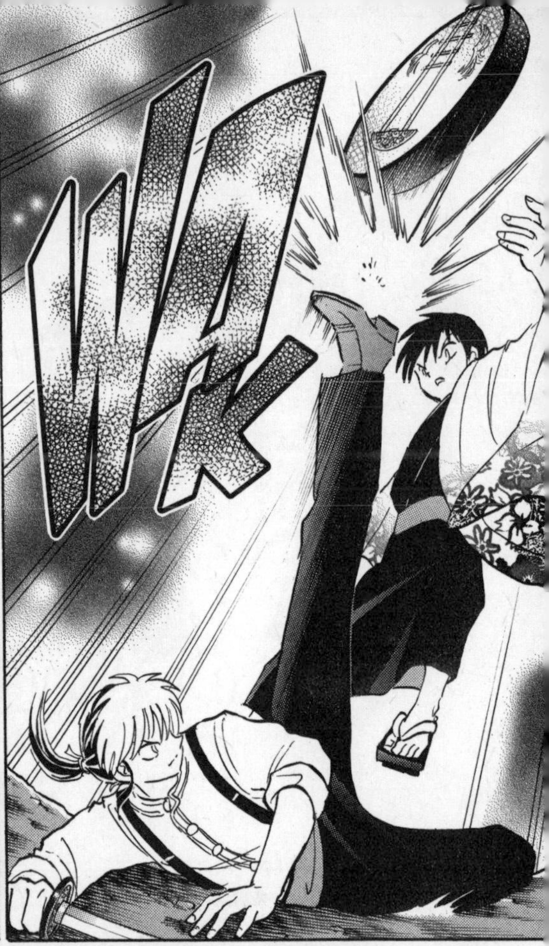
WAK

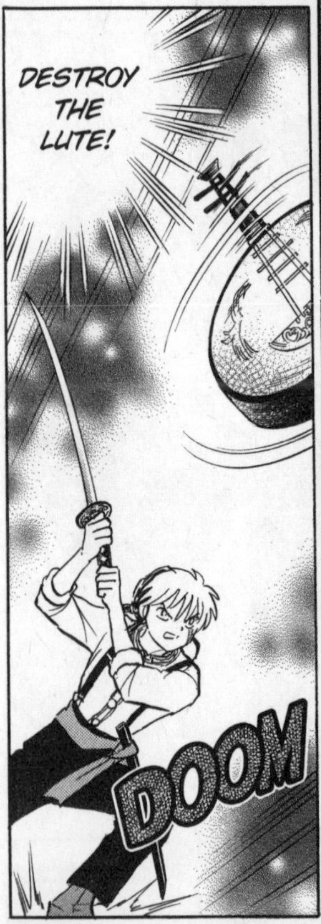
DESTROY THE LUTE!
DOOM

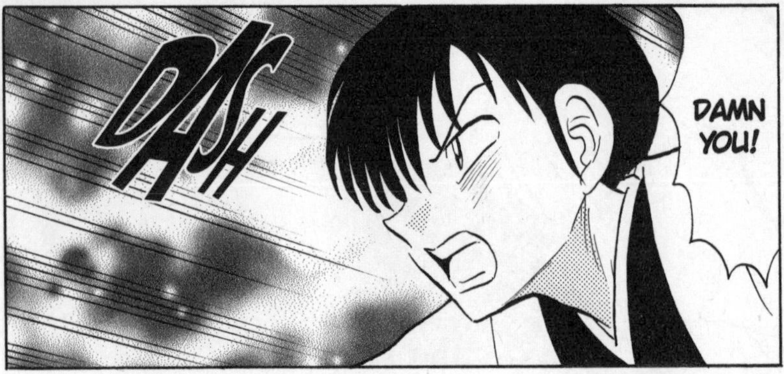
DAMN YOU!
DASH

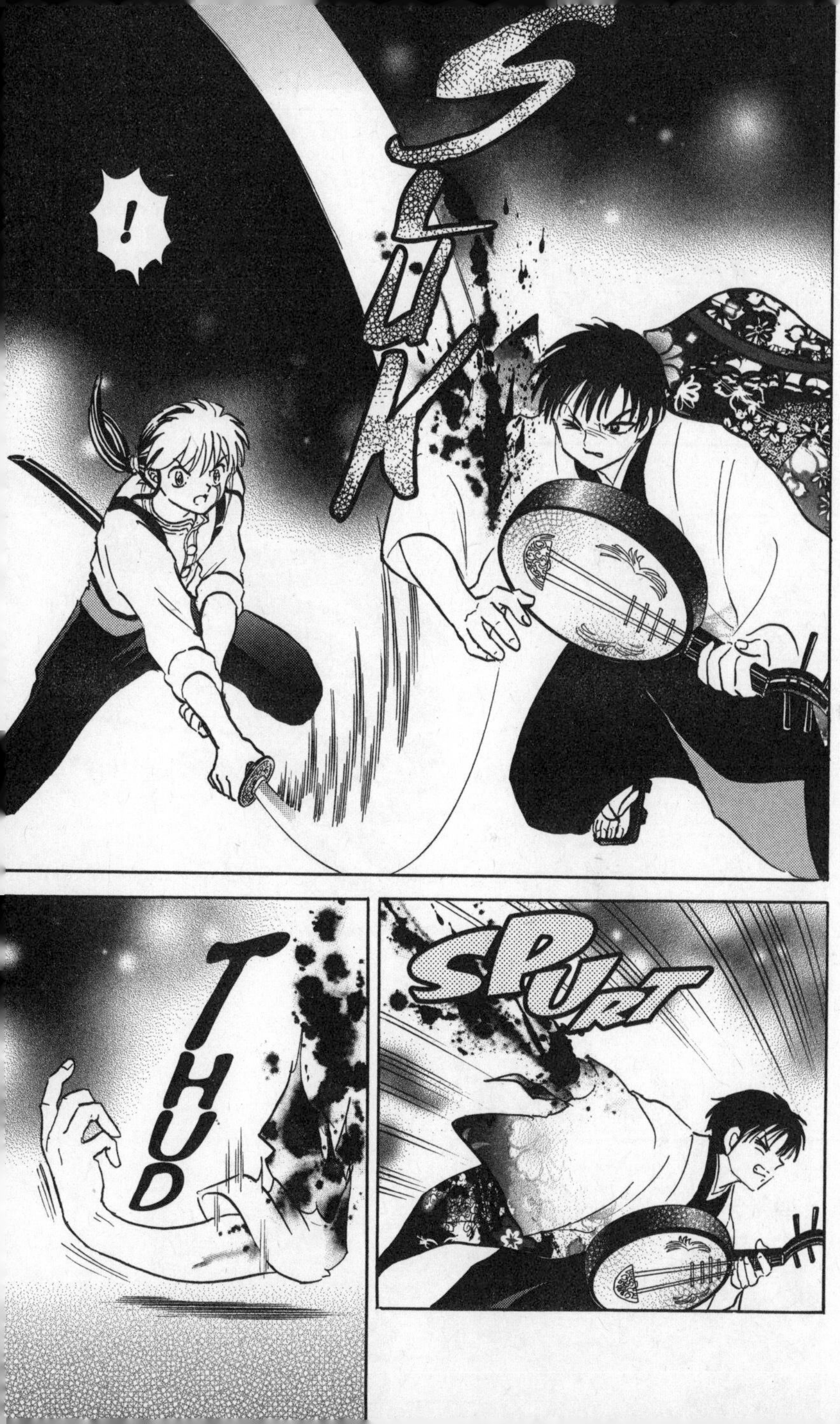
!
SPURT
THUD

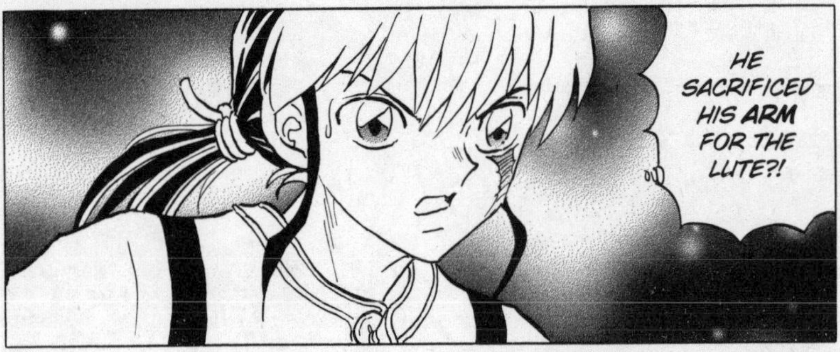
HE SACRIFICED HIS ARM FOR THE LUTE?!

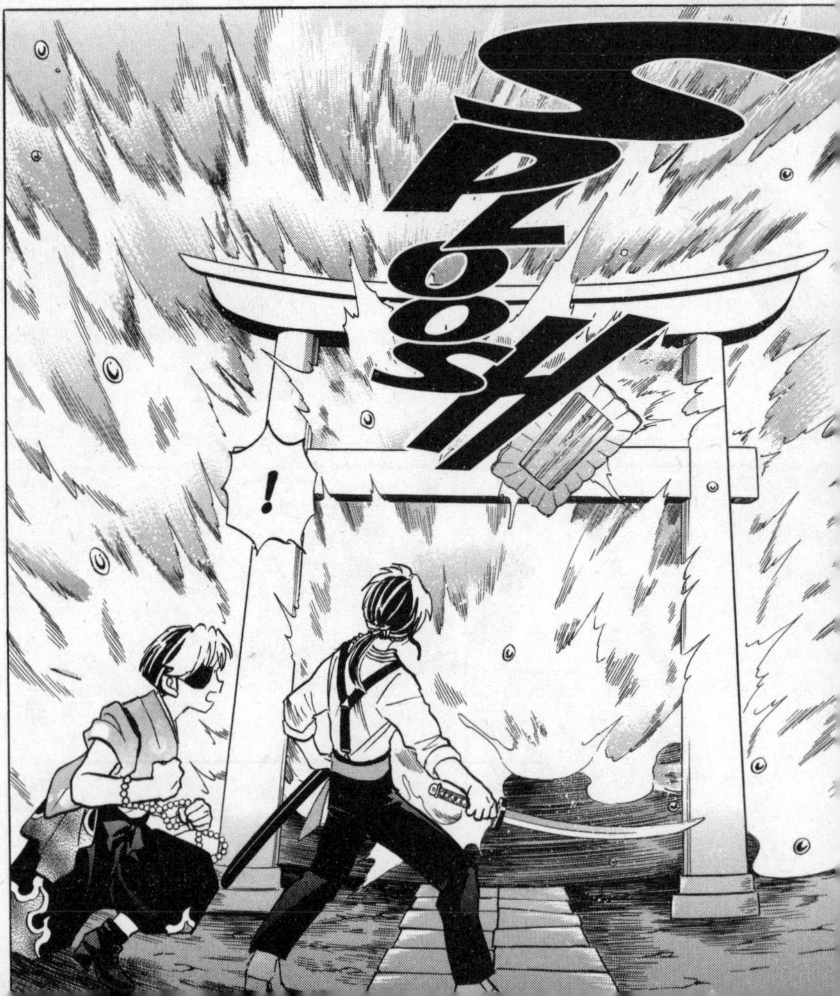
SPLOOSH!
!

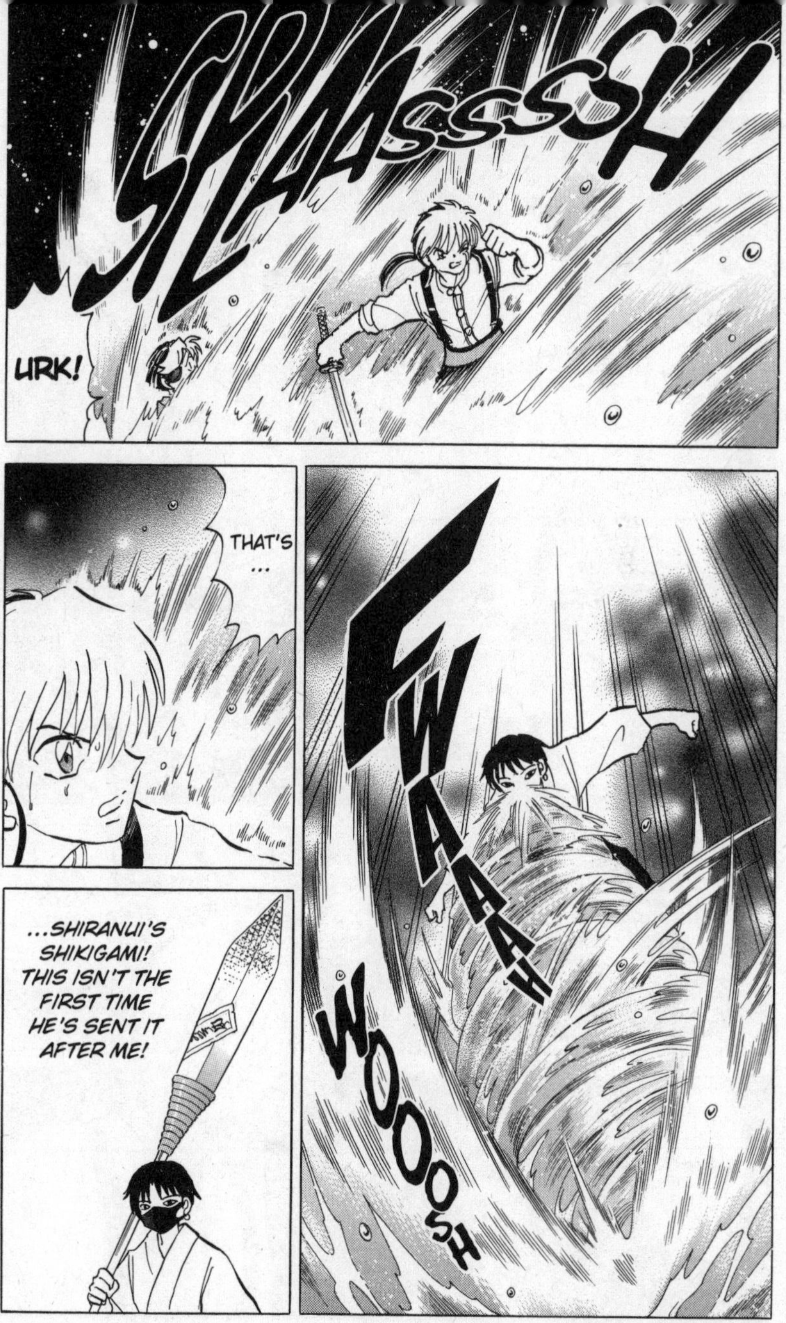
URK!
FWAAAH
WOOOOSH
THAT'S ...
...SHIRANUI'S SHIKIGAMI! THIS ISN'T THE FIRST TIME HE'S SENT IT AFTER ME!

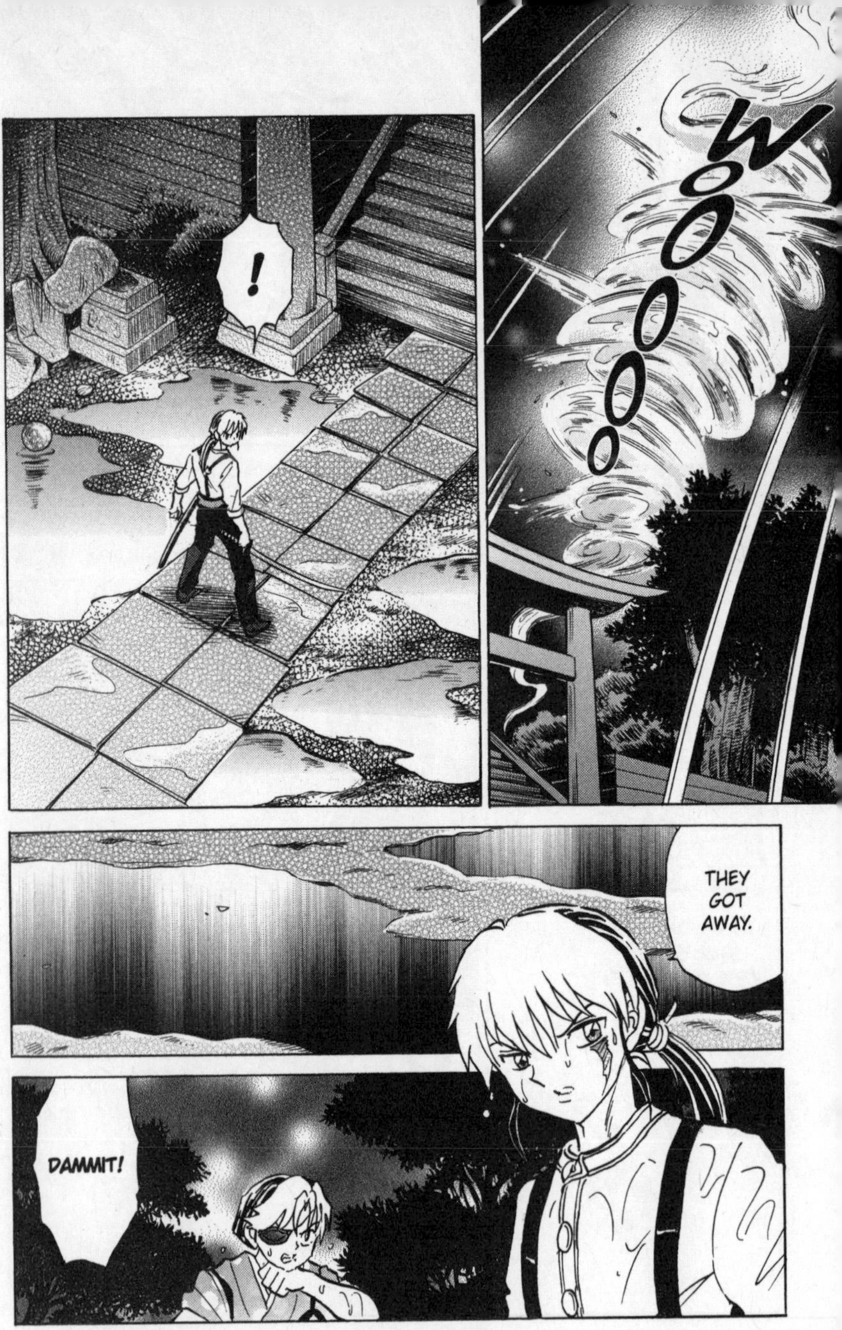
WOOOOOOO
!
THEY GOT AWAY.
DAMMIT!

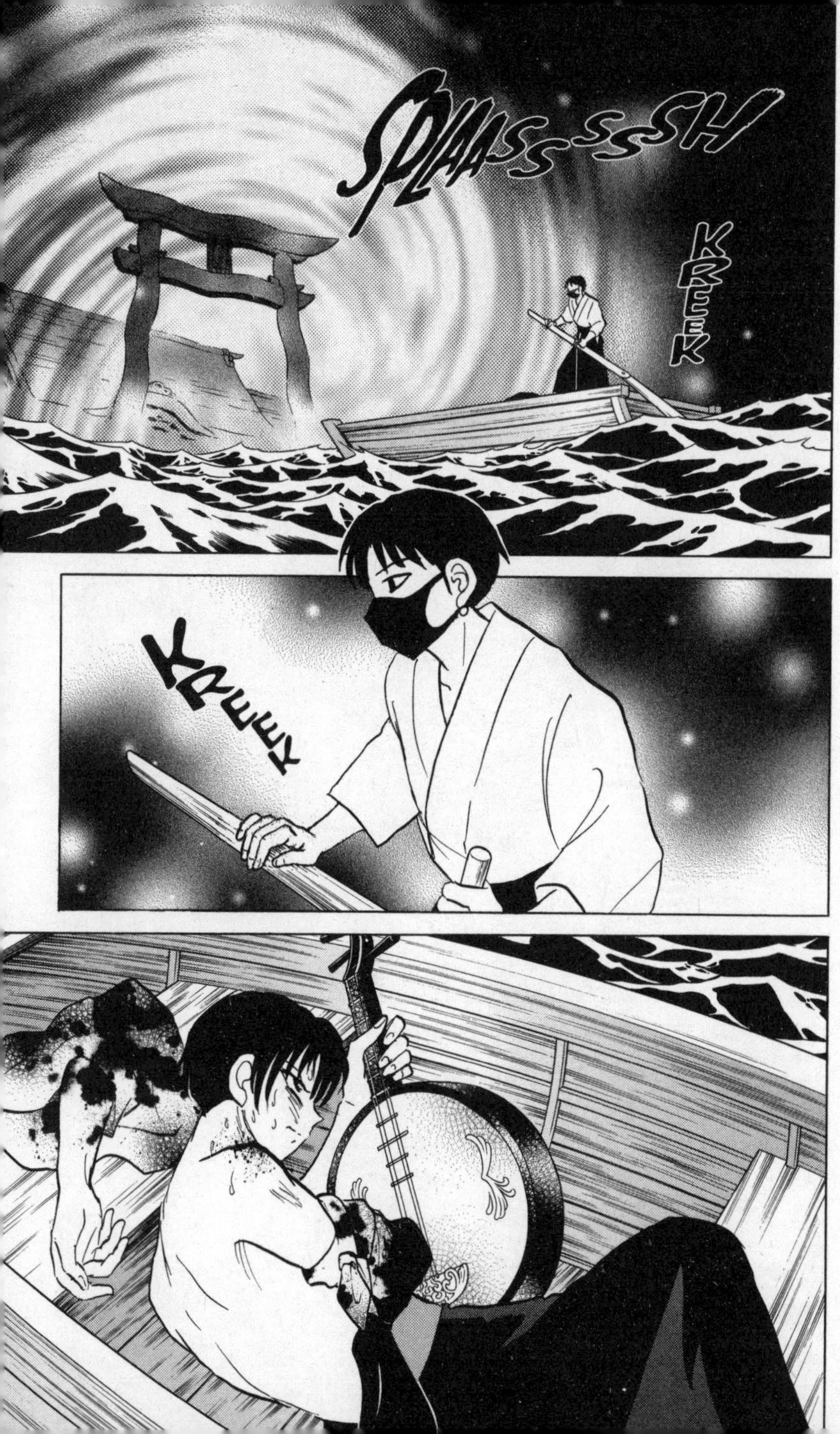
SPLAASS-SSSH
KREEK
KREEK

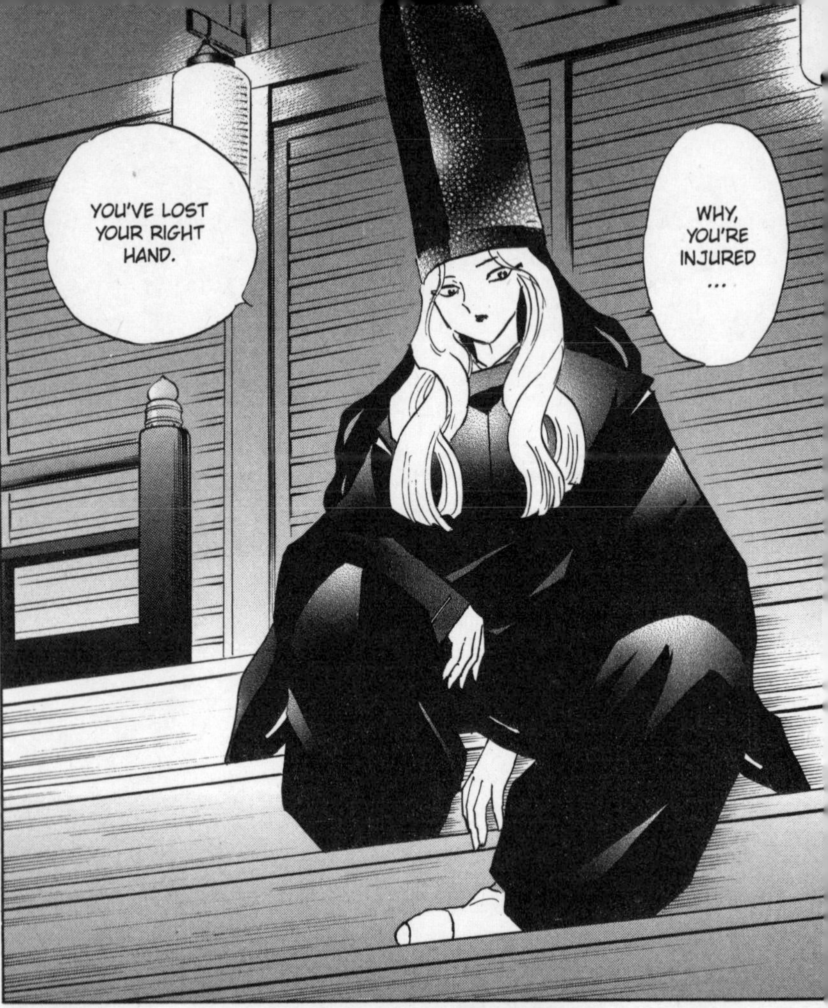
WHY, YOU'RE INJURED ...
YOU'VE LOST YOUR RIGHT HAND.
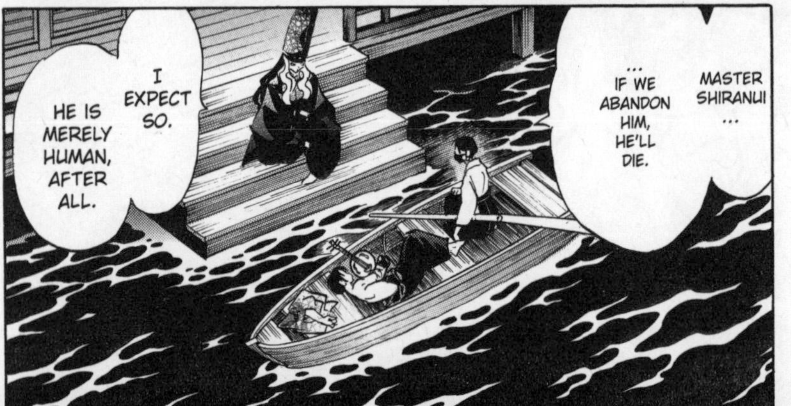
MASTER SHIRANUI ...
... IF WE ABANDON HIM, HE'LL DIE.
I EXPECT SO.
HE IS MERELY HUMAN, AFTER ALL.

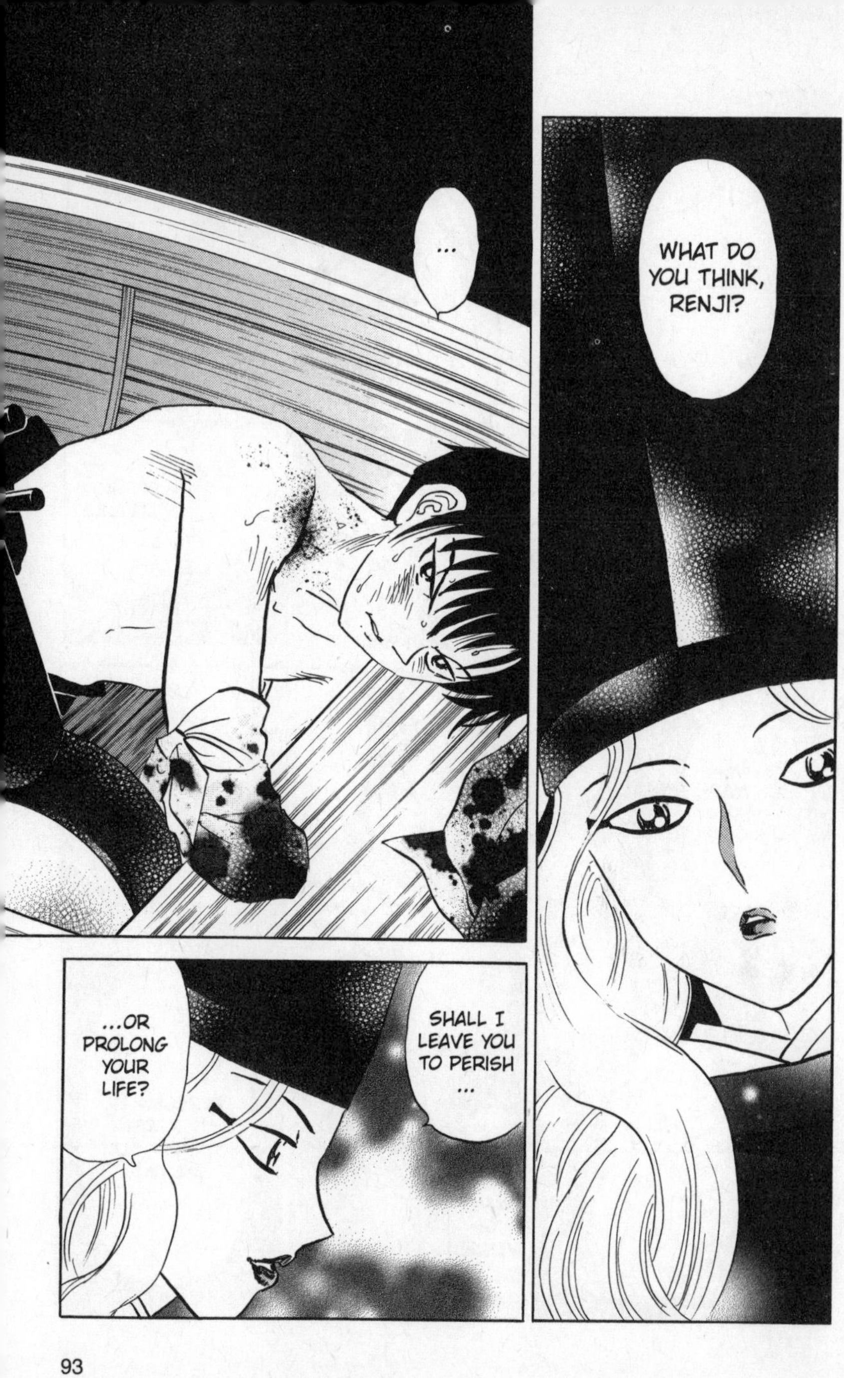
WHAT DO YOU THINK, RENJI?
...
SHALL I LEAVE YOU TO PERISH ...
...OR PROLONG YOUR LIFE?

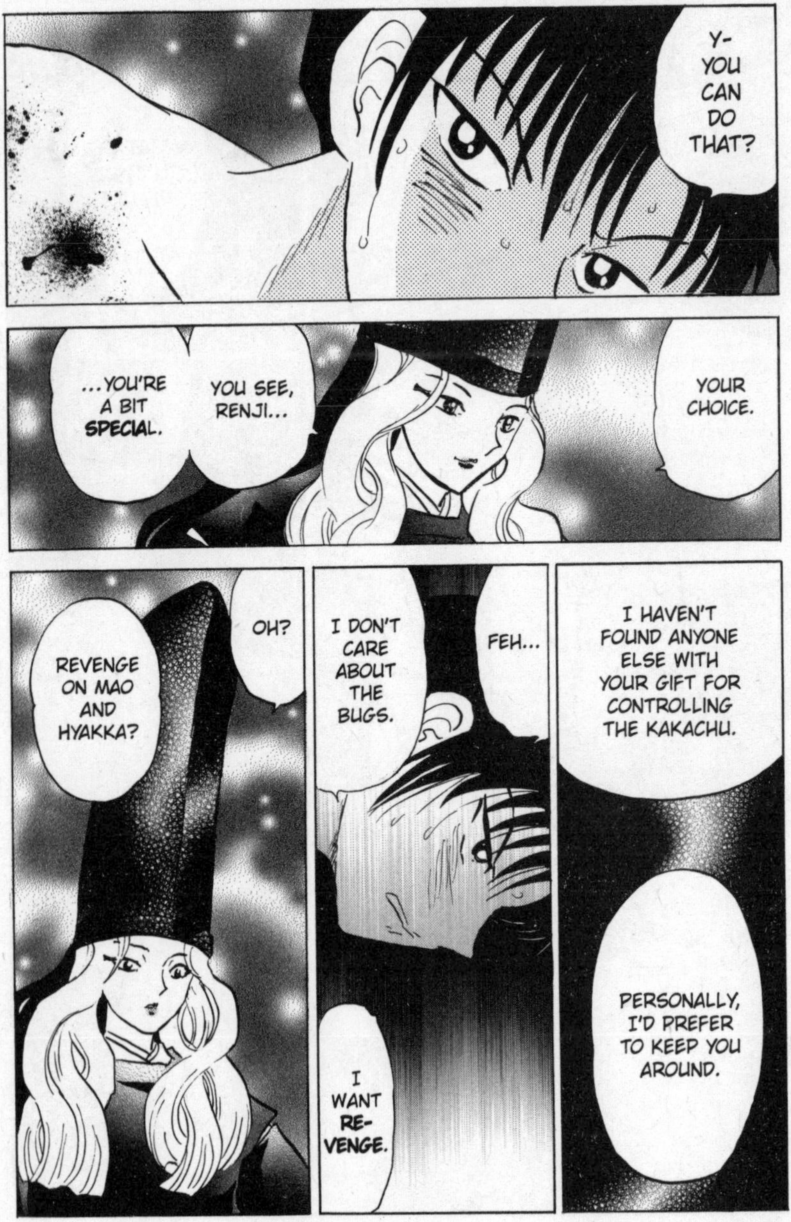
Y- YOU CAN DO THAT?
YOUR CHOICE.
YOU SEE, RENJI...
...YOU'RE A BIT **SPECIAL**.
I HAVEN'T FOUND ANYONE ELSE WITH YOUR GIFT FOR CONTROLLING THE KAKACHU.
PERSONALLY, I'D PREFER TO KEEP YOU AROUND.
FEH...
I DON'T CARE ABOUT THE BUGS.
I WANT **RE-VENGE**.
OH?
REVENGE ON MAO AND HYAKKA?

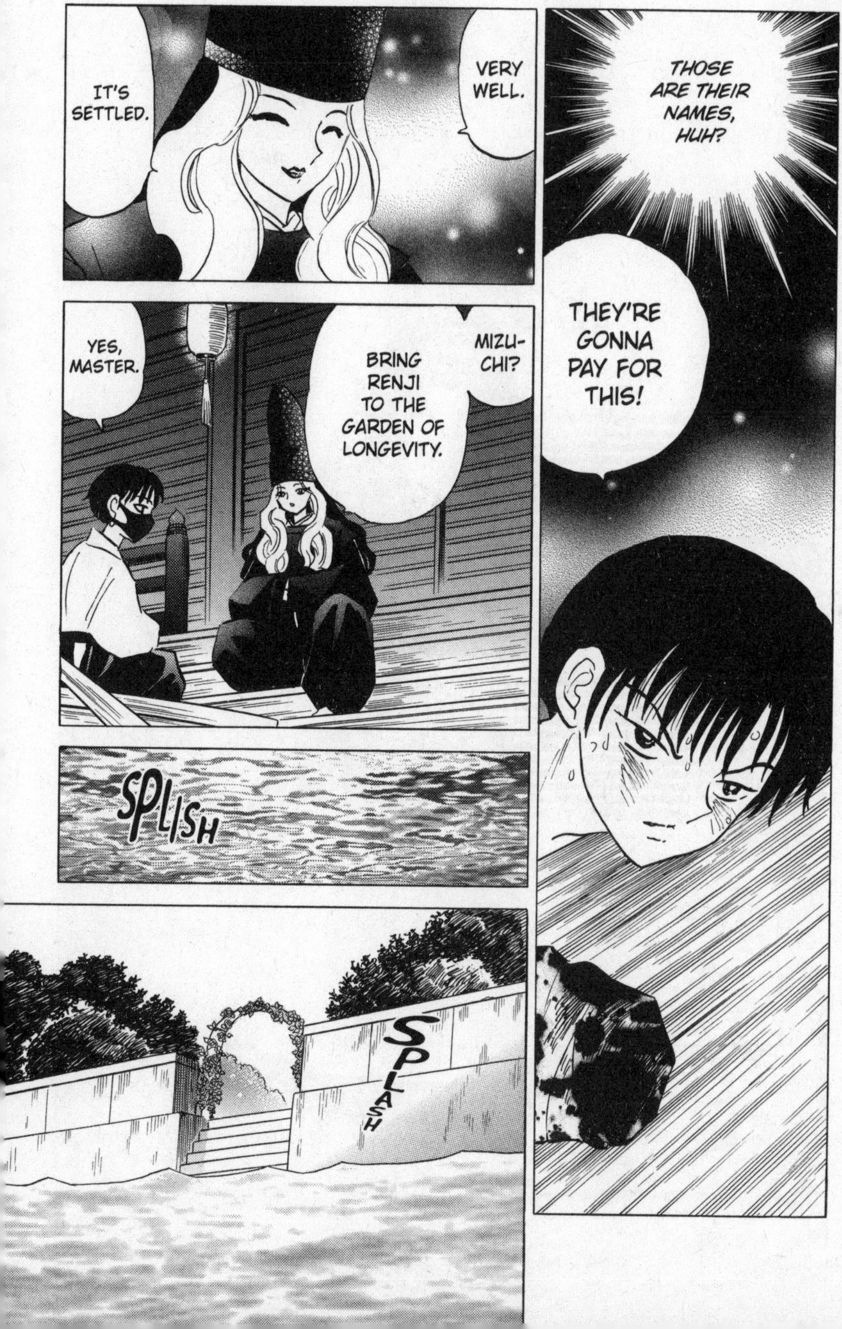
THOSE ARE THEIR NAMES, HUH?
THEY'RE GONNA PAY FOR THIS!
VERY WELL.
IT'S SETTLED.
MIZU-CHI?
BRING RENJI TO THE GARDEN OF LONGEVITY.
YES, MASTER.
SPLISH
SPLASH

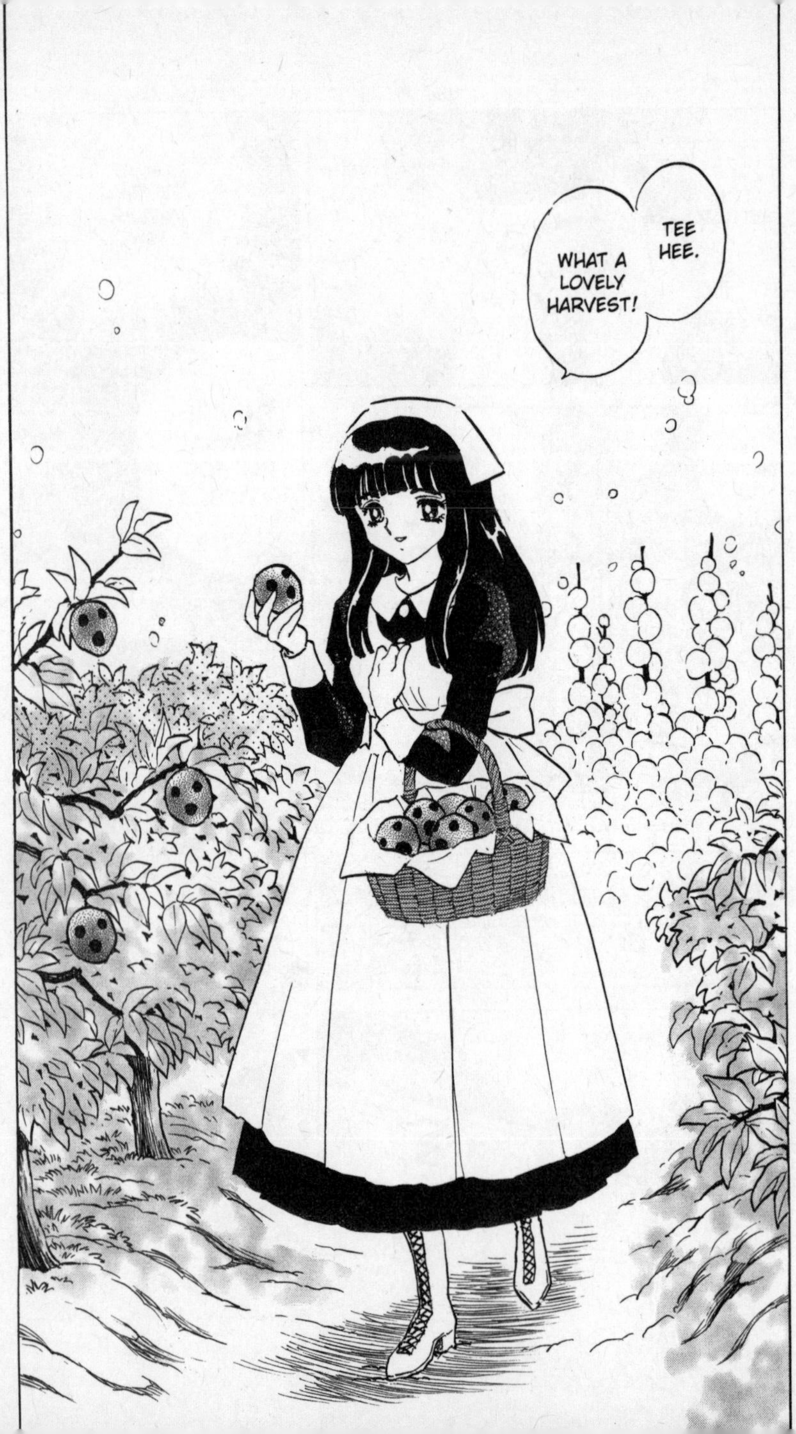
TEE HEE.
WHAT A LOVELY HARVEST!

Chapter 6:

The Garden of Longevity

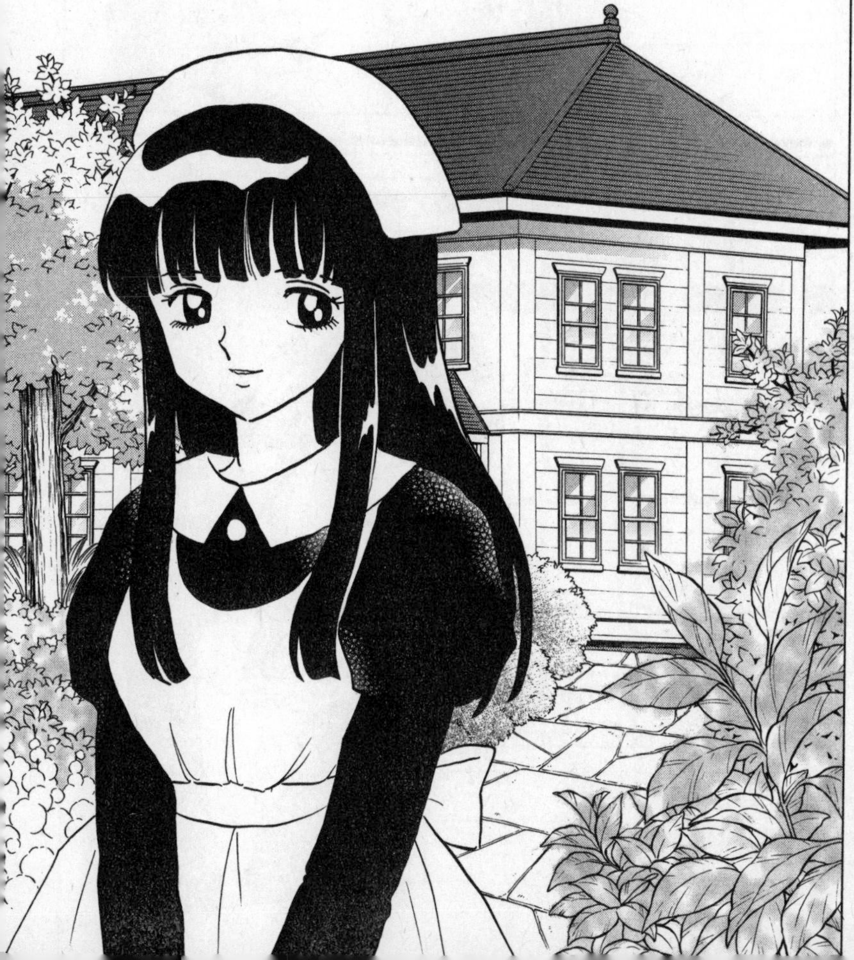

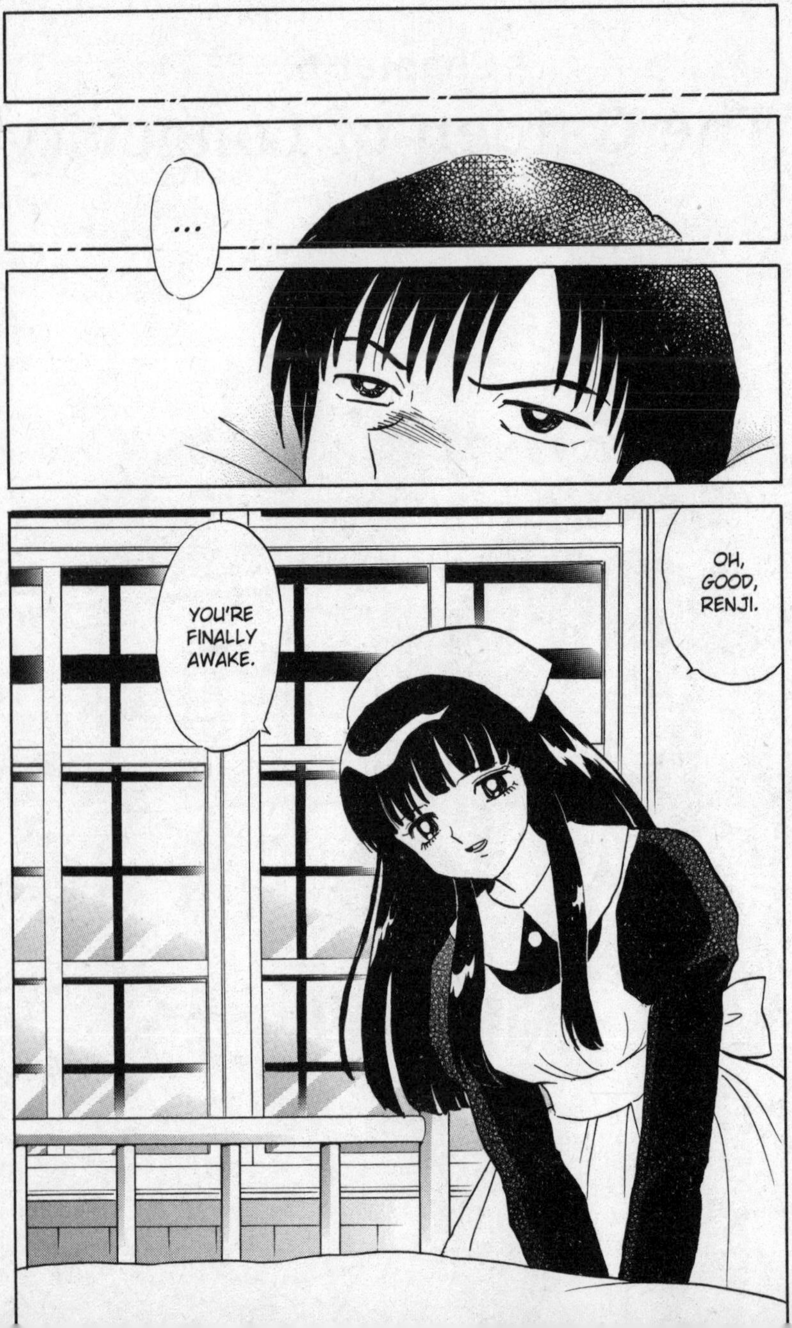
...
OH, GOOD, RENJI.
YOU'RE FINALLY AWAKE.

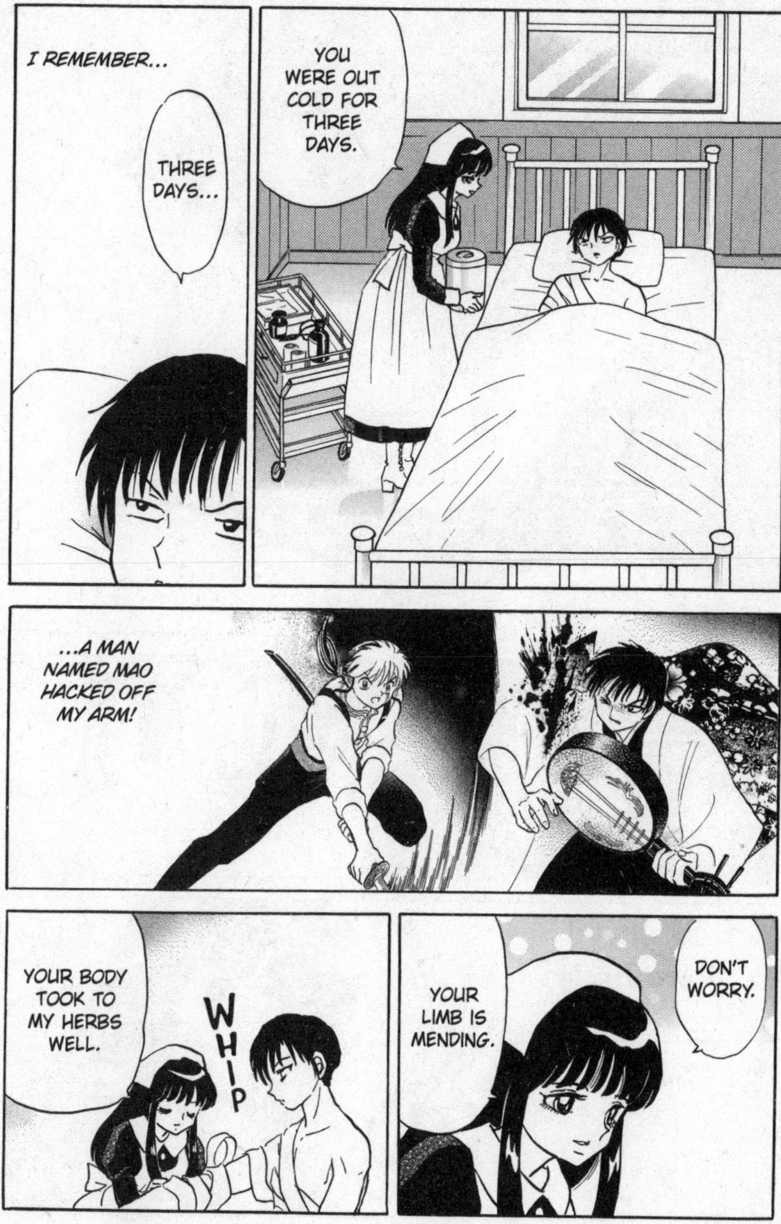
YOU WERE OUT COLD FOR THREE DAYS.
THREE DAYS...
I REMEMBER...
...A MAN NAMED MAO HACKED OFF MY ARM!
DON'T WORRY.
YOUR LIMB IS MENDING.
YOUR BODY TOOK TO MY HERBS WELL.
WHIP

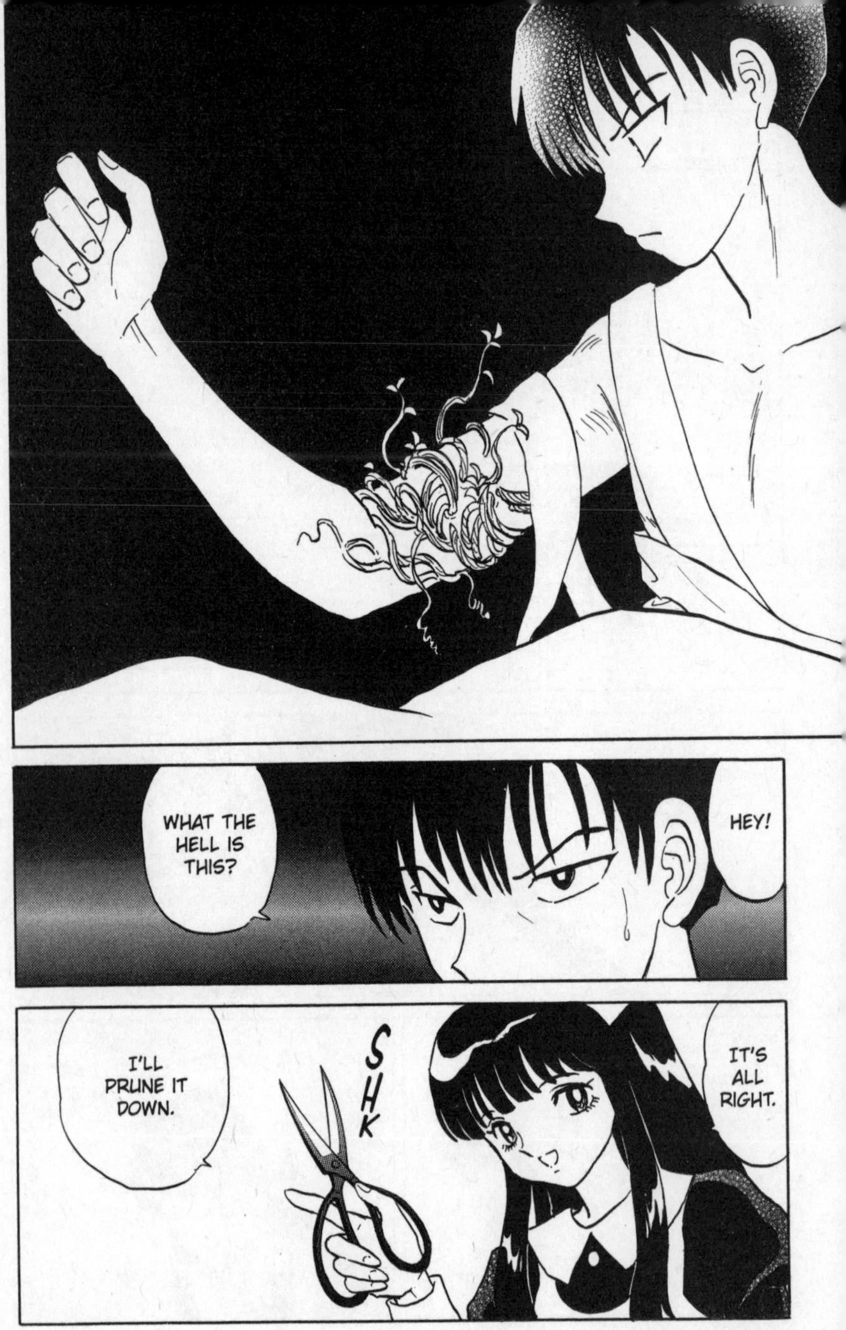
HEY!
WHAT THE HELL IS THIS?
IT'S ALL RIGHT.
SHK
I'LL PRUNE IT DOWN.

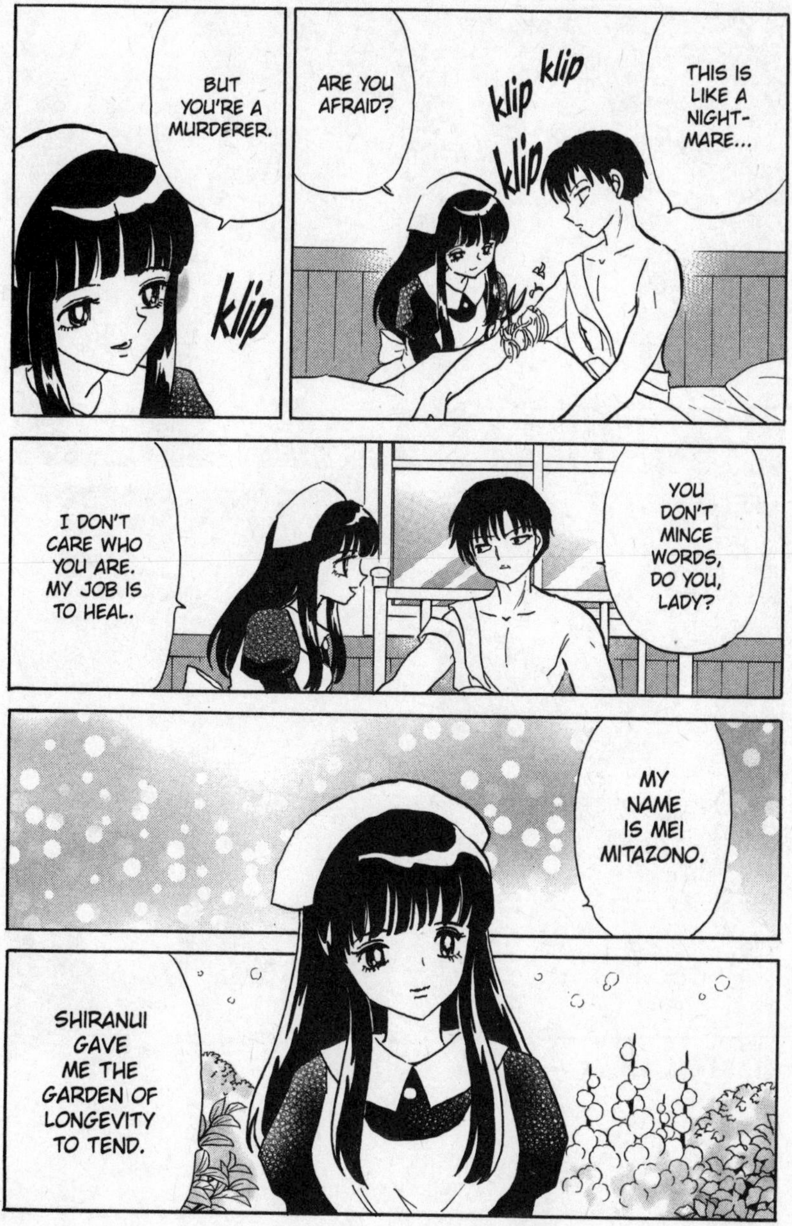
THIS IS LIKE A NIGHT-MARE...
klip klip
klip
ARE YOU AFRAID?
BUT YOU'RE A MURDERER.
klip
YOU DON'T MINCE WORDS, DO YOU, LADY?
I DON'T CARE WHO YOU ARE. MY JOB IS TO HEAL.
MY NAME IS MEI MITAZONO.
SHIRANUI GAVE ME THE GARDEN OF LONGEVITY TO TEND.

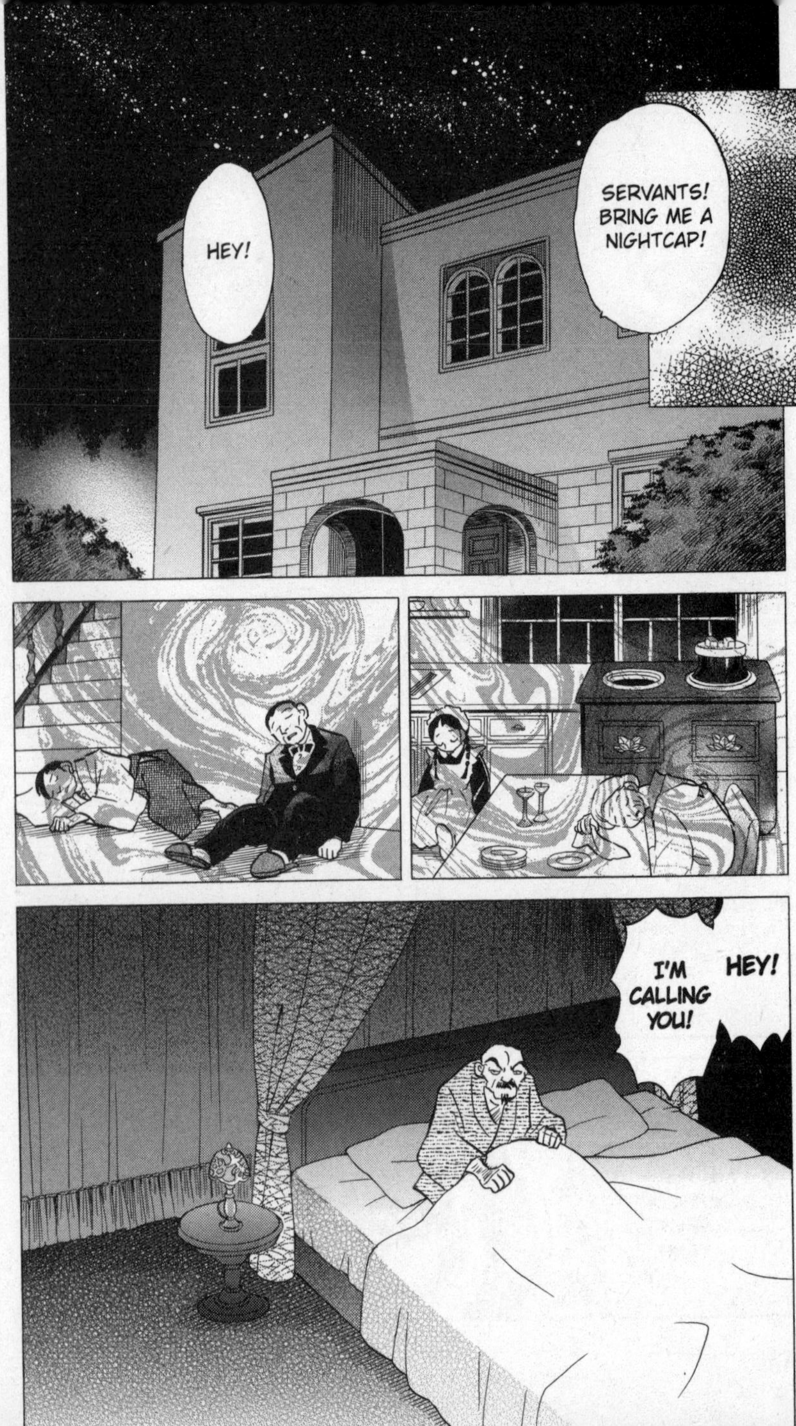
SERVANTS! BRING ME A NIGHTCAP!
HEY!
HEY!
I'M CALLING YOU!

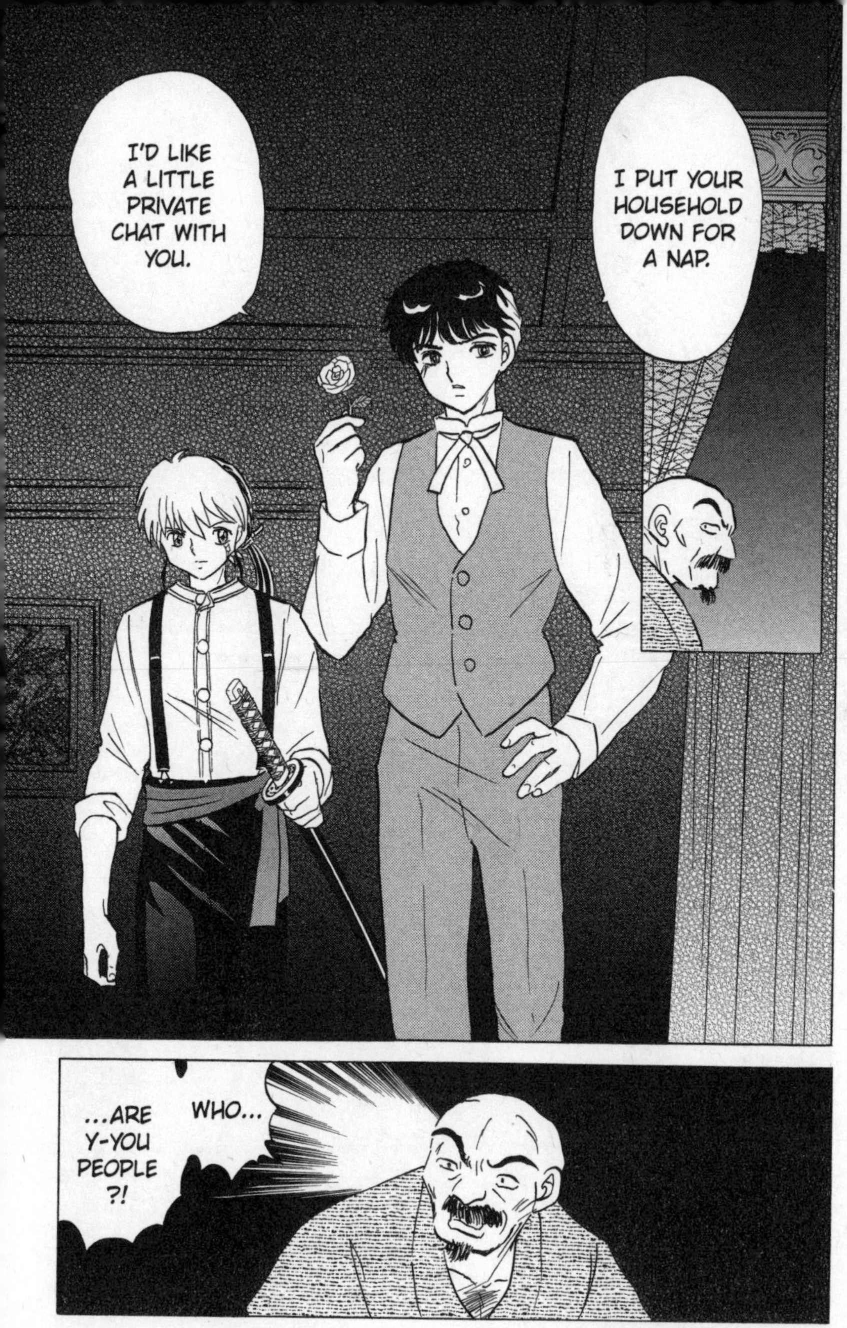
I PUT YOUR HOUSEHOLD DOWN FOR A NAP.
I'D LIKE A LITTLE PRIVATE CHAT WITH YOU.
WHO...
...ARE Y-YOU PEOPLE ?!

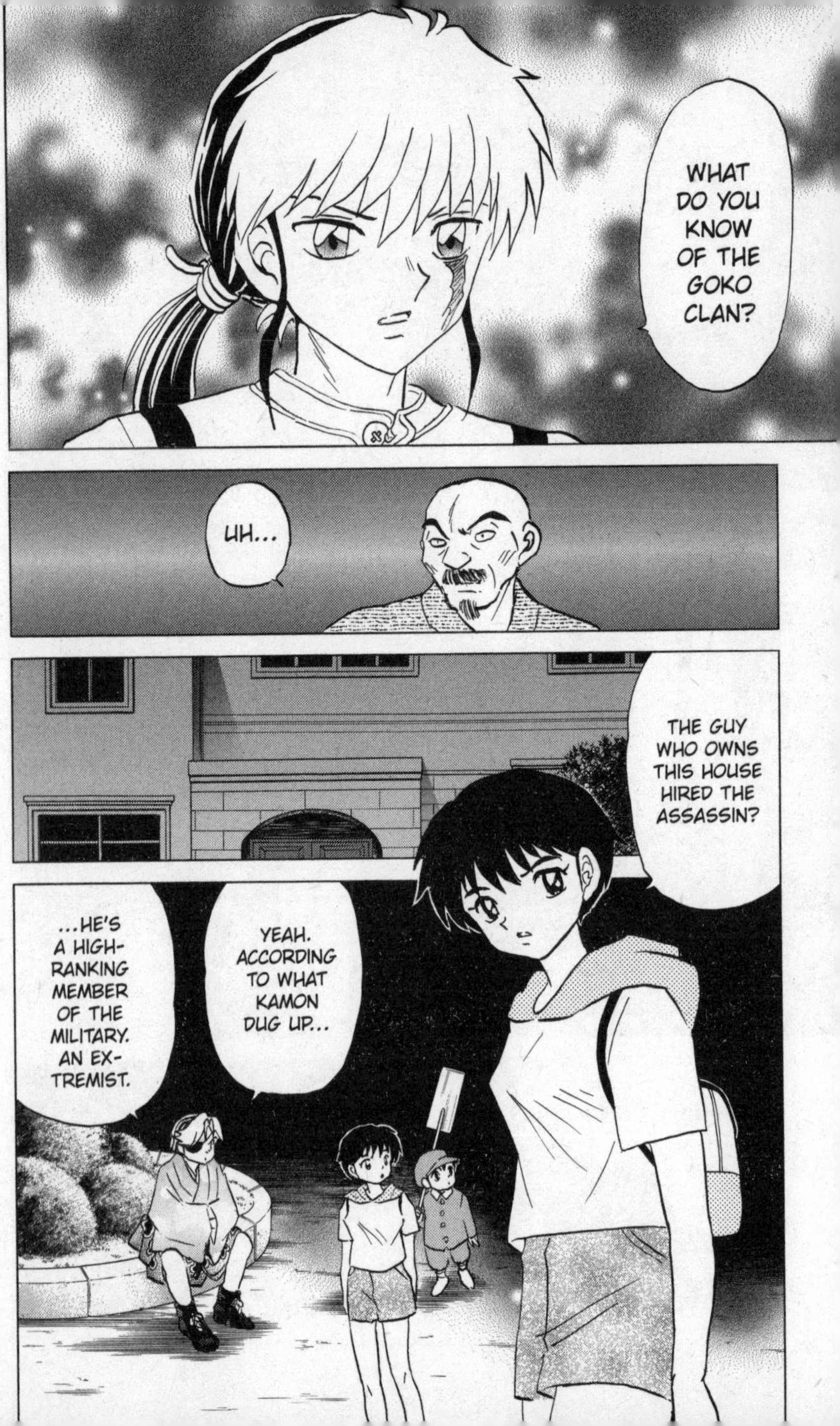
WHAT DO YOU KNOW OF THE GOKO CLAN?
UH...
THE GUY WHO OWNS THIS HOUSE HIRED THE ASSASSIN?
YEAH. ACCORDING TO WHAT KAMON DUG UP...
...HE'S A HIGH-RANKING MEMBER OF THE MILITARY. AN EX-TREMIST.

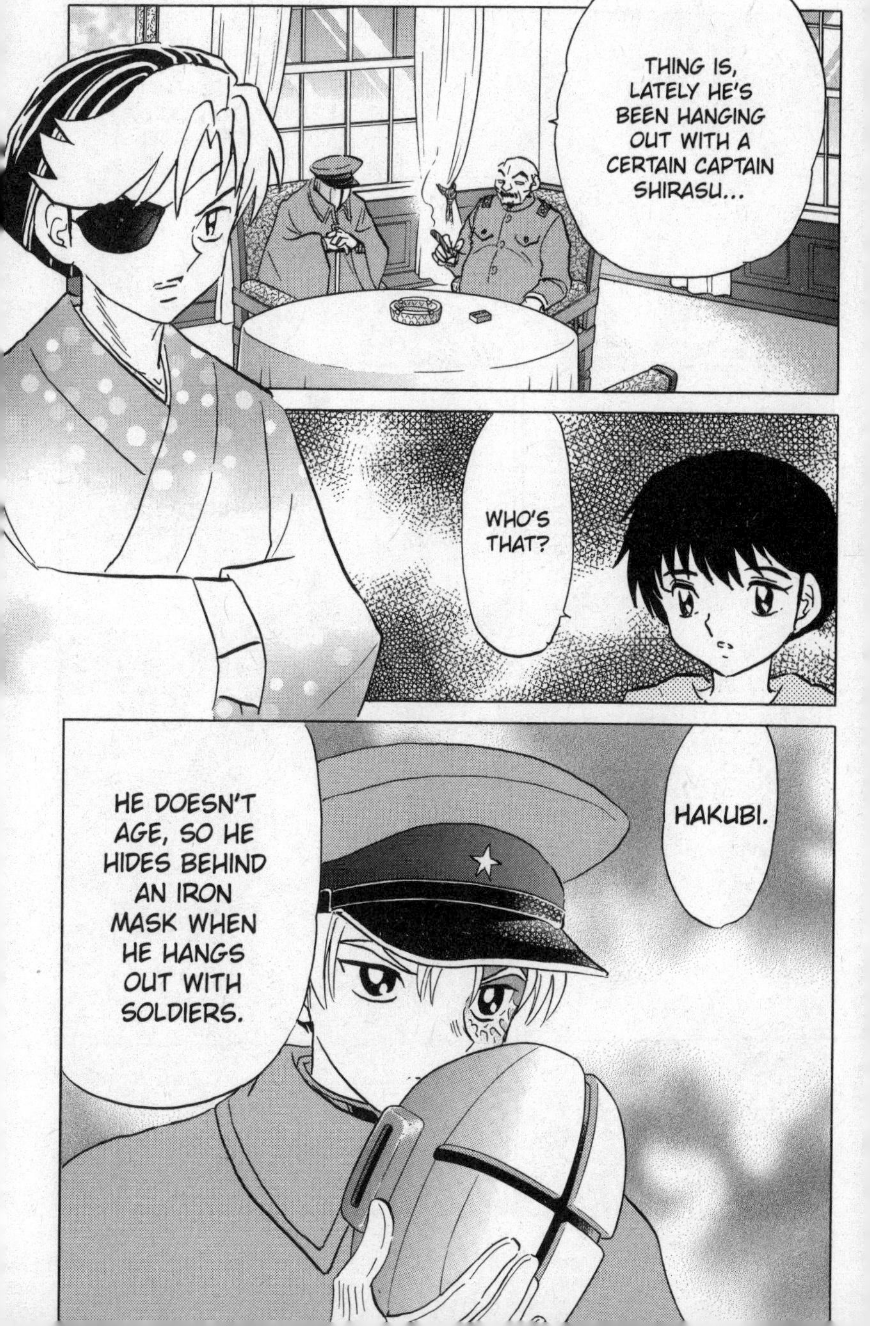
THING IS, LATELY HE'S BEEN HANGING OUT WITH A CERTAIN CAPTAIN SHIRASU...
WHO'S THAT?
HAKUBI.
HE DOESN'T AGE, SO HE HIDES BEHIND AN IRON MASK WHEN HE HANGS OUT WITH SOLDIERS.

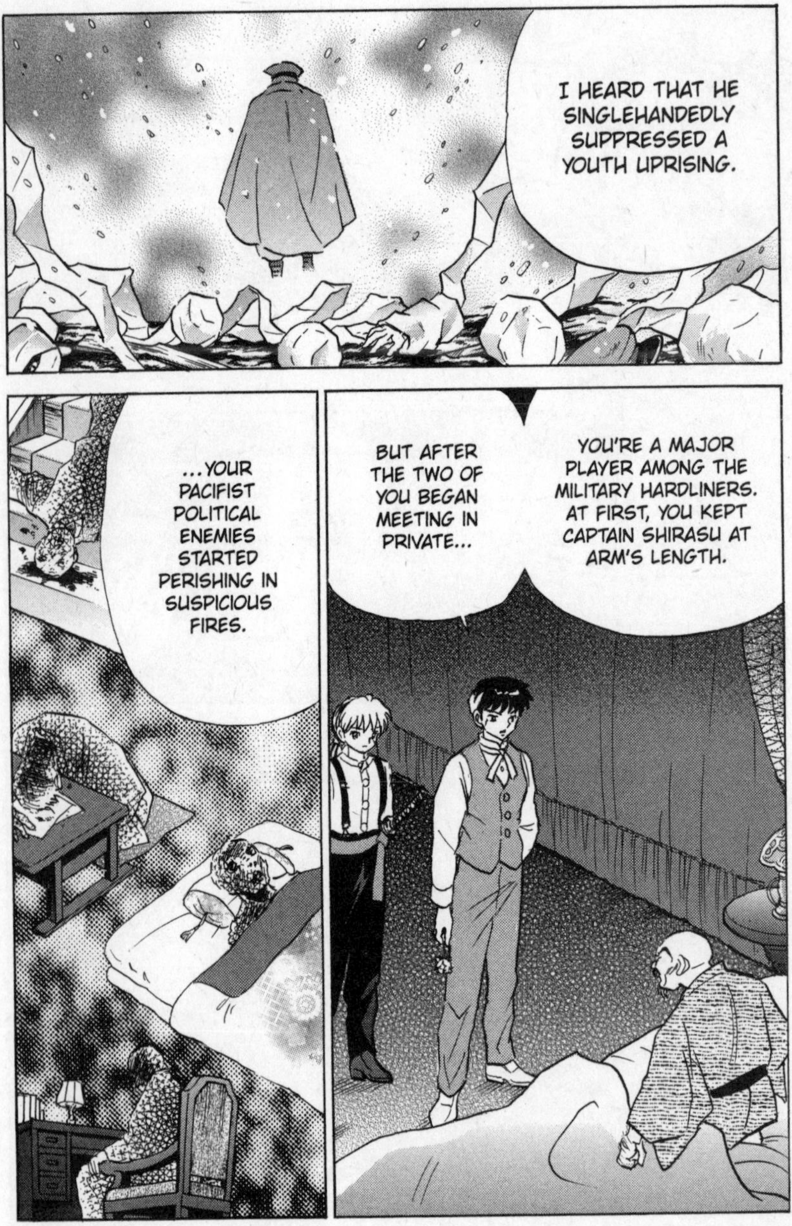
I HEARD THAT HE SINGLEHANDEDLY SUPPRESSED A YOUTH UPRISING.
YOU'RE A MAJOR PLAYER AMONG THE MILITARY HARDLINERS. AT FIRST, YOU KEPT CAPTAIN SHIRASU AT ARM'S LENGTH.
BUT AFTER THE TWO OF YOU BEGAN MEETING IN PRIVATE...
...YOUR PACIFIST POLITICAL ENEMIES STARTED PERISHING IN SUSPICIOUS FIRES.

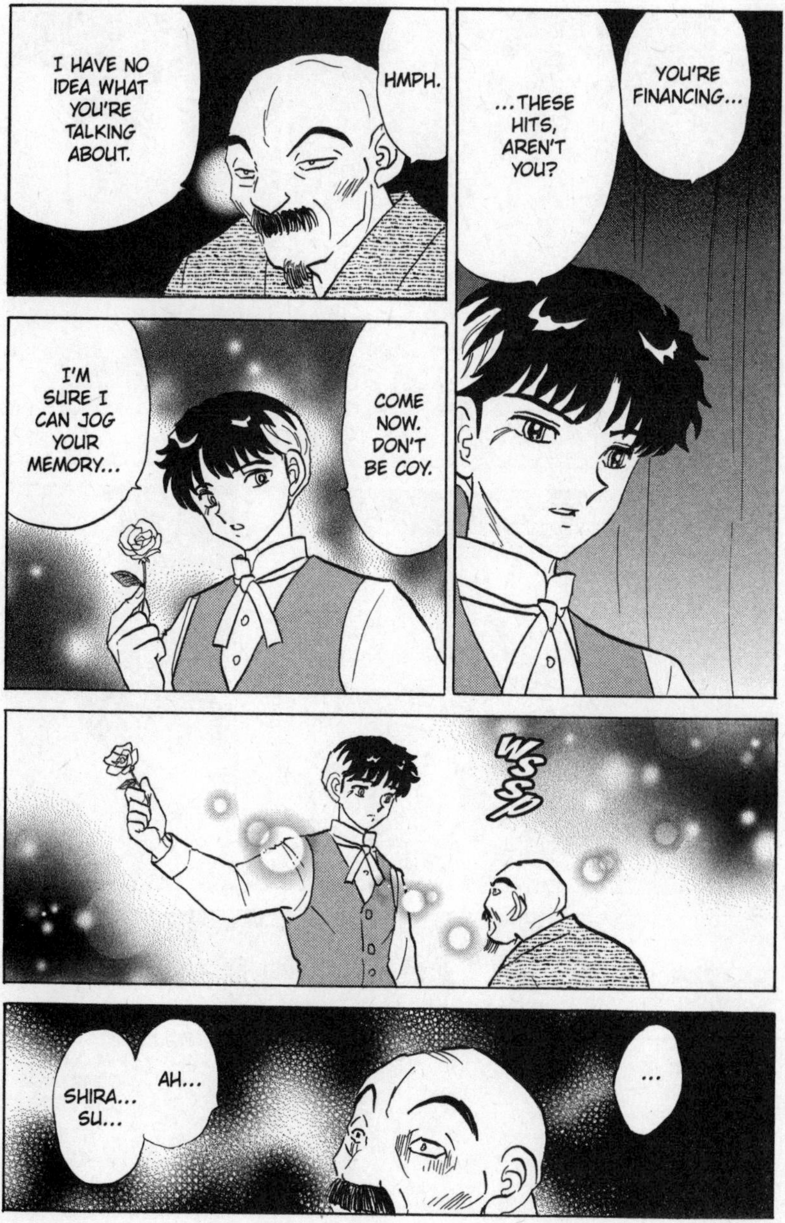
YOU'RE FINANCING...
...THESE HITS, AREN'T YOU?
HMPH.
I HAVE NO IDEA WHAT YOU'RE TALKING ABOUT.
COME NOW. DON'T BE COY.
I'M SURE I CAN JOG YOUR MEMORY...
WSSP
...
AH...
SHIRA... SU...

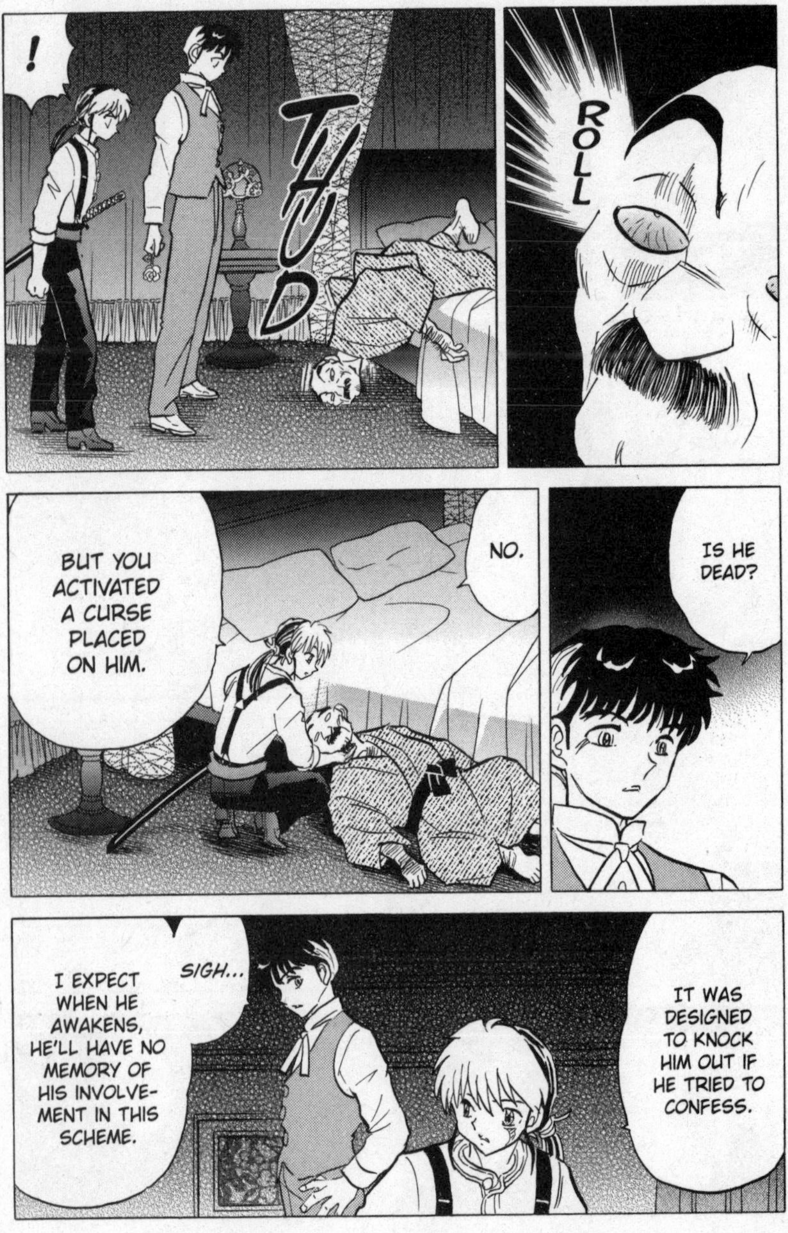
ROLL
!
THUD
IS HE DEAD?
NO.
BUT YOU ACTIVATED A CURSE PLACED ON HIM.
IT WAS DESIGNED TO KNOCK HIM OUT IF HE TRIED TO CONFESS.
SIGH...
I EXPECT WHEN HE AWAKENS, HE'LL HAVE NO MEMORY OF HIS INVOLVEMENT IN THIS SCHEME.

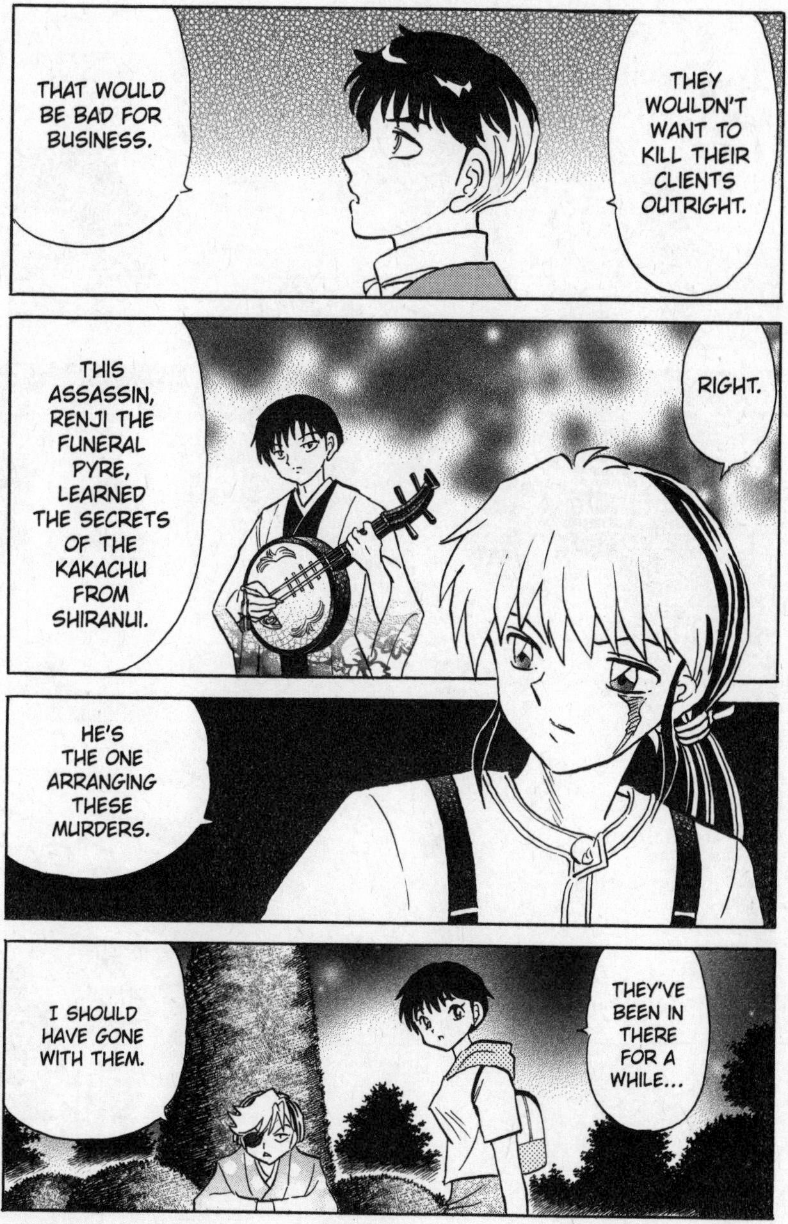
THEY WOULDN'T WANT TO KILL THEIR CLIENTS OUTRIGHT.
THAT WOULD BE BAD FOR BUSINESS.
RIGHT.
THIS ASSASSIN, RENJI THE FUNERAL PYRE, LEARNED THE SECRETS OF THE KAKACHU FROM SHIRANUI.
HE'S THE ONE ARRANGING THESE MURDERS.
THEY'VE BEEN IN THERE FOR A WHILE...
I SHOULD HAVE GONE WITH THEM.

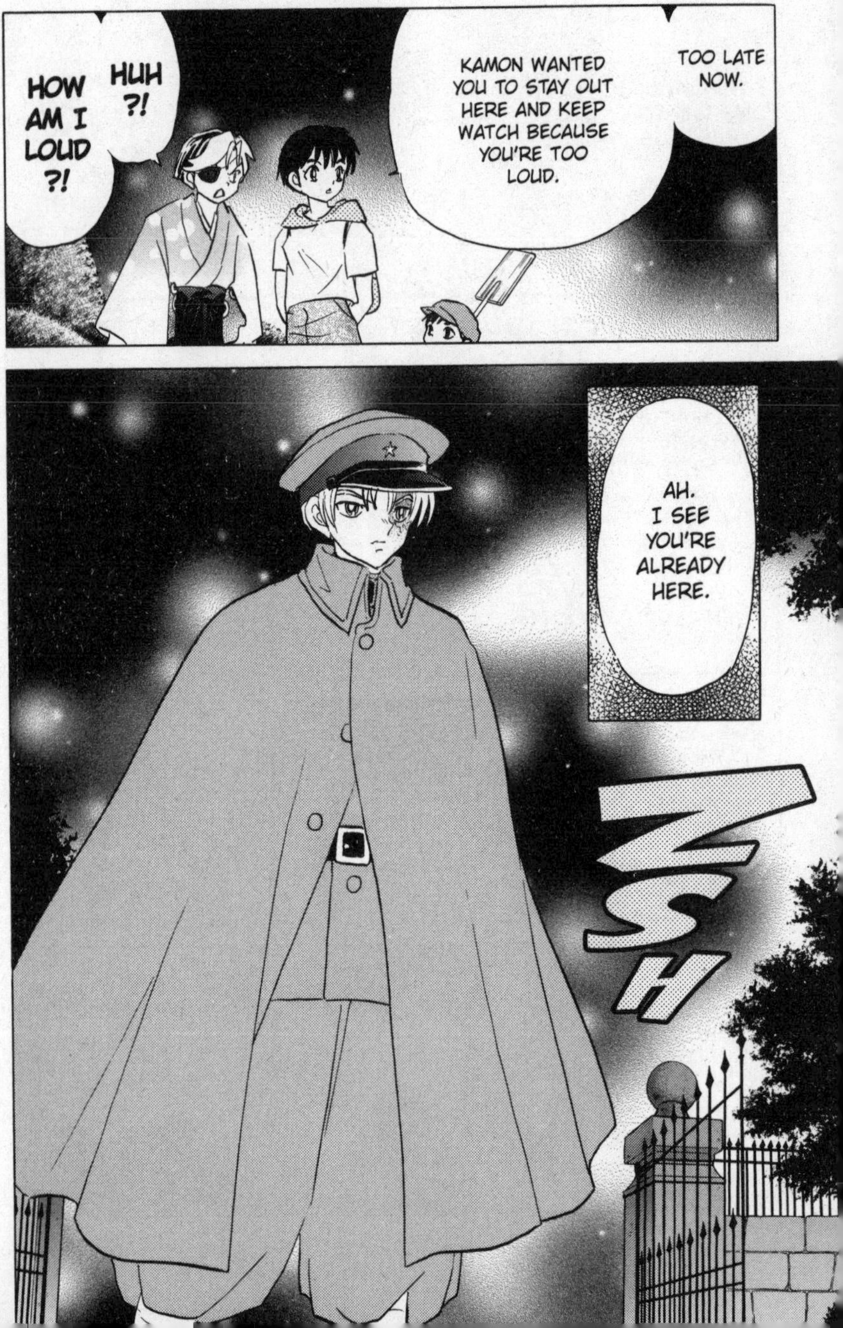
TOO LATE NOW.
KAMON WANTED YOU TO STAY OUT HERE AND KEEP WATCH BECAUSE YOU'RE TOO LOUD.
HUH ?!
HOW AM I LOUD ?!
AH. I SEE YOU'RE ALREADY HERE.
WSH

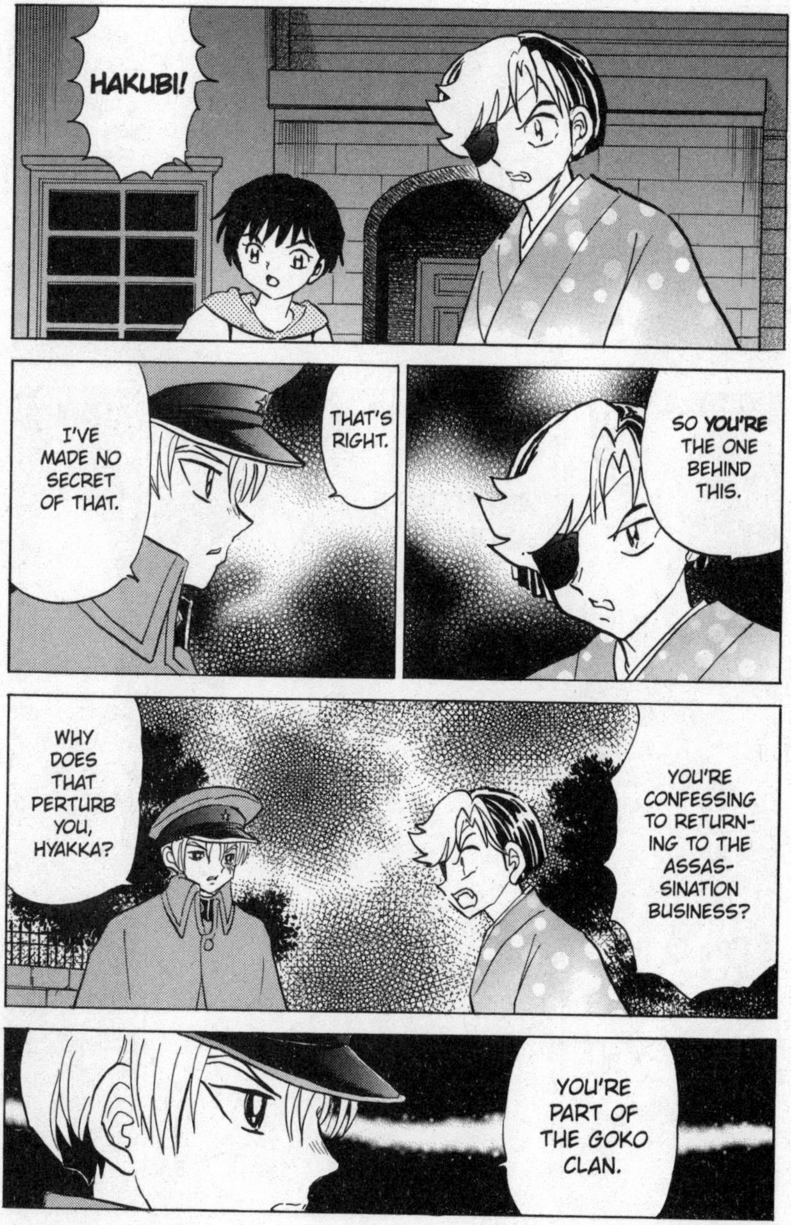
HAKUBI!
SO **YOU'RE** THE ONE BEHIND THIS.
THAT'S RIGHT.
I'VE MADE NO SECRET OF THAT.
YOU'RE CONFESSING TO RETURNING TO THE ASSASSINATION BUSINESS?
WHY DOES THAT PERTURB YOU, HYAKKA?
YOU'RE PART OF THE GOKO CLAN.

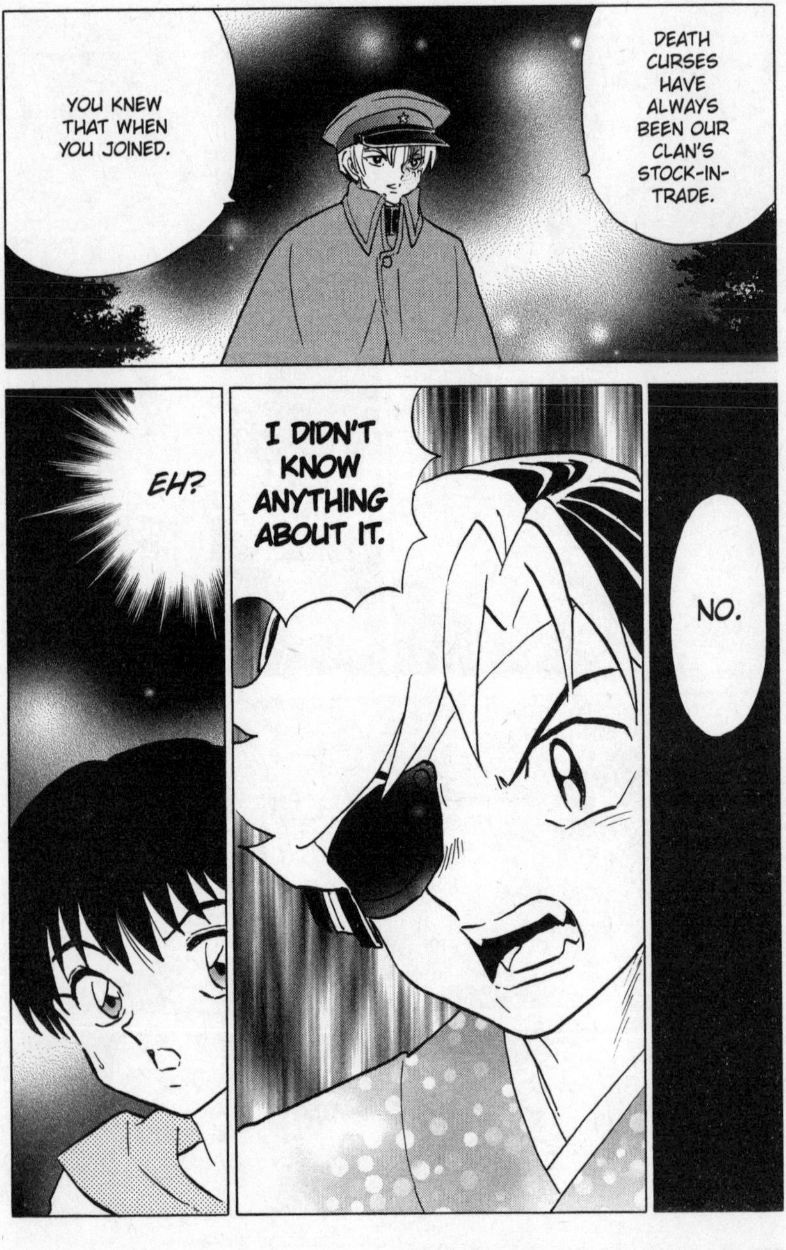
DEATH CURSES HAVE ALWAYS BEEN OUR CLAN'S STOCK-IN-TRADE.
YOU KNEW THAT WHEN YOU JOINED.
NO.
I DIDN'T KNOW ANYTHING ABOUT IT.
EH?

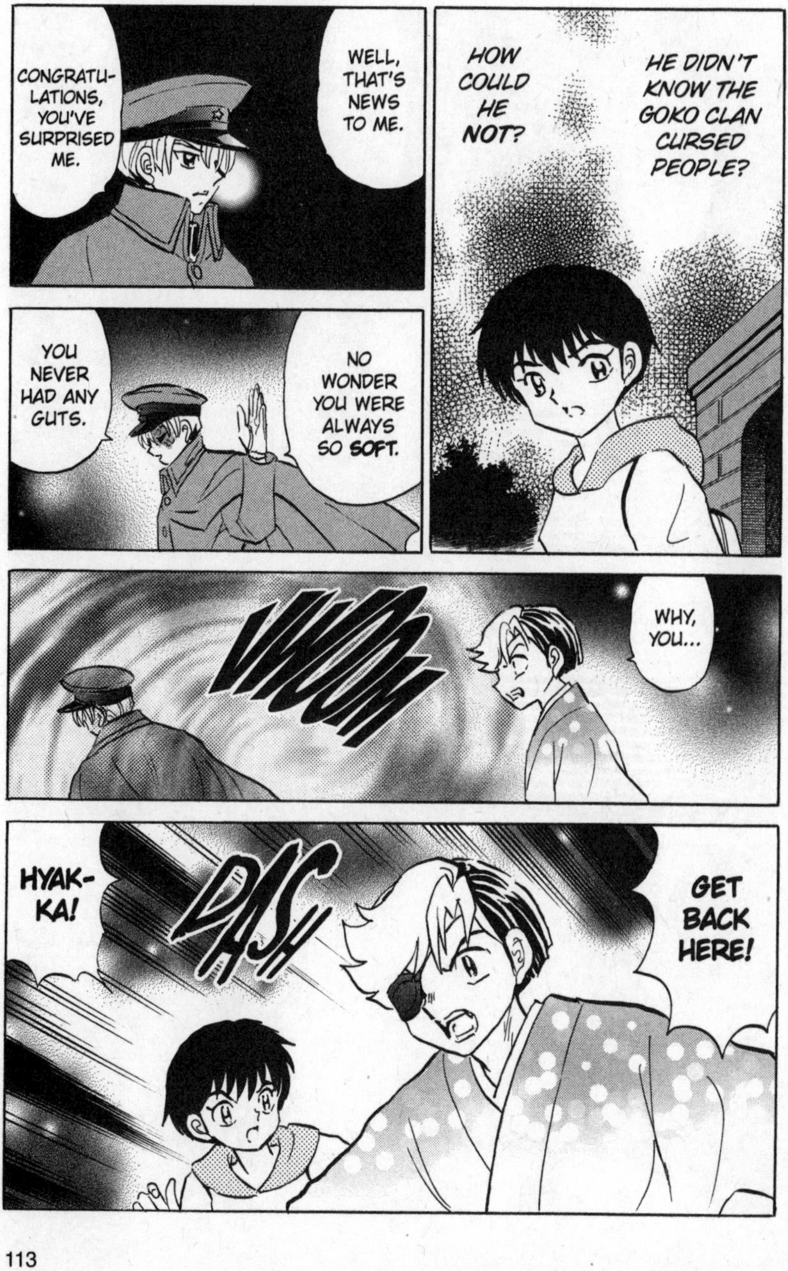
HE DIDN'T KNOW THE GOKO CLAN CURSED PEOPLE?
HOW COULD HE NOT?
WELL, THAT'S NEWS TO ME.
CONGRATULATIONS, YOU'VE SURPRISED ME.
NO WONDER YOU WERE ALWAYS SO **SOFT**.
YOU NEVER HAD ANY GUTS.
WHY, YOU...
VWOOM
GET BACK HERE!
DASH
HYAK-KA!

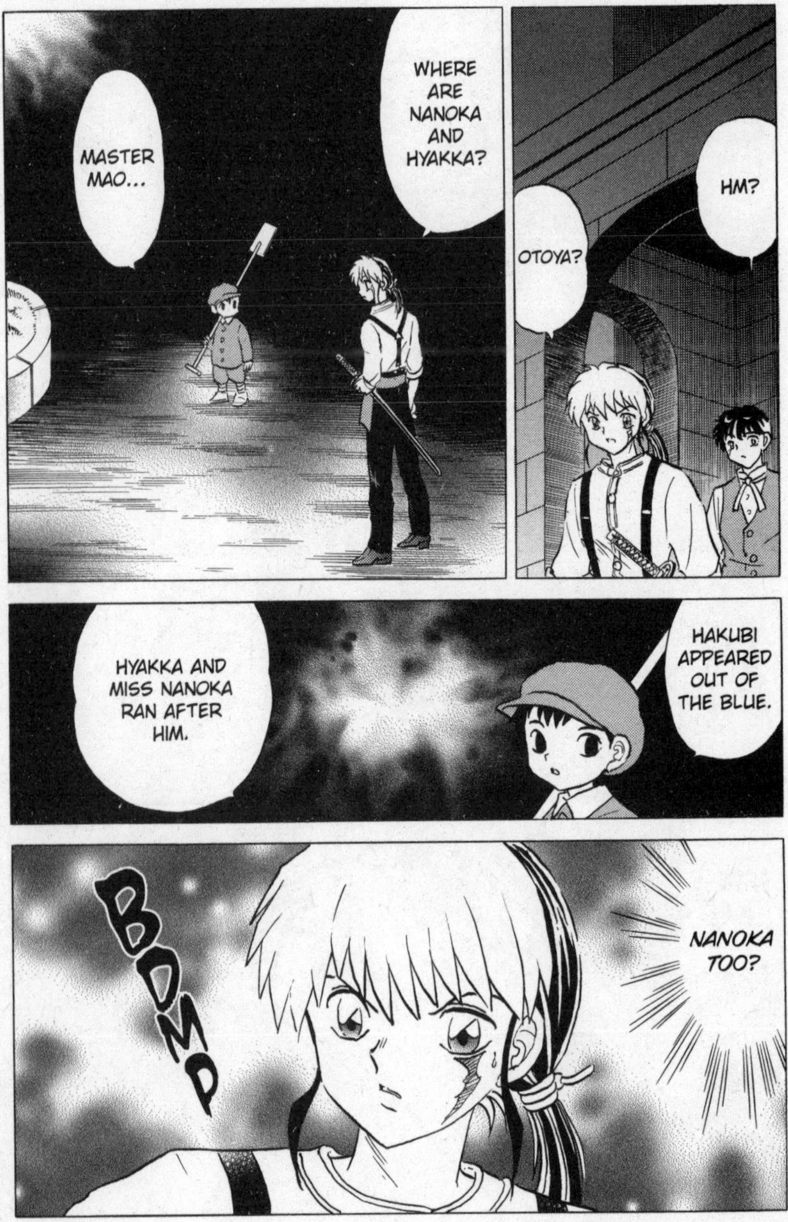
HM?
OTOYA?
WHERE ARE NANOKA AND HYAKKA?
MASTER MAO...
HAKUBI APPEARED OUT OF THE BLUE.
HYAKKA AND MISS NANOKA RAN AFTER HIM.
NANOKA TOO?
BDMP

Chapter 7:
Ambition

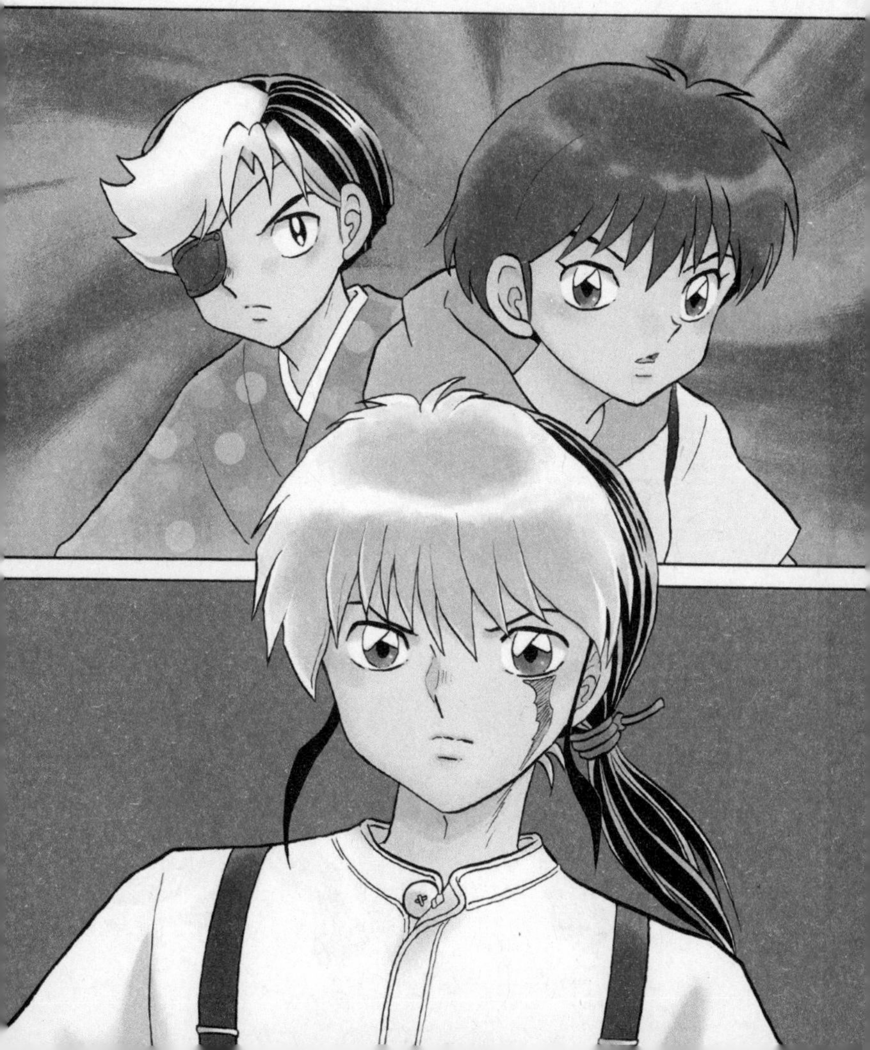

MAO

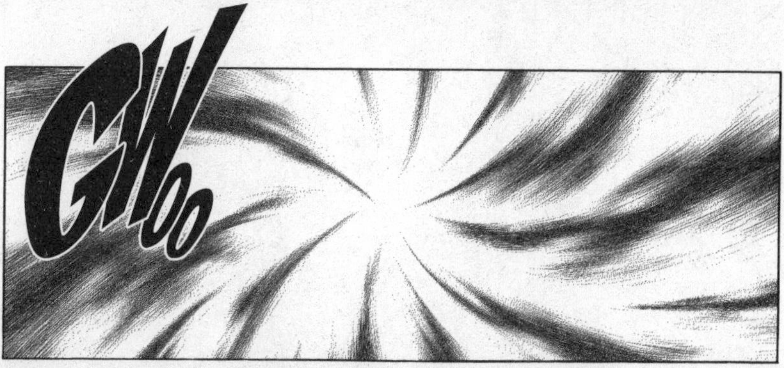
GWOO
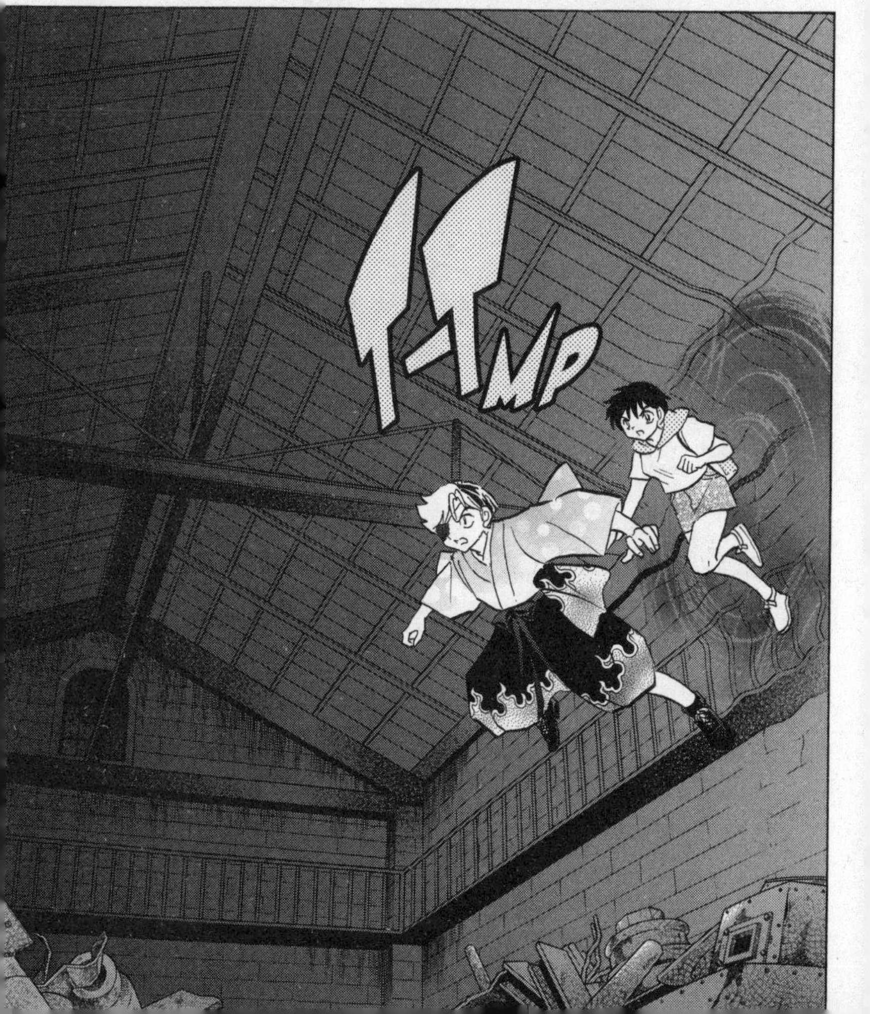
T-TMP

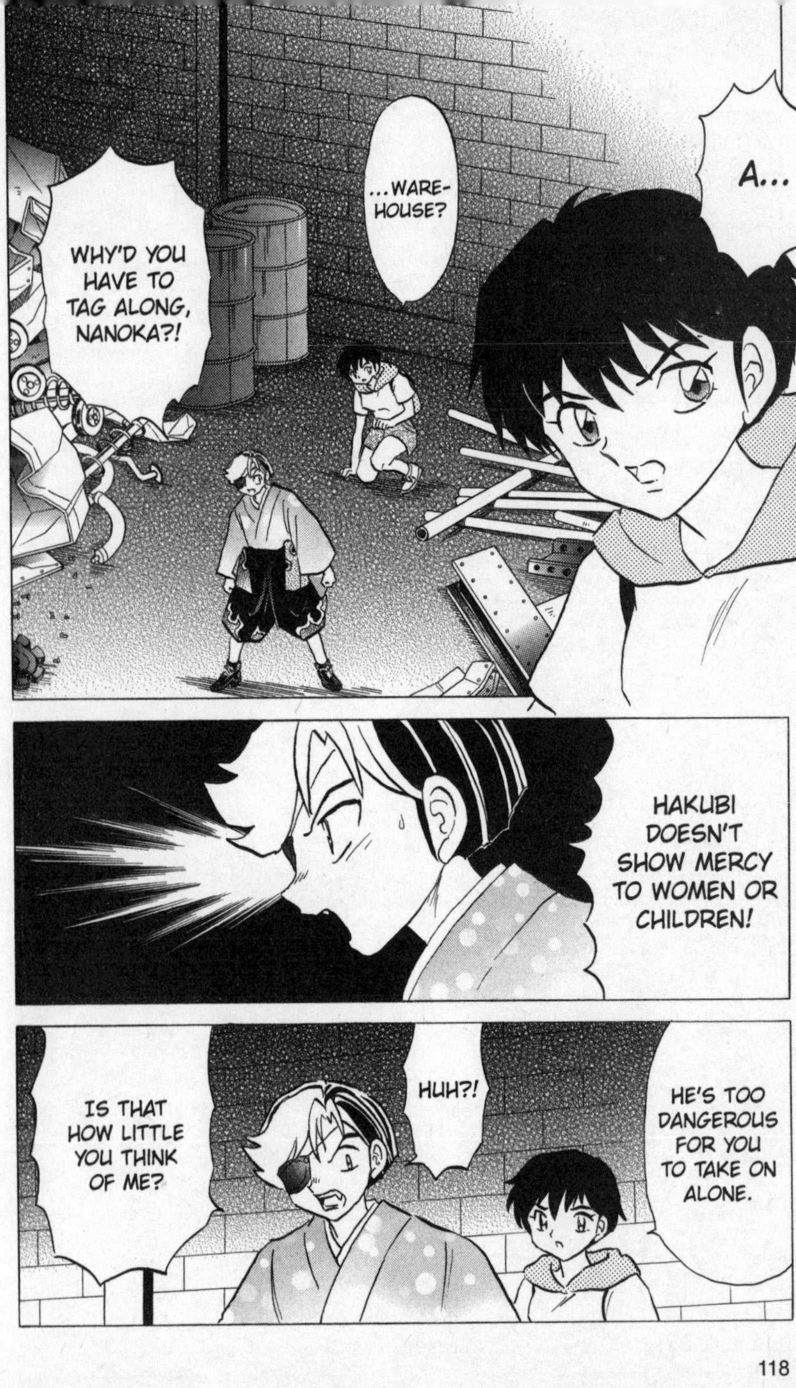
A...
...WARE-HOUSE?
WHY'D YOU HAVE TO TAG ALONG, NANOKA?!
HAKUBI DOESN'T SHOW MERCY TO WOMEN OR CHILDREN!
HE'S TOO DANGEROUS FOR YOU TO TAKE ON ALONE.
HUH?!
IS THAT HOW LITTLE YOU THINK OF ME?

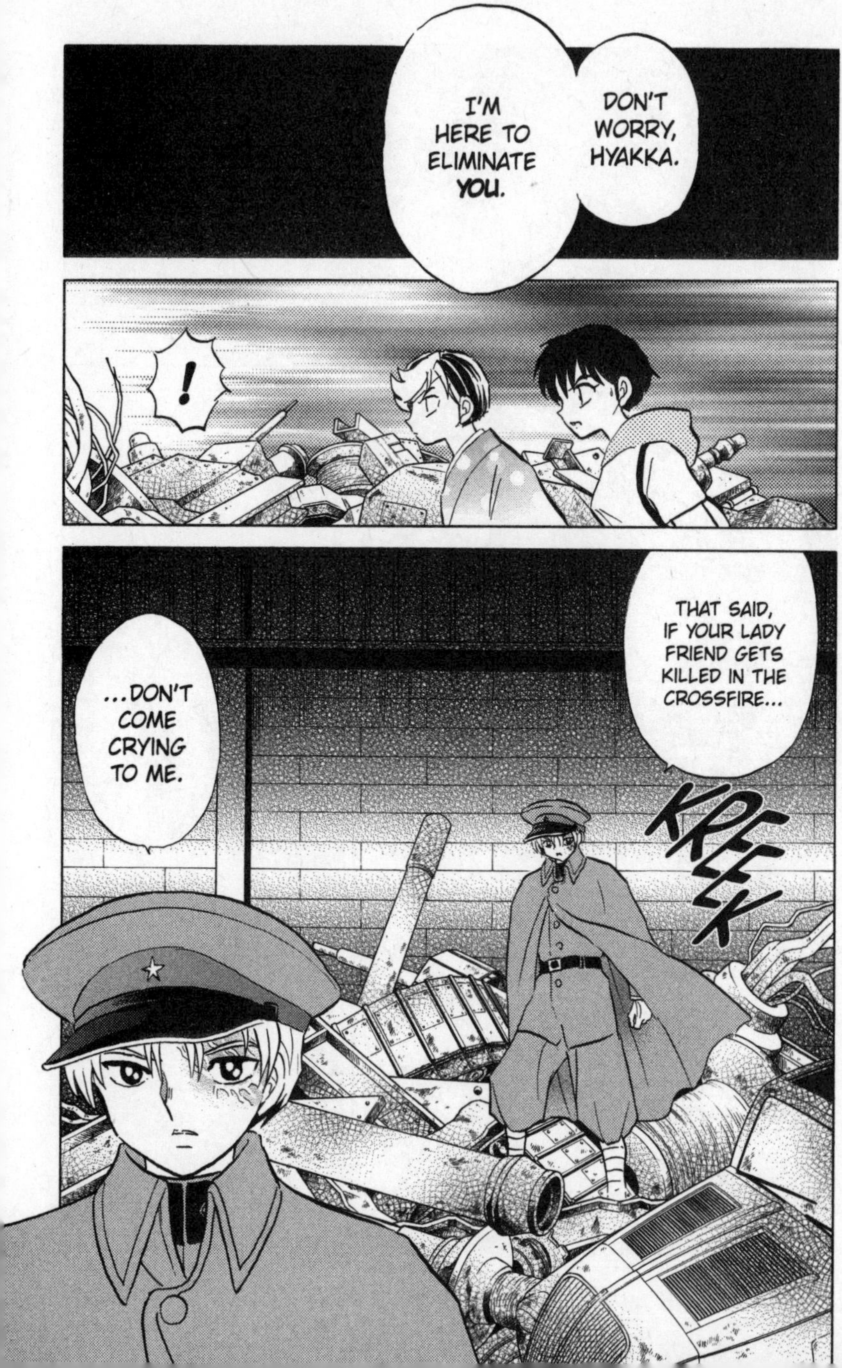
DON'T WORRY, HYAKKA.
I'M HERE TO ELIMINATE YOU.
!
THAT SAID, IF YOUR LADY FRIEND GETS KILLED IN THE CROSSFIRE...
KREEK
...DON'T COME CRYING TO ME.

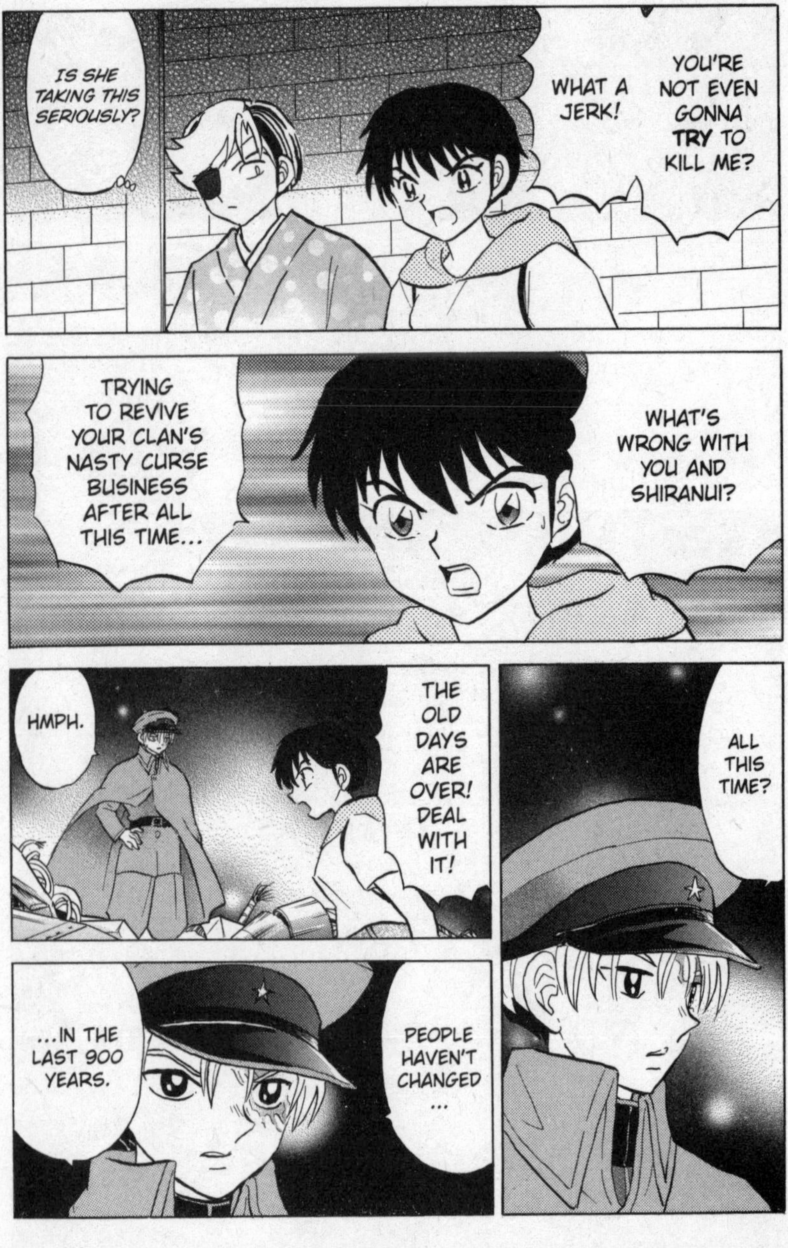
YOU'RE NOT EVEN GONNA **TRY** TO KILL ME?
WHAT A JERK!
IS SHE TAKING THIS SERIOUSLY?
WHAT'S WRONG WITH YOU AND SHIRANUI?
TRYING TO REVIVE YOUR CLAN'S NASTY CURSE BUSINESS AFTER ALL THIS TIME...
ALL THIS TIME?
THE OLD DAYS ARE OVER! DEAL WITH IT!
HMPH.
PEOPLE HAVEN'T CHANGED...
...IN THE LAST 900 YEARS.

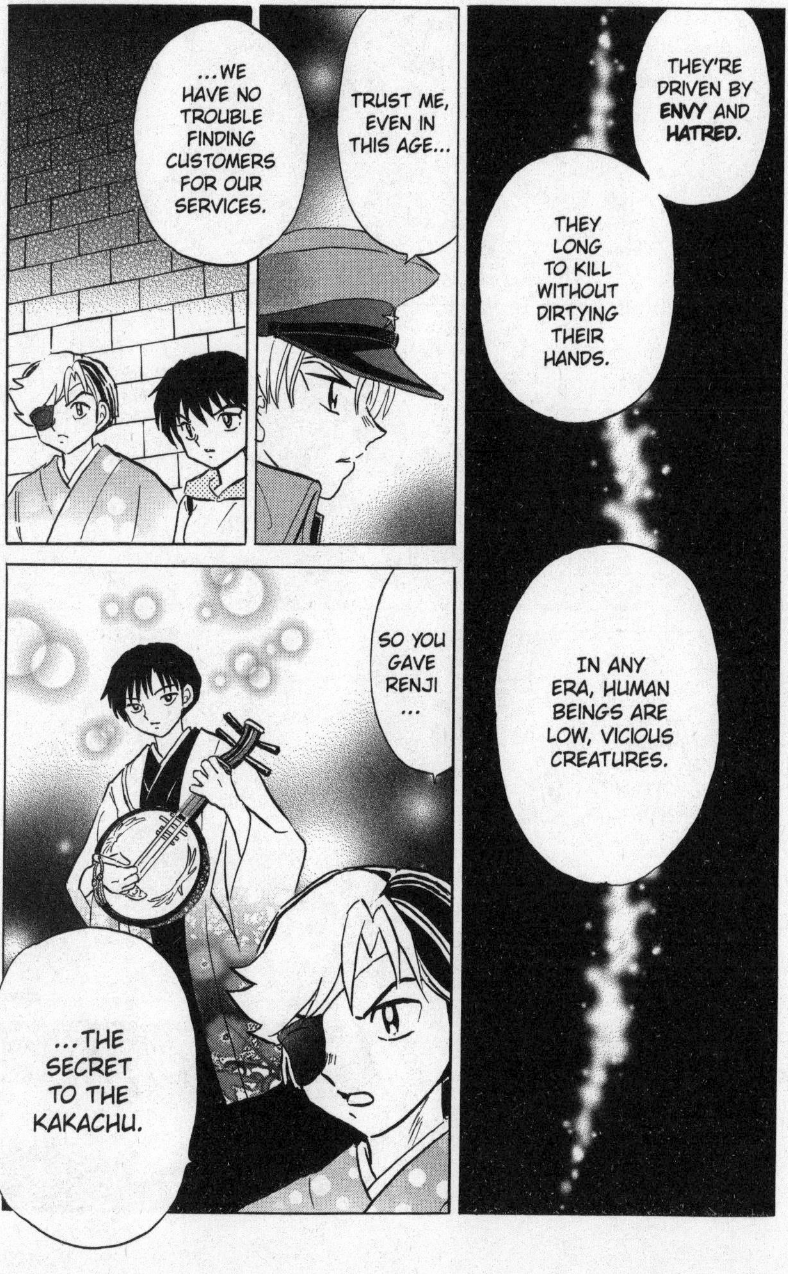
THEY'RE DRIVEN BY ENVY AND HATRED.
THEY LONG TO KILL WITHOUT DIRTYING THEIR HANDS.
IN ANY ERA, HUMAN BEINGS ARE LOW, VICIOUS CREATURES.
TRUST ME, EVEN IN THIS AGE...
...WE HAVE NO TROUBLE FINDING CUSTOMERS FOR OUR SERVICES.
SO YOU GAVE RENJI...
...THE SECRET TO THE KAKACHU.

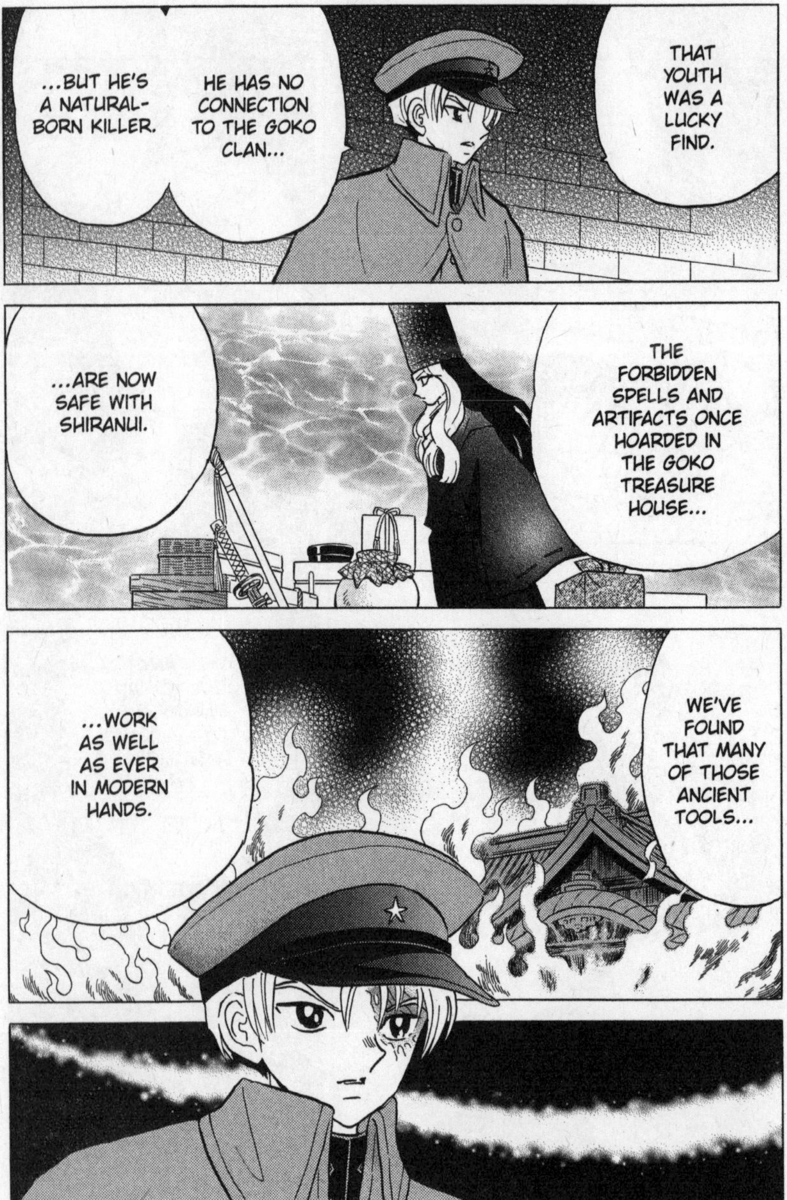
THAT YOUTH WAS A LUCKY FIND.
HE HAS NO CONNECTION TO THE GOKO CLAN...
...BUT HE'S A NATURAL-BORN KILLER.
THE FORBIDDEN SPELLS AND ARTIFACTS ONCE HOARDED IN THE GOKO TREASURE HOUSE...
...ARE NOW SAFE WITH SHIRANUI.
WE'VE FOUND THAT MANY OF THOSE ANCIENT TOOLS...
...WORK AS WELL AS EVER IN MODERN HANDS.

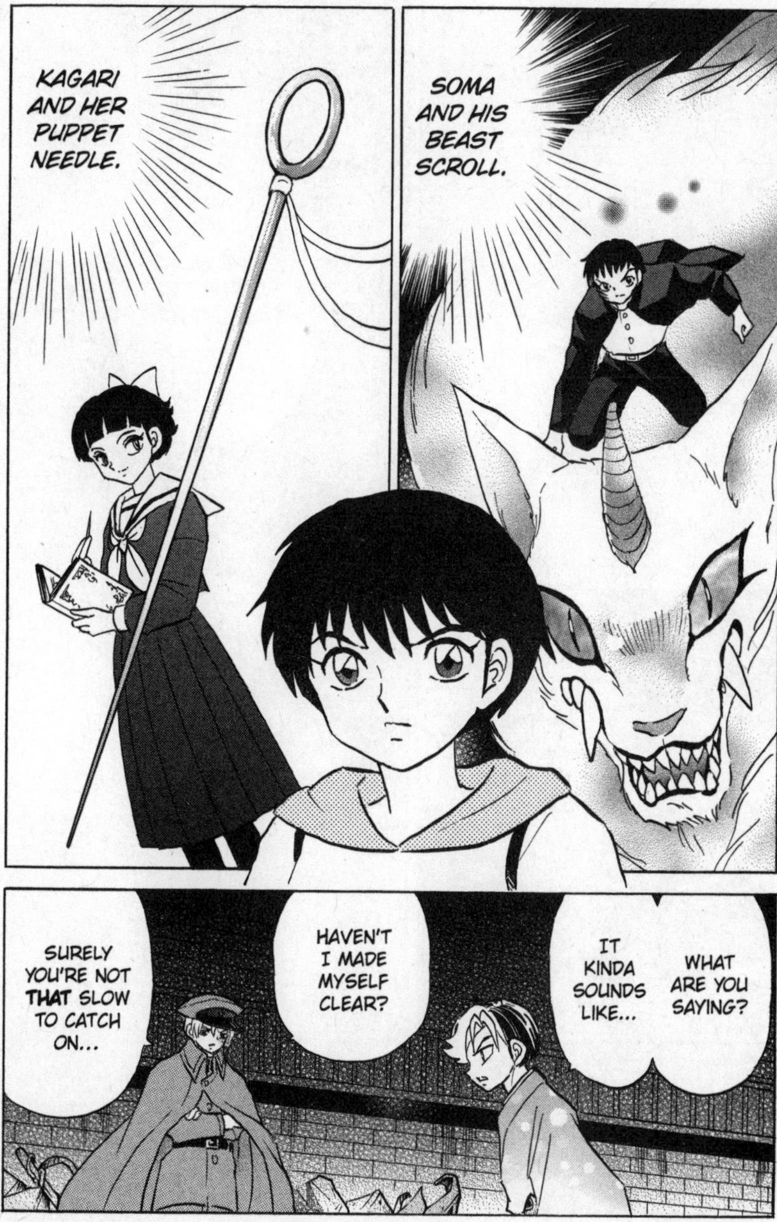
SOMA AND HIS BEAST SCROLL.
KAGARI AND HER PUPPET NEEDLE.
WHAT ARE YOU SAYING?
IT KINDA SOUNDS LIKE...
HAVEN'T I MADE MYSELF CLEAR?
SURELY YOU'RE NOT **THAT** SLOW TO CATCH ON...

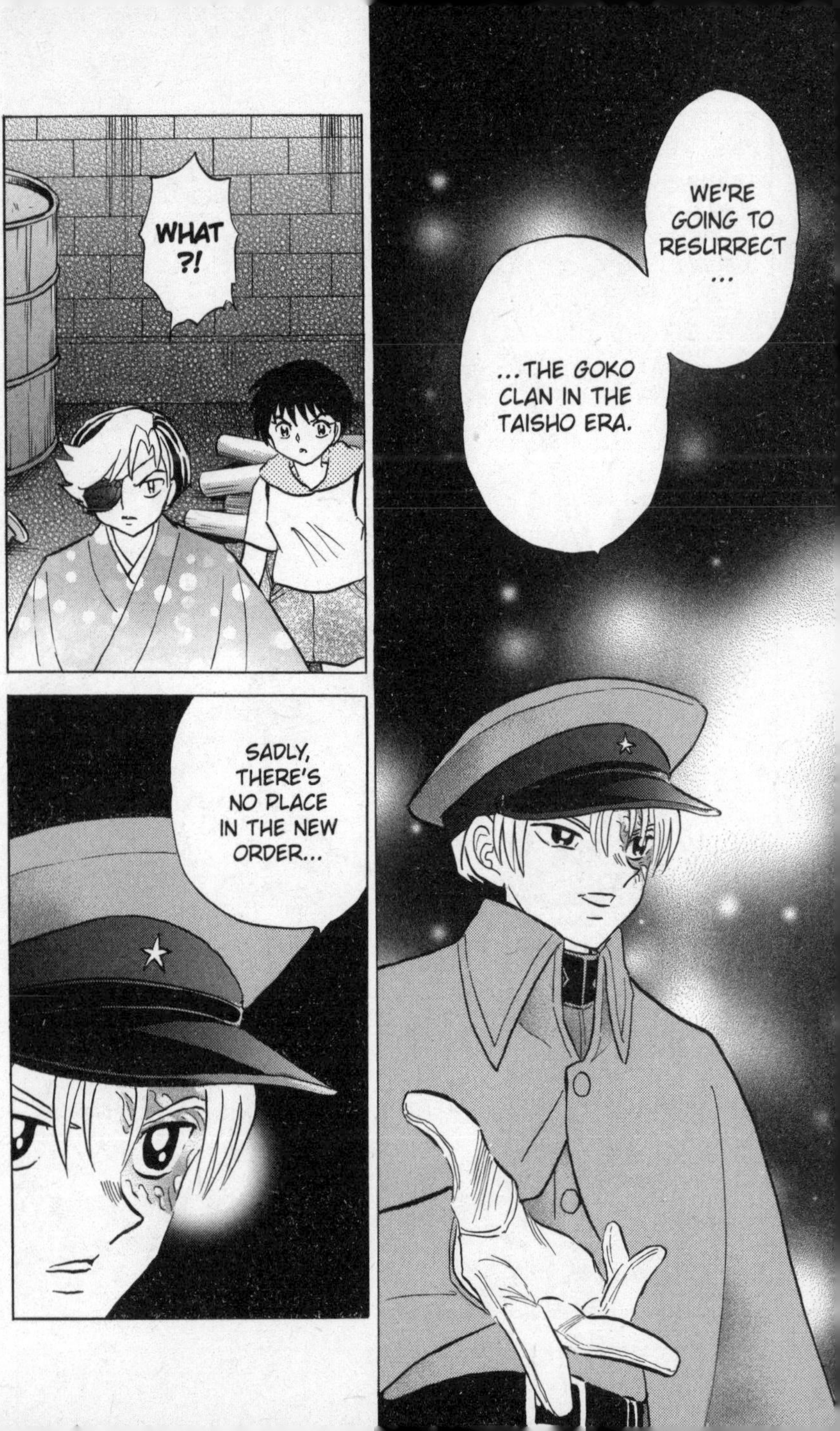
WE'RE GOING TO RESURRECT ...
...THE GOKO CLAN IN THE TAISHO ERA.
WHAT ?!
SADLY, THERE'S NO PLACE IN THE NEW ORDER...

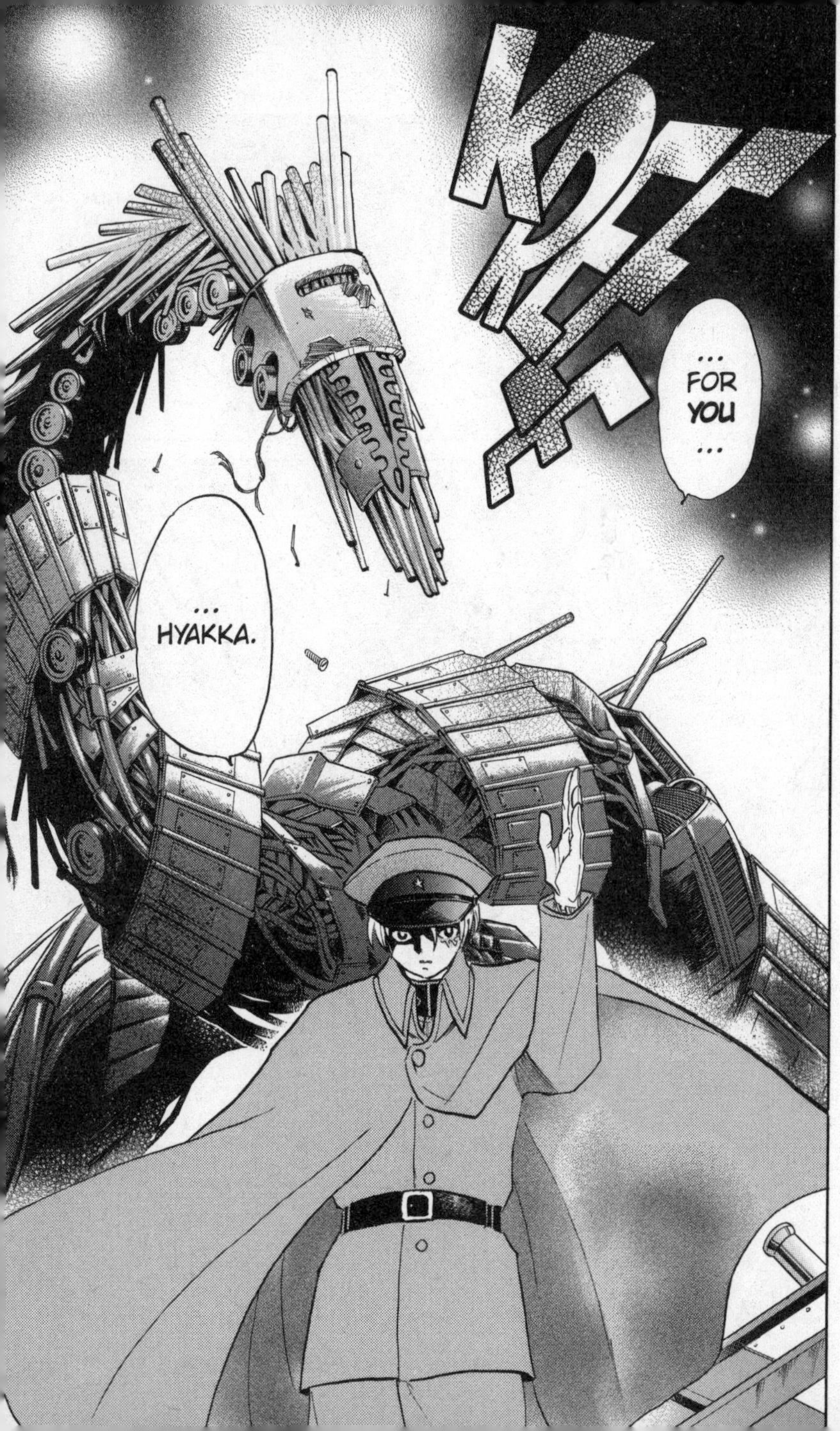
... FOR YOU ...
... HYAKKA.

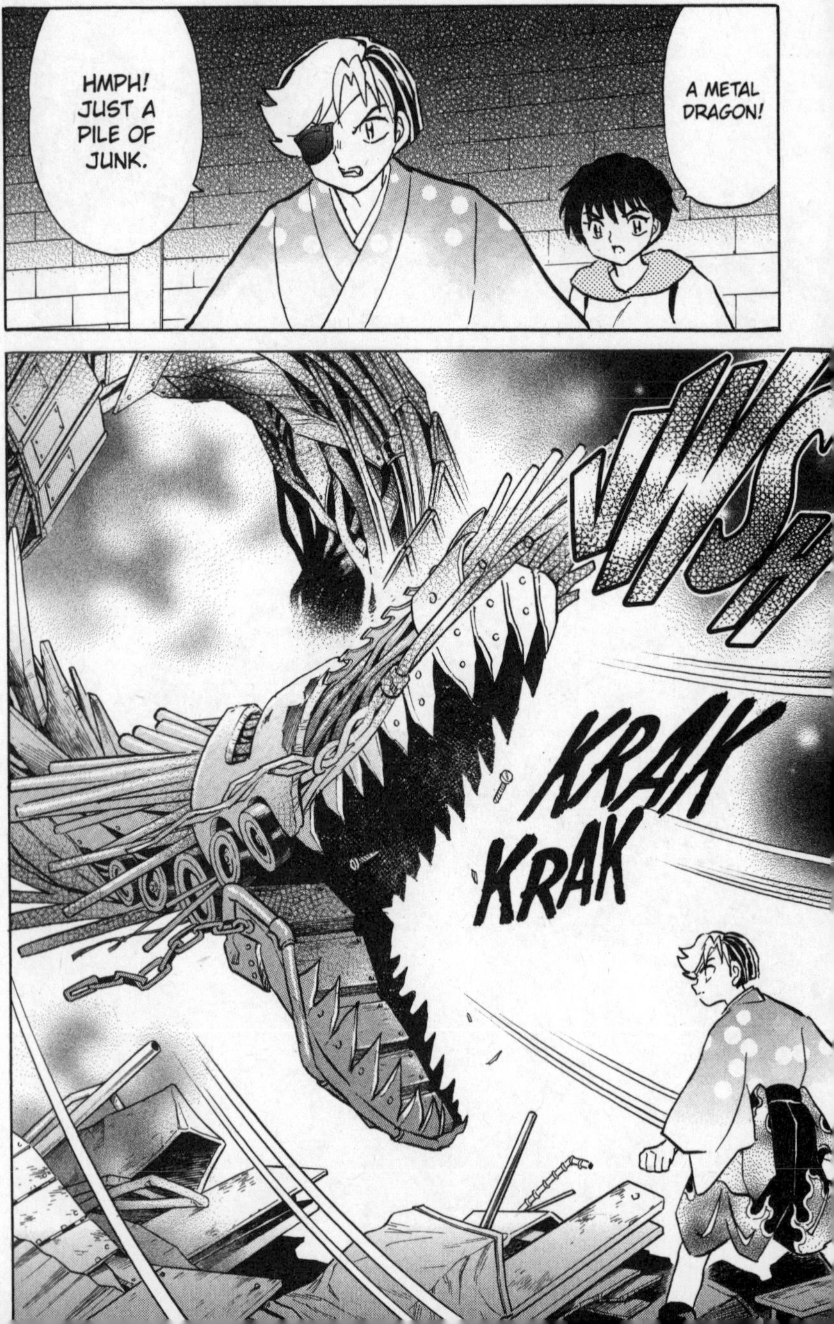
A METAL DRAGON!
HMPH! JUST A PILE OF JUNK.
VWSH
KRAK KRAK

I'LL MELT IT INTO SLAG!

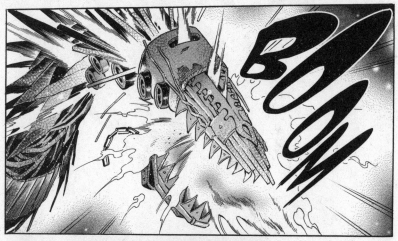

OH, THAT'S RIGHT... FIRE HAS AN ADVANTAGE OVER METAL.

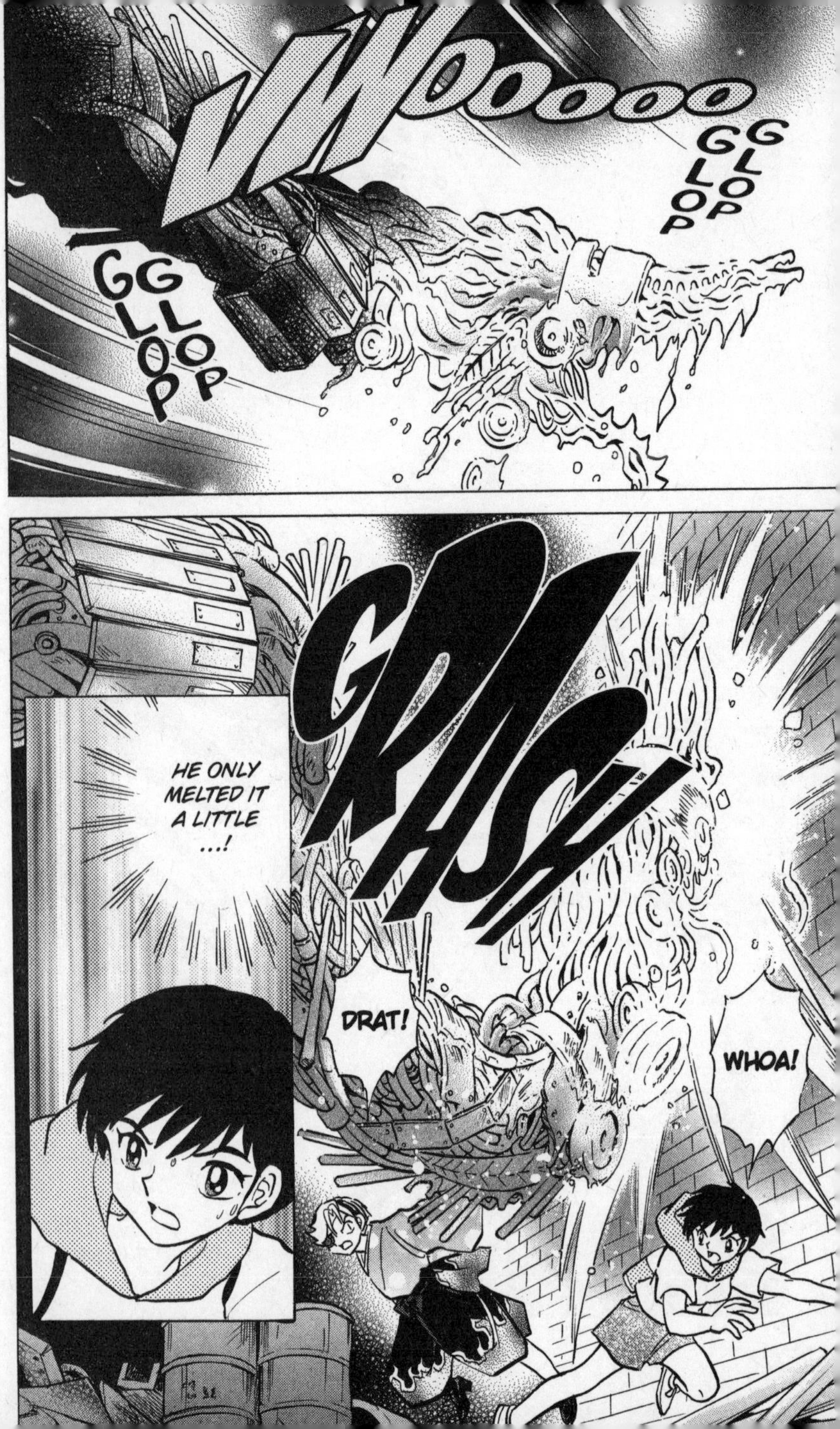
WHOOOOOO
GGLOOP
GGLOOP
GNASH
WHOA!
DRAT!
HE ONLY MELTED IT A LITTLE ...!

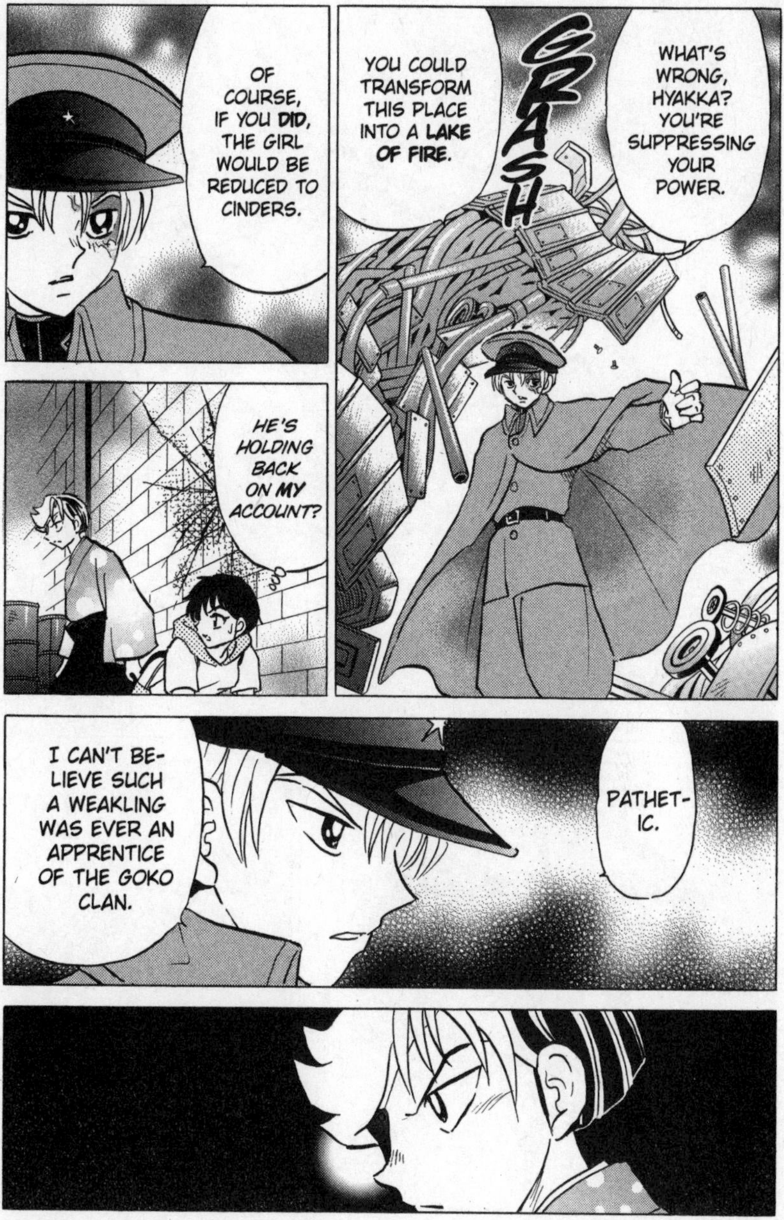
WHAT'S WRONG, HYAKKA? YOU'RE SUPPRESSING YOUR POWER.
GRASH
YOU COULD TRANSFORM THIS PLACE INTO A **LAKE OF FIRE**.
OF COURSE, IF YOU **DID**, THE GIRL WOULD BE REDUCED TO CINDERS.
*HE'S HOLDING BACK ON **MY** ACCOUNT?*
PATHET-IC.
I CAN'T BE-LIEVE SUCH A WEAKLING WAS EVER AN APPRENTICE OF THE GOKO CLAN.

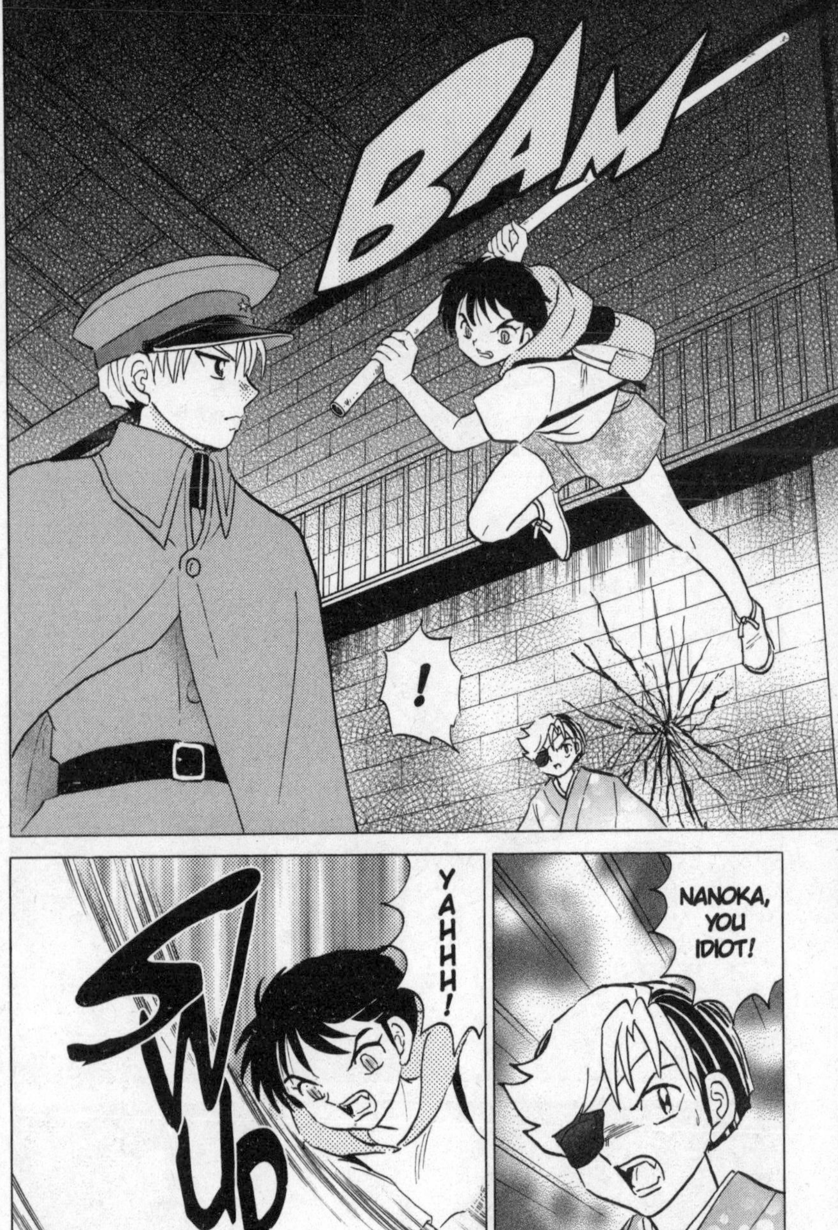
BAM
!
NANOKA, YOU IDIOT!
YAHHH!
SWUP

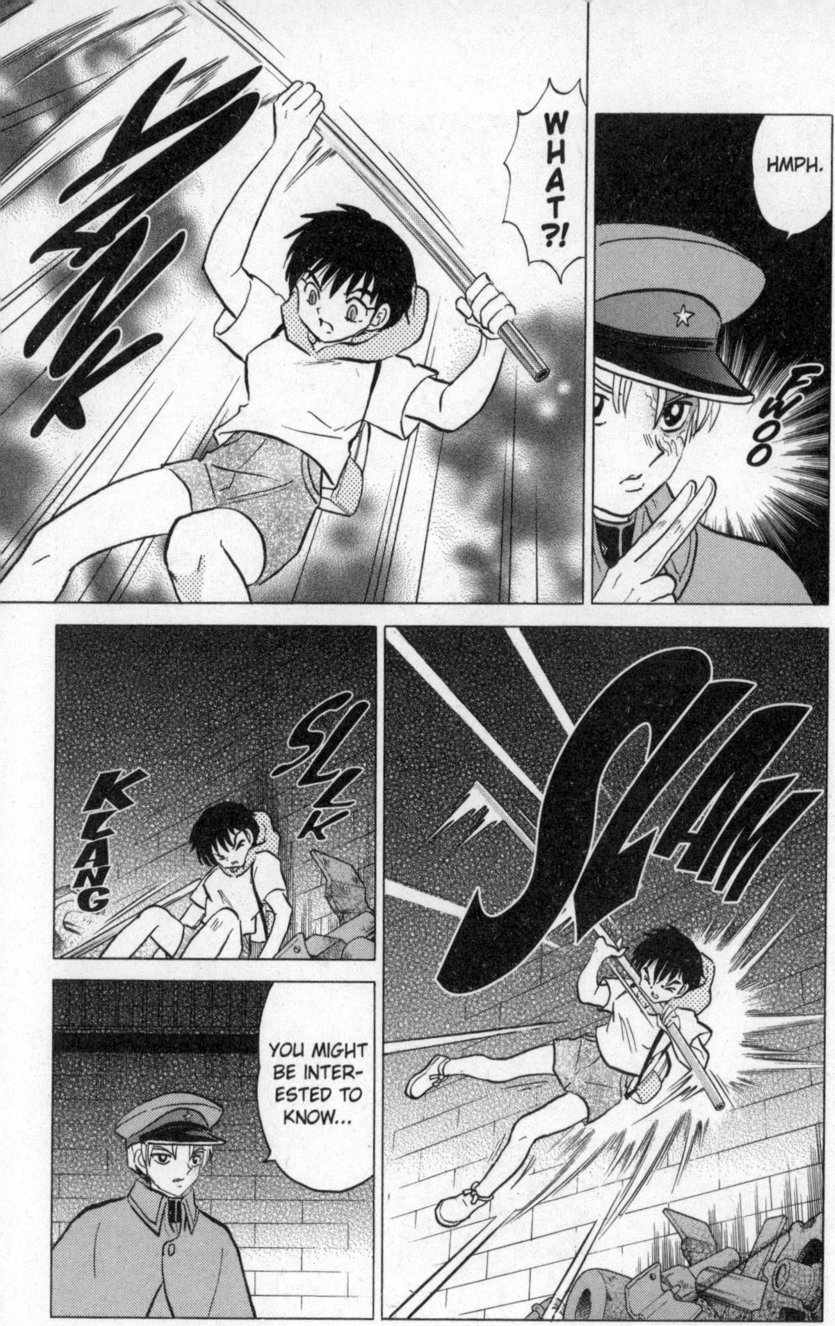
HMPH.
FWOO
WHAT?!
YANK
SLAM
SLLK
KLANG
YOU MIGHT BE INTER- ESTED TO KNOW...

...THAT THIS IS MY PRIVATE MUNITIONS WAREHOUSE.

EVERY WIRE, EVERY SHEET OF STEEL, IS INFUSED WITH MY POWER.

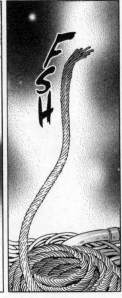

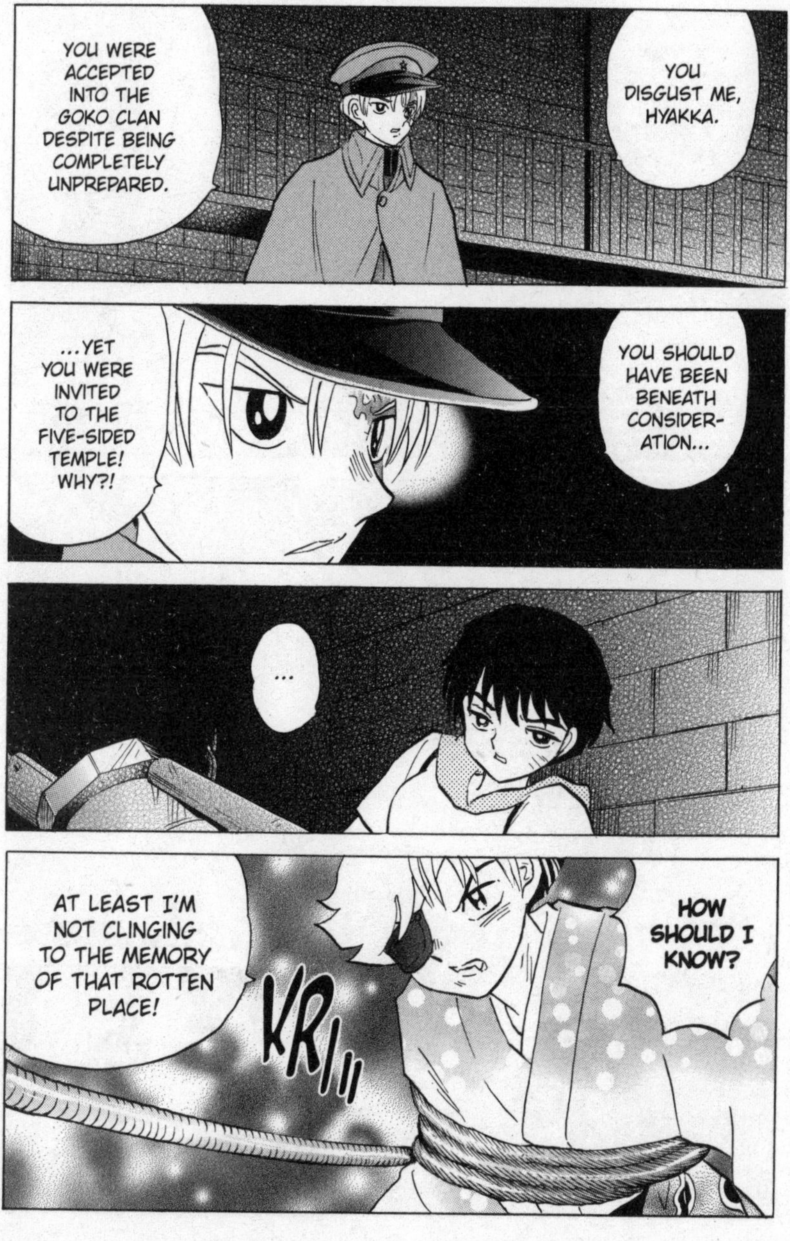
YOU DISGUST ME, HYAKKA.
YOU WERE ACCEPTED INTO THE GOKO CLAN DESPITE BEING COMPLETELY UNPREPARED.
YOU SHOULD HAVE BEEN BENEATH CONSIDER-ATION...
...YET YOU WERE INVITED TO THE FIVE-SIDED TEMPLE! WHY?!
...
HOW SHOULD I KNOW?
AT LEAST I'M NOT CLINGING TO THE MEMORY OF THAT ROTTEN PLACE!
KRI

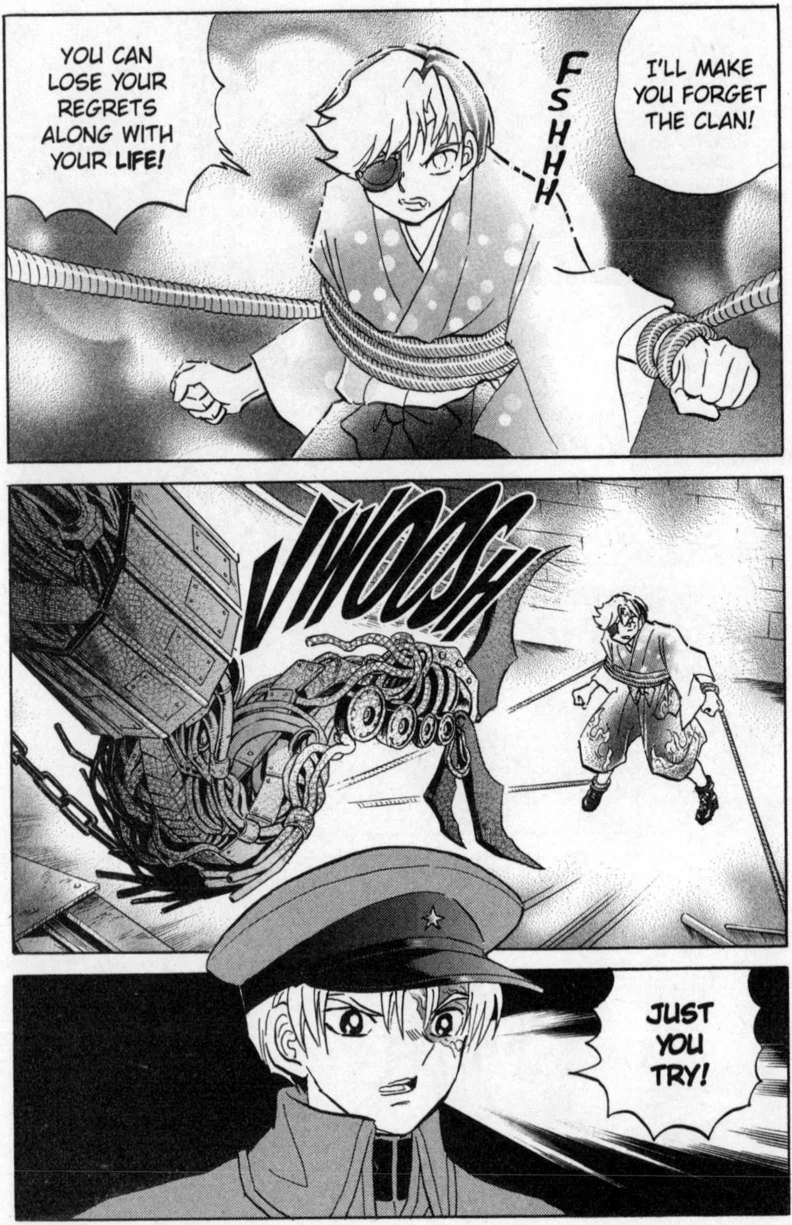
I'LL MAKE YOU FORGET THE CLAN!
FSHHH
YOU CAN LOSE YOUR REGRETS ALONG WITH YOUR LIFE!
WOOSH
JUST YOU TRY!

Chapter 8:
Hakubi's Thoughts

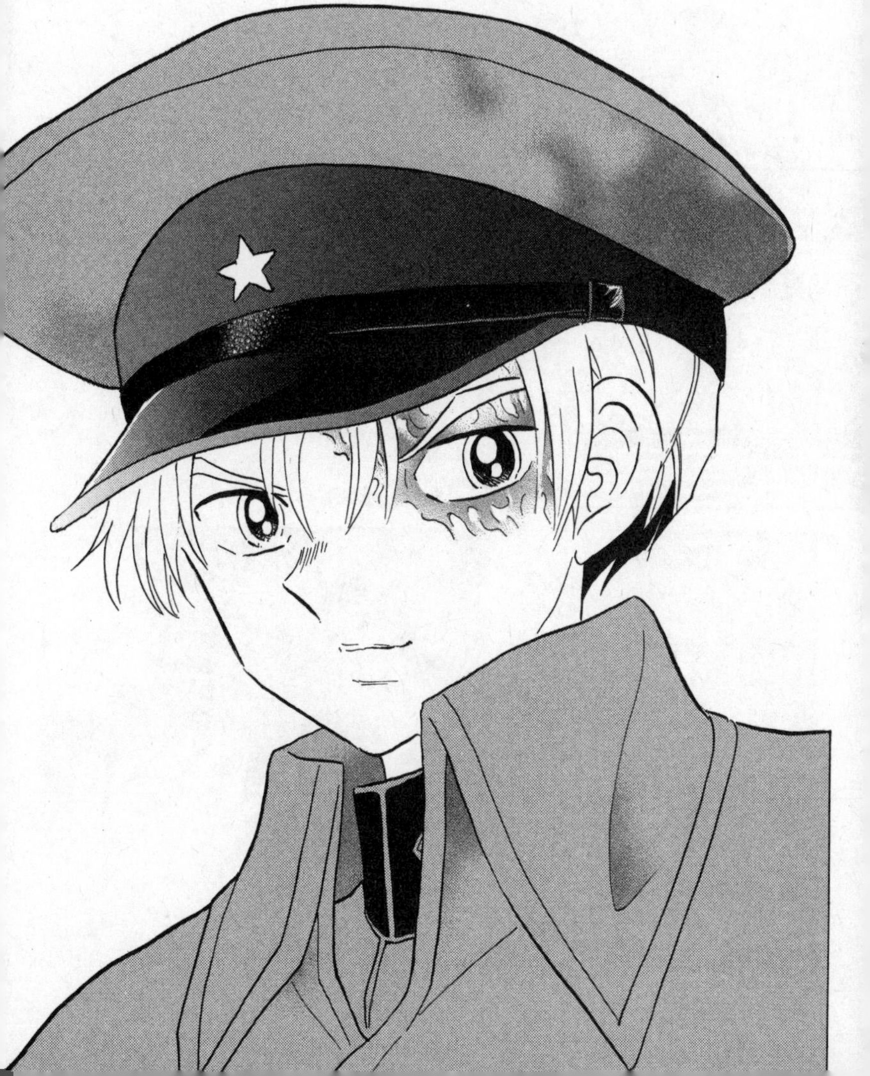

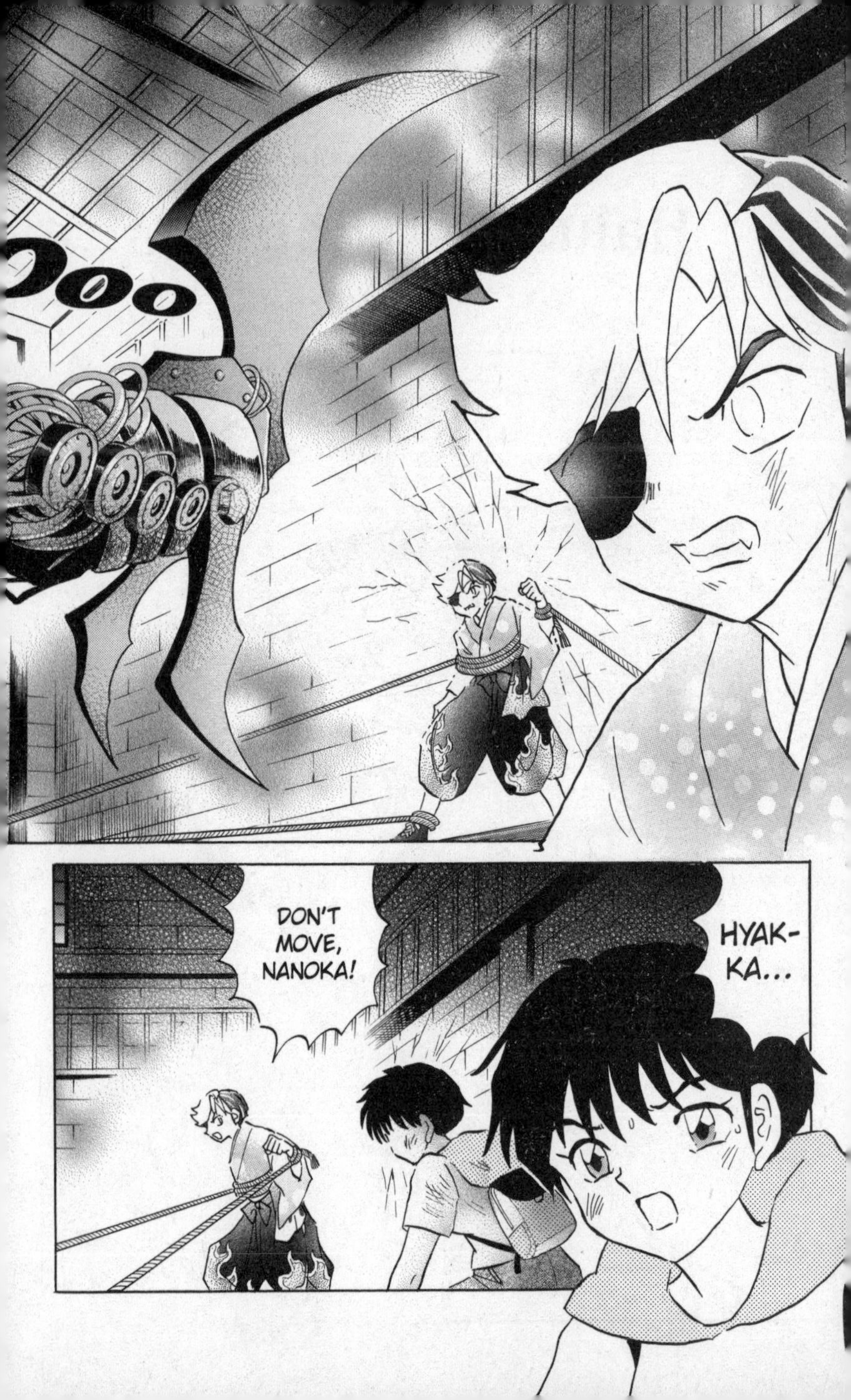
OOO
HYAK-KA...
DON'T MOVE, NANOKA!

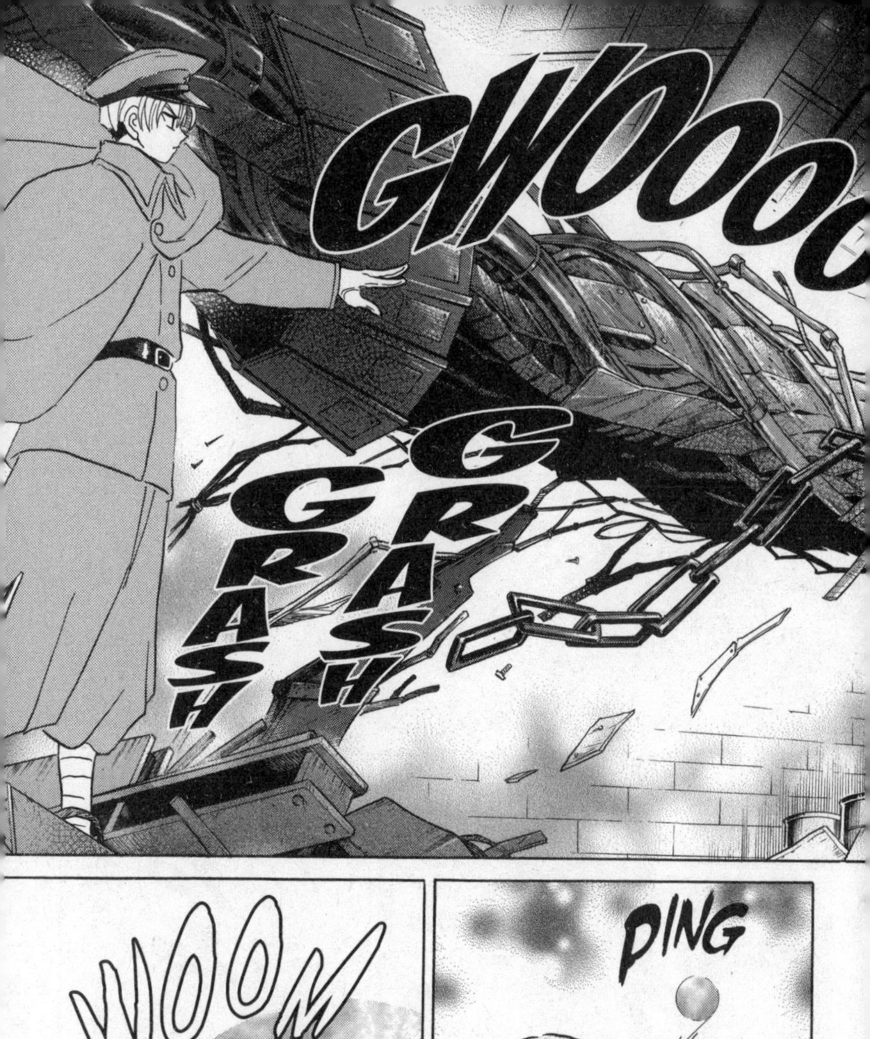
GWOOOO
GRASH
GRASH

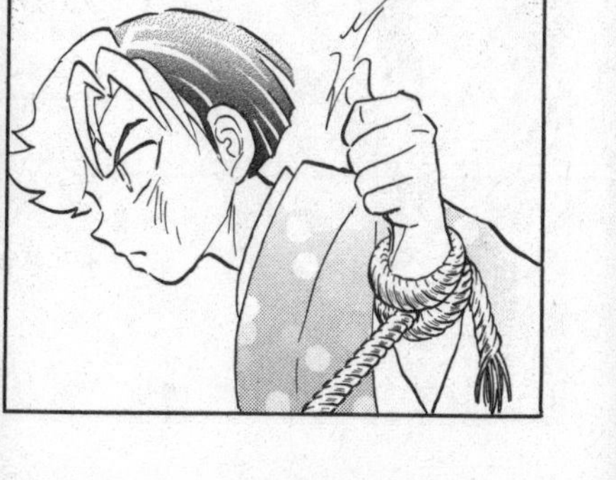
DING

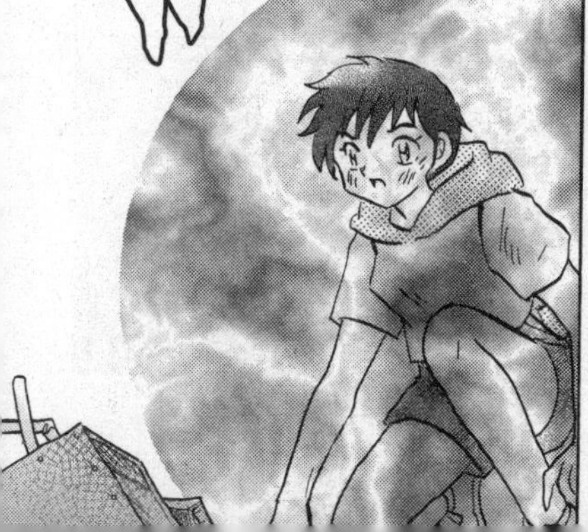
WOOM

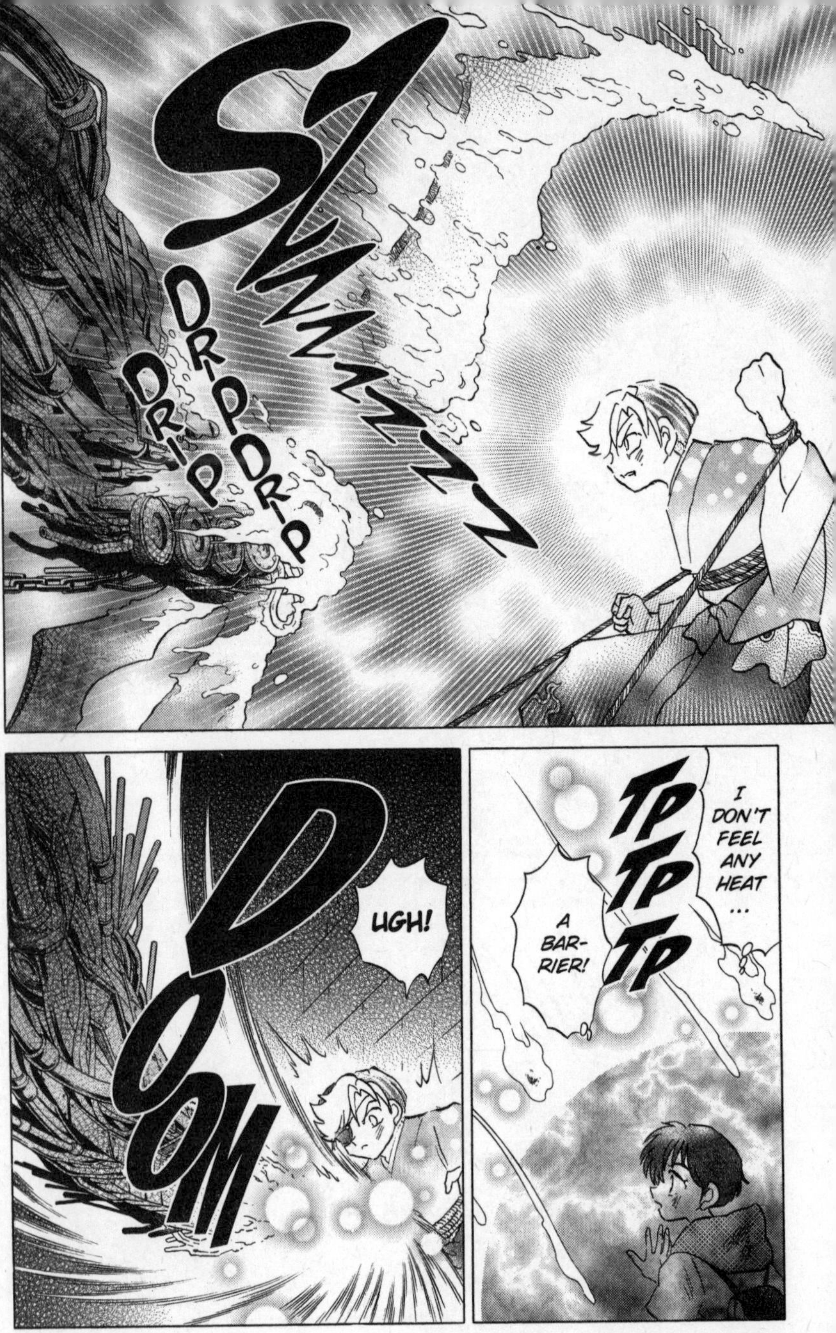
SIZZZZZZ
DRIP DRIP DRIP DRIP
I DON'T FEEL ANY HEAT...
TP TP TP
A BAR-RIER!
DOOM
UGH!

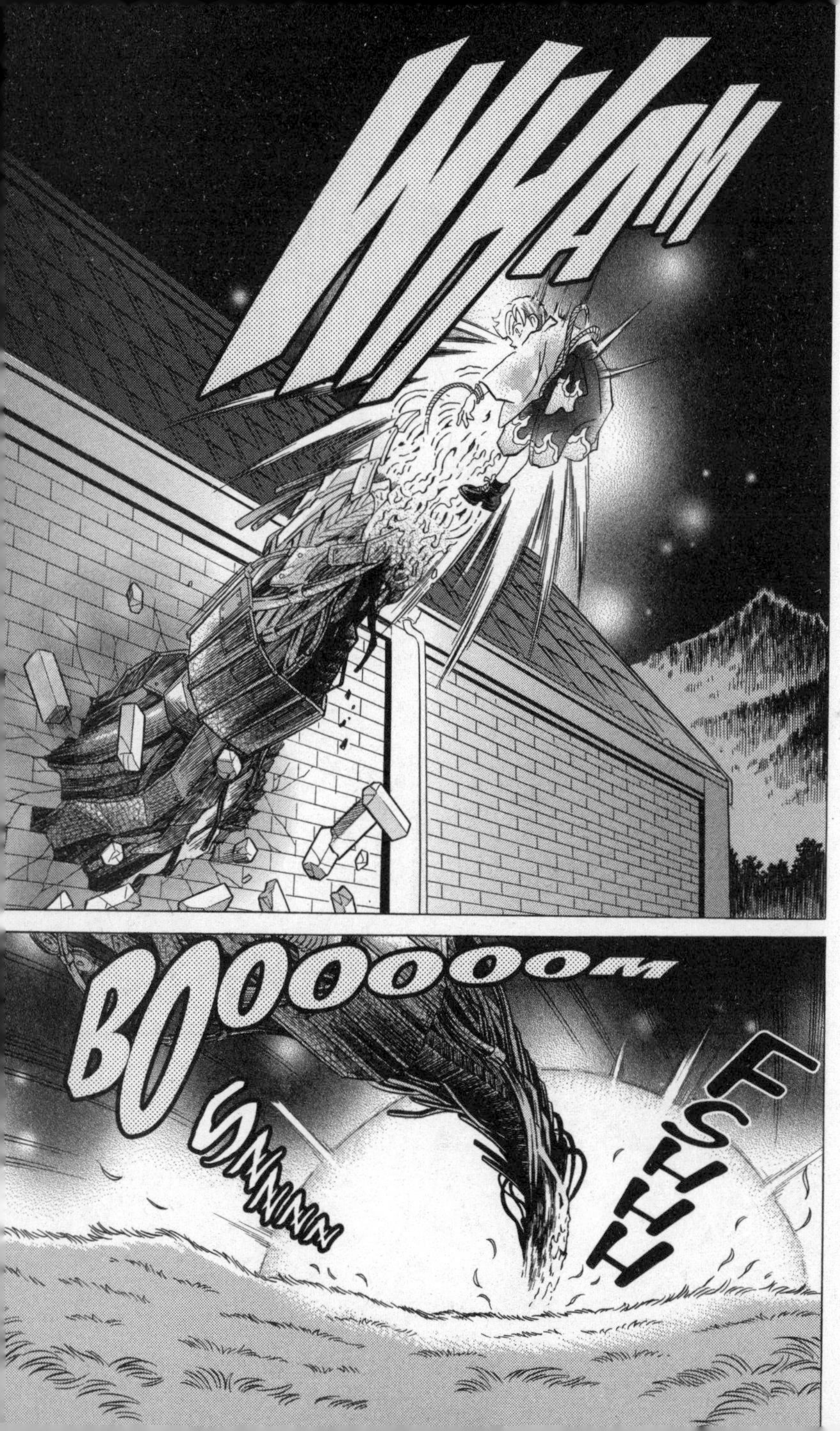
WHAM
BOOOOOOM
FSHHH

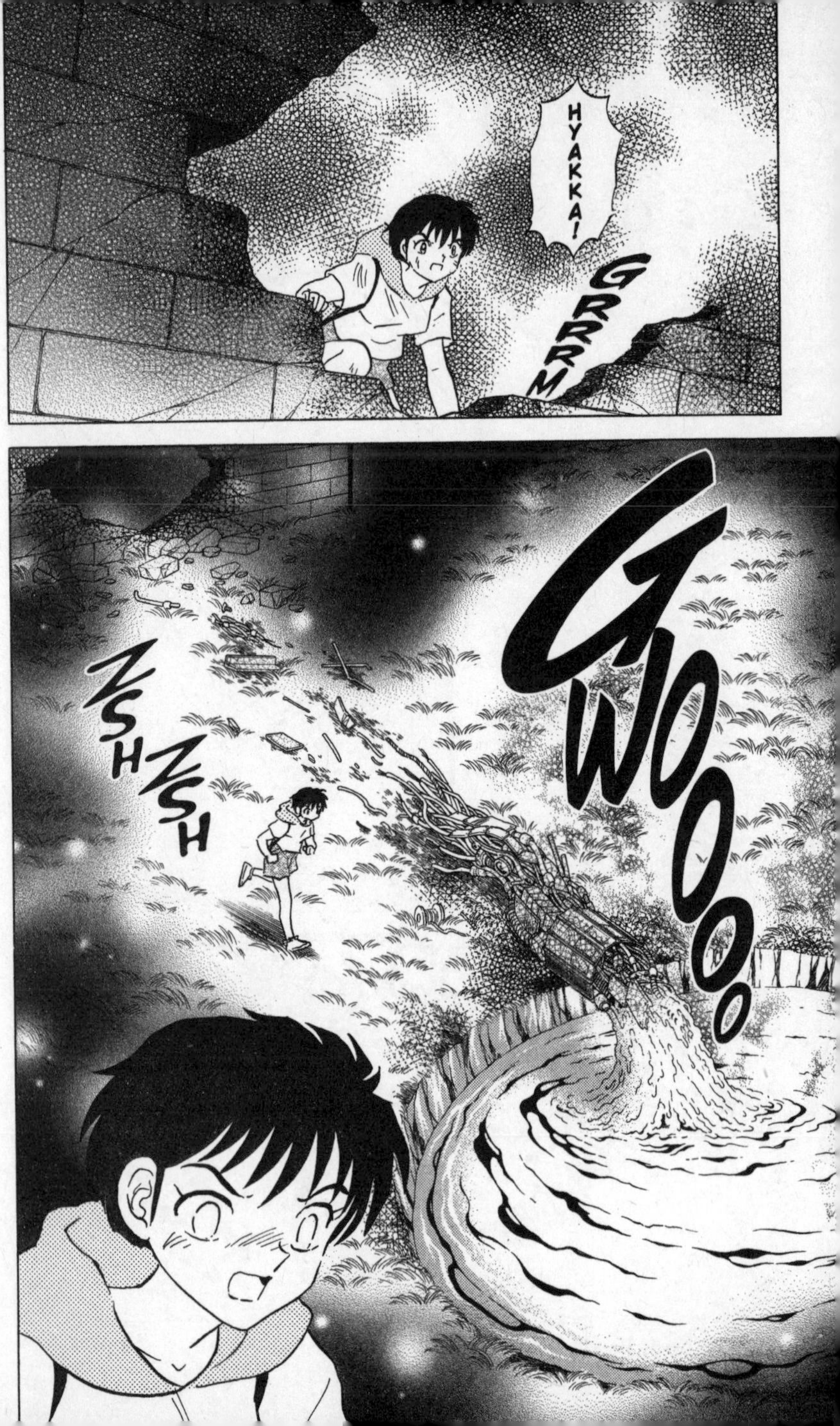
HYAKKA!
GRRRM
GWOOOOO
ZSH ZSH

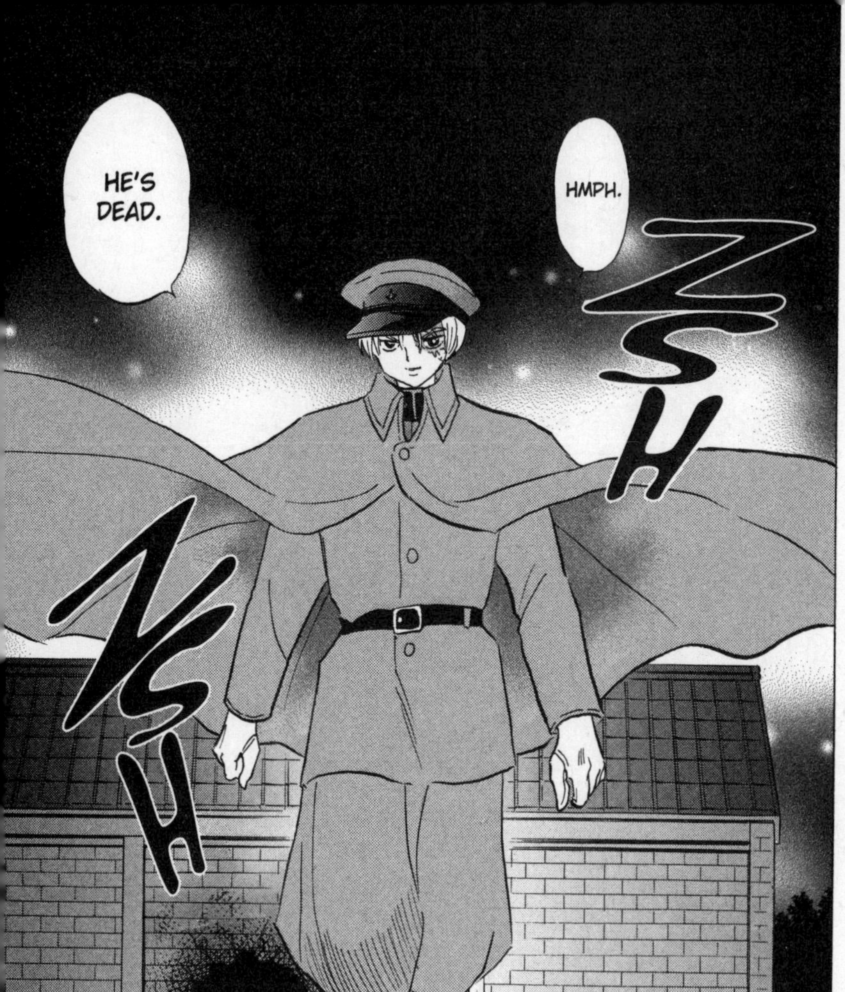
HMPH.
HE'S DEAD.
ZSH
ZSH
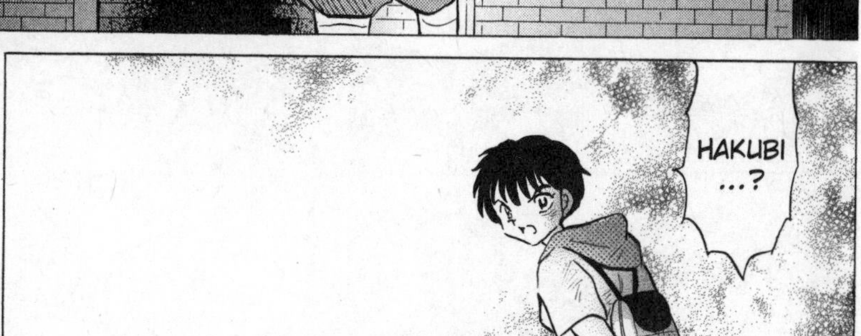
HAKUBI ...?

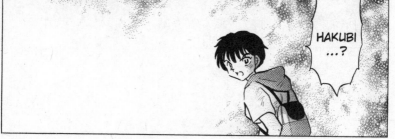

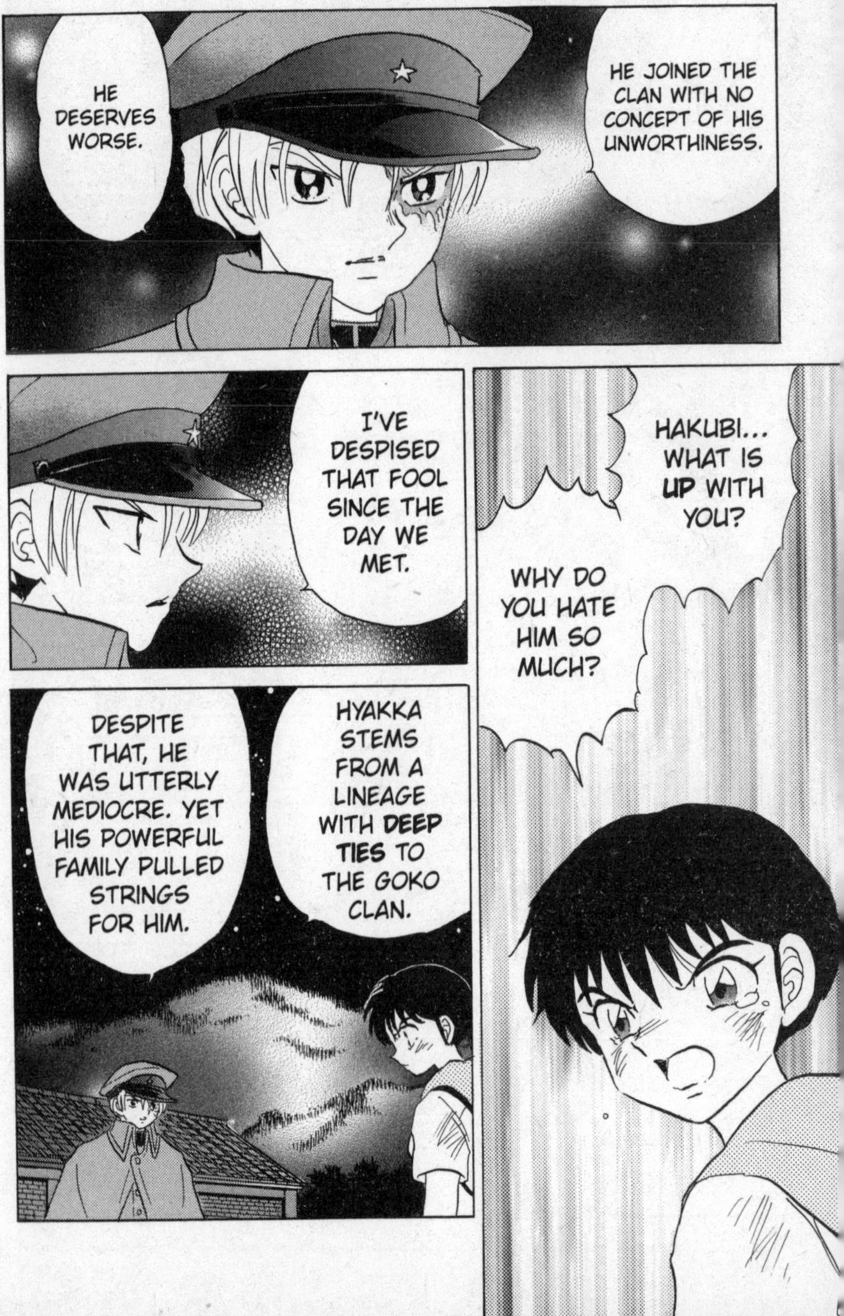
HE JOINED THE CLAN WITH NO CONCEPT OF HIS UNWORTHINESS.
HE DESERVES WORSE.
HAKUBI... WHAT IS **UP** WITH YOU?
WHY DO YOU HATE HIM SO MUCH?
I'VE DESPISED THAT FOOL SINCE THE DAY WE MET.
HYAKKA STEMS FROM A LINEAGE WITH **DEEP TIES** TO THE GOKO CLAN.
DESPITE THAT, HE WAS UTTERLY MEDIOCRE. YET HIS POWERFUL FAMILY PULLED STRINGS FOR HIM.

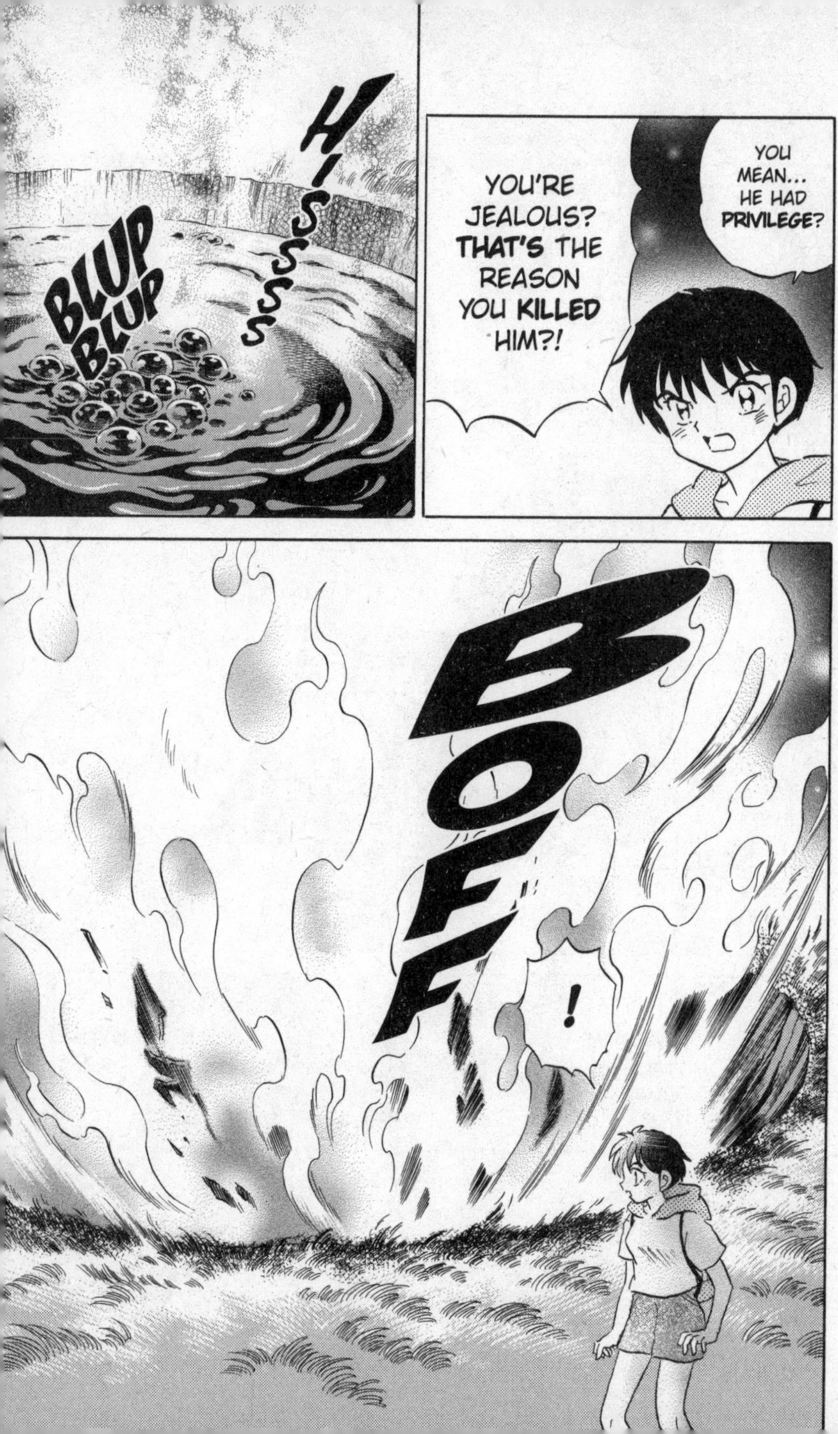
YOU MEAN... HE HAD PRIVILEGE?
YOU'RE JEALOUS? THAT'S THE REASON YOU KILLED HIM?!
HISSSSS
BLUP BLUP
BOFF
!
!

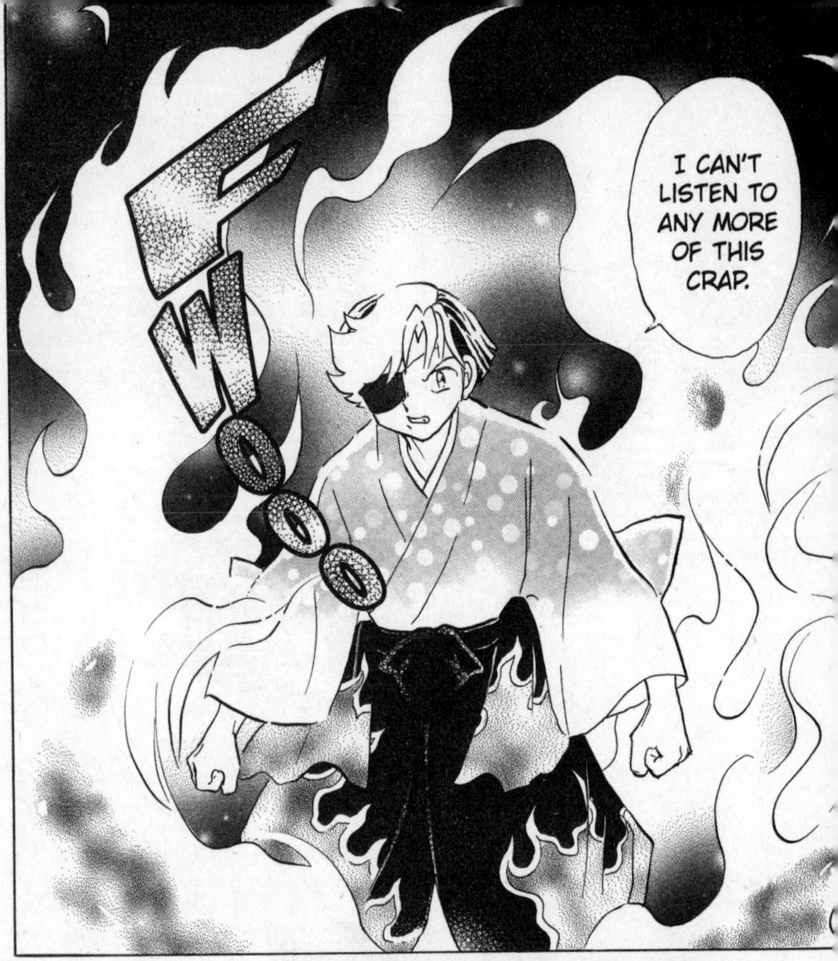
I CAN'T LISTEN TO ANY MORE OF THIS CRAP.
FWOOO
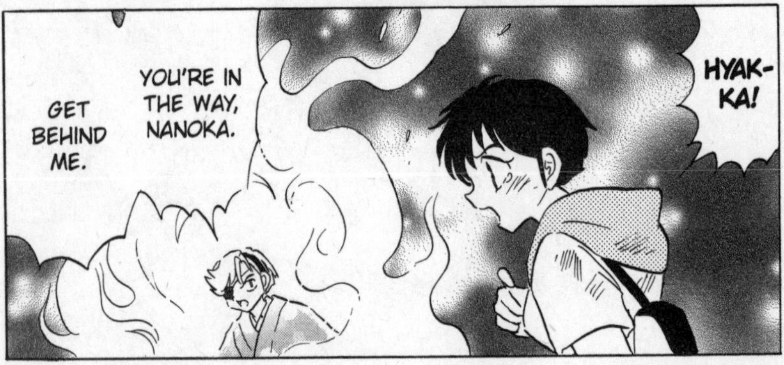
HYAK-KA!
YOU'RE IN THE WAY, NANOKA.
GET BEHIND ME.

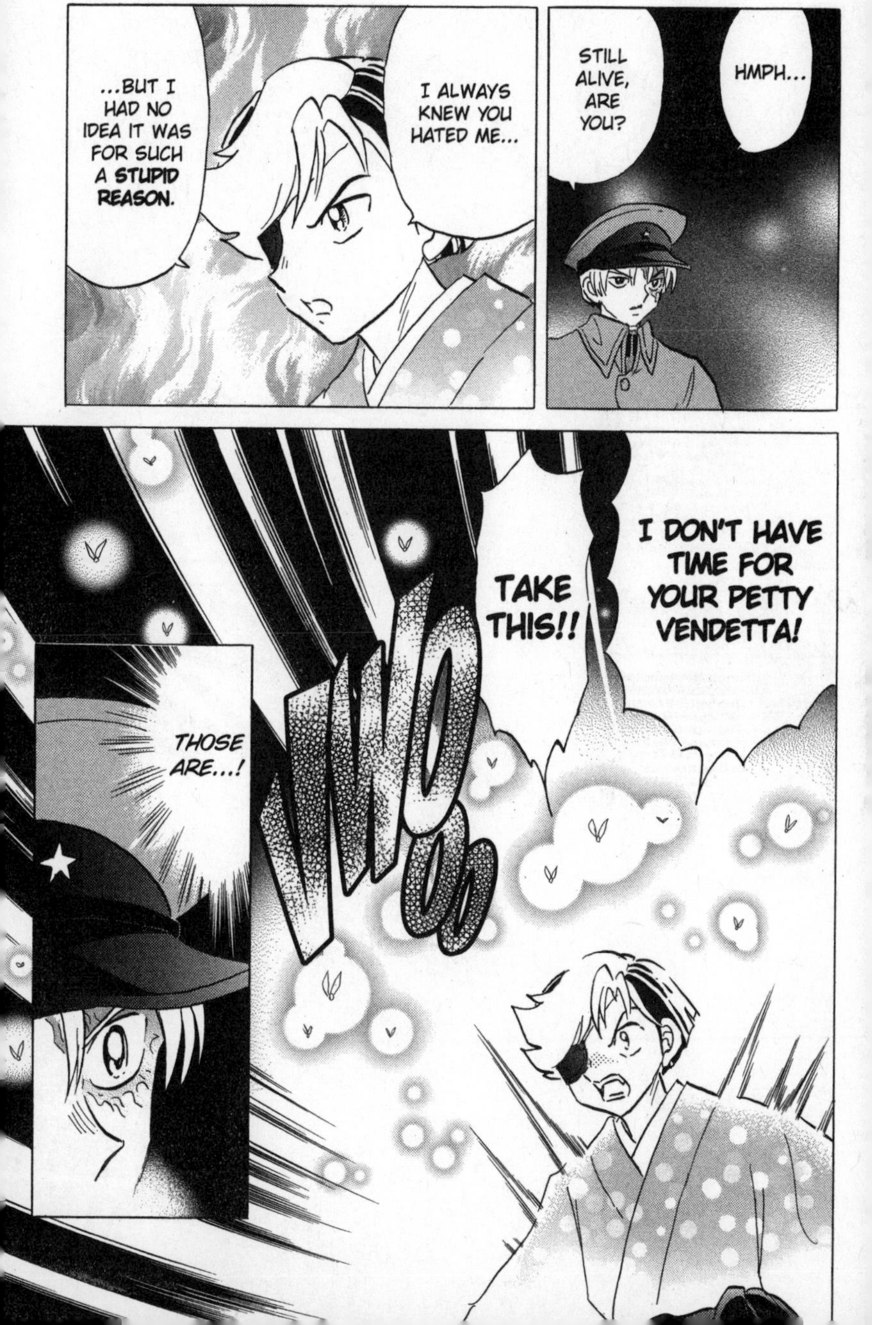
HMPH...
STILL ALIVE, ARE YOU?
I ALWAYS KNEW YOU HATED ME...
...BUT I HAD NO IDEA IT WAS FOR SUCH A STUPID REASON.
I DON'T HAVE TIME FOR YOUR PETTY VENDETTA!
TAKE THIS!!
VWOOO
THOSE ARE...!

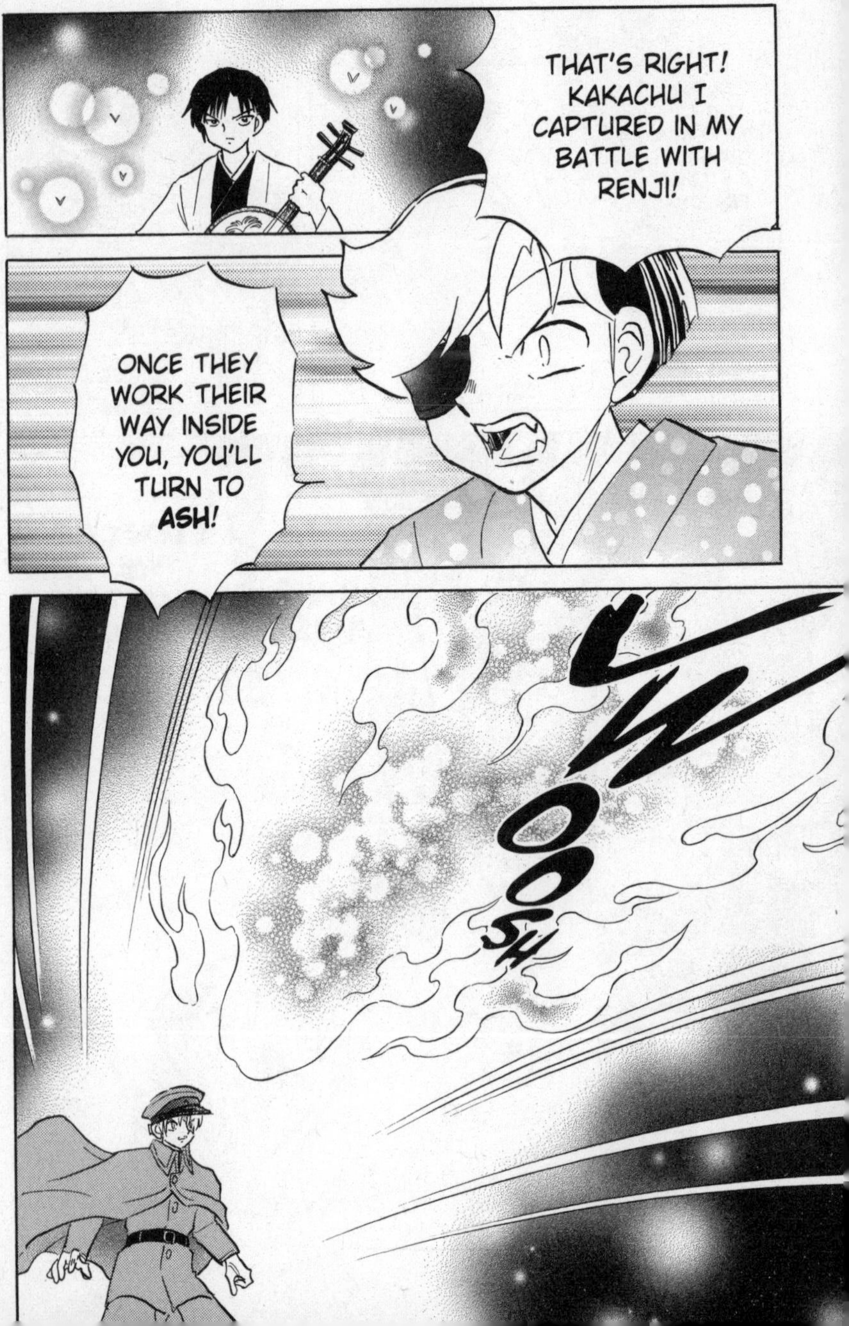
THAT'S RIGHT! KAKACHU I CAPTURED IN MY BATTLE WITH RENJI!
ONCE THEY WORK THEIR WAY INSIDE YOU, YOU'LL TURN TO **ASH!**
WHOOOSH

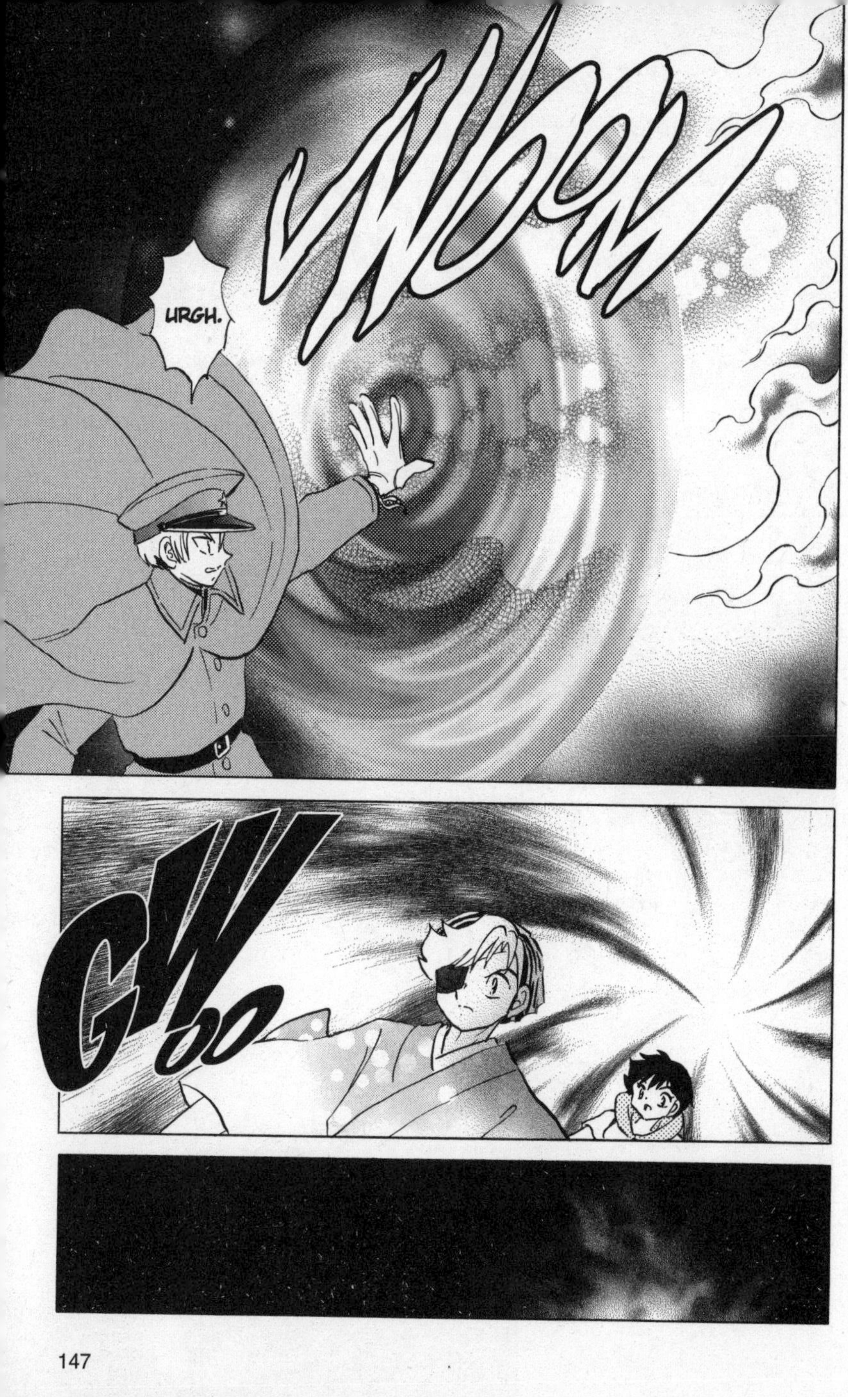

WHOOM
URGH.
GWOO

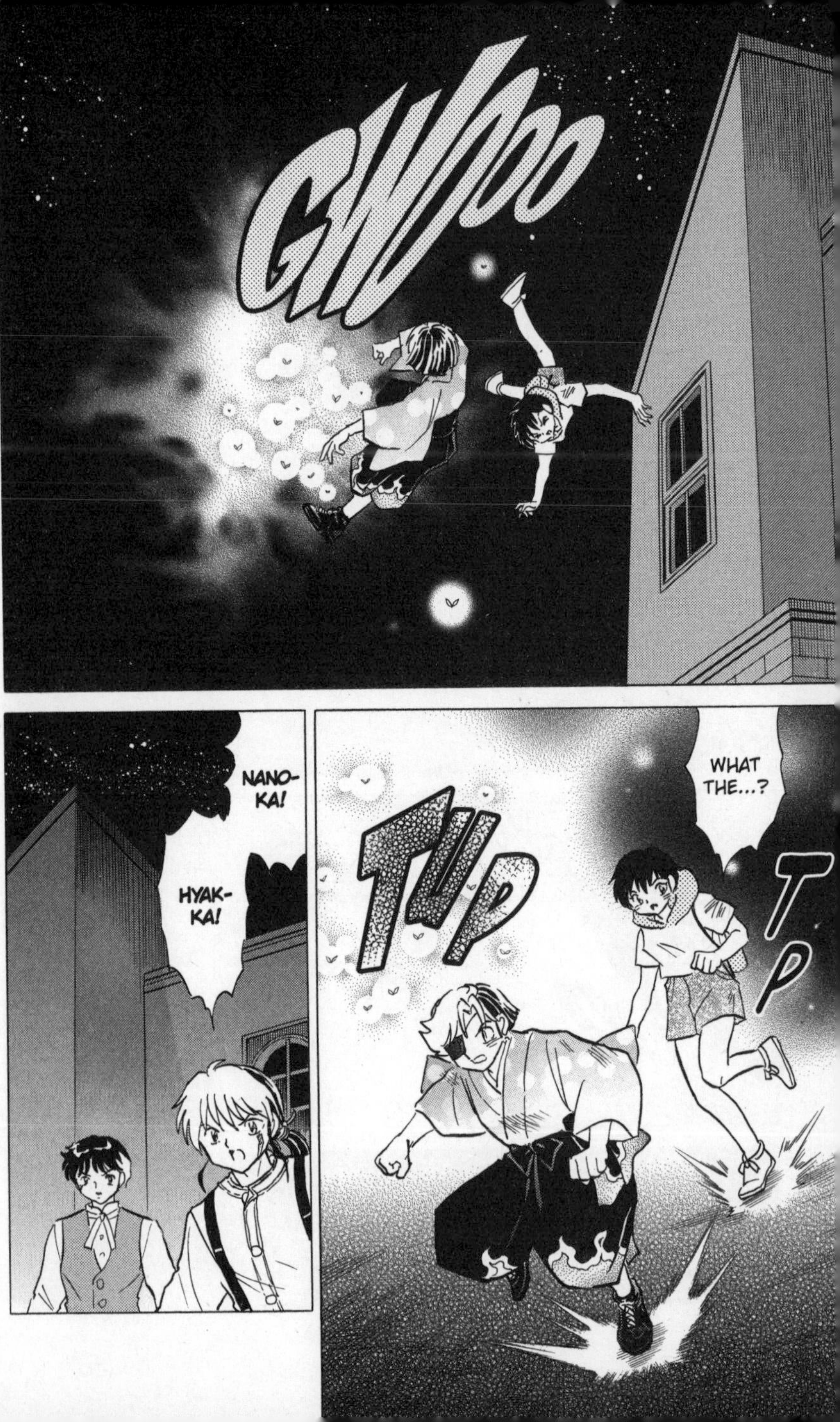
GWOO
WHAT THE...?
TP
TUP
NANO-KA!
HYAK-KA!

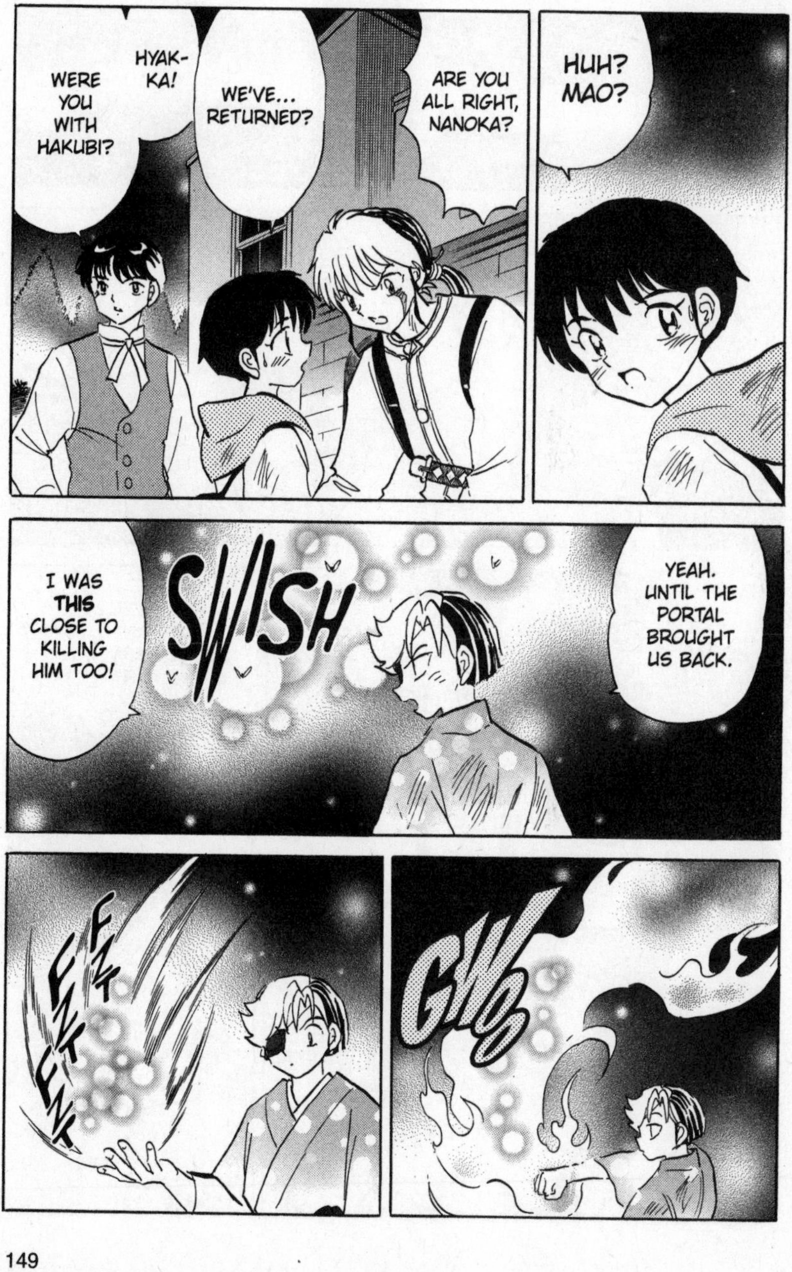
HUH? MAO?
ARE YOU ALL RIGHT, NANOKA?
WE'VE... RETURNED?
HYAK-KA!
WERE YOU WITH HAKUBI?
YEAH. UNTIL THE PORTAL BROUGHT US BACK.
SWISH
I WAS **THIS** CLOSE TO KILLING HIM TOO!

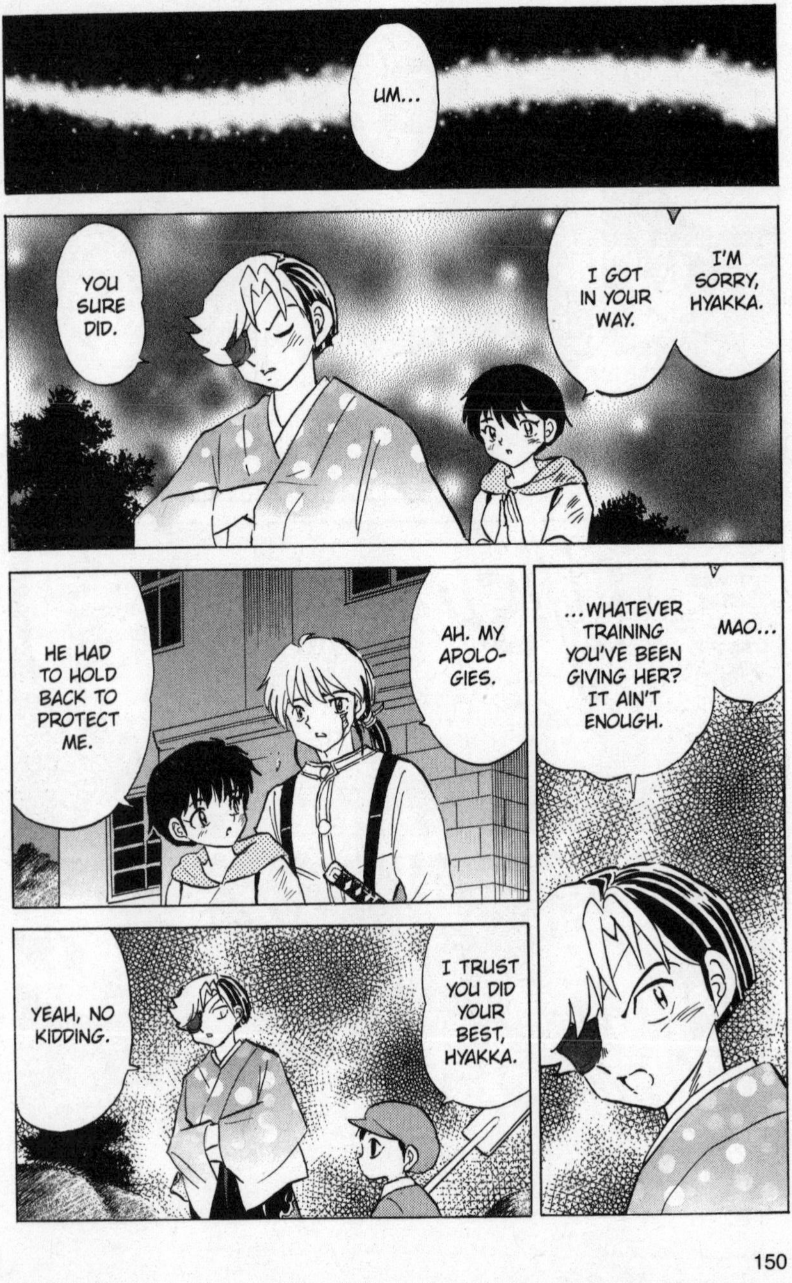
UM...
I'M SORRY, HYAKKA.
I GOT IN YOUR WAY.
YOU SURE DID.
MAO...
...WHATEVER TRAINING YOU'VE BEEN GIVING HER? IT AIN'T ENOUGH.
AH. MY APOLOGIES.
HE HAD TO HOLD BACK TO PROTECT ME.
I TRUST YOU DID YOUR BEST, HYAKKA.
YEAH, NO KIDDING.

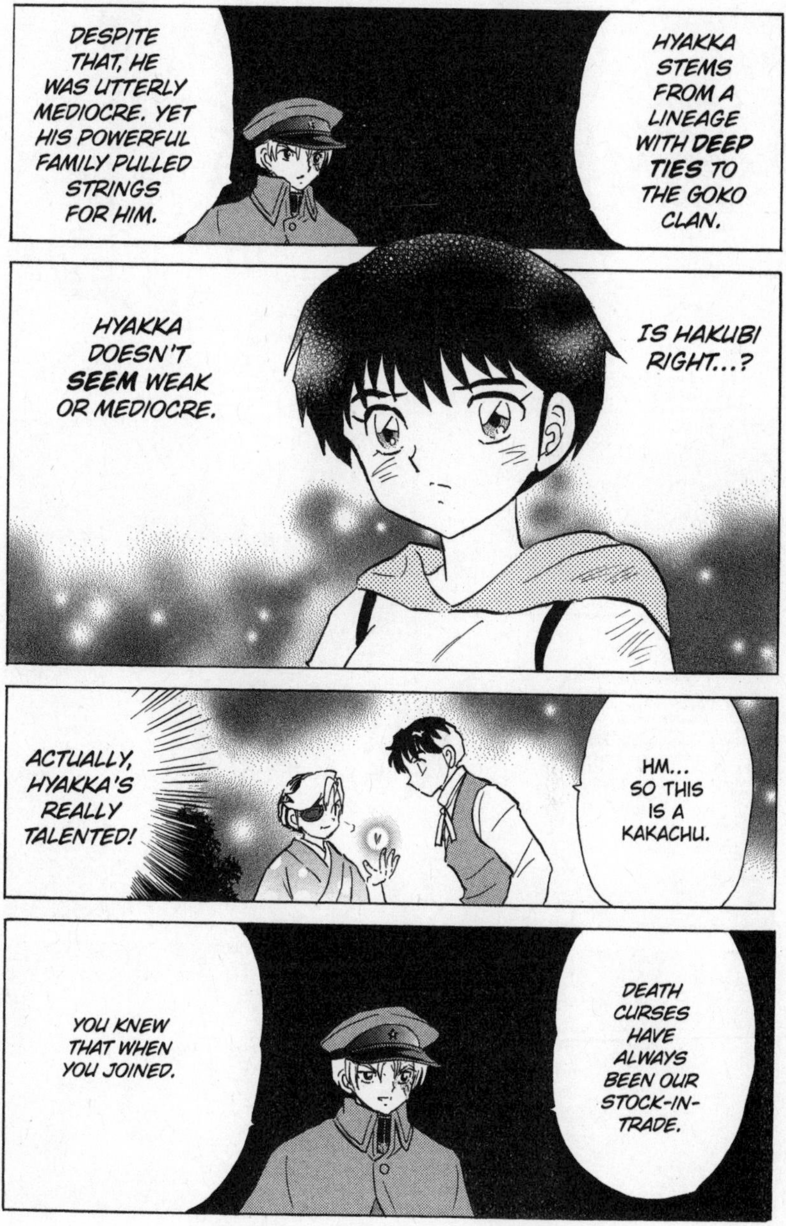
HYAKKA STEMS FROM A LINEAGE WITH DEEP TIES TO THE GOKO CLAN.
DESPITE THAT, HE WAS UTTERLY MEDIOCRE. YET HIS POWERFUL FAMILY PULLED STRINGS FOR HIM.
IS HAKUBI RIGHT...?
HYAKKA DOESN'T SEEM WEAK OR MEDIOCRE.
HM... SO THIS IS A KAKACHU.
ACTUALLY, HYAKKA'S REALLY TALENTED!
DEATH CURSES HAVE ALWAYS BEEN OUR STOCK-IN-TRADE.
YOU KNEW THAT WHEN YOU JOINED.

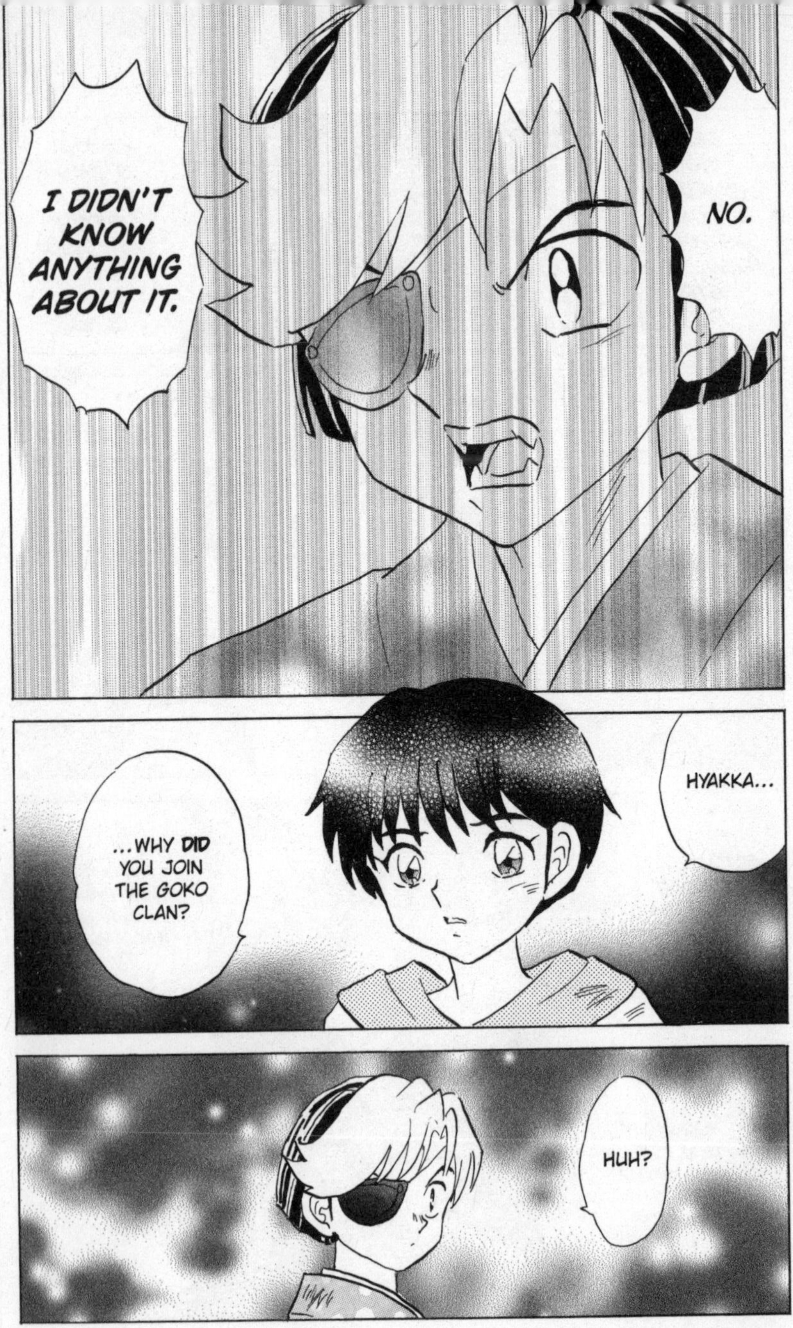
NO.
I DIDN'T KNOW ANYTHING ABOUT IT.
HYAKKA...
...WHY DID YOU JOIN THE GOKO CLAN?
HUH?

Chapter 9:
Otori Family Matters

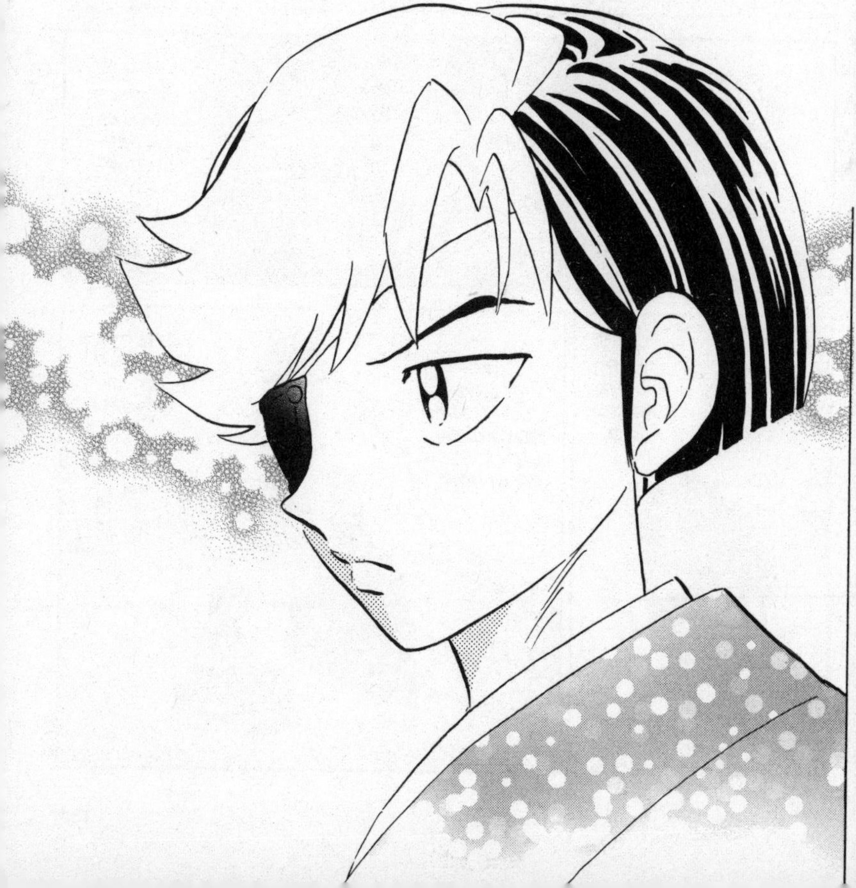

... MY...
BROTHER
...

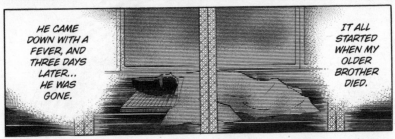

IT ALL STARTED WHEN MY OLDER BROTHER DIED.

HE CAME DOWN WITH A FEVER, AND THREE DAYS LATER... HE WAS GONE.

AFTER THE FUNERAL, MY DAD SUMMONED ME.

YOUR BROTHER...

...WAS TO HAVE JOINED THE GOKO CLAN TEN DAYS FROM NOW.

OUR FAMILIES HAVE A PACT.

ONE OF US MUST GO.

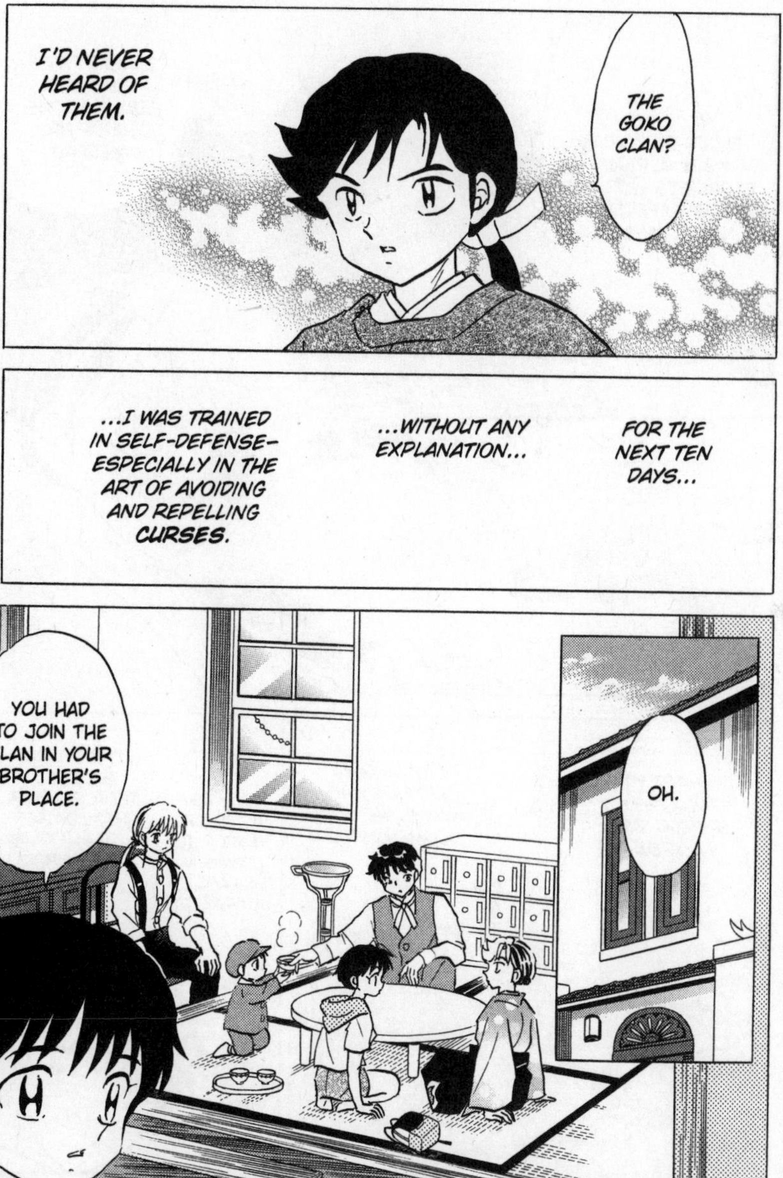
THE GOKO CLAN?
I'D NEVER HEARD OF THEM.
FOR THE NEXT TEN DAYS...
...WITHOUT ANY EXPLANATION...
...I WAS TRAINED IN SELF-DEFENSE-ESPECIALLY IN THE ART OF AVOIDING AND REPELLING CURSES.
OH.
YOU HAD TO JOIN THE CLAN IN YOUR BROTHER'S PLACE.

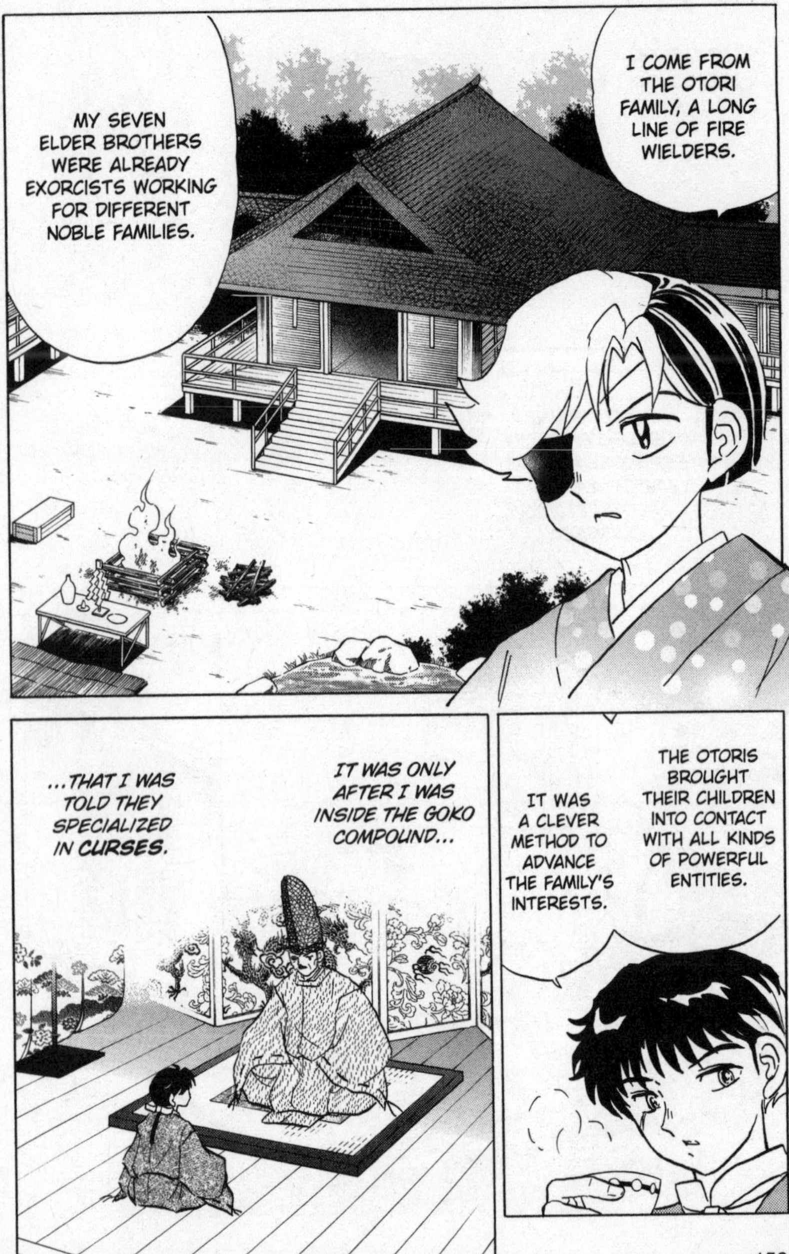
I COME FROM THE OTORI FAMILY, A LONG LINE OF FIRE WIELDERS.
MY SEVEN ELDER BROTHERS WERE ALREADY EXORCISTS WORKING FOR DIFFERENT NOBLE FAMILIES.
THE OTORIS BROUGHT THEIR CHILDREN INTO CONTACT WITH ALL KINDS OF POWERFUL ENTITIES.
IT WAS A CLEVER METHOD TO ADVANCE THE FAMILY'S INTERESTS.
IT WAS ONLY AFTER I WAS INSIDE THE GOKO COMPOUND...
...THAT I WAS TOLD THEY SPECIALIZED IN CURSES.

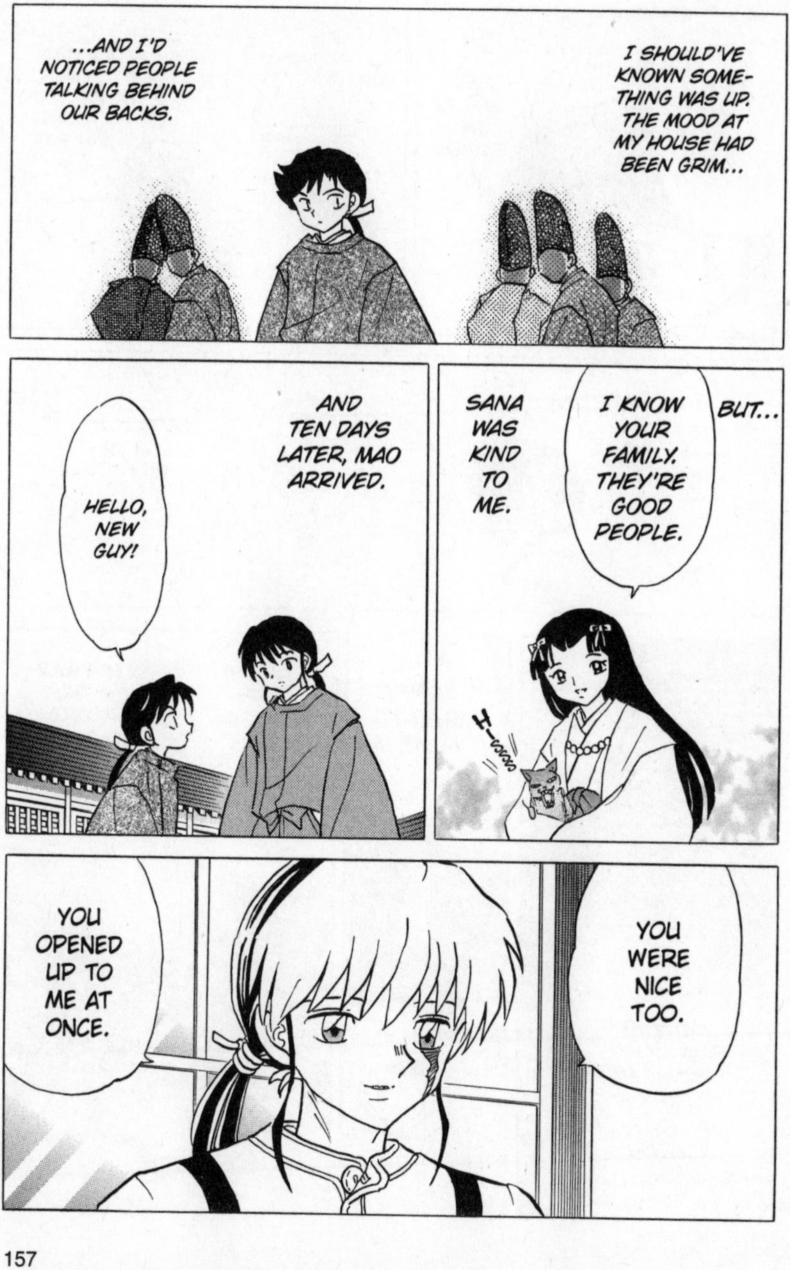
I SHOULD'VE KNOWN SOMETHING WAS UP. THE MOOD AT MY HOUSE HAD BEEN GRIM...
...AND I'D NOTICED PEOPLE TALKING BEHIND OUR BACKS.
BUT...
I KNOW YOUR FAMILY. THEY'RE GOOD PEOPLE.
SANA WAS KIND TO ME.
HISSSS
AND TEN DAYS LATER, MAO ARRIVED.
HELLO, NEW GUY!
YOU WERE NICE TOO.
YOU OPENED UP TO ME AT ONCE.

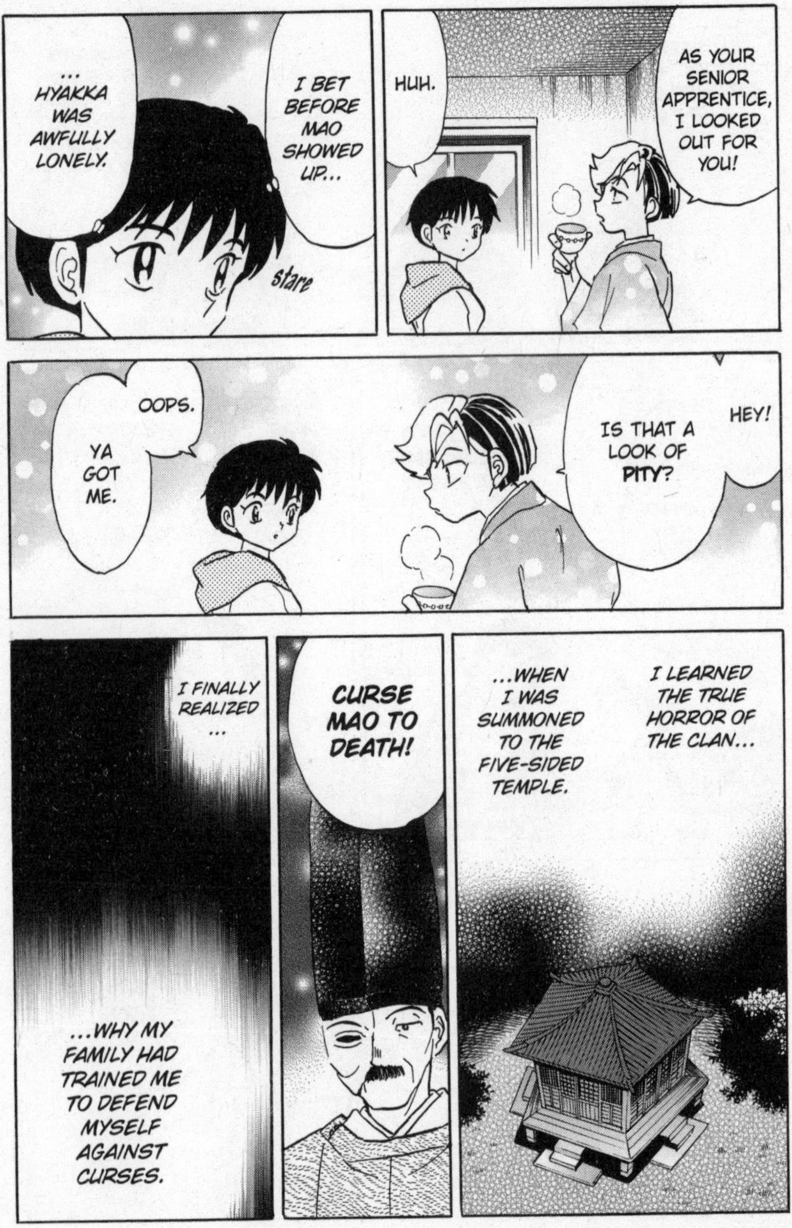
AS YOUR SENIOR APPRENTICE, I LOOKED OUT FOR YOU!
HUH.
I BET BEFORE MAO SHOWED UP...
...HYAKKA WAS AWFULLY LONELY.
stare
HEY!
IS THAT A LOOK OF PITY?
OOPS.
YA GOT ME.
I LEARNED THE TRUE HORROR OF THE CLAN...
...WHEN I WAS SUMMONED TO THE FIVE-SIDED TEMPLE.
CURSE MAO TO DEATH!
I FINALLY REALIZED ...
...WHY MY FAMILY HAD TRAINED ME TO DEFEND MYSELF AGAINST CURSES.

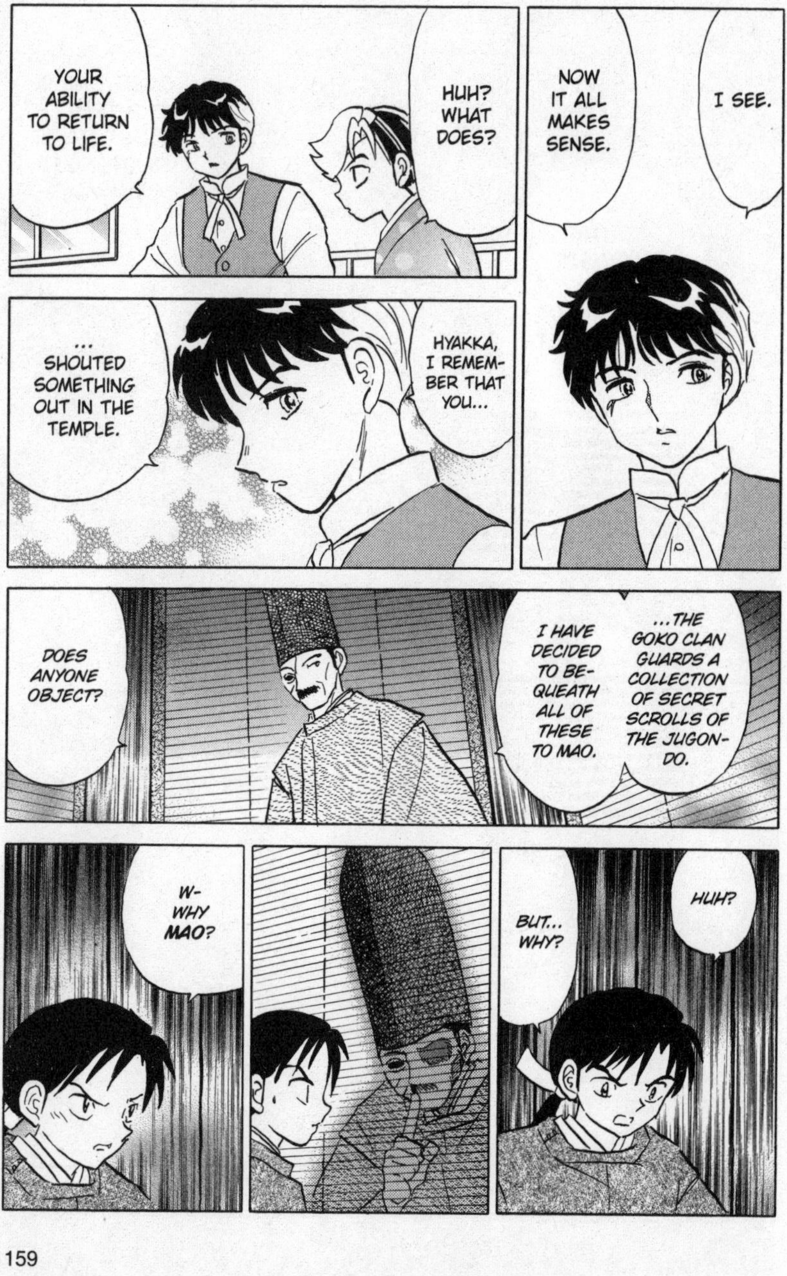

I SEE.
NOW IT ALL MAKES SENSE.
HUH? WHAT DOES?
YOUR ABILITY TO RETURN TO LIFE.
HYAKKA, I REMEMBER THAT YOU...
...SHOUTED SOMETHING OUT IN THE TEMPLE.
...THE GOKO CLAN GUARDS A COLLECTION OF SECRET SCROLLS OF THE JUGON-DO.
I HAVE DECIDED TO BEQUEATH ALL OF THESE TO MAO.
DOES ANYONE OBJECT?
HUH?
BUT... WHY?
W-WHY MAO?

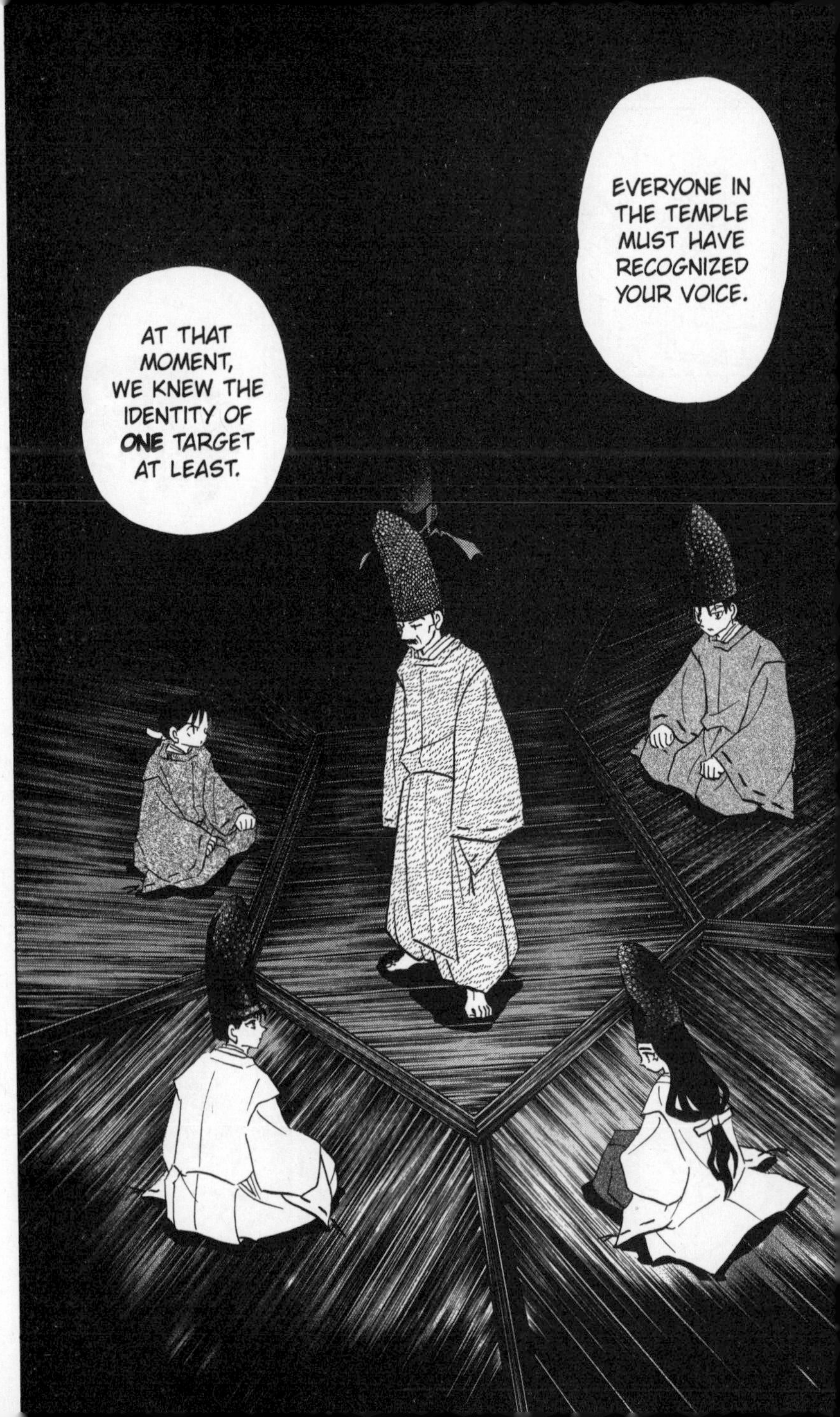
EVERYONE IN THE TEMPLE MUST HAVE RECOGNIZED YOUR VOICE.
AT THAT MOMENT, WE KNEW THE IDENTITY OF ONE TARGET AT LEAST.

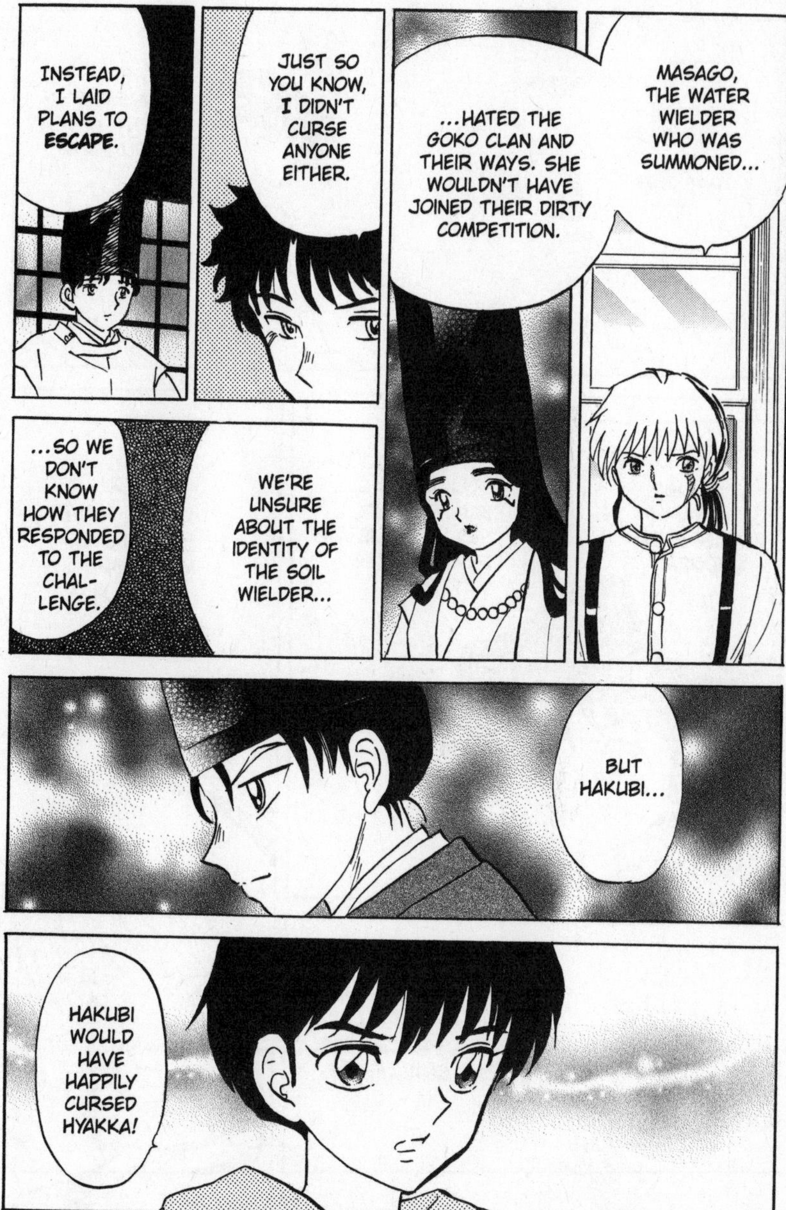
MASAGO, THE WATER WIELDER WHO WAS SUMMONED...
...HATED THE GOKO CLAN AND THEIR WAYS. SHE WOULDN'T HAVE JOINED THEIR DIRTY COMPETITION.
JUST SO YOU KNOW, I DIDN'T CURSE ANYONE EITHER.
INSTEAD, I LAID PLANS TO ESCAPE.
WE'RE UNSURE ABOUT THE IDENTITY OF THE SOIL WIELDER...
...SO WE DON'T KNOW HOW THEY RESPONDED TO THE CHAL-LENGE.
BUT HAKUBI...
HAKUBI WOULD HAVE HAPPILY CURSED HYAKKA!

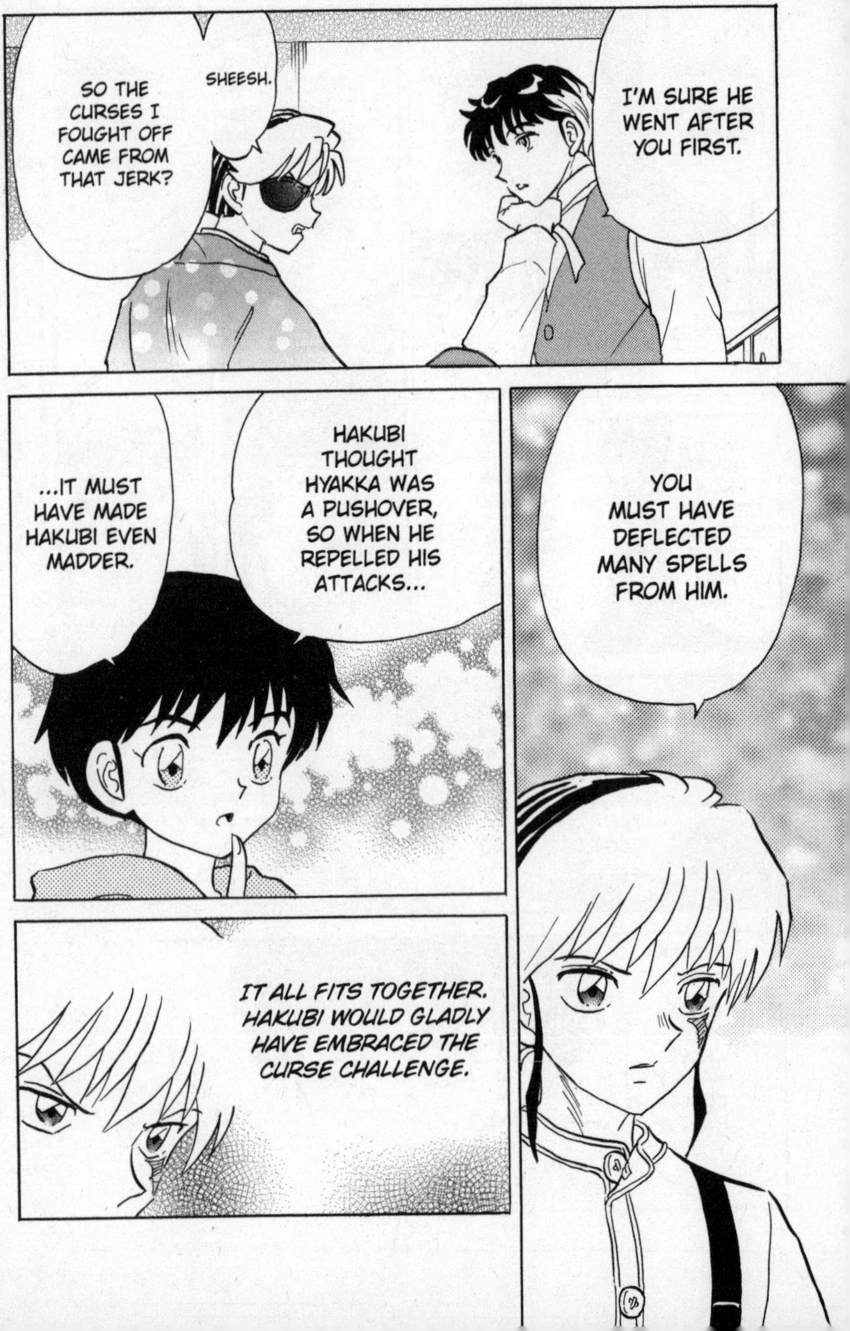
I'M SURE HE WENT AFTER YOU FIRST.
SO THE CURSES I FOUGHT OFF CAME FROM THAT JERK?
SHEESH.
YOU MUST HAVE DEFLECTED MANY SPELLS FROM HIM.
HAKUBI THOUGHT HYAKKA WAS A PUSHOVER, SO WHEN HE REPELLED HIS ATTACKS...
...IT MUST HAVE MADE HAKUBI EVEN MADDER.
IT ALL FITS TOGETHER. HAKUBI WOULD GLADLY HAVE EMBRACED THE CURSE CHALLENGE.

DAIGO...

AND HE WOULDN'T HAVE CARED HOW MANY BYSTANDERS WERE KILLED ALONG THE WAY.

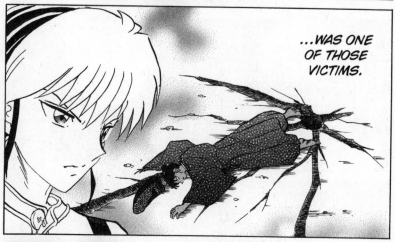

...WAS ONE OF THOSE VICTIMS.

WE'RE GOING TO...

...HAKUBI HASN'T CHANGED AT ALL.

IN 900 YEARS...

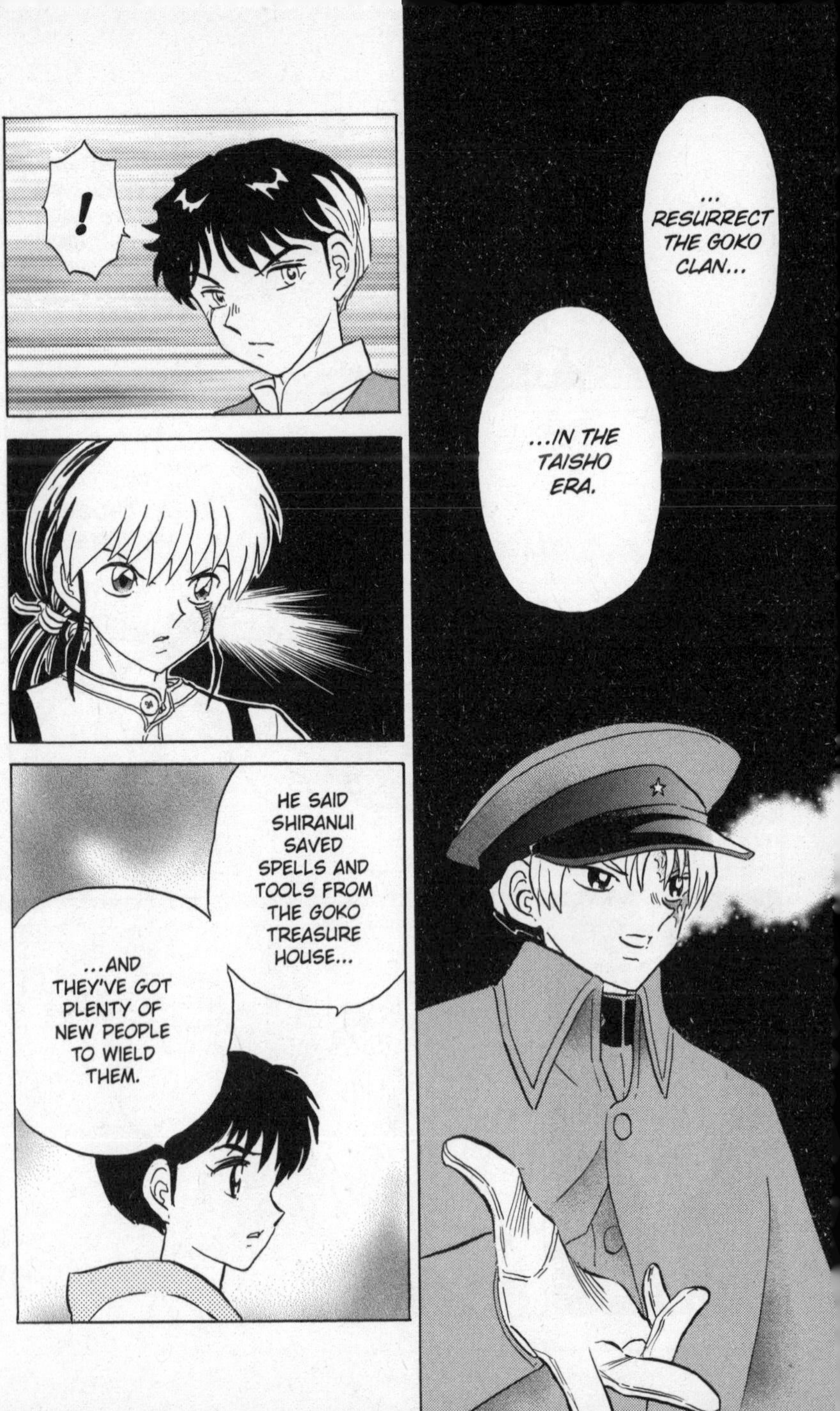
...RESURRECT THE GOKO CLAN...
...IN THE TAISHO ERA.
!
HE SAID SHIRANUI SAVED SPELLS AND TOOLS FROM THE GOKO TREASURE HOUSE...
...AND THEY'VE GOT PLENTY OF NEW PEOPLE TO WIELD THEM.

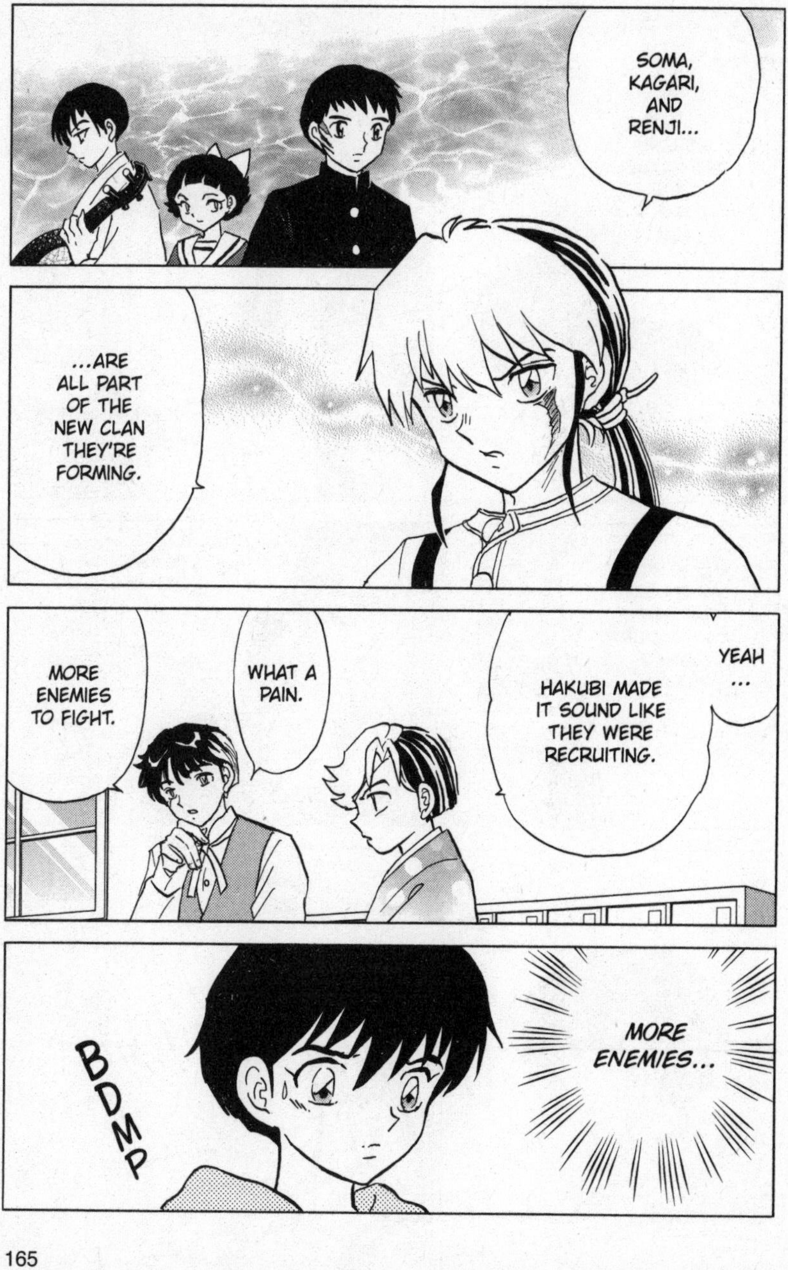
SOMA, KAGARI, AND RENJI...
...ARE ALL PART OF THE NEW CLAN THEY'RE FORMING.
YEAH ...
HAKUBI MADE IT SOUND LIKE THEY WERE RECRUITING.
WHAT A PAIN.
MORE ENEMIES TO FIGHT.
MORE ENEMIES...
BDMP

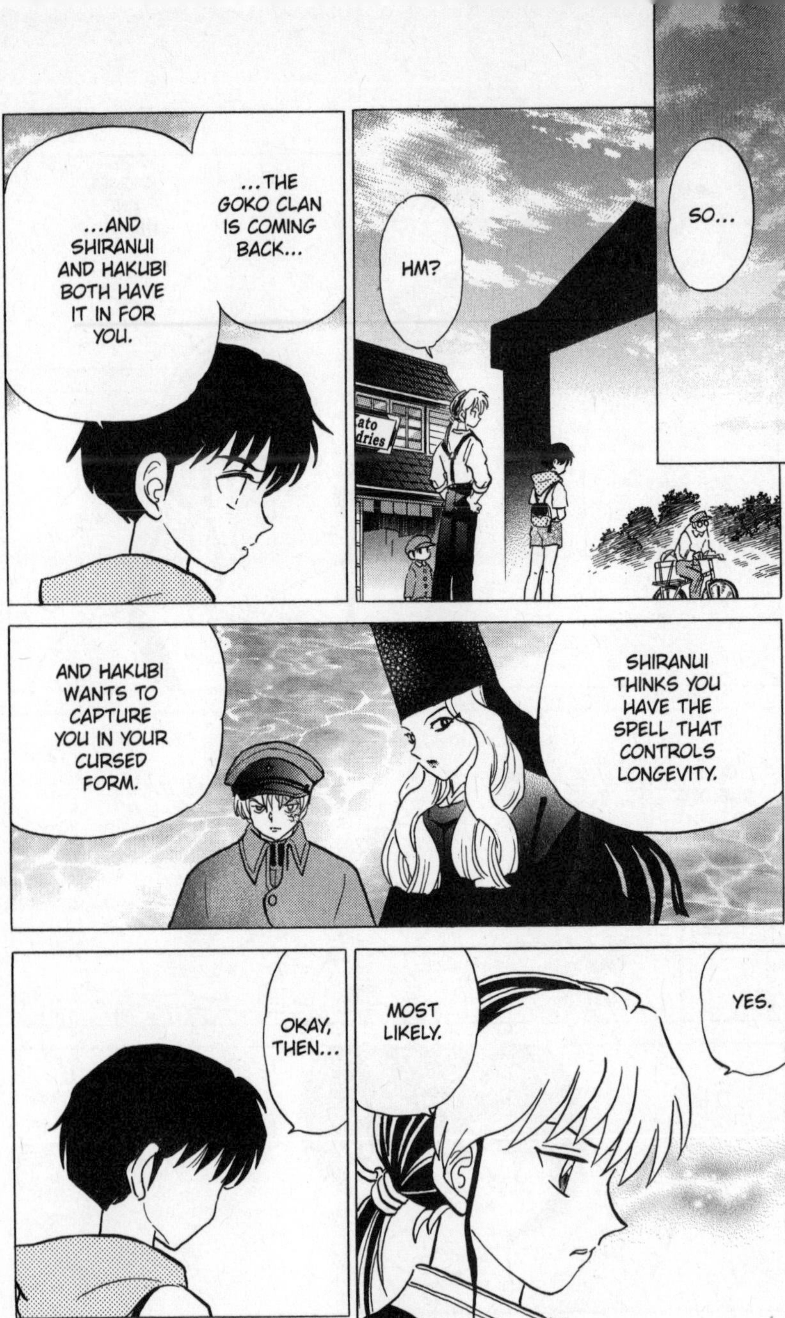
SO...
HM?
...THE GOKO CLAN IS COMING BACK...
...AND SHIRANUI AND HAKUBI BOTH HAVE IT IN FOR YOU.
SHIRANUI THINKS YOU HAVE THE SPELL THAT CONTROLS LONGEVITY.
AND HAKUBI WANTS TO CAPTURE YOU IN YOUR CURSED FORM.
YES.
MOST LIKELY.
OKAY, THEN...

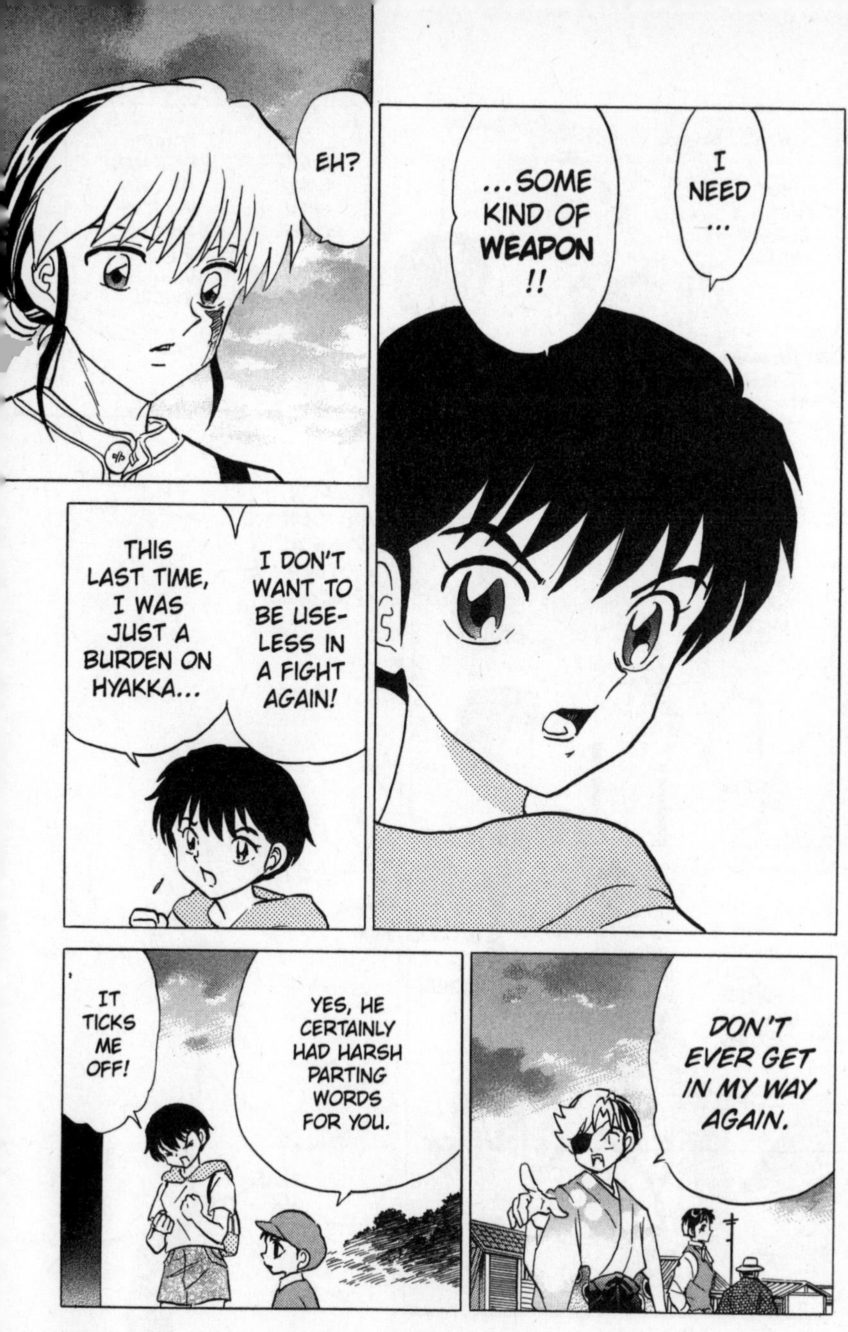

I NEED...
...SOME KIND OF WEAPON!!
EH?
I DON'T WANT TO BE USELESS IN A FIGHT AGAIN!
THIS LAST TIME, I WAS JUST A BURDEN ON HYAKKA...
DON'T EVER GET IN MY WAY AGAIN.
YES, HE CERTAINLY HAD HARSH PARTING WORDS FOR YOU.
IT TICKS ME OFF!

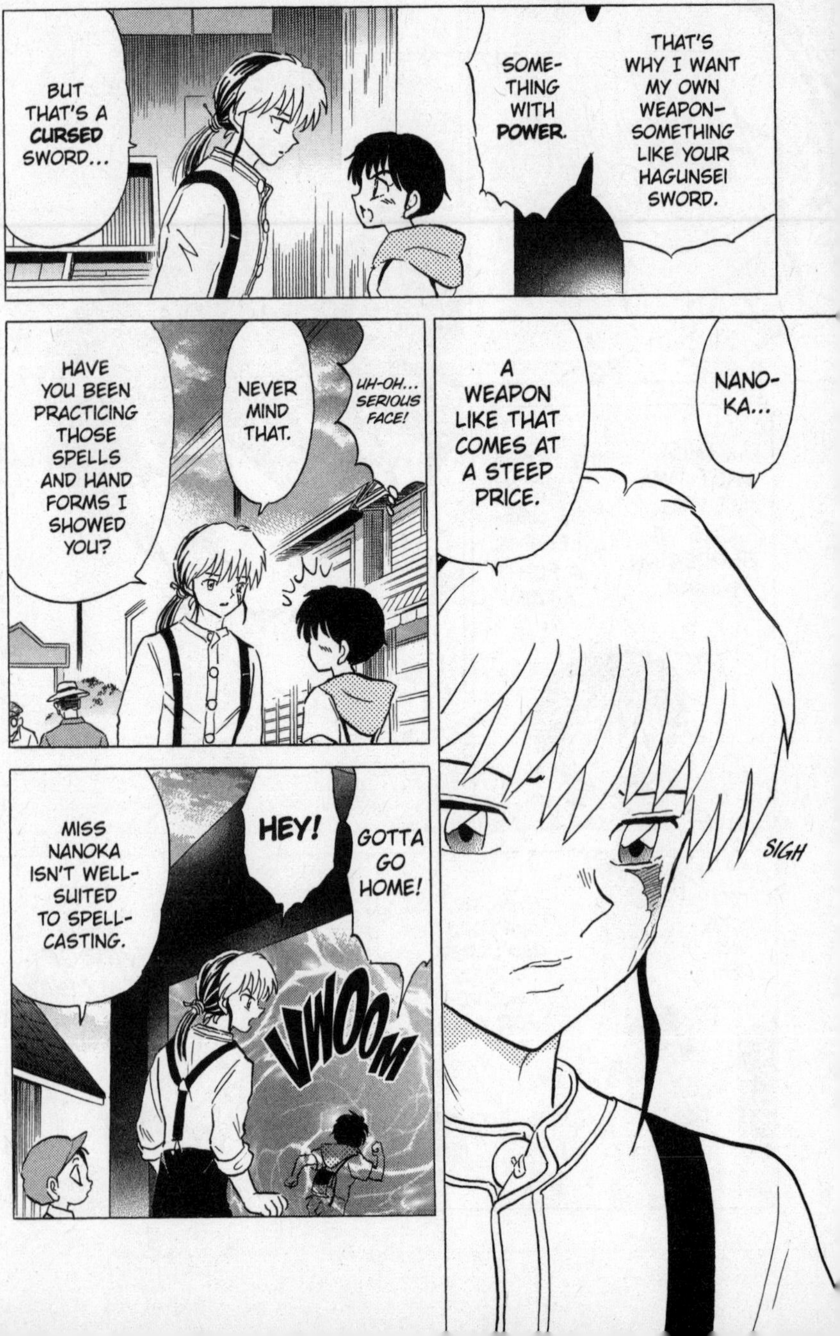
THAT'S WHY I WANT MY OWN WEAPON—SOMETHING LIKE YOUR HAGUNSEI SWORD.
SOME-THING WITH **POWER.**
BUT THAT'S A **CURSED** SWORD...
NANO-KA...
A WEAPON LIKE THAT COMES AT A STEEP PRICE.
SIGH
UH-OH... SERIOUS FACE!
NEVER MIND THAT.
HAVE YOU BEEN PRACTICING THOSE SPELLS AND HAND FORMS I SHOWED YOU?
GOTTA GO HOME!
HEY!
MISS NANOKA ISN'T WELL-SUITED TO SPELL-CASTING.
VWOOM

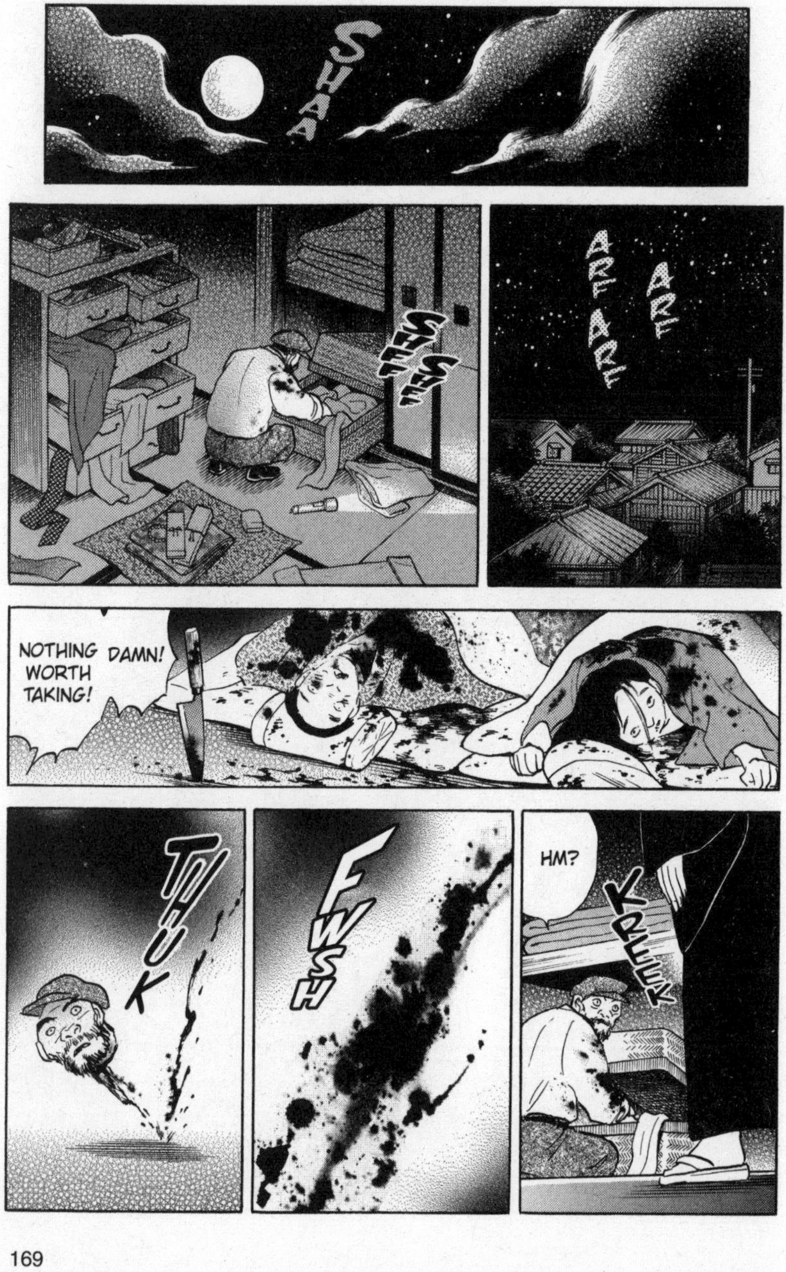
SHAA
ARF
ARF ARF
SHFF
SHFF
DAMN!
NOTHING WORTH TAKING!
HM?
KREEK
FWSH
THUK

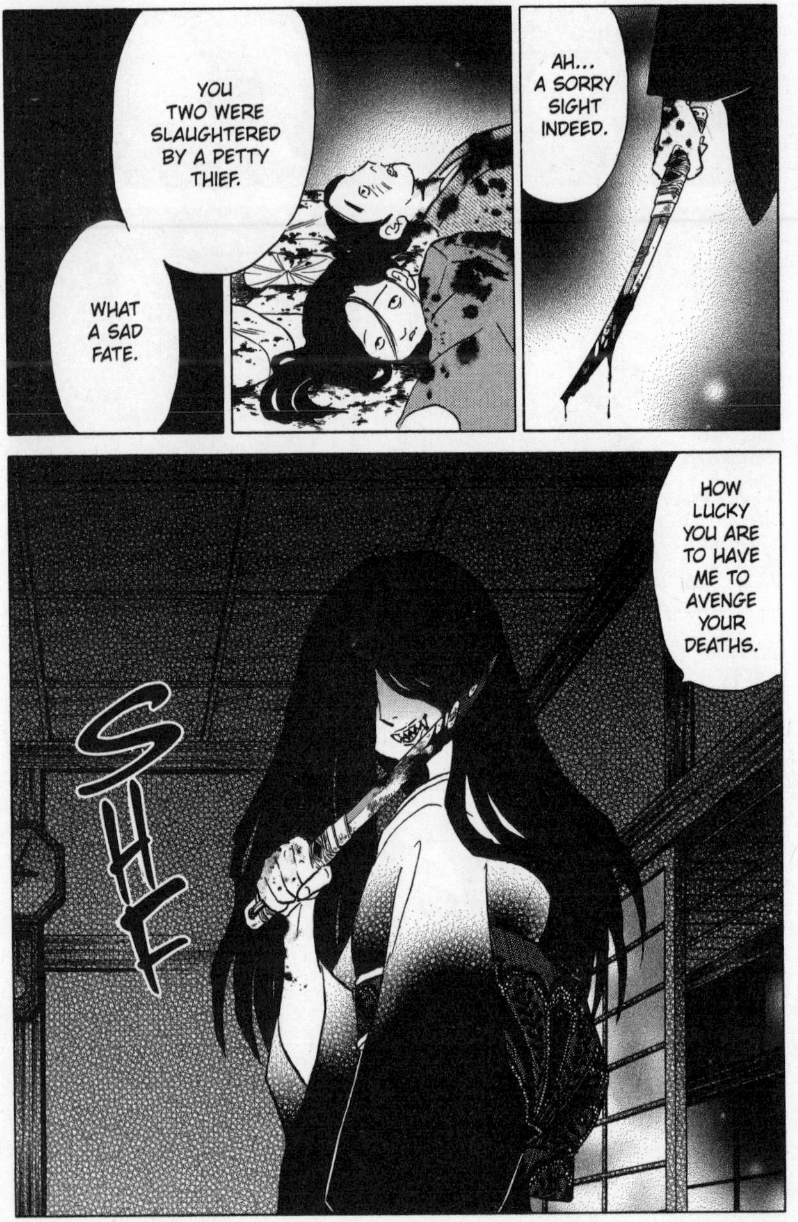
AH... A SORRY SIGHT INDEED.
YOU TWO WERE SLAUGHTERED BY A PETTY THIEF.
WHAT A SAD FATE.
HOW LUCKY YOU ARE TO HAVE ME TO AVENGE YOUR DEATHS.
SHF

Chapter 10:
The First Victim

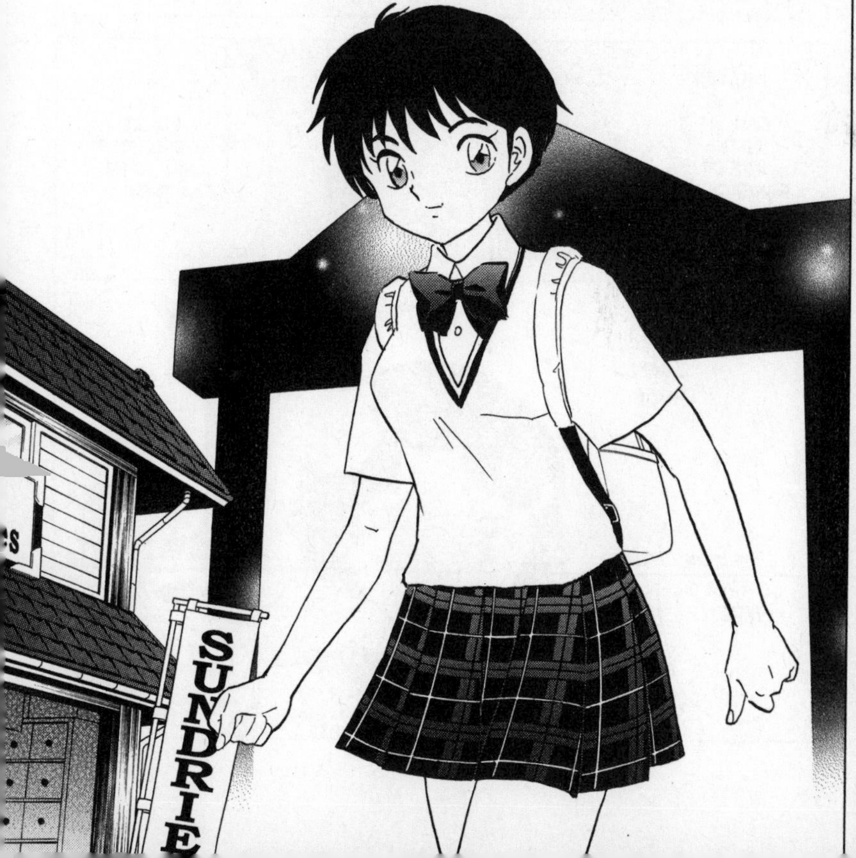
SUNDRIE

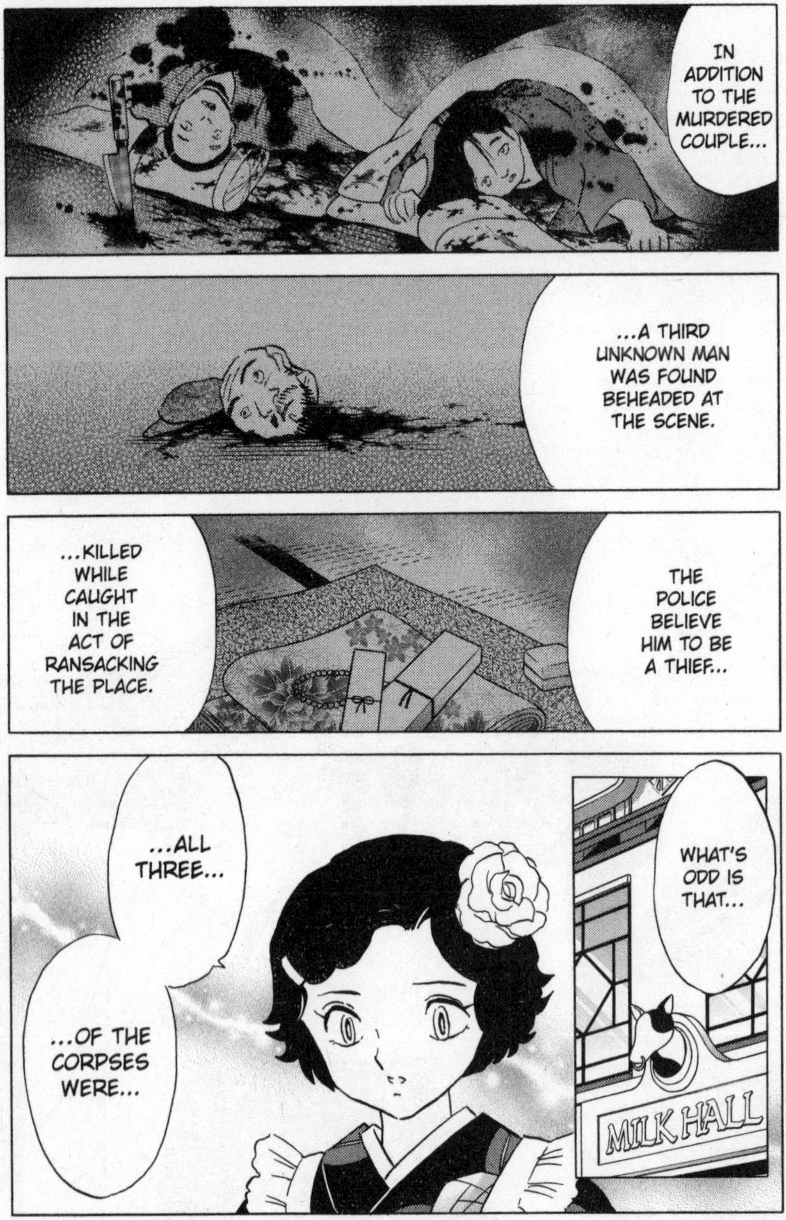
IN ADDITION TO THE MURDERED COUPLE...
...A THIRD UNKNOWN MAN WAS FOUND BEHEADED AT THE SCENE.
THE POLICE BELIEVE HIM TO BE A THIEF...
...KILLED WHILE CAUGHT IN THE ACT OF RANSACKING THE PLACE.
WHAT'S ODD IS THAT...
MILK HALL
...ALL THREE...
...OF THE CORPSES WERE...

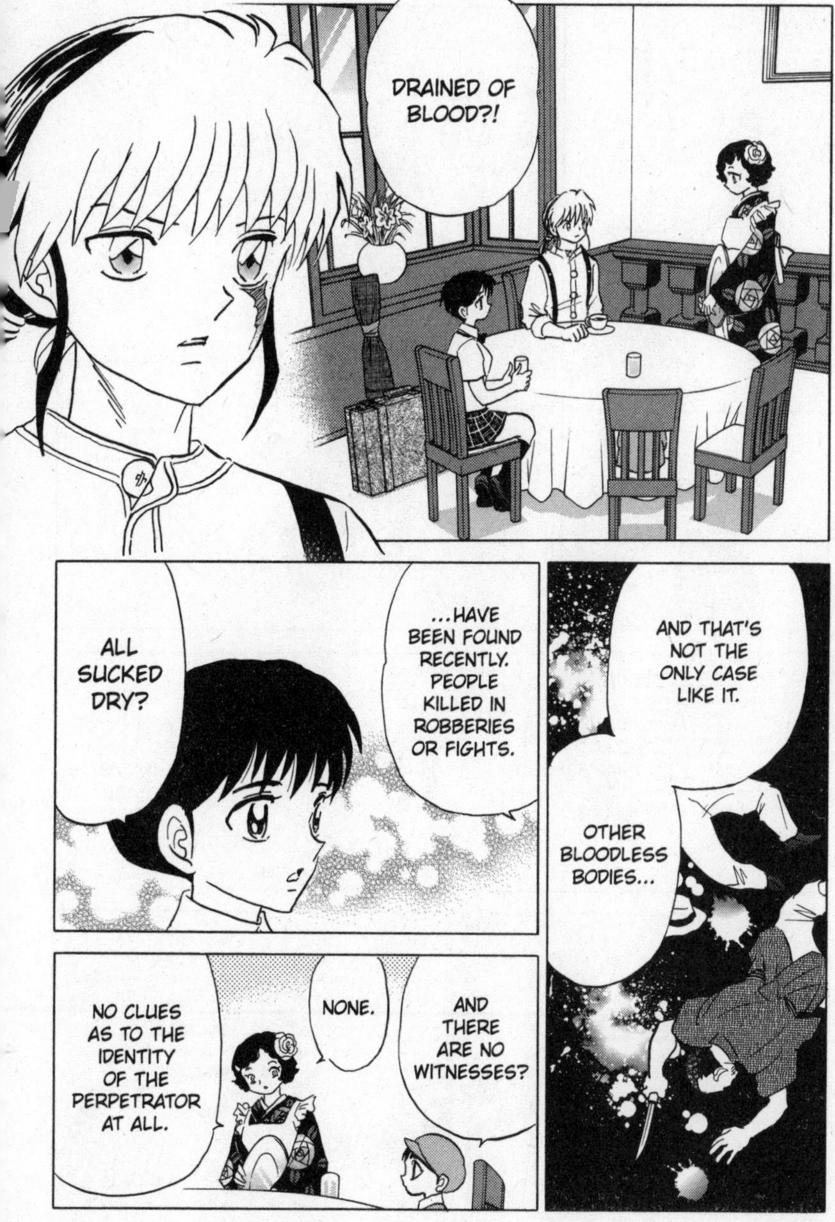
DRAINED OF BLOOD?!
AND THAT'S NOT THE ONLY CASE LIKE IT.
OTHER BLOODLESS BODIES...
...HAVE BEEN FOUND RECENTLY. PEOPLE KILLED IN ROBBERIES OR FIGHTS.
ALL SUCKED DRY?
AND THERE ARE NO WITNESSES?
NONE.
NO CLUES AS TO THE IDENTITY OF THE PERPETRATOR AT ALL.

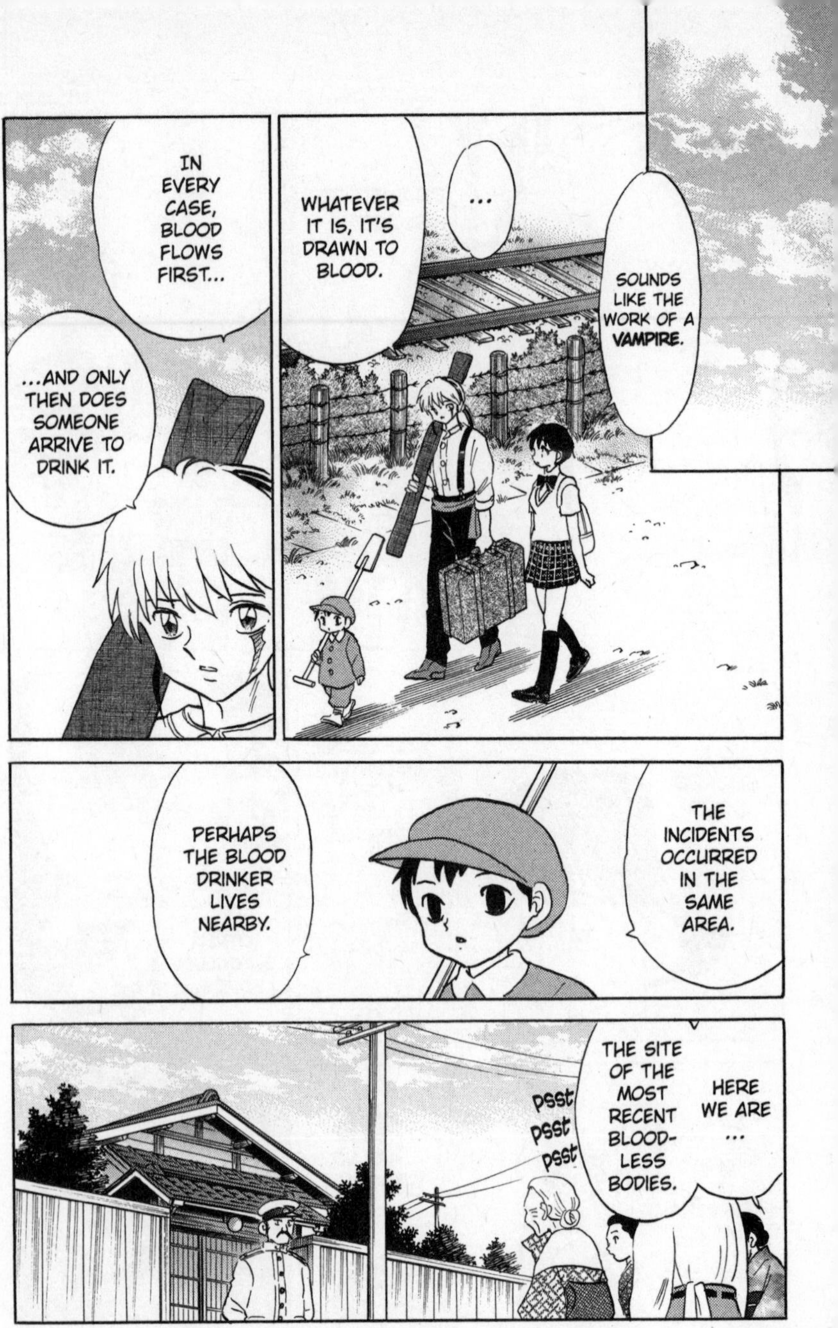
SOUNDS LIKE THE WORK OF A **VAMPIRE.**
...
WHATEVER IT IS, IT'S DRAWN TO BLOOD.
IN EVERY CASE, BLOOD FLOWS FIRST...
...AND ONLY THEN DOES SOMEONE ARRIVE TO DRINK IT.
THE INCIDENTS OCCURRED IN THE SAME AREA.
PERHAPS THE BLOOD DRINKER LIVES NEARBY.
HERE WE ARE ...
THE SITE OF THE MOST RECENT BLOOD-LESS BODIES.
psst
psst
psst

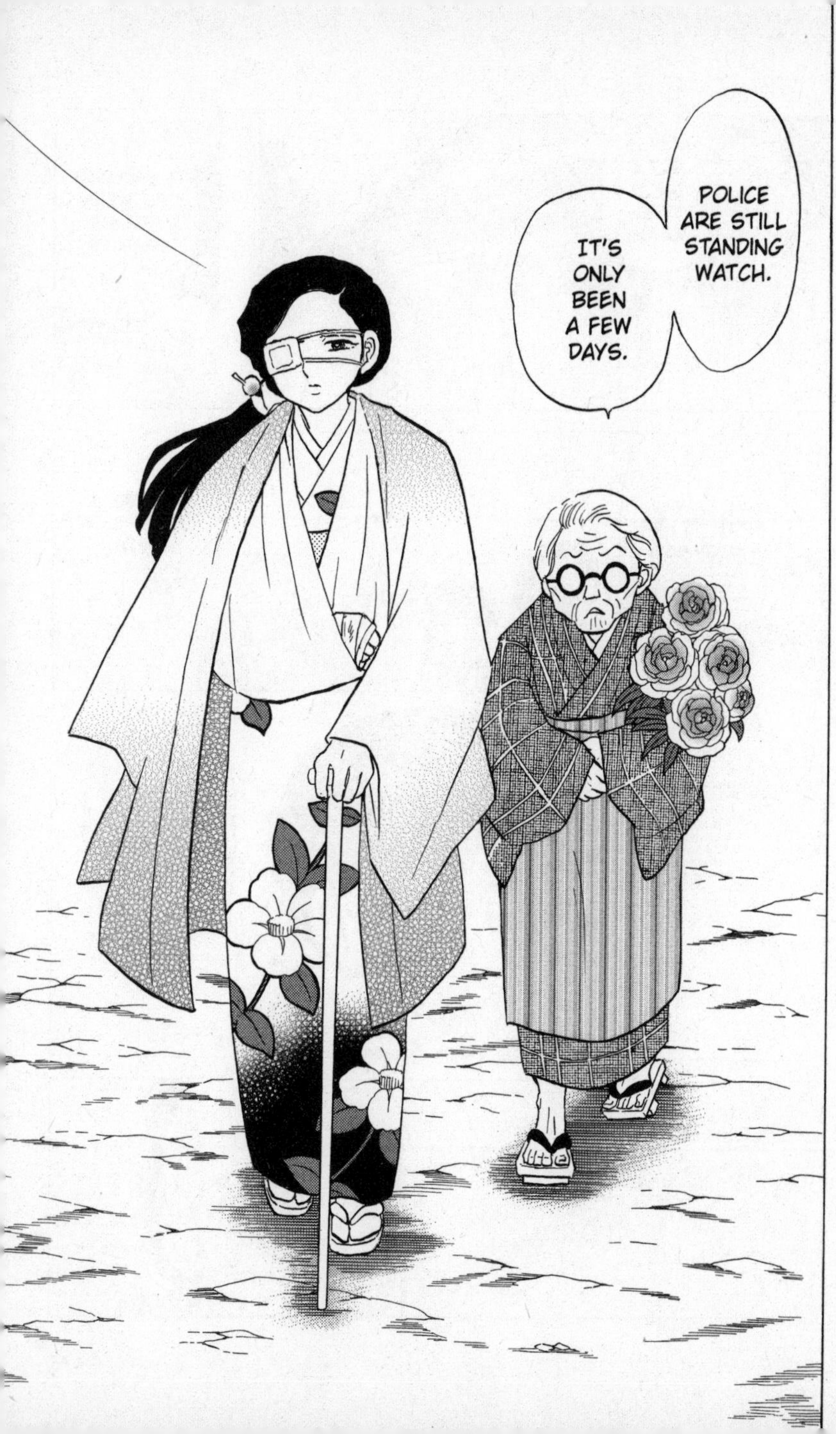
POLICE ARE STILL STANDING WATCH.
IT'S ONLY BEEN A FEW DAYS.

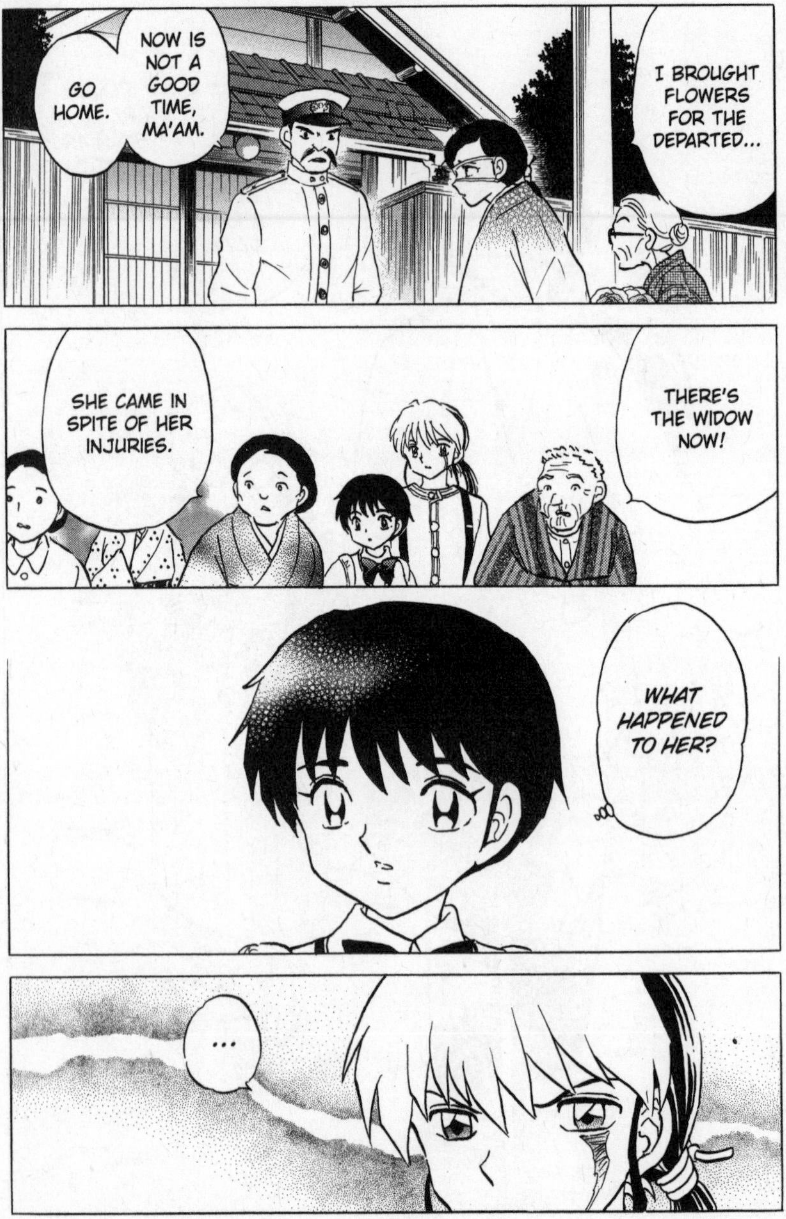
I BROUGHT FLOWERS FOR THE DEPARTED...
NOW IS NOT A GOOD TIME, MA'AM.
GO HOME.
THERE'S THE WIDOW NOW!
SHE CAME IN SPITE OF HER INJURIES.
WHAT HAPPENED TO HER?
...

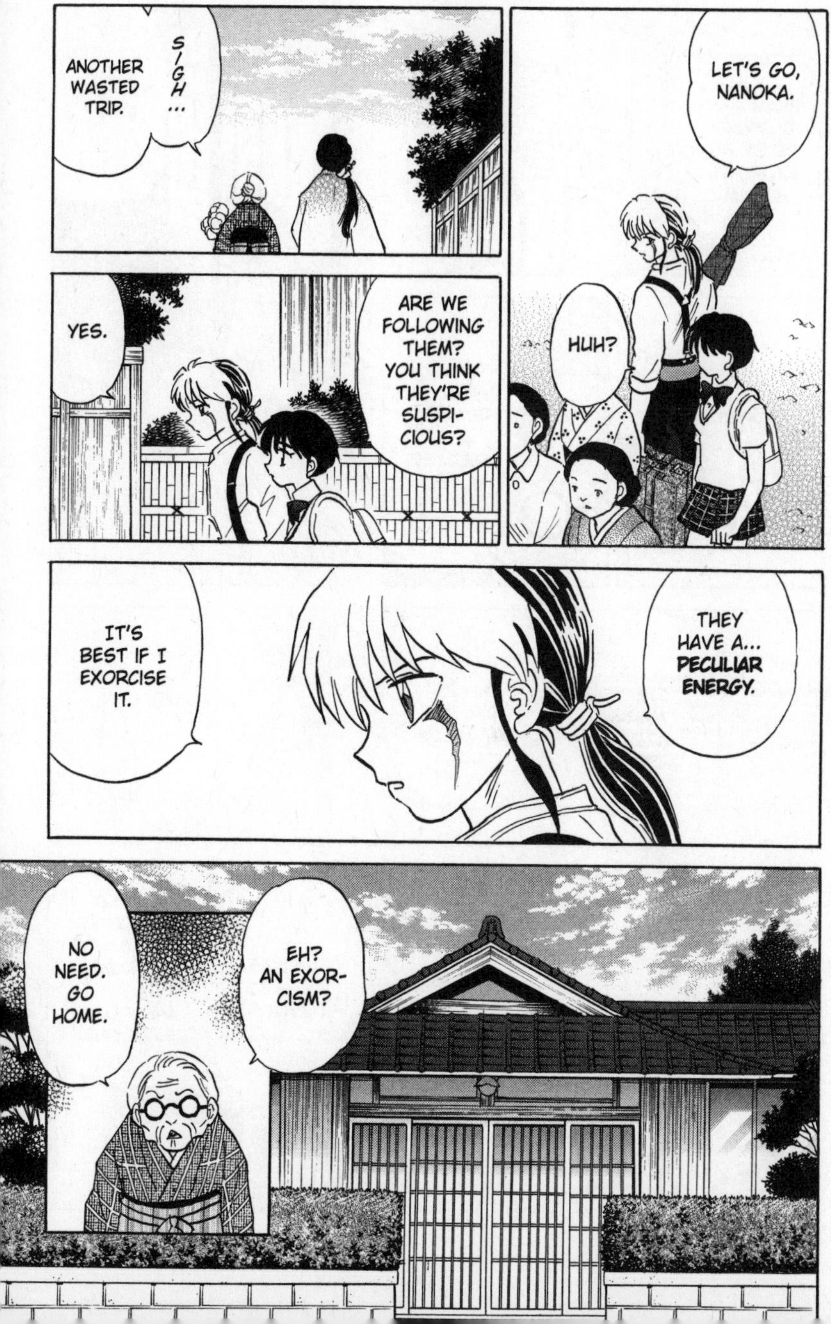
LET'S GO, NANOKA.
HUH?
SIGH...
ANOTHER WASTED TRIP.
ARE WE FOLLOWING THEM? YOU THINK THEY'RE SUSPICIOUS?
YES.
THEY HAVE A... **PECULIAR ENERGY.**
IT'S BEST IF I EXORCISE IT.
EH? AN EXORCISM?
NO NEED. GO HOME.

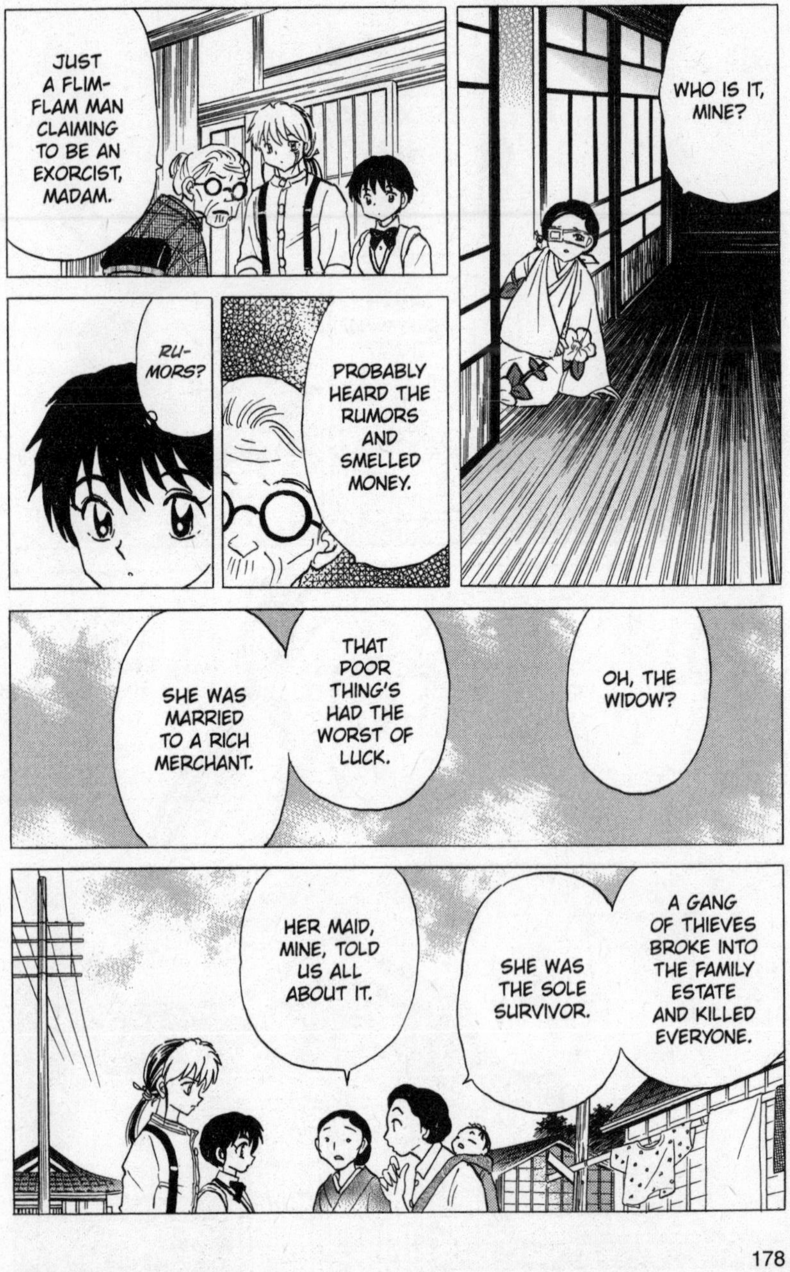
WHO IS IT, MINE?
JUST A FLIM-FLAM MAN CLAIMING TO BE AN EXORCIST, MADAM.
PROBABLY HEARD THE RUMORS AND SMELLED MONEY.
RU-MORS?
OH, THE WIDOW?
THAT POOR THING'S HAD THE WORST OF LUCK.
SHE WAS MARRIED TO A RICH MERCHANT.
A GANG OF THIEVES BROKE INTO THE FAMILY ESTATE AND KILLED EVERYONE.
SHE WAS THE SOLE SURVIVOR.
HER MAID, MINE, TOLD US ALL ABOUT IT.

SHAAA

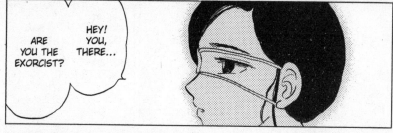

HEY! YOU, THERE...

ARE YOU THE EXORCIST?

OOPS.

UM, SORRY.

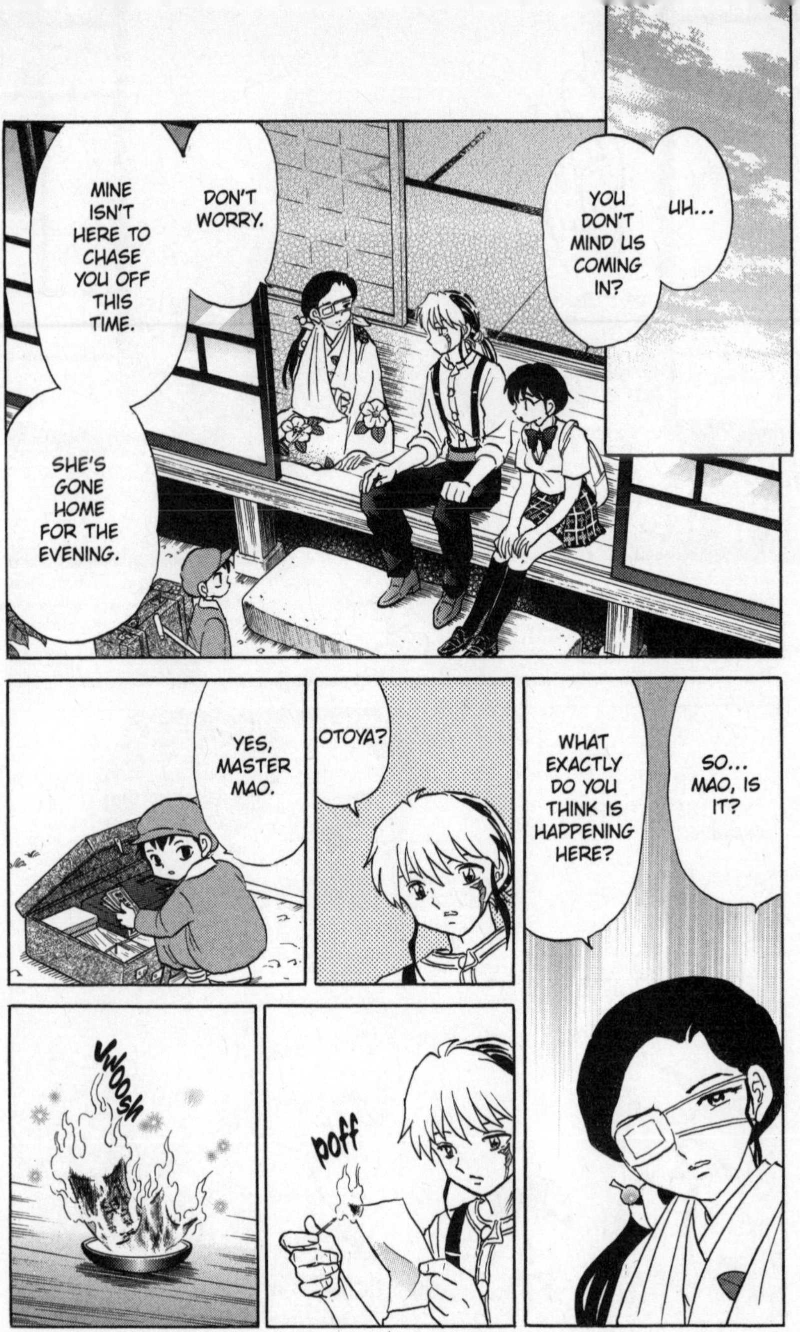
UH...
YOU DON'T MIND US COMING IN?
DON'T WORRY.
MINE ISN'T HERE TO CHASE YOU OFF THIS TIME.
SHE'S GONE HOME FOR THE EVENING.
SO... MAO, IS IT?
WHAT EXACTLY DO YOU THINK IS HAPPENING HERE?
OTOYA?
YES, MASTER MAO.
poff
JWOOSH

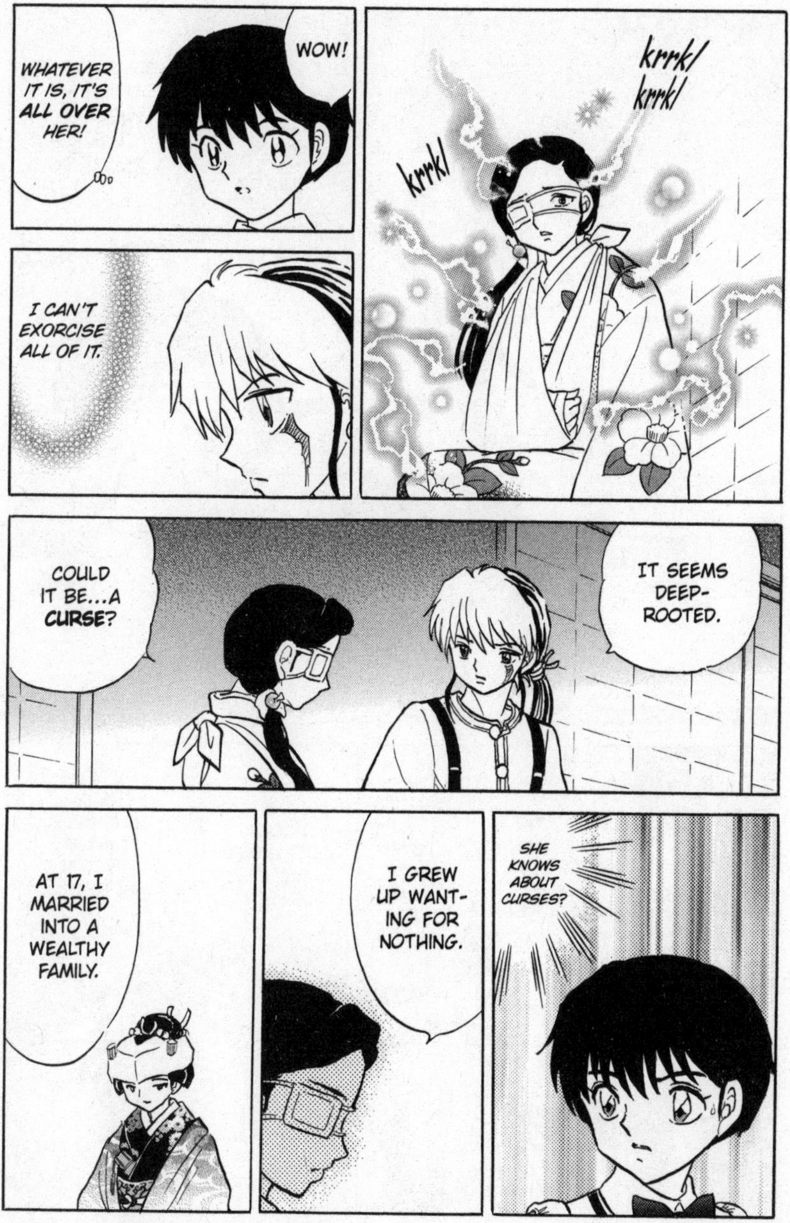
krrk/ krrk/
krrk/
WOW!
WHATEVER IT IS, IT'S ALL OVER HER!
I CAN'T EXORCISE ALL OF IT.
IT SEEMS DEEP-ROOTED.
COULD IT BE...A CURSE?
SHE KNOWS ABOUT CURSES?
I GREW UP WANTING FOR NOTHING.
AT 17, I MARRIED INTO A WEALTHY FAMILY.

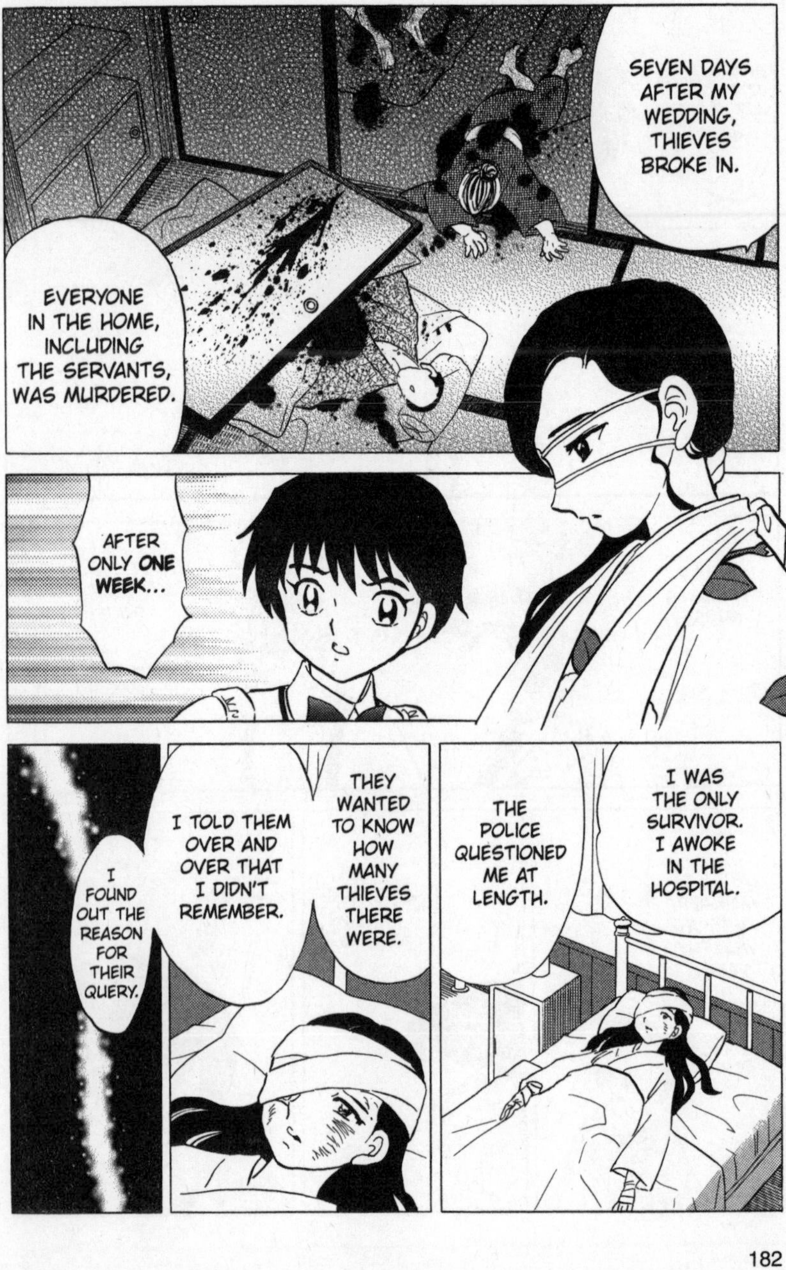
SEVEN DAYS AFTER MY WEDDING, THIEVES BROKE IN.
EVERYONE IN THE HOME, INCLUDING THE SERVANTS, WAS MURDERED.
AFTER ONLY ONE WEEK...
I WAS THE ONLY SURVIVOR. I AWOKE IN THE HOSPITAL.
THE POLICE QUESTIONED ME AT LENGTH.
THEY WANTED TO KNOW HOW MANY THIEVES THERE WERE.
I TOLD THEM OVER AND OVER THAT I DIDN'T REMEMBER.
I FOUND OUT THE REASON FOR THEIR QUERY.

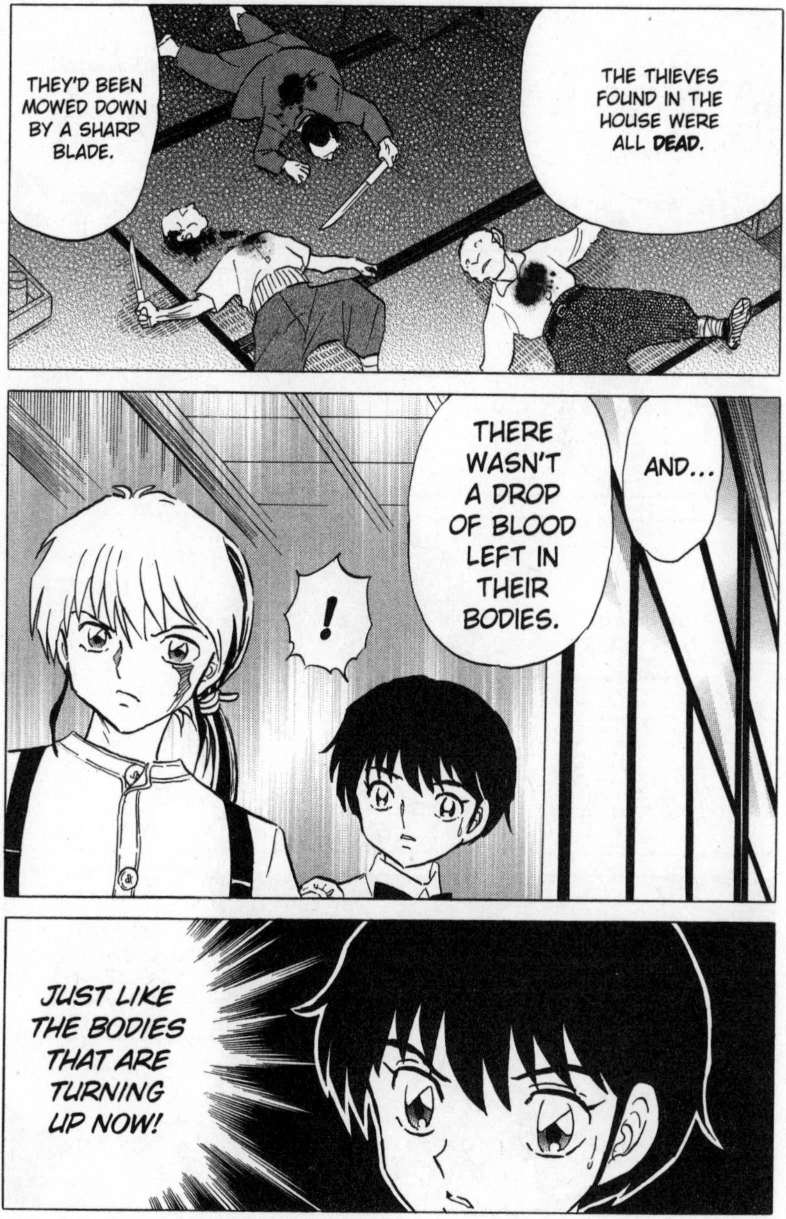
THE THIEVES FOUND IN THE HOUSE WERE ALL **DEAD.**
THEY'D BEEN MOWED DOWN BY A SHARP BLADE.
AND...
THERE WASN'T A DROP OF BLOOD LEFT IN THEIR BODIES.
!
JUST LIKE THE BODIES THAT ARE TURNING UP NOW!

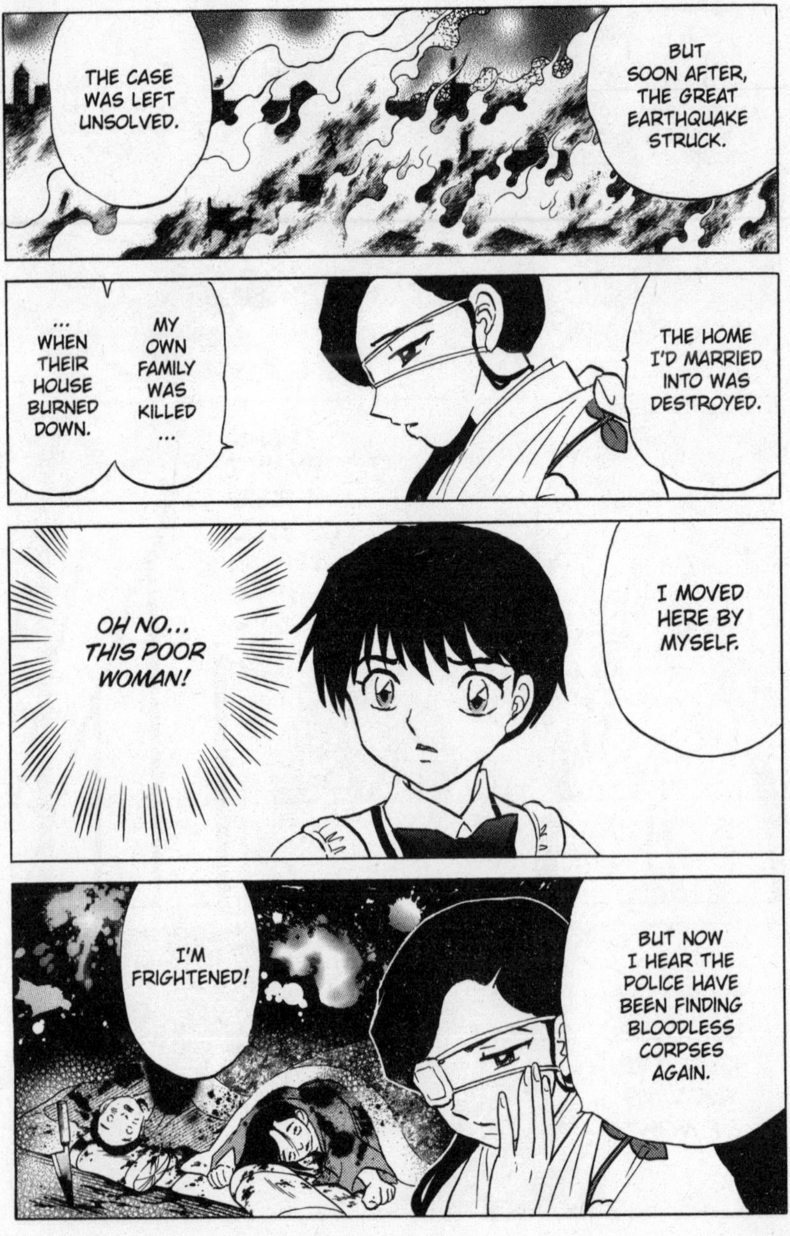
BUT SOON AFTER, THE GREAT EARTHQUAKE STRUCK.
THE CASE WAS LEFT UNSOLVED.
THE HOME I'D MARRIED INTO WAS DESTROYED.
MY OWN FAMILY WAS KILLED ...
... WHEN THEIR HOUSE BURNED DOWN.
I MOVED HERE BY MYSELF.
OH NO... THIS POOR WOMAN!
BUT NOW I HEAR THE POLICE HAVE BEEN FINDING BLOODLESS CORPSES AGAIN.
I'M FRIGHTENED!

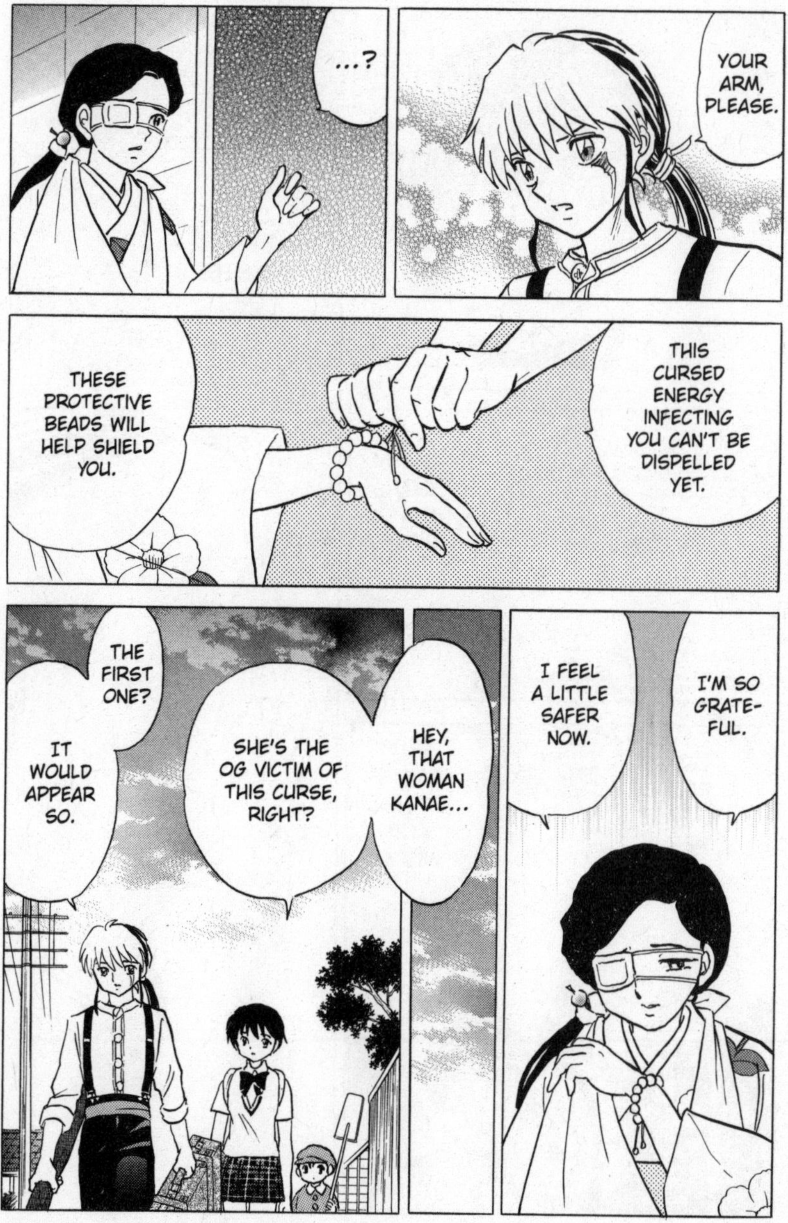
YOUR ARM, PLEASE.
...?
THIS CURSED ENERGY INFECTING YOU CAN'T BE DISPELLED YET.
THESE PROTECTIVE BEADS WILL HELP SHIELD YOU.
I'M SO GRATE-FUL.
I FEEL A LITTLE SAFER NOW.
HEY, THAT WOMAN KANAE...
SHE'S THE OG VICTIM OF THIS CURSE, RIGHT?
THE FIRST ONE?
IT WOULD APPEAR SO.

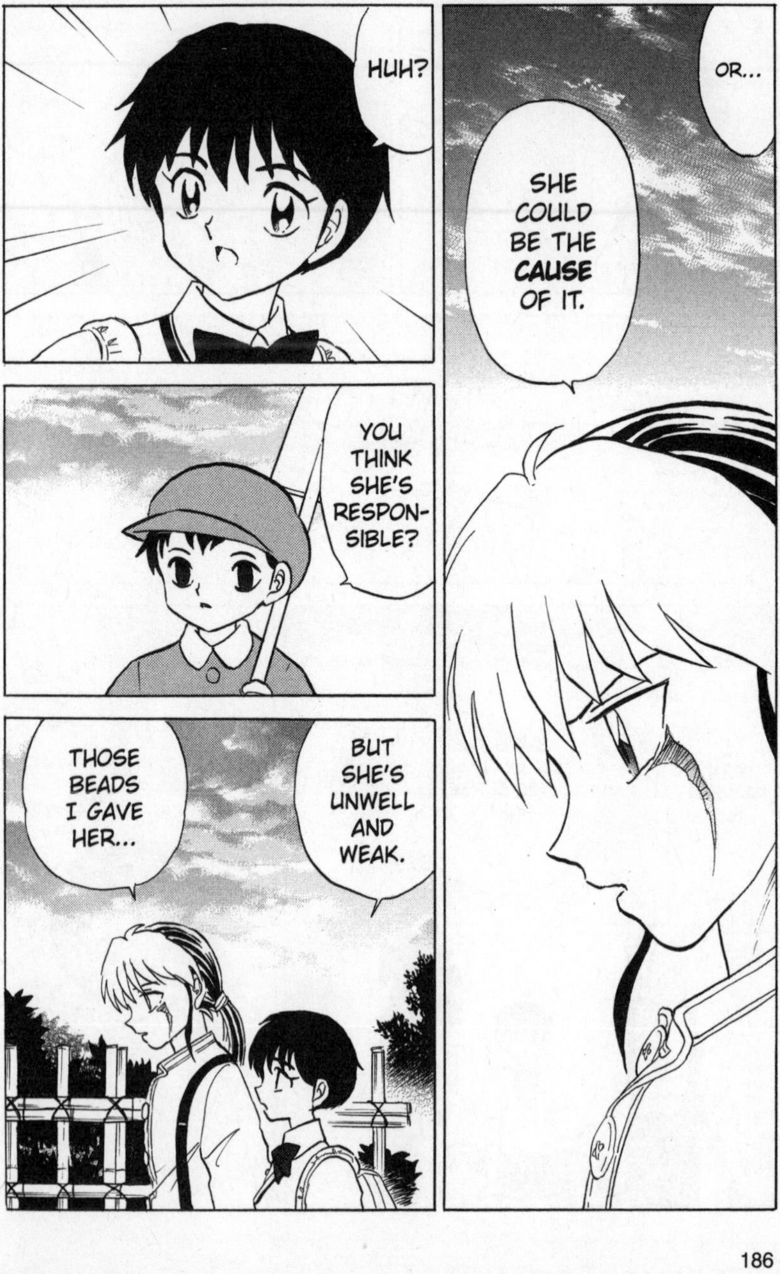
OR...
SHE COULD BE THE CAUSE OF IT.
HUH?
YOU THINK SHE'S RESPONSIBLE?
BUT SHE'S UNWELL AND WEAK.
THOSE BEADS I GAVE HER...

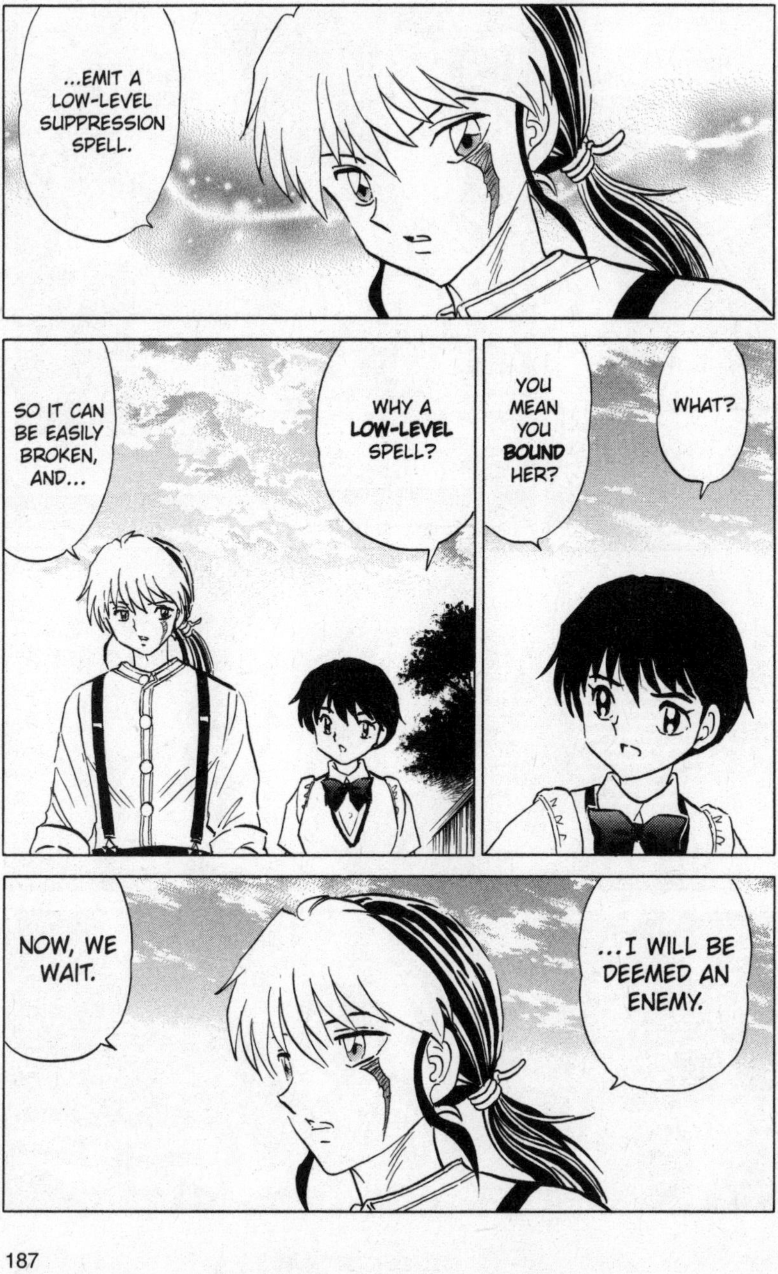
...EMIT A LOW-LEVEL SUPPRESSION SPELL.
WHAT?
YOU MEAN YOU BOUND HER?
WHY A LOW-LEVEL SPELL?
SO IT CAN BE EASILY BROKEN, AND...
...I WILL BE DEEMED AN ENEMY.
NOW, WE WAIT.

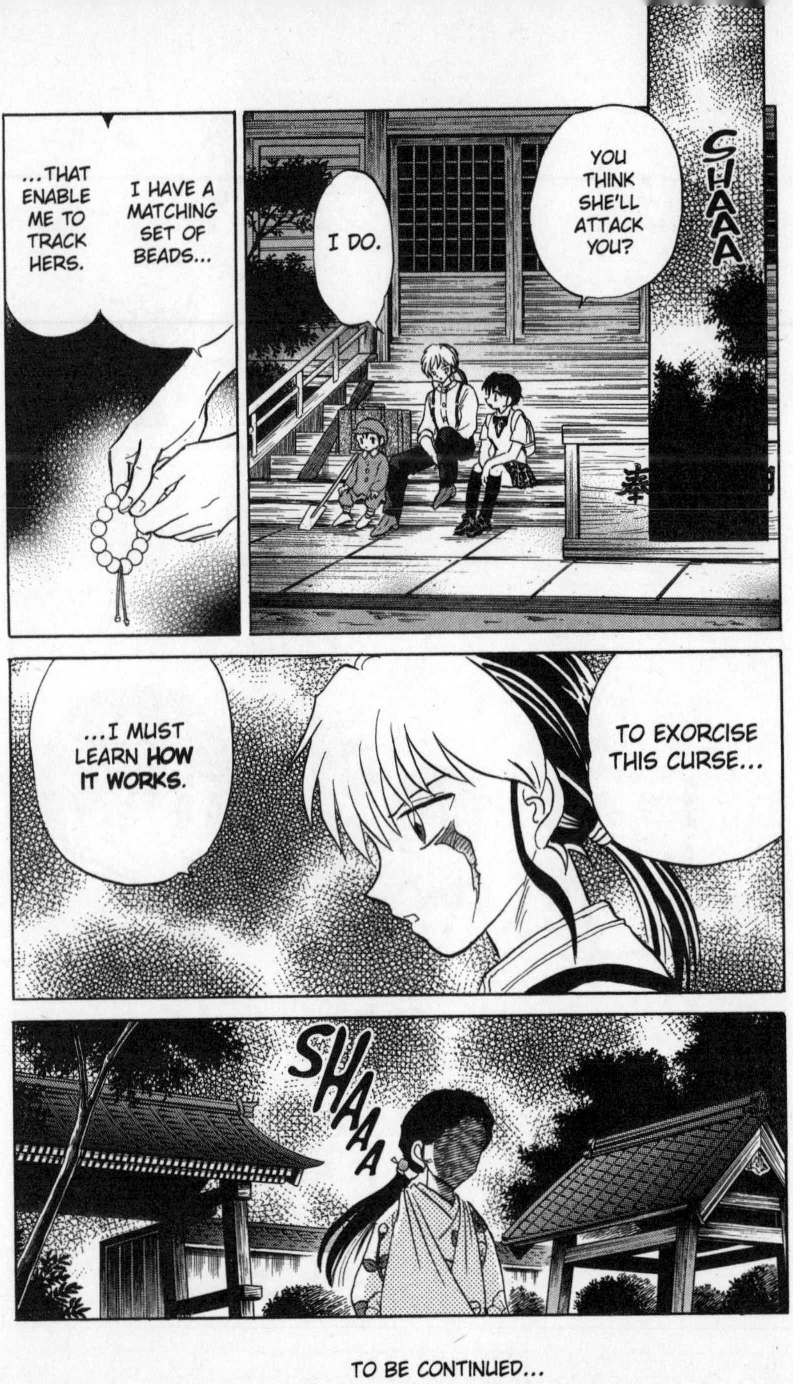
SHAAA
YOU THINK SHE'LL ATTACK YOU?
I DO.
I HAVE A MATCHING SET OF BEADS...
...THAT ENABLE ME TO TRACK HERS.
TO EXORCISE THIS CURSE...
...I MUST LEARN **HOW** IT **WORKS**.
SHAAA

TO BE CONTINUED...

Rumiko Takahashi

The spotlight on Rumiko Takahashi's career began in 1978 when she won an honorable mention in Shogakukan's prestigious New Comic Artist Contest for *Those Selfish Aliens*. Later that same year, her boy-meets-alien comedy series, *Urusei Yatsura*, was serialized in *Weekly Shonen Sunday*. This phenomenally successful manga series was adapted into anime format and spawned a TV series and half a dozen theatrical-release movies, all incredibly popular in their own right. Takahashi followed up the success of her debut series with one blockbuster hit after another—*Maison Ikkoku* ran from 1980 to 1987, *Ranma ½* from 1987 to 1996, and *Inuyasha* from 1996 to 2008. Other notable works include *Mermaid Saga*, *Rumic Theater*, and *One-Pound Gospel*.

Takahashi was inducted into the Will Eisner Comic Awards Hall of Fame in 2018. She won the prestigious Shogakukan Manga Award twice in her career, once for *Urusei Yatsura* in 1981 and the second time for *Inuyasha* in 2002. A majority of the Takahashi canon has been adapted into other media such as anime, live-action TV series, and film. Takahashi's manga, as well as the other formats her work has been adapted into, have continued to delight generations of fans around the world. Distinguished by her wonderfully endearing characters, Takahashi's work adeptly incorporates a wide variety of elements such as comedy, romance, fantasy, and martial arts. While her series are difficult to pin down into one simple genre, the signature style she has created has come to be known as the "Rumic World." Rumiko Takahashi is an artist who truly represents the very best from the world of manga.

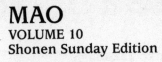

MAO
VOLUME 10
Shonen Sunday Edition

STORY AND ART BY
RUMIKO TAKAHASHI

MAO Vol. 10
by Rumiko TAKAHASHI

Original Japanese edition published by SHOGAKUKAN.
English translation rights in the United States of America, Canada, the United Kingdom, Ireland, Australia, and New Zealand arranged with SHOGAKUKAN.

Original Cover Design: Chie SATO, Eri HAYASAKA + Bay Bridge Studio

Translation/Junko Goda
English Adaptation/Shaenon K. Garrity
Touch-Up Art & Lettering/James Gaubatz
Cover & Interior Design/Ian Miller
Editor/Annette Roman

Printed in the U.S.A.

Published by VIZ Media, LLC
P.O. Box 77010
San Francisco, CA 94107

10 9 8 7 6 5 4 3 2 1
First printing, March 2023

ratings.viz.com RATED T+ OLDER TEEN

PARENTAL ADVISORY
MAO is rated T+ for Older Teen and is recommended for ages 16 and up. This volume contains fantasy violence.

VIZ MEDIA
viz.com

SHONEN SUNDAY
shonensunday.com

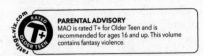

Coming in Volume 11...

Nanoka claims a cursed sword and has it reforged to suit her, but the blade is stolen before she has a chance to wield it. Who does the original weapon belong to, and why do they want it back so badly? Pitched battles ensue, and this time it's Mao's turn to sacrifice himself to save Nanoka... And then Nanoka is taken hostage!

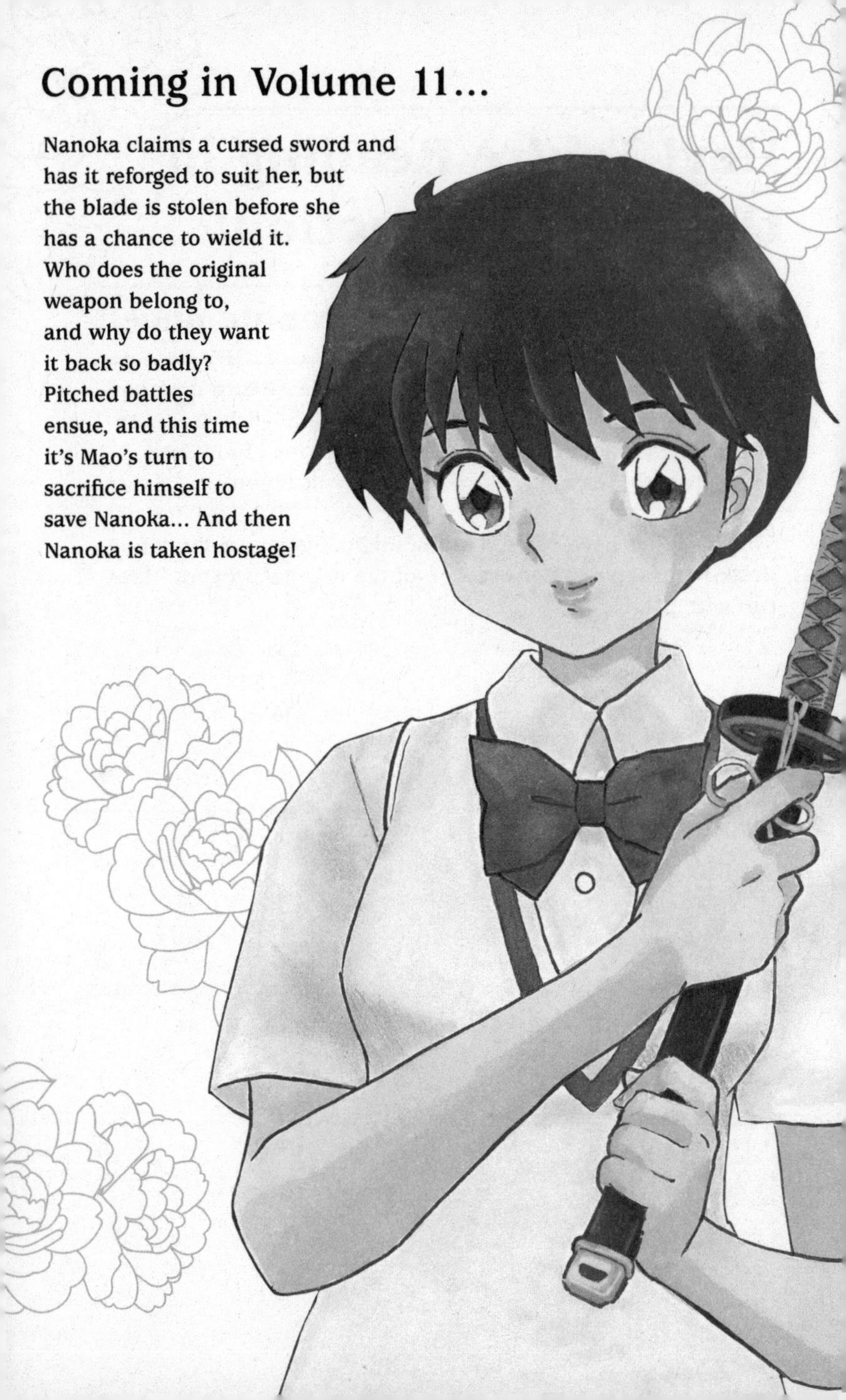

Hey! You're Reading in the Wrong Direction!

This is the end of this graphic novel!

To properly enjoy this VIZ graphic novel, please turn it around and begin reading from right to left. Unlike English, Japanese is read right to left, so Japanese comics are read in reverse order from the way English comics are typically read.

This book has been printed in the original Japanese format in order to preserve the orientation of the original artwork. Have fun with it!

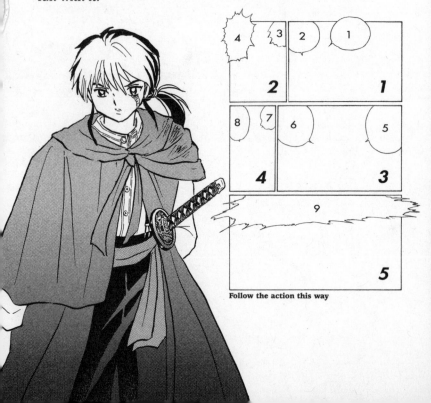

Follow the action this way